AF600693

FEDERAL DEMOCRACIES AT WORK

Federal Democracies at Work

Varieties of Complex Government

EDITED BY ARTHUR BENZ
AND JARED SONNICKSEN

UNIVERSITY OF TORONTO PRESS
Toronto Buffalo London

Toronto Buffalo London
utorontopress.com

ISBN 978-1-4875-0900-2 (cloth)
ISBN 978-1-4875-3949-8 (EPUB)
ISBN 978-1-4875-3948-1 (PDF)

Library and Archives Canada Cataloguing in Publication

Title: Federal democracies at work : varieties of complex government / edited by Arthur Benz and Jared Sonnicksen.
Names: Benz, Arthur, editor. | Sonnicksen, Jared, 1978– editor.
Description: Includes bibliographical references and index.
Identifiers: Canadiana (print) 20210133473 | Canadiana (ebook) 20210133619 | ISBN 9781487509002 (cloth) | ISBN 9781487539498 (EPUB) | ISBN 9781487539481 (PDF)
Subjects: LCSH: Federal government. | LCSH: Democracy. | LCSH: Comparative government.
Classification: LCC JC355.F337 2021 | DDC 321.8–dc23

University of Toronto Press acknowledges the financial assistance to its publishing program of the Canada Council for the Arts and the Ontario Arts Council, an agency of the Government of Ontario.

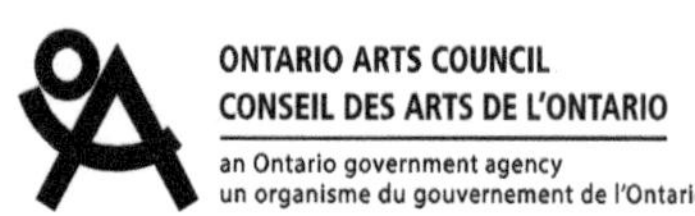

Funded by the Government of Canada | Financé par le gouvernement du Canada | Canada

Contents

Preface vii

1 Introduction 3
ARTHUR BENZ AND JARED SONNICKSEN

2 Federalism as a Yardstick for Democracy 23
THOMAS O. HUEGLIN

3 Linking Federalism and Democracy: An Analytical Framework 37
ARTHUR BENZ

4 Out of Balance: Executive Dominance in Federal Settings 58
JOHN ERIK FOSSUM AND DAVID LAYCOCK

5 Federalism and Democracy in the United States 78
TIMOTHY CONLAN

6 Federalism and Direct Democracy in Switzerland: Competing or Complementary? 99
SEAN MUELLER

7 Germany: How Federalism Has Shaped Consensus Democracy 122
SABINE KROPP

8 Between Co-evolution and Intercurrence: How Democracy Has Shaped Federalism in Canada 142
JÖRG BROSCHEK

9 Party Federalism in Australia 164
ANDREW BANFIELD AND ANTHONY SAYERS

10 Belgium: The Democratic State of the Federation 180
PETRA MEIER AND PETER BURSENS

11 Democracy and Federalism in Spain: Interactions, Tensions, and Compatibilities 197
CÉSAR COLINO

12 Democracy and Federalism in India: Mutually Reinforcing? 218
WILFRIED SWENDEN AND KATHARINE ADENEY

13 Comparing Patterns of Federal Democracy 239
ARTHUR BENZ AND JARED SONNICKSEN

References 263

Contributors 311

Index 315

Preface

As many would agree, federalism and democracy belong together – in principle. In reality, when institutions of government are designed according to these principles, and when governments have to work under the conditions of a two-dimensional division of powers, it apparently depends on the particular institutional pattern whether, as well as how, federalism and democracy go together. In practical governance, tensions and conflicts are bound to arise, but political actors can also use the differentiated structures to manage these challenges. Executives, for instance, have to coordinate policies among jurisdictions, although democracy requires autonomy of governments. They have to come to agreements despite divergent policies, defined in democratic processes at the different levels or constituent units, or have to meet the challenges of inter-jurisdictional competition. Parliaments likewise face the challenge of a complex balancing act. They respond to trends towards executive federalism by holding executives accountable, while avoiding tying the hands of executives engaged in intergovernmental relations. Federalism creates multiple access points for parties, but a territorially fragmented party system can obstruct the integration of a federation. In multinational societies, federalism might be demos-enabling, but it can also increase conflicts among *demoï*, which are to be coped with in intergovernmental relations.

"Federal democracy at work" does not mean that it works, though we agree that, in principle, it does. Yet how it works in reality and under which conditions is a question that is still to be answered in comparative research. So far, tensions, frictions, and dynamics in federal democracies have been revealed by case studies on individual countries, while comparative research on parties, elections, and intergovernmental relations in federal democracies focuses on specific aspects, but hardly considers the systemic nature of federal democracies and their modes of operation and evolution. In this book, we have collected case studies to present a comparative approach. The chapters address the existing varieties of institutional configurations linking federalism and democracy, which emerged during the course of the history of different countries. They analyse the particular tensions and frictions that may arise in federal democracies and the dynamics of structures and practices that result when actors try to cope with these tensions and frictions. These analyses also draw on normative and theoretical reasoning.

This book reaches back to some of the articles we have published during the last few years. We realized that we should broaden our theoretical approach as well as extend the set of federal democracies under consideration. For this reason, we invited colleagues to a workshop, which took place in July 2017. In June 2018, we met in a second workshop to discuss the drafts of the chapters. We are very grateful to our authors for contributing to the project and for working with us so intensely. We also thank Florian Ostertag and Tim Rieth for assisting us in our editorial work. Finally, we thank the reviewers and members of the editorial board of University of Toronto Press for their helpful comments on the manuscript and Daniel Quinlan for his excellent cooperation during the publication of this volume.

Arthur Benz and Jared Sonnicksen

FEDERAL DEMOCRACIES AT WORK

1 Introduction

ARTHUR BENZ AND JARED SONNICKSEN

Federalism emerged as an idea and was entrenched in constitutions long before modern democracy was invented. The existence of federal polities and federalist thinking can be traced back to at least the sixteenth century in Europe, if not to the ancient world (Elazar 1987, 115–53; Elazar and Kincaid 2000; Hueglin and Fenna 2015, 73–82; Karmis and Norman 2005). When the first modern federal state was founded in the United States, it aimed predominantly to limit the power of government. Moreover, although the United States turned into a democracy, federalism was originally not intended to be demos-enabling (Stepan 1999), nor the "Union" government a democracy, but rather a compound political order. For the most part, it was not until the late nineteenth century that linking democracy and federalism became an issue in constitutional debates. Thus, from a historical point of view, there is no necessary connection between federalism and democracy.

Today, many presume that a federal system cannot work without democracy and that federalism actually improves the quality of democracy (e.g., Burgess 2012, 252–78; Watts 2008, 192). Indeed, modern federalism evolved in parallel with the rise of liberal democracy, and both aimed to limit government and include checks and balances to prevent a concentration of power. At present, most federations in the world are democracies. Evidently, there are also states in the world that, according to their constitutions, are federations but have autocratic governments – contemporary Russia and Nigeria, or Brazil and Argentina before democratization, are cases in point – and there are democratic federations where enclaves of authoritative regimes persist at the regional level (Behrend and Whitehead 2016; Gibson 2013). As a rule, however, scholars categorize these states as defect federations or as federations only on paper, not in practice (see, e.g., Lane and Ersson 2005). Since federalism limits power by ensuring a division of competences and checks and balances, it would appear incompatible with a concentration of power in the hands of a president or central government, as is usually the case in an autocracy (Obydenkova and Swenden 2013).

However, the link between federalism and democracy is anything but uncomplicated. When we consider democratic states with a federal structure, we find continuous debates on executive dominance or problems of multi-level governance caused by party competition or divides among elected governments in the constituent units. Certainly, federalism has its values for democracy, particularly in view of the increasing plurality of post-industrial societies. As Thomas O. Hueglin (chap. 2) convincingly argues, democracy in the sense of majority rule faces limits – not least with a view to the actual economic, social, and cultural disparities among places and people – and, thus, discrepancies between formal and substantive equality. From this point of view, federalism provides an essential corrective against a policy that presumes the unrealistic ideal of a homogeneous demos (Breton 1998). In contemporary societies, equality needs to effectively take diversity into account by decentralizing power and by protecting the interests and governance capacities of distinct groups or territories. To mitigate the inequality among individuals caused by the places in which they live, federalism establishes the principle of solidarity. To safeguard diversity against the unitarizing trend of majority rule, federalism stipulates that fundamental decisions should be approved by all or at least acceptable for all.

Yet from an empirical point of view, considerable ambivalence remains about how rules, decision procedures, and mechanisms of policymaking interact. The different rules, procedures, and mechanisms as well as their interactions result from the division and sharing of powers among levels of government on the one hand and from relations between the executive and legislature within levels of government on the other. They may complement and even reinforce one another or cause conflicting policies or decisions due to diverging rules of policymaking. As of yet, we have not been able to gain definitive answers about under which conditions we can expect compatibility or conflict. Depending on the analytical perspective, scholars have tended to view federalism and democracy as either mutually reinforcing or contradicting one another: from the former perspective, for instance, because both foster self-rule and liberty (see, e.g., Levy 2007; Oates 1972) or, in the latter view, because the two dimensions of government follow contrasting logics of operation (see, e.g., Lehmbruch 2000) or since the vertical division of powers hinders effective democratic governance (see, e.g., Gerring and Thacker 2008). What is certain, therefore, is this: the combination of federalism and democracy in one polity produces a series of tensions.

Hence, we have good reason to address the question of what makes federal democracies work. We are aware that this is an age-old question raised in comparative federalism since at least the days when the US model was transferred to parliamentary democracies. Moreover, debates on the democratic deficit of the European Union (EU), which shares many features of modern federal systems, has contributed to this debate (see, e.g., Fossum and Jachtenfuchs 2017). Yet there is still a need for systematic, comparative research on the various complex governments that combine different patterns of democracy and federalism, as the following review of the state of research demonstrates.

State of Research

The assumption that federalism coexists with democracy and that both are mutually supportive is strongly influenced by normative political theories (Dahl 1983; Føllesdal 2018; Hueglin 2013a; Levy 2007; K. Scott 2011; Whitaker 1992). Following Montesquieu (see, e.g., Ward 2007) and the Federalists (Hamilton, Madison, and Jay [1787] 1989), protagonists of liberal democracy praise the division of powers as a safeguard against despotism and, hence, a way to protect individual liberty against the encroachment of a powerful government. Scholars who advocate a republican concept of democracy, building upon proposals by the Anti-Federalists or taking into account observations made by Alexis de Tocqueville, accentuate decentralization as a precondition of citizen participation and a strong civil society (Jörke 2019). Outside the US context, federalism is justified as a means to protect minorities or to integrate distinct societies or multiple nations, provided that it allows an asymmetrical allocation of power and the right of secession (Gagnon and Tully 2001; Kymlicka 2005).

In general, federalism has been regarded as a constitutional principle that supports individual liberty or equality of citizens, one that enables citizens to participate in a political system without being discriminated against. Moreover, federalism is advocated as a means to protect minorities against the "tyranny of the majority" (Tocqueville [1835–40] 2010, 410), to mobilize citizens to participate in politics (K. Scott 2011; Weinstock 2001), or to manage conflicts between groups peacefully and fairly (De Schutter 2011; Levy 2007). Notably, however, while modern political theory highlights its positive effects for liberty and participation, scholars have rarely considered federalism as a design principle in theories of representative government. Nor do these theories tell us how federalism and democracy interact in reality.

Other normative approaches to federalism make the case for decentralization either as a condition for efficient or effective governance or as an institutional design that makes governments serve the people, thus emphasizing *output legitimacy*. The first reasoning finds expression in the economic theory of federalism. It explains why decentralization and competition between governments of different jurisdictions is conducive to the efficient provision of public services (Oates 1972). However, inter-jurisdictional competition responds to the mobility of taxpayers and, thus, privileges those groups in a society that profit from the low costs of mobility. The turn of economists towards the idea of "laboratory federalism" (Breton 1998; Oates 2005) introduced a new perspective on competitive federalism as a governance regime that facilitates policy innovation and best practices and, thus, establishes a sort of "democratic experimentalism." The second approach associates federalism with *subsidiarity*, a principle that gives precedence to decentralization of power. Yet although federalism implies decentralization, the smaller, constituent units of a federation are always embedded in a multi-level structure of governance and cannot solve the problems of modern societies on their own.

This "stratification" and the relations between levels of government are reflected in concepts that consider federalism as covenant (Elazar 1987) and as a consociational polity (Lijphart 1979), ideas that surfaced in the sixteenth and early seventeenth centuries in the context of Reformed Protestantism. The most elaborated version of this theory, published by Johannes Althusius ([1614] 1995), was rediscovered by Carl Joachim Friedrich (1975) and later by Thomas Hueglin (1999), both of whom explicated its relevance as a theory of federal democracy. They reformulated federalism as a process of continuous negotiation among representatives of small communities that had joined to form a government by contract. Instead of accentuating competition or decentralization, this line of theorizing links federalism to consensus democracy resulting from a sequence of negotiated agreements within and between jurisdictions. It reformulates the principle of subsidiarity from a legal rule privileging decentralization into a negotiation principle, a "political guideline for negotiated task assignment" (Hueglin and Fenna 2015, 140; see also Hueglin 2016, 270–2). Accordingly, division of power turns into a matter of democracy, even though it constitutes an essential feature of federalism. Yet it is not the consensus that results, but the quality of the processes of negotiation, that turns out to be the essential requirement of democratic federalism.

Consociational theory is relevant for a normative approach to federalism since it takes intergovernmental relations, or multi-level governance, into account (K. Scott 2011, 15). This fundamental feature is widely neglected in other normative theories. As far as they reflect on relations between levels or constituencies, as in the concept of checks and balances, they emphasize the constraining effects of a division of powers. On the other hand, theories that focus on subsidiarity, decentralization, or the protection of minorities assume that powers can be contained in territorial units. In consequence, they underrate the need to manage interdependence or to deal with the external effects of policies that cut across the boundaries of jurisdictions as well as the relevance of the institutions, procedures, and power appropriate to achieve these tasks.

In fact, federalism must be considered as a principle requiring a division of power *and* the coordination of policies made by governments exerting divided power, a principle stipulating differentiation *and* integration or diversity *and* unity. In consequence, a federation implies patterns of multi-level governance – that is, structures and processes of intergovernmental coordination, either through mutual adjustment or negotiation. It goes without saying that executives tend to predominate these processes, not least under conditions of modern government and public administration. Although executives can be influenced by parliaments, parties, and civil society associations, be it by providing input into agenda-setting or policy proposals, by ratifying agreements, or by monitoring executive policymaking, multi-level governance is based on a functional differentiation between intergovernmental and "domestic" politics. Accordingly, federalism and democracy refer to distinct institutional components of a polity. Whereas democratic legitimacy results from institutions and procedures linking government to the people within a jurisdiction, federalism concerns the division of powers among governments of different jurisdictions and the coordination of these powers. The structure of a federal democracy differentiates the procedures that create democratic legitimacy within the boundaries of jurisdictions and the intergovernmental politics and policymaking that span these boundaries.

Although many scholars have researched and written on federalism and democracy at least implicitly, they have rarely examined the question of how both interact in the institutions of government designed according to these principles. Surprisingly, this "subject has been a strangely neglected one in comparative political science," as Michael Burgess and Alain-G. Gagnon rightly pointed out in the preface to the most important publication in this context (Burgess and Gagnon 2010, xiii; see also Detterbeck and Hepburn 2018; Kincaid 2011). Indeed, in the many strands of research related to federalism, ranging from case studies on individual countries to comparative works, few publications have dealt explicitly with the impact of federalism on democracy or the question of how democracy affects federalism. Explicitly, the issue has been addressed mainly for particular states (for Canada: Simeon and Nugent 2008; for Australia and Canada: Sharman 1990; for Germany: Benz 2015; Lehmbruch 2000; for Switzerland: Vatter 2018b; for the United States: Robertson 2012), but rarely in broader comparative perspective (Stepan 1999).

The only book that addresses the research nexus between federalism and democracy is the above-mentioned volume, *Federal Democracies,* edited by Michael Burgess and Alain-G. Gagnon (2010). Without a doubt, this publication by two leading scholars in the field provides an extremely rich source of further research, combining theoretical contributions, case studies, and comparative analyses. However, the authors are interested mainly in conceptualizing "federal democracies" rather than analysing their particular operation. Moreover, the concept of democratic legitimacy applied in the volume shifts between the liberal and the republican model and between representation and representativeness. Although several authors mention the tensions between federalism and democracy, they neither analyse these tensions in detail nor take them as a starting point for better understanding how federal democracies operate. Thus, the volume provides an excellent overview of the state of research, but also reveals its limits and the need for further research.

In a further book, the late Michael Burgess elaborated the concept of federal democracy, again drawing on the ideas of liberalism, constitutionalism, and republicanism, the latter leading him to emphasize the "federal spirit" and a particular political culture founded in civil society (Burgess 2012). This attempt to integrate institutionalist and society-centred approaches (see, e.g., Livingston 1956) to federalism warrants further elaboration, although we should not ignore the tensions inherent in the institutions and causal processes of federal democracies.

A series of books produced by the Forum of Federations covers nearly all relevant aspects of the variations in the most important federal systems in the world. Although the issue of federalism and democracy has not been explicitly dealt with so far, two of the volumes in this series touch upon this nexus. The book edited by Klaus Detterbeck, Wolfgang Renzsch, and John Kincaid (2016) analyses the role of parties and civil society organizations in federations and the changes in party systems – thus, to a certain degree, focusing on the interplay of democracy and federalism. Another volume, edited by Johanne Poirier, Cheryl Saunders, and John Kincaid (2015), addresses various patterns of intergovernmental relations, using country studies and ending with a brief discussion of the problems for democracy that result from intergovernmental relations. Yet both the books and the series as a whole describe structures, operation, and development. They provide empirical material for comparative research, but they do not systematically explain the operation of federal systems in connection with democratic government.

A particular approach to federal democracy has emerged in research on multinational federalism, multinational democracies, and citizenship in multicultural societies (Requejo and Caminal 2012; Gagnon and Tully 2001; Requejo 2005). This literature is about democracy as a precondition of solving disputes in multinational societies and about the effects of the diversity of these societies on the concept and practices of constitution, federalism, and democracy. As such, this research strand contributes to the topic of our volume, but addresses a specific problem, usually from a particular, normative perspective of political philosophy (Kymlicka 2001; Tully 1995).

In contrast with scholars working on multinational federations, we start from the assumption that each federal system divides the demos into *demoï*, whether minority groups or different regional nationalities exist or not. Moreover, although research on democracy in federations has to address minority rights or the representation of distinct societies and the expression of the diversity of cultures, we also need to study the institutions of government and the operation of governance to understand how disputes are resolved. While the specific challenges faced by deeply diverse societies (e.g., due to language, regional identities, ethnicities, or religion) are of interest and significantly affect the intensity of tensions in federal democracies, we propose an analytical framework to study patterns of federal democracy that can travel across the various sociopolitical and cultural conditions under which federal democracies operate.

The relevance of federalism has found expression in a growing literature on multi-level governance. Related research has been propelled by a number of developments, such as the simultaneous processes of globalization and regionalization, the decline of the state as a dominating political order, and the rise of multi-level, multinational, territorially differentiated polities or regimes. In this context, scholars have discussed the dilemma of effective governance and democratic legitimacy that is becoming apparent in these new political orders (Dahl 1994; DeBardeleben and Hurrelmann 2007; Papadopoulos 2010; Scharpf 1999; Sørensen and Torfing 2007). However, scholars have identified and discussed this dilemma mainly in research on governance beyond the state or in the multi-level system of the EU – thus, from the outset, with particular political regimes in mind (Piattoni 2015). Only a few have taken advantage of the potential of comparative research on federal democracies to better understand how the combination of federalism and democracy can work under the condition of modern governments and societies.

Worthy of mention are the volume edited by Kalypso Nicolaïdis and Robert Howse (2001) and the books by Sergio Fabbrini (2005) and Joseph Lacey (2017). Lacey compares the EU with the Belgian and Swiss federal democracies. Interested in how a demos can emerge in a multilingual political system divided into demoï, he makes the claim for establishing a multiple and multifaceted "voting space compound," consisting of elements of representative and direct democracy, but he neglects intergovernmental relations in general and the problem of executive dominance in multi-level governance in particular. Fabbrini focuses on the United States and actually presents a study on how democracy is linked to federalism in this case. Nicolaïdis and Howse present articles that deal with general or theoretical issues or compare the EU with the United States. Their volume – in particular, the concluding chapter by Nicolaïdis – emphasizes the need for flexibility and balance in a federal democracy and provides an impetus to further develop the concept of "demoïcracy," elaborated in other publications (see, e.g., Cheneval and Schimmelfennig 2013). As interesting as this concept might be, it refers mainly to the input side of democratic legitimacy. In contrast, our book also considers the need for policy coordination and the problems of effective governing in a multi-level democracy, and it intends to uncover the logics of the political system in federations.

Considering comparative research, there are certainly quantitative studies on the quality of democracy in different states of the world. However, they largely ignore the impact of federalism. An exception is the study by Pippa Norris, who was particularly interested in the effects of power-sharing (Norris 2008). Using statistical data analysis, she established a positive correlation between a federal state organization and the quality of democracy, which she determined using different indexes. She also found the quality of democracy to be higher in parliamentary systems than in presidential ones. Lane and Ersson, on the other hand, concluded that there was no link between federalism and democracy and asserted that this was the reason for the inherent tensions that exist in a federation (Lane and Ersson 2005).

Scholars also came to different conclusions as to whether effective and legitimate governance required power concentration (Gerring and Thacker 2008) or power diffusion (Bernauer and Vatter 2019). Apparently, these differences in findings arise from the conceptualization of government systems or the measurement of the quality of democracy. Nevertheless, these studies call for further examining the interrelationships between federalism and democracy in more detail, but this requires more in-depth analyses of patterns of federal democracy. Hence, a considerable research desideratum becomes apparent. With a view to the many political developments of recent years, it would seem that questions of territorial organization and democracy could hardly be more topical. Consequently, it is necessary to establish more analytical clarity about the relations between federalism and democracy. Moreover, we need sound empirical evidence on how they interact in reality and how they vary in different federations. Certainly, our volume cannot close this research gap. However, it is intended to take some first steps in advancing research in this important field.

The Approach of This Book

Compared with other publications in this research field, the contributions in this volume take a distinct approach. First, they conceive democracy and federalism as design principles realized in two divergent, but closely related, institutional dimensions of government. Regardless of the particular patterns resulting from constitutional design and evolution, they establish different arenas of politics, include different actor constellations, and imply different logics of operation. Both democracy and federalism involve a structural, functional, *and* territorial organization of politics and contribute to the legitimacy of governance, but by fulfilling different purposes – in short: democracy by governing according to the will of the people, federalism by integrating diverse communities of citizens by mutual recognition and cooperation.

Second, we suppose that how these two dimensions are linked, how different processes of politics and policymaking interact, and whether the inevitable tensions turn into frictions or imbalance ultimately depend on how specific institutions operate and how governance actually works. Therefore, we have to focus on the mechanisms of decision-making that prevail in the institutional setting of the particular federations (concerning the relations between governments at different levels) and patterns of democracy (concerning decision-making within a government). Third, the concept of coupling is used to capture various types of interlinkage between federalism and democracy as well as the dynamics between them that result from tensions and the efforts of actors to cope with them.

Finally, we reformulate the concept of democratic legitimacy insofar as we include – in addition to the basic democratic criteria of equality, inclusion, representation, and accountability (see, e.g., Dahl 1998) – the balance of power, or non-domination (Pettit 2012), which we understand, for our intents and purposes, to be a decisive, normative standard referring to the relative impact of multi-level coordination and democratic procedures on final decisions. In consequence, the challenge of federal democracy is to maintain this balance against the forces inherent in complex, multi-level, democratic systems of government: those originating from parliaments and parties and those set off by executives, bureaucrats, or special interest groups.

Having this perspective on the systemic character of federal democracy, our approach is not designed to provide information about the quality of participation by citizens, the protection of their freedoms or individual rights, or the overall characterization of different polities as federal or democratic. Therefore, we do not follow the research ambition behind a number of indexes that measure either the quality of democracy or the degree of decentralization and/or federalism. Nor does our collaborative study aspire to propose a single-model case of federalism, one that is optimal for improving democratic quality or other aspects of system or policy performance. Historical analyses of the development of federal systems, similar to the emergence and evolution of different democratic government forms, should make us aware that context and dynamics, rather than the "rational choices" of institutional design, have determined the different federal models in different countries. Nonetheless, choices are by no means irrelevant, particularly when institutional and policy learning and adaptation over time are concerned (Benz and Broschek 2013a, 379–82). This insight constitutes a fundamental point of departure for this volume. Moreover, it connects research on how different federal democracies develop with an analysis of the various arrangements of interlinkage and governance designed for coping with and effectively managing the tensions between the two regime dimensions.

To provide answers to these questions, this book presents an analytical approach and basic assumptions about the operation of federal democracies that guide the selected studies. They focus on the following aspects:

1. Taken as political ideas, democracy and federalism provide corresponding normative reasons for the legitimacy of political power. To delineate in condensed, and by no means exhaustive, fashion: democracy links power to the will of the people, federalism acknowledges the existence of multiple demoï; democracy presumes equality of citizens, federalism emphasizes equality of peo-

ples of states or state-like political units; in democracy, the majority rules, federalism empowers minorities and requires power-sharing; democracy is based on individual freedom, federalism aims for solidarity (see also Hueglin, chap. 2).[1]

Hence, federal democracies should not be evaluated merely in terms of a liberal order that limits governments; they also constitute polities that integrate multiple communities and manage the plurality of the interests expressed by society. Yet corresponding ideas or values are not identical; they concern different aspects, and correspondence does not rule out discrepancies or conflicts. In complex political systems, corresponding values need to be balanced. As regards federalism, we find this need expressed by the notions of unity versus diversity, integration versus differentiation, or self-rule versus shared rule. In the same manner, normative propositions derived from the ideas of federalism and democracy have to be considered.

2. In existing federal democracies, these propositions are transformed into different institutional settings. As mentioned, these institutional settings of federalism and of democracy establish distinct contexts of politics and actor constellations. Accordingly, politics and decision-making reveal distinct logics of operation – that is, mechanisms of political interaction. These institutions and processes materialize in various forms and composite structures of governance. However, to analyse whether and how they concur or interfere with each other, we can identify basic characteristic processes in modern democracies and federal systems.

   As a set of core institutions guaranteeing legitimized political power, democracy is defined as government by representatives, who are elected by the people, are accountable to the people, and, thus, are motivated to govern according to the will of the people – provided that citizens are able to freely express their opinion about political issues in public. Democratic government has to be organized in a territorially defined jurisdiction that establishes a certain congruence between the scope of power that governments are in charge of and the community of those affected by power and participating in elections and public communications. A federal system divides jurisdictions, creates a two- or three-tiered order, and, accordingly, constitutes a demos at the federal level and demoï at the sub-federal levels.

   While governance in a democracy is, in principle, bound to territorial jurisdictions, federal governance concerns the relations among governments, particularly for the purpose of coordinating policies that cut across territorial boundaries, not least in order to cope with unjustified disparities and accepted diversities. While powers are separated or shared by constitutional rules and legislation mainly creates distinct realms of law, interdependences between policies are dealt with by executives and intergovernmental relations, be it by mutual adjustments of unilateral policymaking at the different levels or by various kinds of interaction or cooperation. Democracy, in contrast, establishes other mechanisms of politics, which are determined to make governments accountable to the people and empower the people to control governments by elections, party politics, public debates, and contestation of power and policies.

3. These institutional dimensions are linked, and so are the processes and the mechanisms of policymaking. Their interlinkages are structured by institutions or emerge from practice. In a federation, democratic governments making policies in their jurisdiction have to consider the external effects on other governments caused by this autonomous policymaking and adjust their policies to those effects or coordinate their policies in intergovernmental relations – de facto, at the latest, when cross-jurisdictional problems are concerned and certainly when cross-level coordination is prescribed by constitutional law. Depending on the type of democratic government, executives involved in these external relations are responsible to parliaments – for example, their majority party or coalition, in particular, or the legislature as a whole – or directly to citizens. In principle, they have to take into account the will of their party or party coalitions supporting them or the will of parliament or the electorate in general.
4. The different mechanisms of politics and governance generated by particular institutions of federalism and democracy, or inter- and intra-governmental patterns of politics, are linked, and the respective processes mutually interfere. As a result, they regularly cause tensions in the interface of the arenas of democracy and federalism. Party politics in parliaments or the party affiliation of executives can cause confrontational behaviour in intergovernmental negotiations and obstruct policy coordination by mutual adjustment and policy learning among governments. Negotiated intergovernmental agreements achieved by executives or specialized civil servants can be contested in parliaments when the majority and the opposition parties emphasize the presumed interests of their electorates. When a plurality of parties requires coalition governments or issue-specific agreements among parties in minority governments, intergovern-

mental coordination by policy adjustment or negotiations can be hampered by the countervailing commitments of executives or uncertainty about parliamentary support.

Uncertainty about the majority for a decision is also inherent when intergovernmental agreements have to be ratified by a referendum. Power separation between the executive and the parliament reduces party political constraints in intergovernmental relations, which can reinforce executive dominance. However, direct elections of leaders of the executive can also intensify party politics and confrontation affecting the interplay of executive-legislative and intergovernmental relations.

At first glance, power separation and self-rule in federalism may seem to be compatible with democratic politics in parliamentary and presidential governments. But since governmental autonomy is reinforced by democracy, coping with policy interdependences between levels and constituent units in a federation can become extremely difficult. As these examples illustrate, tensions turn into frictions when enduring impasses and instability either reduce the effectiveness of governance or lead to a deficit in democratic legitimacy. The first problem appears if parliaments, parties, or popular democracy dominates; the second one results from executive dominance.

5. Tensions are inherent in federal democracies, while frictions can be avoided. Whether actors are able to cope with tensions depends on the patterns of linkages between the institutional dimensions. Linkages differ according to the intensity of their coupling between structures and processes constituting federal democracies and, in particular, the degree of autonomy or dependence of the executives who are involved in both the intragovernmental and the intergovernmental arenas.

   In some cases, we find a clear separation of powers. If this applies in the federal system, institutions permit only voluntary intergovernmental coordination, non-binding agreements, or mutual adjustment. In the executive-legislative dimension of non-parliamentary systems (e.g., presidential governments), the executive's hands are not tied by majority parties in parliament, although it has to cooperate with members of the legislature or party leaders. Accordingly, inter- and intragovernmental processes are, at best, linked by informal processes involving not only multiple levels but also multiple branches of government. In contrasting cases of tightly coupled federal democracies, institutions of federalism establish power-sharing in compulsory negotiations among governments, which depend on the will of the majority in the parliament they are accountable to. In consequence, executives' discretion is strongly constrained by the rules of intergovernmental and democratic politics.

These patterns of weak or tight coupling are vulnerable to arbitrary power asymmetries caused by the actual "strength of weak ties" (Granovetter 1985) or the predominance of actors who are subject to strong ties. Beyond these cases, we find systems of loose coupling characterized by redundant linkages and communicative relations, which make institutional constraints flexible and processes in the different arenas transparent. These systems allow actors to make effective and legitimate policies by balancing their commitments in the federal (intergovernmental) and democratic (intragovernmental) arenas.

6. For this reason, we suggest considering structures and processes that link democratic politics and (multi-level) governance in federalism as a decisive condition for balancing the corresponding normative standard of democracy and federalism. In cases of balance, a federal democracy would conform to input and output legitimacy, but – more important – it would also avoid a domination of actors profiting either from interactions in multi-level relations (executive federalism) or from predominating parties or particular interest groups at the central or regional level.

For these reasons, linkage structures constitute essential conditions for making federal democracies work. The different intensities of coupling determine how tensions between federalism and democracy can be coped with and how and in what direction federal democracies develop (e.g., towards balance or imbalance). Coupling is affected by structural parameters and institutional configurations, but also, in political practice, by governance and the strategic action of political actors. Conceptualizing coupling arrangements between federal and democratic institutions and processes provides an enhanced approach to understanding what makes federal democracies work. It also allows us to capture the various patterns of federal democracy and foster a richer comparative analysis of the varieties of federalism. What is certain in this regard is that federal democracies, on account of their mutual, concurring, and in part contradictory principles and logics of operation, have to strike a balance: not only between self-rule and shared rule, competition and cooperation, but also, and especially, autonomy in democratic government and comity in multi-level governance.

By emphasizing the relevance of balance, we take into account the fact that particular conditions and the inherent dynamics of federal democracies can cause imbalance. No federal democracy is inherently immune from this risk, as some of the case studies collected in this volume demonstrate. To further identify the conditions that cause different kinds of imbalance warrants further research, for which this volume aspires to contribute fruitful groundwork.

Structure of the Book

This volume is divided into two main parts. The first part consists of chapters on cross-cutting theoretical and conceptual issues. It provides, in particular, basic analytical categories that guide the empirical studies. These studies are collected into the second part, which includes chapters on selected federal democracies. In the final chapter, we summarize the main findings in a comparative perspective and draw conclusions on the operation of federal democracies.

The three theoretical contributions that form the first part of this volume address three basic questions, already outlined above. From the perspective of normative political theory, *Thomas O. Hueglin* suggests taking neither federalism as an obstacle for democracy or a demos-constraining institution nor liberal democracy as the yardstick for assessing federalism (i.e., in how far federalism promotes democracy, etc.), but rather including the federal principle in defining democratic legitimacy. Federalism can indeed mitigate the deficits of real democracies, yet not by limiting the power of government but by constituting a republican democracy based on solidarity among citizens and communities, consensus on basic matters of dispute, and subsidiarity. This concept of federalism inspires theorizing on democracy and provides yardsticks for democratic legitimacy on its own terms.

Taking this as an appropriate normative foundation, *Arthur Benz* addresses federal democracy as a particular political system and emphasizes the structural diversity and conflicting mechanisms that characterize federal democracies and cause the tensions outlined above. His chapter outlines the different ways of linking the two institutional dimensions of federalism and democratic government – in particular, by describing three types of coupling: decoupling, tight coupling, and loose coupling. The chapter explains that loosely coupled structures linked by various processes promise to improve the quality of democratic legitimacy and coordinated governance in federal democracies. As Benz concludes, the challenge in loosely coupled patterns is to balance the institutional arrangements, powers, and mechanisms of politics in the democratic and federal arenas of governance.

The chapter by *John Erik Fossum* and *David Laycock* focuses on this problem, starting from the republican ideal of democracy as non-domination. They argue that loose coupling of federalism and democracy cannot guarantee self-determination of the federal demos and the demoï of the constituent units of a federation, as is revealed by the typical problem of executive dominance. To find ways to avoid this imbalance, the authors analyse different causes and instances of federalism dominated by the executive.

As the three chapters in the first part of the book explain, federal democracies operating in accordance with the normative standards of a republican democracy – of solidarity, consensus, and subsidiarity, or non-domination – cannot be designed by constitutional rules alone. While constitutions and institutions certainly matter, much depends on linkage structures like the party system, public communication, and civil society as well as on political practice, the way actors in the executive and in parliaments interact, and how intergovernmental coordination is achieved. Hence, our approach implies that empirical research has to address the following aspects: In which various ways can institutions of federalism and democracy be loosely coupled? Can actors in federal democracies manage the tensions of tightly coupled or disconnected structures and, if so, how? How do these structures evolve and change over time as a consequence of the actors' responses to inherent tensions? If developments point towards, for example, decoupling and fragmentation or, rather, tight coupling and inflexibility, how might they turn into loosely coupled patterns? And, if not, what might the consequences be?

The second part of our volume comprises case studies on eight federal democracies, each of which can be considered a well-established system of federalism and democratic government. We also selected cases that, taken together, cover both a considerable extent of commonalities and parallels and a sufficient spectrum of variance. They include the oldest democratic federations (Switzerland and the United States), which, at the same time, represent modern democracies that are not parliamentary governments, and younger federations, which mostly have parliamentary systems. The cases cover monolingual, multilingual, and multinational federal democracies, but also those conventionally typified – according to the widely adopted concept by Lijphart (2012) – as consensus democracies (Switzerland), majoritarian democracies (e.g., Canada and Australia), and mixed forms of democracy (Germany, Belgium, India, United States). This collection of selected cases allows not only for informative individual studies but also for meaningful comparison.

The case studies are informed by the conceptual framework set out in the first part of the book, but they certainly cannot deal with all normative or theoretical issues. They focus on the structures of a particular federation and patterns of intergovernmental policy coordination and democracy, and they analyse how they have co-evolved, what kind of tensions have materialized, and whether and to what extent this situation threatens the balance of the federation and the quality of democracy. In general, the case studies show the variety of patterns that can be categorized according to the extent of arena coupling (see the concluding chapter). Beyond that, they emphasize the particular patterns, problems, and practices characterizing the individual cases and, therefore, reflect the variety of federal democracies.

Thus, *Timothy Conlan* examines the evolution of federalism and democracy in the United States by drawing particular attention to informal institutions that link an institutionally disconnected dual federalism with a presidential democracy, elaborating three significant trends that have had – and are having – significant implications for the federalism-democracy relationship in the United States – political nationalization, polarization, and delegitimation of government – implications that reflect the problematic effects of tightly coupled systems. *Sean Mueller* highlights the particular features of direct democracy and decentralized federalism in Switzerland. He explains how both combine to form a loosely coupled system in which federalism has enabling and constraining effects on democracy, but where that democracy also enables and constrains the operation of governance in that federalism. As in the United States, the recent polarization of party politics may threaten this arrangement and its balance.

For a long time, scholars regarded power-sharing in federalism and parliamentary democracy as incompatible, though with different reasoning. For Germany, constitutional theory as well as political scientists diagnosed a fundamental conflict between joint decision-making and party competition in parliamentary democracy. *Sabine Kropp*'s more nuanced study reveals different combinations of both institutional dimensions of government. They are linked in various ways and have sometimes increased the tensions inherent in democratic federations, but they also generate an elasticity of power structures. Recent changes in party politics tend to threaten this elasticity, which explains the push for constitutional reform as well as the constraints of joint decision-making on a redistribution of power and financial resources.

As *Andrew Banfield* and *Anthony Sayers* demonstrate for Australia, moderate changes in election rules or the institutional setting of intergovernmental relations can avoid frictions in a federation with a joint-decision system coupled with party competition in the context of a parliamentary government. They also emphasize the role of bureaucracy, expert councils, and the High Court, which moderate the impact of party competition and induce governments to adopt a pragmatic approach to cope with the tensions of a federal democracy. This is less possible in Canada, where, as *Jörg Broschek* argues, Westminster democracy has shaped the institutional foundations of federalism by promoting a drift towards self-rule. This condition, combined with the need to manage the interdependence between the federal and provincial governments, has caused intergovernmental dynamics by generating cyclical swings between unilateralism and cooperation. The effect is that the intensity of the coupling between the democratic and federal arenas has become looser, but with the consequence that federal democracy is always threatened by imbalance.

Jörg Broschek's chapter and the last three country studies concern federal democracies in multinational states. In the comparative research on federalism, the distinction between multi- and mono-national societies has been considered highly relevant for explaining constitutional evolution and change, party politics, even stability and disintegration in federations. Regarding democracy, the existence of regions dominated by a population claiming minority rights and speaking a distinct vernacular has particular impacts on democracy. As the last three case studies show, politics centred on these differences can shift the balance towards federalism, but with problematic consequences for democracy. For Belgium, *Petra Meier* and *Peter Bursens* argue that the rationale underlying the restructuring of the Belgian state has never been to enhance democracy but rather to federalize the political system to appease the conflict between the ethnolinguistic communities. In consequence, the federal party system has dissolved, and the notion of demoï now dominates over that of a demos, while the tight coupling of executives to party politics undermines the integrative function of intergovernmental coordination.

For Spain, most researchers have emphasized the tensions arising from conflicts between the central government and the autonomous communities, which are striving for more power or independence. However, until recently, these conflicts were tightly connected to a dualist party competition between the Social Democrats and the Conservatives. As *César Colino* reveals, tensions between party politics and relations between the central government and the autonomous communities intensify in moments of absolute majority at the central level. However, they tend to soften in situations of minority government through a series of mechanisms that facilitate intergovernmental coordination among governments, without the parties and parliaments losing control.

This impact of changes in the party system on the linkage between parliamentary democracy and multi-level governance is also confirmed by *Wilfried Swenden* and *Katharine Adeney* for multi-ethnic India. The case study shows that accountability to subnational electorates in the divided society is contingent on the nature of the party system and the style of interaction among the party elites but also on administrative relations across multiple levels. Recent developments in Spain and India demonstrate that, under particular conditions, tensions turn into frictions, which can destabilize a federal democracy.

Based on the book's analytical framework, the concluding chapter brings the case studies together in a comparative perspective. It highlights the varieties of, and changes within, federal democracies that affect the tensions between intergovernmental coordination and the power of parliaments, parties, and citizens against the executive. The conclusion focuses on the tensions inherent in structures of intergovernmental relations and democratic politics. As the empirical studies collected in the second part of this volume reveal, these tensions have evolved in particular institutional configurations. These institutional configurations and the related structures set the framework for linking processes, and they do this in a way that is more or less open for loose, flexible coupling. Workable connections depend less on institutions than on party systems, networks of executives or patterns of interaction in intergovernmental relations, and relations between executives and parliaments as well as on strategic action in the processes of decision-making, control, and revision – all of which shift the policies among the different arenas. Hence, as the empirical studies indicate, loose coupling can be achieved in various ways, in spite of institutional constraints. Since the case studies cannot cover these manifold patterns and practices in sufficient detail, the final chapter outlines only theoretical conclusions and avenues for further research. It is meant to foster a better understanding of not only the tensions, frictions, and imbalances of federal democracies but also the options and implications of loosely coupled structures and processes.

The democratic federations included in our comparative analyses rank relatively high in all indexes that measure the quality of democracy. We are aware of the differences that exist among them in that regard. We also recognize the crisis of democracy or increasing divides in federalism, which have hit some of the countries included in this volume more than others in recent years, such as revived secessionism by Catalonia in Spain, almost unprecedented polarization in the United States, and the authoritarian tendencies of the central government in India. We do not intend to explain their particular causes or conditions, although the analytical approach in this volume can prove beneficial in this regard because such recent developments may reveal case-specific failures to cope with the tensions inherent in federal democracies. Rather, we address a more basic problem and aspire to understand how federalism and democracy can be reconciled despite their different functions and modes of operation and despite the obvious tensions caused by incompatible institutional structures and interfering mechanisms.

We believe that our approach is not only of theoretical relevance. It also implies the practical consequences for institutional reform in federalism as well as, more generally, the search for ways to manage institutional tensions and balance the requirements of democratic legitimacy and effective intergovernmental governance. As such, the volume raises some of the most cardinal and yet persistently current questions for political science in general and the comparative study of federalism and democracy in particular. They concern what makes complex systems work as much as what "holds them together." While we cannot answer these questions definitively, the following studies pave the way for future research to approach the answers.

NOTE

1 Surely the democratic theoretical spectrum can be conceived as being much broader, to include other variants and perspectives – be they more deliberative, civil-society-oriented, or otherwise participatory, among others. However, we consider federal democracies as political systems and therefore focus on the core institutions of the different varieties of these systems. We do not rule out the processes of interest intermediation or citizen participation, which can change the way politics in federal and democratic institutions are linked.

2 Federalism as a Yardstick for Democracy

THOMAS O. HUEGLIN

Investigating patterns of federal democracy means exploring the tensions that exist between political institutions and practices that are usually labelled federal, characterized by a division of power among different orders of government as well as rules for separating and/or sharing these powers, and political institutions and practices usually labelled democratic, with some form of accountability in a system of representative government. As Benz and Sonnicksen show convincingly, this is an entirely useful exercise. Conventional assumptions, according to which federalism promotes or inhibits democracy, and democracy as a prerequisite for federalism, give way to expressions of a more nuanced relationship between federalism and democracy that is characterized by multiple tensions (Benz and Sonnicksen 2017).

I want to argue, however, that characterizing the relationship between federalism and democracy as tension is somewhat misleading. Tensions are typically explored between concepts with equal claims to validity, such as a tension between, say, individual liberty and community. I do not think that this is quite so in the case of federalism and democracy. Inherent in conventional investigations into the compatibility of federalism and democracy is a conceptual predisposition, according to which democracy is a priori good in a normative sense, whereas federalism needs to be questioned critically as to whether it contributes to the primary objective of democratic goodness. In this way, if the values of democracy in theory and practice are not questioned themselves, a critical analysis of federalism can quickly become based on rather naïve assumptions about democracy.

In this chapter, then, I want to turn the tables by asking whether democracy in theory and practice provides a useful yardstick for a critical assessment of federalism as a normative good in itself. For this purpose, I will first debunk some of the myths that usually hold for democratic legitimacy. I will then describe where I see democratic and federal legitimacy parting ways and, finally, offer a conceptual approach to evaluating the political legitimacy of federalism on its own, normative terms.

Democratic Myths

Canadians are often told that theirs is a country whose origins are less legitimate than those of the neighbouring United States of America because the first Canadian Constitution, the British North America Act of 1867, was cobbled together as a compromise among elites and without popular consent. It is quite true, of course, that the Americans had their Constitution ratified by elected conventions in the several states. But the entire process, in the United States as much as in Canada, was controlled and driven by those enfranchised, a small fraction of the population due to property qualifications. The difference is that the propertied classes got to decide twice in America in comparison to just once in Canada. The Americans were better only in creating a myth of popular consent (Russell 2004, 8).

Notwithstanding lofty declarations to the contrary, the meaning of popular sovereignty was, at least initially, not much more than a rather nebulous claim of "we the people" conjured up in bourgeois revolutions against the prior claim of the divine sovereignty of kings. Kings at least had the advantage of knowing for themselves what they wanted. The people had to be told. As even the great champion of popular sovereignty, Jean-Jacques Rousseau, admitted, the people needed a lawgiver who was not one of their own because "the public must be taught to recognize what it desires" (Rousseau [1762] 1968, bk. 2, chap. 7). And only when these desires were fully instilled in the entire populace could the "people's deputies" truly become its "agents" (ibid., bk. 3, chap. 15).

What about accountable representative government, then, so vehemently rejected by Rousseau ([1762] 1968)? In most so-called democracies, the candidates for parliamentary election are anointed by their parties. They then go door to door in their respective constituencies, promising to be faithful agents of the local interest. Once elected, however, they become obedient tools of party discipline, driven by political expediency, if not corporate interest. Disillusioned with the entire process of democratic politics, voters may eventually fall victim to the siren songs of populist leaders. It was Plato who first contended that democracy inevitably ends up in tyranny.

And majority rule? It was Tocqueville, in turn, who first observed that the will of the majority would qualify as a stand-in for democracy only when it was given the halo of moral rather than merely quantitative superiority (Tocqueville [1835–40] 2000, vol. 1, pt. 2, chap. 7). And that moral superiority is nowadays almost routinely bestowed upon elected governments by a minority of eligible voters. Moreover, the electoral systems in democratic countries distort whatever the will of the majority may be. While majorities are grossly exaggerated or even artificially created by first-past-the-post systems, they may be beholden to minority blackmail in the inevitable coalition requirements created by proportional representation systems.

One would nevertheless assume, finally, that accountable, representative, majoritarian governance should be democratic at least in the sense that it cannot blatantly cater to the privileged few. And, indeed, the accountable, representative majoritarian democracies have all established policies for the many, from public education to social security and health care. In most, if not all, these democracies, however, and particularly over the period of the last thirty years or so, albeit to varying degrees, the distribution of income and wealth has grossly favoured a tiny minority. After the 2008 financial crisis, popular movements such as Occupy Wall Street achieved nothing. Indeed, US President Barak Obama, who galvanized what may well have been a genuine majority with his electoral slogan of "Yes, we can," bailed out banks instead of people.

Some eighty years ago, Harold Laski wrote about the "obsolescence of federalism." The balkanization of political power in federal systems, he argued, would prove to be helpless against the forces of giant capitalism ([1939] 2005). As it turns out, the two industrialized democracies showing the greatest levels of income inequality are the United States and the United Kingdom. One is a federal state, the other is not. Federalism, it would appear, is not to blame. What holds for democracy is.

It would seem, then, that the ubiquitous reference to democracy as the yardstick of all that is good in politics is a little bit like Plato's magnificent myth or noble lie. In *Politeia*, when Glaucon is sceptical about how people would accept a political system in which justice means minding one's business in a rigid class society, Plato has Socrates suggest to tell them how the qualities of gold, silver, and bronze have been instilled in people by the gods, or by nature, and that, at least over several generations, they will come to believe it (Plato [n.d.] 1955, 414b–15c). As Christopher Morrissey (2016), a philosophy professor in British Columbia, writes about Socrates's ruse in "The Imaginative Conservative," a newsletter edited by the president of the Free Enterprise Institute: "It is not an untruth. Instead, it is a tradition that *all* the citizens have come to see, on the basis of their shared experience, as best approximating the hard-to-discern fullness of truth about their place in the world" – fake news becoming fake truth.

I am not trying to make a case against democracy. It may well be, as Churchill famously said, that democracy is "the worst form of government except all other forms that have been tried from time to time" (Churchill 1947). Plato actually kind of agreed. In *Politikos*, where he first admits that all existing political forms will inevitably fall short of his ideal, he provides an insightful analysis of the different forms that have been tried. The rule of one is best, Plato declares, when it is a lawful monarchy, but worst as a lawless tyranny. At the other end of the spectrum, he continues, democracy as rule of the many is the weakest form of government when it is lawful, but also the most harmless when it is lawless. Democracy is, in fact, the most liveable among lawless regimes because "under it offices are distributed in small portions among many people" (Plato [n.d.] 1997, 302d–3b).

I am also not suggesting that the democracies under which we live are lawless. In fact, I would argue that what we most commonly mean by democracy, apart from periodic elections, is not captured by the usual fuzzy incantations such as inclusiveness, responsiveness, or accountability. Instead, I think that what most clearly distinguishes democracy from non-democratic regimes is exactly this: the comfortable knowledge that there are rules that will be followed or, as first preformulated by Thomas Hobbes, that "in all kinds of actions, by the laws praetermitted, men have the Liberty, of doing what their own reasons shall suggest, for the most profitable to themselves" ([1651] 1991, chap. 21, original p. 109). Even if these laws are often toothless when it comes to social justice, democracy, or at least what is liberal about democracy, is, in this sense, less harmful than other forms of government.

But is it democratic? It may be more appropriate, in fact, to see what holds for democracy as a mixed republican regime, which Machiavelli described as a fragile balance between an upper class with "a great desire to dominate" and a lower class driven by "merely the desire not to be dominated" ([1531] 1970, bk. 1, chap. 5). The great Florentine realist also observed that "all legislation favourable to liberty is brought about by the clash between them" (ibid., bk. 1, chap. 4). The deregulatory destruction of labour power since the 1980s, the delusional search for a third way by progressive parties since the 1990s, and the hollow appeals to a shrinking middle class by politicians of all shades ever since do not inspire much hope for legislation favourable to liberty.

Democratic and Federal Legitimacy: Where Is the Problem?

One of the conventional ways in which the legitimacy of political systems can be discussed in a less value-laden and more systematic fashion is by distinguishing between input and output legitimacy, in the tradition of David Easton (1965) and Fritz Scharpf (1970). *Input legitimacy* in terms of democracy means elections and representative government. *Output legitimacy*, in turn, means effective governance in terms of problem-solving capacity and citizen satisfaction.

On both counts, the established federal systems are as legitimate as any other political systems generally classified as democratic and, with regard to input legitimacy, perhaps more so. Input legitimacy is about the participatory quality of politics, and federal systems double down on both elections and representative government by offering choice at two levels of government. A range of political decisions, as prescribed by federal constitutions, will be made closer to the people.

In terms of output legitimacy, the effectiveness of federal systems has sometimes been questioned. Yet, in regionally divided societies such as Canada, unitary governance is not an option, and even in highly homogeneous societies such as Australia, it is not desired. Moreover, taking the modern welfare state as one important yardstick of output effectiveness and citizen satisfaction, the comparative record of federal systems measures up quite well, at least over time. While "institutional blockage" may have slowed down social policy development in its earlier formative phase, it now also puts a brake on neo-liberal dismantling (Obinger, Leibfried, and Castles 2005).

In discussing input and output, therefore, it appears superfluous to engage in elaborate investigations about suspected incompatibilities or even tensions between federal and democratic legitimacy. And, indeed, the democratic discontent with federalism stems from elsewhere, from the political process itself, the way decisions are made and final authority may be contested. For this reason, Vivien Schmidt has suggested "throughput" as a third normative category of democratic legitimacy (2013).

Despite the well-established and long-standing distinction between majority and consensus, or consociational, democracies (Lijphart 2012), the kind of democratic throughput legitimacy that is usually held up as a critical yardstick for evaluating federal systems essentially means parliamentary supremacy or, more precisely, supremacy of the parliamentary majority. In large part, this is so because democratic discomfort with federalism is a particular characteristic in the so-called parliamentary federations such as Canada and Australia, where the Westminster tradition of parliamentary absolutism has remained a strong focal point of political legitimacy. In presidential federations such as the United States of America, by comparison, the normative focus is more on the system of republican checks and balances, with federalism as its legitimate vertical dimension.

From a perspective of majoritarian parliamentary supremacy, however, the democratic-throughput credentials of federalism are suspect because "any functioning federal system denies by its very processes that the national majority is the efficient expression of the sovereignty of the people" (Whitaker 1992, 167). This denial comes in several ways.

First, national parliamentary majority decisions can be second-guessed by the second legislative chamber. The senates in both Canada and Australia are regarded with democratic suspicion, albeit for different reasons. The Canadian Senate is government-appointed and lacks political legitimacy even in basic democratic terms. The directly elected and partisan-driven Australian Senate, in turn, is seen as lacking federal political legitimacy because it does not perform any discernible function as a regional chamber, as is the case with most, if not all, directly elected second chambers.

Second, majority decisions at either level of government can be invalidated by the courts. One of the main pro-Brexit arguments was to get out from under the shadow of the European Court of Justice to "end the supremacy of EU Law in Britain" (Allan and Parker 2017). Since federal systems are, by definition, systems of divided powers, everyone understands that there has to be some kind of final arbitration in the case of power conflict. But for purists of parliamentary supremacy, "judicial power is a frightening third estate in a federal system" (Saywell 2002, 308).

Third, all federal systems inevitably rely on intergovernmental relations, conducted by the executive branch of government. Intergovernmental relations are inevitable because the theoretical assumption of classical federalism, that the division of powers allows the two orders of government to operate in separate, autonomous spheres of jurisdiction, has proved, in practice, to be an illusion. The reality is that both orders of government in modern federations are simultaneously active in almost all policy fields. Minimally, this amounts to a need for administrative coordination, but, more often than not, it requires intergovernmental processes of joint decision-making, leading to negotiated agreement on compromise. Such agreements, however, like international agreements, are not typically justiciable. To the extent that they are concluded on the basis of existing law, they also do not always require majoritarian approval by the respective legislatures. And, even if they do, the accusation is that the people's representatives are involved only ex post facto, signing off on executive deals in the gestation of which they had no hand or voice. As Donald Smiley (1979, 107) put it for Canada: executive federalism contributes to "non-participatory and non-accountable processes of government."

So where is the problem? If democracy really comes down to not much more than accountability of the executive to the elected representatives of the people, then federalism would appear to stray only very little from this path of democratic righteousness. The bicameral process of "compound majoritarianism" (Elazar 1987, 19) can be criticized in terms of federalism because – except perhaps for the German Bundesrat, which is composed of subnational government delegates – second chambers rarely represent the collective interests of the federated entities. But in terms of democracy, it means only that lawmakers have to contend with two possibly conflicting manifestations of the popular will. And only someone rather naïve about the democratic serenity of the people's representatives would seriously question the political legitimacy of an independent judiciary watching over the rule of law.

What remains is the discomfort with executive federalism, stereotypically depicted as late-night deals behind closed doors. As I have tried to show elsewhere, however, the lack of transparency and inclusion does not automatically make the intergovernmental process undemocratic (Hueglin 2013a). Federalism is more than just a constitutional division of powers. It also and essentially rests on the normative assumption that the members of a larger union have a right to pursue their particular collective interests and, in doing so, to be represented by their democratically elected governments. The intergovernmental process provides an entirely legitimate forum for the articulation and cooperative coordination of such interests.

It is for this reason that I think that the conventional democratic criticisms of federalism are misguided and that the political legitimacy of federalism must be tested and critically evaluated on its own normative terms.

Federalism on Its Own Normative Terms

With some degree of simplification, one might say that, from time immemorial, political organization among humans has been grounded in either one of two basic ideas. One of these is the idea of empire, according to which political stability requires the dissemination of exclusive authority from one single source. The best-known ancient examples are

Egypt, Persia, and Rome. During the European Middle Ages, the idea of a universal Christian empire was superimposed upon a plurality of territorial rulers with overlapping powers. Imperial unity was fragile as all rulers were to have as much power in their own realm as had the emperor in his (*rex imperator in regno suo*). When the Reformation destroyed even this pretense of imperial unity, the idea of empire was turned inward as each ruling prince's absolute territorial sovereignty. And when the rising bourgeois classes wrested power away from these princely rulers, claiming to do so in the name of the people, the idea of popular sovereignty gained ground as the idea of one people and one government. In this sense, democracy and empire are two sides of the same coin.

The other idea is federalism. Its trajectory from ancient to modern times is less linear and, therefore, more difficult to force into a – however foreshortened – narrative. The opposite of empire was the autarkic polis, grounded in the ancient Greek ideal of living in self-sustaining, small communities. These communities sometimes entered into leagues, or alliances, for trade or defence purposes. But the Greeks never developed the idea of combining several such communities into a larger political union. The Holy Roman Empire of the Middle Ages, with its undefined boundaries of overlapping powers, likewise cannot be considered, as such, a political union, although its emperors knew that the unity they claimed to represent ultimately depended on agreement: what pertained to all had to be approved by all (*quod omnes tangit, ab omnibus approbetur*). It was only at the beginning of the modern age of territorial absolutism that the need arose to think about how to protect the autonomy of smaller communities from being absorbed into larger, territorial states. In particular, this was a matter of survival for smaller communities of religious minorities at a time when the Peace of Augsburg, the religious peace treaty of 1555, allowed those rulers with claims to territorial sovereignty to determine their own faith as the exclusive state religion (*eius regio, cuius religio*).

The quest for autonomy brought forth a new wealth of survival doctrines focusing on the right of resistance against tyranny (Kingdon 1994). Only the *Politica Methodice Digesta* of Johannes Althusius, however, amounted to a first systematic theory of federalism by providing principles of political organization that would allow smaller and larger communities to coexist in what would later be called a system of self-rule and shared rule (Althusius [1614] 1995). These principles can be identified as subsidiarity, social solidarity, and consensus. As I will argue, they also allow for an adequate and self-sufficient, critical evaluation of political legitimacy in federal systems.

Subsidiarity

As a test of political legitimacy, the principle of *subsidiarity* asks whether decisions are taken as closely as possible to the citizens affected by them. In doing so, it in fact questions the legitimacy of the centralized, unitary, territorial state regardless of whether it is constituted in formal, democratic terms. Federalism, thus understood as a form of political organization that distinguishes between universal and particular, or national and local, matters to be decided, becomes the default option for political legitimacy.

When it comes to the current understanding of subsidiarity, however, one needs to be careful. It is commonly thought to have its origin in Catholic social doctrine, where the purpose of its invocation was to protect Christian civil society from being absorbed into the state. Paul Ryan, for instance, Republican majority leader and speaker of the American House of Representatives (2015–18), elaborated on its meaning for federalism as "having a civil society" in which the common good is advanced "through our civic organizations, through our churches, through our charities, through all of our different groups where we interact with people as a community" (Brody 2012).

Yet, when subsidiarity was first recognized as a guiding principle for European Union (EU) governance in the 1992 Maastricht Treaty, the research team of then European Commission president Jacques Delors identified its Protestant rather than Catholic origins: in the formulations of the 1571 General Synod of the Dutch Reformed Churches in the East Frisian city of Emden and in the early seventeenth-century political theory of Johannes Althusius (Endo 1994, 630–1; Luyckx 1992; Riklin 2006, 218–19).

The difference is significant. While Catholic social doctrine is primarily concerned with safeguarding the "bounds of the private sphere," the European and Althusian meaning of subsidiarity aims at a principled "allocation of power within the public realm" (Barber 2005, 313). At Emden, the General Synod resolved that "provincial or general assemblies must not deliberate on matters already decided at a lower level" and that "they shall concern themselves only with such matters as pertaining to all churches generally" (Goeters [1571] 1971, 79–83; own translation). Althusius, in turn, formulated the idea that majority rule may apply "in the things that concern all orders together, but not in those that concern them separately" (Althusius [1614] 1995, chap. 8, para. 70), which effectively granted individual members of a composite union veto power over matters particular to them. Contrary to Catholic social thought much later, these formulations were not just about the protection of societal autonomy. They clearly established procedural principles of pluralized governance.

When it found its way into the Maastricht Treaty, subsidiarity was initially derided as mere "Euro-froth" (Diez 1995, 14), a principle for all seasons that could be invoked by Christian democrats, German federalists, and British nationalists alike (Peterson 1996). And from the hallowed perspective of "seasoned federalism like that of the United States," finally, "the notion of subsidiarity" was even ridiculed as somewhat immature, with a "hollow, even foolish, ring to it" (Bermann 1994, 442). Yet subsidiarity has nevertheless become a linchpin of EU governance. As an elaborate procedural mechanism (Protocol 2, Treaty on the Functioning of the European Union), it provides member-state parliaments with an "early-warning system" (Kiiver 2011) for detecting transgressions of the boundaries of what might well be particular. It does so by means of an "enhanced inter-institutional dialogue" (Horsley 2012, 269) and thus "plays a promising role in structuring the democratic process" (Barber 2005, 315).

In Canada, a leading scholar of constitutional law has written that the principle of subsidiarity, while not regular subject matter in political discourse, nevertheless "does offer some useful ways of thinking about the Canadian Constitution" (Hogg 1998, 112). More importantly, the Supreme Court of Canada has referred to subsidiarity in a string of recent decisions (Arban 2013), and, in the first of these, it affirmed that "matters of governance are often examined through the lens of the principle of subsidiarity. This is the proposition that law making and implementation are often best achieved at a level of government that is not only effective, but also closest to the citizens affected and thus most responsive to their needs, to local distinctiveness, and to population diversity" (Supreme Court of Canada 2001).

At its core, subsidiarity as a normative value of federalism safeguards spatial identity and autonomy. It not only demands that political decisions should be taken at the lowest possible level of government. It also means that subsidiarity considerations may deliberately overrule political efficiency considerations that would favour centralization. It does not, however, override – let alone replace or determine – the constitutional division of powers in federal systems. Subsidiarity can provide auxiliary guidance only when this division is under dispute, either before the courts or in processes of intergovernmental negotiation.

Social Solidarity

Federalism is, at its core, also an agreement among equal members to coexist by sharing common resources fairly and for the benefit of all. This not only presupposes adherence to the principle of subsidiarity as a safeguard of member autonomy, it also requires a commitment to social solidarity. Subnational decision makers must be able to provide their citizens with equitable living conditions across the federation. Solidarity considerations may thus overrule the allocation of resources by market forces.

Taken together, subsidiarity and solidarity constitute what the Germans call federal comity (*Bundestreue*), first developed by the German Federal Constitutional Court as an unwritten constitutional principle: "The reciprocal obligation of the federation and the Länder to behave in a pro-federal manner, governs all constitutional relationships" (quoted in Kommers and Miller 2012, 92). In Canada, J.A. Corry alluded to it as "constitutional morality" (quoted in Dupré 1985, 27). The obligation to maintain a federal order, in other words, not only pertains to the explicitly institutional division of powers between different levels of government but also includes an implicitly procedural commitment to federal comity in the sense that the members of a federation have an obligation to act in such a way as to make the maintenance of the federal order meaningful to all in an existential as well as material sense (Hueglin 2015). As Althusius put it at a time when mutuality was a matter of survival in an early modern and pre-industrial, economic zero-sum game: the essence of politics among equal members in a composite commonwealth was "mutual communication" not just of common rights but also of the "things and services" necessary for a "harmonious exercise of social life" (Althusius [1614] 1995, chap. 1, paras. 2, 7).

Under conditions of modern market capitalism, such communication, to maintain at least a semblance of political as well as material balance among the members of a federation, inevitably means what Yanis Varoufakis (2016, 37) recently called a "political surplus recycling mechanism." Without such a mechanism, as the then Greek finance minister tried in vain to explain to Dr Schäuble, his German counterpart, the EU may qualify as an economic and monetary union, but not as a legitimate federal union because, with reference to what the Athenians famously told the Melians, in such an incomplete and unequal union, "the strong do what they can and the weak suffer what they must" (Thucydides [n.d.] 1934, bk. 5, chap. 89).

What the recycling amounts to is fiscal redistribution from richer to poorer jurisdictions. The most important mechanism for such redistribution in federal systems is fiscal equalization. According to some fiscal need- or cost-based formula, revenue is redistributed so that "subject to local preferences, all persons or firms in a country can obtain comparable public services at comparable tax rates" (Blöchliger and Charbit 2008, 2). Apart from footing the bill for revenue-equalizing transfers to poorer jurisdictions in cases of so-called vertical fiscal equalization (see ibid., 5–15), national governments also engage in a variety of other fiscal-transfer activities with redistributive effects. They may offer conditional grants to subnational governments in areas of national policy interest; they may enter into joint-financing-policy programs with the subnational governments; and they may set up their own programs of directly assisting individuals, firms, or other organizations, with the objective of advancing social stability and/or regional development (see Shah 2007).

This use of the so-called federal spending power (Watts 1999) is one of the main sources of contention and conflict in federal systems to the extent that such transfers can be made, and routinely are made, in areas formally under subnational jurisdiction. It is here that solidarity and subsidiarity as markers of political legitimacy can conflict. While the spending power may, in general, serve legitimate purposes of social solidarity by supporting national programs or regional projects in the name of equitable living and working conditions for all citizens, it may at the same time violate the principle of subsidiarity by transgressing into policy areas where subnational entities can, in principle, act on their own. This is a tension that cannot be resolved by turning to some abstract concept of democracy (similarly Noël 2009, 277). The crucial legitimacy test for federal systems, therefore, is whether, how, and to what extent the governments and societies of a federal union can agree on where to strike a balance or equilibrium between subsidiarity and solidarity considerations.

Consensus

In its classical or coordinate understanding, federalism is not supposed to require consensus. Each order of government is meant to tend to the responsibilities under its jurisdiction separately and without interference from the other order. Federalism, in this way, should be based on "well-established constitutional rules" and not depend on compromises and agreements that work around these rules (Gagnon and Iacovino 2007, 157). What is more, the kind of consensus that is needed for intergovernmental agreements, based on second-best compromise rather than common vision, is precisely what is generally thought to stand in the way of political efficiency as well as legitimacy in federal systems. It blurs accountability and leads to federalism's most famous defect, the joint-decision trap (Scharpf 1988).

Yet, as Daniel Weinstock has pointed out, this classical, coordinate, or "side-by-side" form of federalism does not exist in practice because "the whole idea of a policy 'domain' is a theoretical creation rather than a reflection of reality" (2006, 172). Federalism in practice is "overlapping federalism" (ibid.) and therefore needs cooperation and coordination based on agreement. It also needs a common vision as the predisposition to federal comity. Aristotle said it first: "It is the sharing of a common view ... that makes a household and a state" ([n.d.] 1962, 1253a7). And it was Althusius ([1614] 1995, chap. 19, para. 49) who translated this vision into federalism: "The fundamental law" establishing union is "nothing other than certain covenants by which many cities and provinces come together and agree to establish and defend one and the same commonwealth." Althusius also provided the formula meant to transform common vision into joint decision-making by availing himself of that old Roman law formula, according to which "what touches all ought also to be approved by all" (ibid., chap. 4, para. 20; see also chap. 17, para. 60).

Modern federal systems have replaced the old confederal consensus requirement with high-threshold majority rule in the name of efficiency, "compound majoritarianism" in the United States (Elazar 1987, 19), or "qualified majority voting" in the case of the EU (Lewis 2013, 150–1). Constitutional amendment in federal systems, which amounts to a change of the original compact of union, requires supermajorities in all federal systems. Underlying all these provisions, however, remains a commitment to consensus as the ultimate normative predisposition necessary for a federation to function and hold together.

Consensus does not mean harmony. It also does not mean the absence of power imbalances between rich and poor, between large and small members of a federation, and/or between these members collectively and a federal government endowed with superior fiscal clout. What it does mean, as a critical yardstick of political legitimacy in federal systems, however, is that the process of decision-making must be carried out by a common predisposition to negotiation, cooperation, and agreement, perhaps even agreement to disagree, which might lead to a "crystallization of the divergences expressed by different governments" (Rocher 2009, 93).

If there are power imbalances, as there inevitably are, consensus and the commitment, in principle, to engage in negotiated agreement rather than resorting to unilateral action, however deeply entrenched in a political culture of federal comity and a spirit of mutual respect, is not enough. A critical yardstick of federal political legitimacy, therefore, is the extent to which there are "institutional preconditions" for dialogue (Neyer 2003, 688), underpinned by "clear and consensual rules" (Noël 2006, 67).

There will always be an ultimately irresolvable tension between the political legitimacy of agreement among the members of a diverse union and the efficiency-driven provisions for – however qualified – majority rule. In Canada, for instance, the 7/50 formula for constitutional amendment for most matters related to the division of powers adopted in 1982, requiring the approval of a minimum of seven provinces representing at least 50 per cent of the Canadian population, will likely never be used because even this high approval threshold would not be considered legitimate by the mostly francophone province of Quebec. Even that province's most recent pro-federalist, liberal government of Philippe Couillard remained committed to demanding a constitutional veto (Canadian Broadcasting Corporation 2017). In the EU, by comparison, all treaty changes require the approval of all member states to begin with.

In terms of ordinary legislation in matters of overlapping jurisdiction or joint-financing programs, and in the absence of a legitimately functioning bicameral legislature at the national level, the Canadian federation routinely relies on intergovernmental agreements; there are some 1,500 in effect at any given time (Simmons and Graefe 2013). Only a minority of these constitute multilateral agreements involving the federal and all provincial or territorial governments, and it is in these instances that Quebec is usually granted some degree of asymmetry or opting out (e.g., Health Canada 2004). In Germany, by comparison, the subnational Länder governments possess a powerful and direct co-decision right in federal legislation that affects their constitutional interests based on weighted majority rule in the second-chamber Bundesrat. Nevertheless, the legislative process on matters of particular gravity, such as the recent changes to the German fiscal equalization formula, is usually preceded by a drawn-out process of reaching intergovernmental agreement. In the EU, again, possible qualified majority votes in the Council of Ministers are avoided as much as possible; about 90 per cent of Council decisions are taken by agreement (Lewis 2013, 151).

Conclusion

Let me come to an end in this way: in a deeply divided world of diversity, demystified from liberal assumptions about individual equality under conditions of social homogeneity, subsidiarity as a principle of safeguarding particular autonomies, social solidarity as a principled commitment to sustaining these autonomies materially, and consensus as a principled mode of inclusive decision-making carry weight reaching far beyond the federal form. To the extent that these principles are derived from that federal form, federalism becomes a critical yardstick for democracy.

3 Linking Federalism and Democracy: An Analytical Framework

ARTHUR BENZ

Democracy has been generally defined as government according to the will of the people or, in Abraham Lincoln's famous formulation in the Gettysburg Address, as "government of the people, by the people, for the people" (see Wills 2006). Since the French Revolution, the people have been designated a community of free and equal citizens, with everyone having the same right to participate in public affairs. Accordingly, democracy has been presumed to be a nation state in which equal citizens constitute a people and organize their government. Lincoln expressed his definition of democracy at a time when the first federal state, which had been created by the American Revolution, was on the brink of failure. His concern was democracy, not federalism, which was not compatible with the unitarist understanding of *the people* that had prevailed in the debates during the French Revolution. However, when the US federation was founded by "the people," as declared in the Constitution's preamble, it was meant not as a democracy, but as a government with constrained powers to safeguard individual liberty.

A democratic federation dividing a government into levels constitutes not one demos, but more *demoï*, and it thus institutionalizes the undeniable diversity of societies. Often reduced to the phenomenon of multinationalism, diversity is a ubiquitous reality that finds expression in location patterns of industries and business, in social disparities among people living in different territories, and in cultures shaped by the history, language, or practices of communities. Certainly, democracy requires that all citizens forming the people participate in politics on an equal basis, but democracy in the sense of governing for the people also requires that real diversities are taken into account in formulating policies. Of course, dividing the people into peoples according to the principle of federalism never conforms to the real diversity of societies, but it is a way to accommodate diversity in politics. This is, as Thomas

O. Hueglin (chap. 2) has explained in detail, the purpose of federalism for democracy, a purpose that is relevant not only in so-called multinational democracies since all societies are diverse in various respects.

By extending the opportunities of citizens to control public power, a federal structure of government has "demos-enabling" effects, but federalism also constrains the power of democratic government. Checks and balances between levels institutionalized in a federal system are only one reason for this (Stepan 1999). The other reason is the need to accommodate the interests of diverse communities, expressed by the peoples of the constituent units, with the general interest of the people of the federation. For this reason, *federalism* means not only the division of power but also the coordinated exertion of power and solving conflicts. Beyond decentralization and subsidiarity, it implies intergovernmental interaction, regardless of the way governments coordinate their policies – be it by negotiated agreements, fair contests for best practices, or mutual adjustments. In practice, therefore, federal systems are both demos-enabling and demos-constraining, and thus not necessarily compatible with democracy. Rather, federal democracies inherently institutionalize the tensions between these institutions and the processes that make democracy and federalism work.

In line with historical approaches to studying the sequential evolution of institutions or political order (Orren and Skowronek 2004; Pierson 2004), empirical research on governance and policymaking in federal democracies has drawn attention to these tensions, which necessarily emerge in modern federations between democratic politics and intergovernmental relations (Benz 2009; Benz and Sonnicksen 2017; Burgess and Gagnon 2010; Brock 2003; Lehmbruch 2000; Sharman 1990). Apparently, how these tensions materialize depends on the particular institutional designs of a federal democracy, but, irrespective of these varieties, they cannot be avoided outright. They find expression in continuous shifts of power between legislatures or parliaments and intergovernmental politics as well as between party politics, intermediation of interests, or citizen participation within jurisdictions and executive policymaking, which cuts across levels or jurisdictions. These dynamics can lead to an imbalance of power, not unlike the continuous struggles for power carried out among political actors interested in either centralization or decentralization, processes that can destabilize federalism (Riker 1964). Scholars have framed the problem as a dilemma between effective governance and democratic legitimacy.

This dilemma materializes in different ways and with different consequences, depending on the organization of a federal democracy. The particular combination of various types of federal and democratic systems also determines how the dilemma is coped with in politics and policymaking. Therefore, to uncover the particular causes of these tensions, the conditions under which they arise, and the ways in which actors cope with them, and to understand whether and how federalism can support democracy or the other way around, we have to engage in comparative research on the varieties of federalism and democracy, regarding both institutions and political processes.

This chapter presents a framework for comparative research. First, it outlines a concept of democratic federalism by adjusting the idea of democratic legitimacy to the conditions of a federation and by explaining the purpose of a federation with regard to democratic legitimacy. The notion of *democratic federalism* is used to designate a normative concept of democracy suited to a federal context. In contrast, a *federal democracy* indicates a particular polity characterized by democratic institutions and a division of government into two or more levels, a democratic government operating under the conditions of a federal structure, and intergovernmental policymaking designed to manage the interdependence among policies that affect different jurisdictions. Federal democracies exist in different varieties, and understanding their operation requires an appropriate analytical approach. This will be outlined in the second part of this chapter.

Democratic Legitimacy in a Federal Context

When considering a federal context, a theory of democracy has to address three basic issues: First, it has to explain how people can be governed according to their will. Second, it has to justify federalism as a way to improve the quality of that democracy. Third, if federal democracy is deemed preferable to democracy in a unitary state, it needs to be investigated whether governance in federalism and in democracy are compatible. At first glance, this seems to be obviously the case. Yet the answer is not that easy. In principle, federalism relates to the territorial organization of the state, and democracy relates to the people. But for a government to exert power over a people and the people to control their government, both have to act in a congruent space.

Thus far, a federal organization of government seems to accord with democracy, not least because democratic governance at the different levels contributes to discovering and coping with diverse interests and inequalities in societies. However, problems to be dealt with and policies made at the different levels often span the boundaries of jurisdictions. Hence, whereas governing in a democracy is bound to a territory, governing in a federal system actually transcends territories, for functional reasons. In addition, policy coordination in intergovernmental relations violates the congruence principle of democracy, which requires that those affected by governmental power should participate in legitimizing this power. Hence, federal governance and democracy operate in different territorial contexts of governing. The ensuing tensions are reinforced by different mechanisms of politics and policymaking in both institutional arenas.

How the People Can Govern Themselves

In a democracy, *the people* incorporates all citizens of a political community. Citizens enjoy the fundamental rights to be free, subject to limits defined by law, and to participate in political processes on an equal basis. Although these rights apply to individual persons and protect their autonomy, their significance materializes for citizens as members of a republican community. It is in this context that they realize their liberty by understanding and acknowledging the liberty of others and the necessary limits of their own. In the course of collective action, they experience their equality despite their distinctness as human beings. Thus, liberty and equality constitute the basic requirements of democracy, but, at the same time, democracy sets the context that allows citizens to realize and exercise these rights (Habermas 1992, 112–35). Therefore, the demos has to be conceived as a community of citizens based on the existence and acknowledgment of rights.

Although citizens constitute a rights-based community, they are not able to act collectively. Rights connect individual citizens, but the demos is a virtual entity without a will and unable to govern. The people can govern themselves only through representatives, and the demos cannot express its will; only individual citizens can. The public interests of a demos cannot be discovered by summing up the will of citizens when they cast a vote, be it the will of all or of a majority of individuals. Instead of the "*volonté de tous*," it is the "*volonté général*" that defines the standard of democratic legitimacy (Rousseau [1762] 1966, 66). Unanimity, or the majority of a vote, can serve as an ideal or pragmatic standard of democratic legitimacy only if the substance of a decision results from public deliberation (Habermas 1992, 349–98). Yet deliberation is also an ideal, if not due to the unequal bargaining power of the participants, then because of the sheer number of participants in a demos, notwithstanding other conditions that prevent reason from prevailing over interests or power in public communication.

The mechanism that generates a meaningful public discourse on the public interest is anchored in the relations between the represented citizens and their representatives who hold power (Urbinati 2006). Those elected to govern by legislative and executive power are called to account by the people in competitive re-elections. To maximize the chance of re-election against competing candidates or parties, they are induced to govern according to the will of at least a majority of citizens. Since the common will of a majority is uncertain and cannot be expressed other than by voting, those in power are motivated to govern in a way that can be accepted by as many citizens as possible and to justify their policies as conforming to the public interest. Those competing for office have to engage in a public discourse in the shadow of a majority decision in elections, which will determine who can be trusted most to act for the people. In view of this shadow of elections, representatives have to anticipate the "will of the people" (Friedrich 1937, 16) and to make explicit in their proposals, programs, and actions what they presume this common will to be.

A similar shadow of majority decision, including the uncertainty about the will of a majority, characterizes referendum democracy. While referendums might be used by governments to support their policies in party competition, it is necessary that policy proposals submitted to voters are developed in public discourse, if not negotiated among the representatives of different parties and civil society. By negotiating a policy proposal, those interested in the outcome of a referendum try to anticipate the – uncertain – will of a majority of the people. For this reason, referendum democracy aims to achieve negotiated agreements among representatives of different interests, whereas electoral democracy selects representatives from among competing parties or candidates who promise to best fulfil the presumed common will of the people.

Both types of democracy operate in a recurrent, sequential process whereby officeholders or candidates for elected office claim to act for the people, the public deliberates on these claims, and the electorate votes. This process links the government with the demos. Accordingly, it has to be organized in a territorially delineated jurisdiction, where the scope of output of governing, and the community defining the demands and supporting a government, correspond and where those responsible for the consequences of their policies are held accountable by those affected by these policies. The congruence of jurisdiction and the community of citizens is the first essential condition for democracy; the difference between representatives and represented is the other (Pitkin 1972). As the will of the many citizens is not identical to the public interest, and as the latter can be expressed only by representatives, the collective will of the people is achievable only in public discourses that lead to mutual adjustment between citizens and their representatives. Hence, democracy must be conceived as a process of continuous learning.

Although this concept of democracy can work in reality, it is still a model. It presumes a territorially defined, homogeneous community of citizens in which all interests are appropriately expressed and have an equal chance to be considered. Yet real interactions in societies, like trade and communication, and real problems generated in societies transgress jurisdictional borders, and societies are, as mentioned, diverse. Therefore, the congruence principle is increasingly undermined by this reality. Furthermore, the public discourse between represented and representatives is distorted by the selective processes of information-sharing by the media and their power to influence communication. One way to cope with these problems is federalism.

How Federalism Enhances Democracy

Federalism is not equivalent to democracy. However, as Thomas O. Hueglin has outlined (chap. 2), it provides guidelines to be taken into account to make democracy work in diverse and complex societies. If these are taken seriously in the design of institutions and processes, a federation can increase the probability that citizens are governed according to the public interest, for the following reasons:

1. Federalism improves the congruence between a demos and the scope of policies by differentiating the boundaries defining a community of citizens. In modern societies with their complex problems, the congruence principle often speaks for enlarging the territory of a jurisdiction and for centralizing power. In contrast, federalism provides a differentiated territorial structure and, in line with the principle of subsidiarity, allows smaller communities to govern their own affairs, to raise their voice in politics, and to effectively influence political decisions at the federal level. In multilingual societies, citizens can express their opinion and political will in their own language and, thus, participate in the larger polity.
2. A federal organization of government unveils externalities caused by governments, industry, and consumers, and federalism provides procedures to cope with them without "internalizing" – and thus concealing – them by centralization. Externalities are uncovered by governments in smaller or neighbouring jurisdictions that are directly affected. In a federation, they are in a position to set these negative effects on the political agenda of the federal government or to initiate intergovernmental coordination. Thus, federalism

allows conflicts to be managed in a consensual spirit, whereas, in unitary states, these issues might be neglected.
3. While democracy is designed to transform the plurality of private interests into a public interest (the "general will"), federalism must accommodate the diverse "general wills" that arise in a complex and functionally and territorially differentiated society. In such a society, general decisions often disregard justified distinctness or unjustified inequalities. Economic and cultural development is best fostered by specialization and clustering of activities in regions or localities, but an integrated society needs some level of distributive justice and solidarity among people living in different regions. A federal polity provides better conditions for addressing diversity and distributive justice than a central government. Thus, federalism does not place limits on a central government for the protection of liberty, a long and commonly held theoretical premise. Rather, it creates institutional arenas in which people can express their distinct claims for rights and resources and establishes procedures for finding a balance between them.
4. Federalism induces policy learning, which, as outlined above, is essential in a democracy. From time to time, any decision resulting from democratic politics needs to be adjusted to consider ongoing political disputes or changes in society. A federal system fosters continuous adjustment of policies since it organizes conflict and countervailing power. Furthermore, it stimulates experimental policymaking, innovation, and diffusion of innovation, as explained by theories of laboratory federalism (Breton 1998; Oates 2005). It generates policy alternatives beyond those arising in party competition and allows new policies to be tested on a limited scale before being introduced into other jurisdictions or at the federal level.

A federal system that fulfils these democratic functions has to divide powers, but not separate them. It is the linkage between the levels of democracy that unveils externalities and disparities, that allows conflicts to be managed in accordance with the principles of subsidiarity and solidarity, and that invigorates policy learning by governments and citizens. This concept of federalism emerged in the political theories of Reformed Protestantism; its most elaborated version appeared in the *Politica* of Johannes Althusius ([1614] 1995). Against Jean Bodin's centralist notion of sovereignty, he argued for a consociation of smaller and larger units of government. These units should fulfil different societal functions in a process of continuous cooperation and mutual support (Friedrich 1975; Hueglin 1999). By considering the interdependence of tasks in a multi-level polity, this concept provides a better guideline for a democratic federation than the model of a dual federalism with a separation of powers. However, it also raises the question of how democratic politics within territories, and intergovernmental politics that cut across territorial boundaries, can operate in a complementary way.

Tensions in Federal Democracies

Explaining that federalism contributes to the quality of democracy does not mean that politics and policies in a federation are democratic or that policies made through democratic processes are compatible with the rules and procedures of a federal system. As indicated, democratic politics materializes in public deliberation, party competition or competition of candidates for office and in majority rule in institutions and processes related to a territorial context. In a federation, government is divided between levels and territories. However, not only are real federations characterized by overlaps of competences and functions, more or less sharing of powers, and intergovernmental coordination, it is also the interaction between levels of governments that makes federalism relevant for democracy.

In a federal democracy, the people are divided into different demoï, which coexist with the demos. Democratic legitimacy needs to be founded on a dual or multiple representation ("compounded representation"; Tuschhoff 1999) of citizens as members of a federal and regional or local demoï. The institutional design of representation and the procedures of inclusion and accountability vary, but they need to guarantee that the interests of peoples in constituent units are considered in federal politics and policymaking and that the multiplicity of the demoï is taken into account on an equivalent basis.

These modes of representation must be linked to political processes that coordinate policymaking at the different levels. It has been argued that, in decentralized federations that guarantee the autonomy of regional or local governments, citizens may be able to limit the power of a government by threatening to vote with their feet or by actually leaving a jurisdiction (Tiebout 1956). In reality, however, it is more likely that they face high costs of mobility and that their liberty is actually constrained by the external effects of policies executed in another jurisdiction. These effects cannot be ruled out by separating power into "watertight compartments" since they are caused by the application of power. Moreover, they often come with unjustified inequalities – for instance, if economic development is concentrated in particular locations, while other places are losing a competition with the centres of growth. These negative consequences of decentralization can be avoided only if the relevant powers are centralized or if policies are coordinated among jurisdictions.

Irrespective of the institutional solution, policymaking turns into an intergovernmental process. This is obvious if externalities or disparities are coped with in inter-jurisdictional coordination. If powers are centralized within a federation, the demoï abandoning power in favour of the centre can claim to be compensated by obtaining a voice in federal decision-making. In either case, equality of political participation might be at risk since the effective political power of the demoï depends on how they are involved in intergovernmental politics. According to the principle of federalism, coordination between governments acting for the demos and the demoï precludes a unilateral exertion of power, while both negotiations and mutual adjustment in competitive relations promise to lead to a fair resolution of conflicts.

Constitutions and practice in federations that conform to standards of democracy regularly meet the requirement of dual representation, while the appropriate coordination of policies between governments is more problematic. On the one hand, externalities between levels and jurisdictions are often not coped with in established procedures or institutions because constitutions usually set out a separation of powers, but rarely how to manage interdependences. On the other hand, where formal intergovernmental institutions exist, accountability relations between representatives and represented are either indirect or weak (see the case studies in Poirier, Saunders, and Kincaid 2016). And where they are strong, the commitments of governments to parliaments or the people can constrain the governments' capacity to cope with conflicts caused by externalities (Lehmbruch 2000, 27–30). In consequence, the necessary linkage of input and output legitimacy is not guaranteed.

These tensions between the institutions and decision-making in federalism and democracy materialize in different ways. They affect democratic processes as well as governance in federalism and, thus, both input and output legitimacy. On the one hand, compounded representation at the different levels can infringe the principle of equality of citizens. In elections, the effective weight of one vote is affected by the relative number of citizens in the constituent units of a federation. In second chambers, equality of demoï conflicts with equality of citizens. In multinational federations, individual rights and group rights might diverge as well. Considering accountability, executives tend to avoid taking the blame for making joint decisions instead of assuming responsibility for tasks or decisions that reach beyond their domain, particularly if citizens or parliaments induce them to maximize the interests of their constituency.

Regardless of the division of power, the interdependence of policies between levels or jurisdictions requires governments to share responsibility, while this multi-level character of policies leads to public debates that obscure competences and responsibility. On the other hand, fair coordination among governments cannot be taken for granted in intergovernmental politics, which not only aims to solve problems and dispense justice but also tends to foster power games among the officeholders involved. This contest for power is caused by the personal ambitions of political leaders. Yet it is also a consequence of democracy, which requires that political leaders act in the best interests of the people they represent in intergovernmental policymaking. Therefore, party competition and competition between governments for competences or resources can obstruct intergovernmental coordination, as does the presumption of parliaments to decide autonomously.

To conclude: as a principle, federalism has its value for democracy. And in view of the diversity in society, there are good reasons to prefer federal democracy to unitary democracy. Its territorial structure conforms to the diversity of society, provided that power is distributed with a significant degree of decentralization. Moreover, intergovernmental coordination allows interdependence to be managed in a fair and solidary way, and continuous mutual adjustments among governments can stimulate policy learning and balance powers. A federation fulfils these functions by establishing structures and procedures that complement democracy rather than by being democratic on its own.

A democratic government and a federal order constitute different institutional dimensions and arenas of governance. Whereas a division of powers and intergovernmental coordination adjust the structures of a government to conform to the complexity of a plural and diversified society, they can, at the same time, hamper the democratic mechanisms designed to reveal a public interest of the people, be it the demos of the whole federation or the demoï of the lower-level units. Democracy, on the other hand, does not per se encourage actors to cope with the interdependence of policies made at the different levels in a federal system; rather, it can thwart intergovernmental coordination. Whether structures and policymaking in a federation obstruct or enhance democratic legitimacy, and whether politics in a democracy supports or weakens intergovernmental policy, depend on how the institutions of federalism and democracy, and the processes of multi-level and democratic governance in the related arenas, are linked and interoperate.

How Federal Democracies Operate

To answer the question of how federal democracies work, we need to look at particular federations and the particular mechanisms of governance generated by these different institutional settings. Moreover, we have to investigate how these mechanisms interact and how such interaction influences their operation. Generally speaking, it is the intensity of the interference of one mechanism in another, depending on the kind of coupling, that affects the coherence and co-evolution of federalism and democracy. Interference causes tensions that policymakers are confronted with and have to manage. The effects of these tensions can vary: they can obstruct policymaking, but they can also create dynamics if actors adjust processes and modify institutions to cope with the resulting tensions. Finally, concerning the quality of federal democracy, we need to determine whether its dynamics lead to a balance between federalism and democracy or whether one mechanism dominates the other. The following sections elaborate on this framework for comparative research in greater detail.

Institutions and Mechanisms of Politics and Policymaking

Like the institutional structures of a political system in general, the institutions of democracy and federalism enable and constrain power, shape action orientations, and guide the behaviour of actors. Moreover, they make collective action feasible by providing rules or procedures and by coordinating the actions of the relevant participants in politics and policymaking. These rules and procedures, both those written down in law or statutes and those acknowledged as norms of appropriate behaviour or standard operating procedures, constitute social mechanisms. They enable the interaction of participants and create particular modes of interaction that, under otherwise equal conditions, generate specific outcomes. Mechanisms are abstract representations of usually very complex processes that highlight the essential causal relations among institutions, interaction, and outcomes (Bunge 1997; Hedström and Swedberg 1998; Mayntz 2004). Understanding these causal relations is essential to comprehend and explain how institutions work.

In view of the variety of democratic governments and federations, the analysis can start by distinguishing basic types of democracy and federalism, both of which refer to the mechanisms of negotiation and competition (Lijphart 2012). Consensus democracies oblige policymakers in a jurisdiction to find agreement among parties and associations that are pursuing diverse interests and policies; the outcome of negotiations is normally influenced not just by the majority of parties in parliament and government but by other veto players as well. In a majoritarian democracy, policymakers' behaviour is determined by party competition, and a government is committed to implementing the will of the majority party or parties in parliament. The leaders of the executive in majoritarian democracies are powerful as long as they can rely on the support of their party or coalition, in contrast to leaders in a consensus democracy, who have to find wider support for particular policies. Yet party competition can compel the executive to stand for a given party policy, while consensus democracy provides room for policy adjustment. These institutional conditions and mechanisms of governance, illustrated here as ideal types of democratic government, affect processes of intergovernmental coordination in the federal context.

In turn, federalism constitutes institutional conditions on its own, conditions that affect processes in the democratic institutions. For instance, if powers are shared according to a federal constitution, governments will, in many cases, be obliged to settle an agreement on a joint policy; otherwise, they find themselves in a political stalemate and cannot fulfil their task. In reality, participants avoid policymaking deadlock, but actors who prefer the status quo are in a stronger position and can use their veto power to prevent far-reaching policy change (Scharpf 1988). Different outcomes are to be expected, if intergovernmental policies are made by voluntary cooperation, because individual governments may opt out of making joint decisions and pursue their own policy, while others may resume negotiations and find a more or less exclusive agreement (Scharpf 1997, 127–8). In a federal constitution, which separates the domains of the central government from the constituent units, intergovernmental coordination can be achieved by unilateral action or mutual adjustment in a competitive process. Depending on whether governments compete for the necessary resources (e.g., tax competition) or for best practices ("yardstick competition"; Salmon 2019), mutual adjustment either compels governments in the individual jurisdictions to implement a particular policy or stimulates policy innovation in response to intergovernmental relations (Benz 2012).

Certainly, institutional constellations and mechanisms in federal democracies are more complex than outlined so far. Moreover, they do not determine policy outcomes since mechanisms operate under particular conditions, such as the constellations in a party system, the impact of powerful interest groups, the rise of social conflicts, or a particular economic situation or development. What is important, though, is that intergovernmental mechanisms interfere with the mechanisms of democratic government. They have to be linked according to the principles of democratic federalism, which require multiple actors at multiple levels to consider and accommodate the will of the people of the federation and the peoples of the constituent units.

As a rule, it is executives who participate in both arenas – in democratic government and in intergovernmental policymaking – who link institutions and mechanisms. These linkages are crucial for legitimizing intergovernmental policymaking through democratic processes and for effectively coping with the external effects produced in the democratic processes within a jurisdiction. Yet political executives involved in both arenas are more or less constrained by the rules established by the institutions of federalism and democracy, and these rules may demand incompatible behaviour. Usually, the actors in these boundary-spanning positions are committed to parties or powerful interest groups and, at the same time, their partners in intergovernmental negotiations (Putnam 1988). However, the impact of these constraining conditions depends on how institutions and processes in federalism and democracy are coupled.

Coupling Federal and Democratic Institutions and Processes

The concept of *coupling* stems from system theory. Scholars researching public or private organizations have applied it to the patterns of inter-organizational relations or linkages among policy sectors (Trein 2017). Coupled units operate according to their own logics, but are linked more or less intensely – that is, more or fewer variables that impact the operation of one unit are modified by the operation of another unit (Weick 1976, 3). In theories of federalism and multi-level governance, the concept refers to the type and degree of structural and functional interlocking among levels and arenas of democratic and intergovernmental politics (Benz 2000; Landau 1973, 190). In other words, coupling describes the intensity of ties affecting the "mechanisms" (or logics of politics) that decision bodies or actors underlie. For the purpose of comparative analysis, three basic types of coupling between democratic government and intergovernmental relations appear to be relevant.

Arenas of federalism and democracy are *decoupled* if the inherent mechanisms operate separately, without effective mutual interference.

Tight coupling means that one logic of politics determines or at least strongly influences the operation of another mechanism and, accordingly, policymaking in the other arena.

Loose coupling signifies that mechanisms influence each other, without having determining effects. It allows them to "combine connectedness and autonomy" (Orton and Weick 1990, 216) – that is, to manage the interdependence among independent organizational units, policy sectors, or, as in democratic federations, the policies of different governments.

The conditions of coupling are laid out in institutions or emergent norms, which enable or constrain the autonomy of actors – that is, by the rules separating or interlocking their power or by the commitments resulting from policy networks or negotiated agreements. In federal democracies, the linkages or divides inherent in the party system constitute additional structural conditions determining the coupling of federalism and democracy. Effective coupling is shaped by continuing processes that cut across the boundaries of arenas and the actors in boundary-spanning positions. In combination, structures and processes constitute linkages, while processes regularly modify tightly coupled or disconnected structures to become loosely coupled arenas.

With regard to institutions, the mode by which powers are divided in a democratic government and in a federal system is an essential condition.

In a government that separates powers between executives and parliaments, democratic processes tend to be decoupled from intergovernmental policymaking because executives can engage in intergovernmental negotiations without requiring the support of parliaments or parties, whereas special interest groups may participate in multi-level policymaking and strengthen the executive. In the federal arena, decoupling is more likely if powers are separated between levels of government and a federal organization lacks institutionalized or continuous intergovernmental relations – something that is particularly reflected in rather autonomous fiscal policies. These structural divides between federalism and democracy avoid the tensions that result from the interference of the mechanisms of politics. However, they can increase political conflict since policy interdependences or substantive inequalities among territories tend to be neglected, with the consequence of serious legitimacy deficits.

The strong interference in a tightly coupled system regularly undermines the operation of one mechanism, or even both. This can occur in federations with parliamentary democracies, where executives and parliaments share powers. In the majoritarian type, parliaments can tie the hands of the executive, whereas in the consensus type, a government is bound by coalition agreements. Both have the same constraining effects on policymaking as executives have to anticipate the vetoes of their parliament when coordinating policies in intergovernmental relations and as adjusting the will of the majority party or coalition agreements to the outcomes of intergovernmental policymaking is difficult.

These are instances of tight coupling, which can be intensified by formalized or extensive de facto sharing of powers between the federal and sub-federal governments (Lehmbruch 2000). This power-sharing is often reflected in rather compounded or "entangled" fiscal relations between governmental levels and finds particular expression in compulsory intergovernmental negotiations (joint decision-making). Like uncoupled arrangements, tight coupling bears the risk of turning tensions into frictions because actors are subject to contradictory logics of action when they are compelled to cooperate.

Loose coupling depends on flexible institutional settings, which enable actors to adjust their strategies or policies in case they interfere with the rules or established patterns of politics in the other arena. A loosely coupled federal democracy divides powers, but enables the shared execution of power within governments and between the federal and sub-federal governments, with political executives enjoying discretion to shape decisions in both arenas. However, institutional division of power is not sufficient to create a loosely coupled federal democracy; rather, it is politics and processes that matter.

Party politics plays an important role in coupling democracy and intergovernmental relations (Detterbeck and Hepburn 2018). Individual parties provide a venue for communication and negotiations, since members of parliaments and executives, at least those in higher ranks, are active in parties, often holding leading positions. In integrated parties, which participate in central, regional, and local elections, representatives of different levels can meet and informally prepare negotiations in the federal arena. In this way, they bridge parliamentary and intergovernmental politics. In contrast, a division between regional and statewide parties regularly reinforces divides between levels.

Moreover, the party system can cause competitive or antagonistic relations between governments if elections at the central and regional levels bring competing parties or party coalitions to power. This outcome is not unusual in federal or regionalized states (Hough and Jeffery 2006). In the United States, the consequences have been discussed as "divided government" at the federal level, but in federations with parliamentary systems, they materialize in "divided governments" because it is not the executive-legislative dimension of democracy, but intergovernmental relations, that are affected by party competition. Whereas intra-party linkages create opportunities for informal communication and negotiations, which help to circumvent the institutional constraints within the intragovernmental arena of democracy or the intergovernmental arena, the party system can intensify these constraints.

In a polarized party system, confrontation can obstruct both legislative-executive relations and multi-level policymaking, whereas pluralist or multiparty systems facilitate compromises and various coalitions, which in a federal system constitute overlapping cleavages. In other words, vertically integrated parties and party competition have different effects, with the first fostering loose coupling and the second tight coupling. Furthermore, the polarization of a party system tends to shift the balance towards tight coupling – in particular, in combination with vertically integrated parties, which, in an intense competition for votes, enables leaders to close party ranks. Disjointed party organizations with strong regional, intra-party groups or the existence of regional parties can reinforce the divides between levels of governments if politics is polarized, whereas in pluralist party competition, a loosely coupled constellation is likely to emerge.

The institutions and structures of a party system constitute essential conditions for linking the distinct logics of democracy and federalism, but, in actual policymaking, they are linked by the relations among actors and processes spanning the boundaries of institutions and arenas. Processes are particularly relevant in loosely coupled structures. Moreover, they can contribute to managing interference among the logics of politics in tightly coupled structures. In the same way, they can be used to manage the external effects of democratic politics in different jurisdictions, although powers are separated.

Coping with Tensions: Loose Coupling and Federal Dynamics

As mentioned, politics and policymaking in the arenas of democracy and in intergovernmental relations follow different logics. Sometimes, we find similar mechanisms, such as negotiations in consensus democracy and intergovernmental cooperation, or competition among parties in a democracy and between jurisdictions in federalism, but they affect different actors and do not necessarily operate in harmony. In other cases, the same actors are subject to different mechanisms – for example, if party leaders negotiate intergovernmental agreements, but compete in elections. Irrespective of the particular constellation, there is a need to harmonize decisions made in different institutional settings and actor constellations. The diverging mechanisms of politics inherent in structures of federal democracies can cause conflicting decisions, not only due to the divergent interests of the actors but also due to incompatible "governance systems" (Lehmbruch 2000). In any case, they create tensions among actors committed to the different arenas of democracy and federalism, which add to tensions arising from conflicting interests.

However, these tensions do not prevent governments from making policies and fulfilling their functions. Politics is about coping with conflicts or dilemmas of collective action, and, in a federal democracy, this includes dilemmas caused by the necessary linkage of modes of governance operating in a different manner and producing different outcomes. Responsible policymakers have to find ways to come to decisions despite these tensions, and they have to see to it that tensions do not cause frictions, which may lead to political instability, an erosion of institutions, or a disintegration of a polity. Tight coupling or decoupling of federalism and democracy threatens to turn tensions into frictions, whereas the flexibility of loose coupling is a condition that is essential for coping with them. In consequence, beyond the appropriate institutions, processes or patterns of interaction are essential to combine federalism and democracy appropriately. They emerge from iterated interactions and are often established by actors who try to cope with the uncertainties of mutual adjustments in dissociated structures or to avoid threatening deadlocks in tightly coupled arenas.

A common way of loosely coupling institutions and politics in different areas is informal communication. In executive-legislative relations – in particular, if powers are divided, members of the executive or heads of government meet members of the legislature to make sure that a policy is not voted down in parliament or second chambers. Informal meetings are also typical for intergovernmental relations, which are regularly supported by networks of civil servants. These processes reduce the risk that governments exerting separate powers will run into a process of "thrust and riposte" (Painter 1991, 275), and that governments engaged in shared powers will end in the "negotiation dilemma" (Scharpf 1997, 124), or that those negotiating under the condition of polarized party politics will run into the "joint-decision trap" (Scharpf 1988). In competitive relations, informal communication supports lesson drawing and policy transfer.

Committees and intergovernmental councils (Behnke and Mueller 2017) constitute an additional layer of interaction. Like informal communication, they turn disconnected or tightly coupled structures into a loosely coupled constellation. They often assemble actors from different arenas, parties, or governments. In a similar vein, groups of experts or institutionalized expert councils can fulfil a boundary-spanning function because they include actors not committed in any of the linked arenas of democratic government or intergovernmental relations. Consultation by experts can help executives to avoid the uncertainty, confrontation, and collective-action dilemmas they are exposed to in their "double-edged" position between intergovernmental relations and democratic politics. A less common, but still appropriate, way to loosely link intra- and intergovernmental politics is the inclusion of interest groups or civil society organizations. Beyond providing alternative ways to exchange views on contested issues, these patterns of policy-making can contribute to balancing the impact of party politics and to moderating confrontation or strategic bargaining in intergovernmental politics.

As mentioned, parties link executives and intergovernmental policymaking to the democratic process, but they can cause divides and confrontation. The shift of policymaking from political executives to administration has the opposite effect on multi-level governance. Political executives are elected and directly accountable in the democratic process. In contrast, civil servants are accountable within their department to their minister or higher-ranking officials. They are expected to abide by rules and professional standards, regardless of whether they contribute to political decisions or legislation or whether they implement the law or programs of a government. In consequence, administration makes policies, but does so at a certain distance from party politics. If multi-level policymaking shifts from the political executive to the administration, this restructuring detaches the processes within and between governments and thus reduces the constraining effects of tightly coupled structures. This differentiation of politics and administration seems particularly relevant in joint-decision systems, which, under the condition of redistributive conflicts or party polarization, are prone to deadlock.

Multi-level relations of parliaments are an additional channel of communication linking executive intergovernmental politics to democratic arenas. They have been discovered in the European Union and in international regimes (Crum and Fossum 2013), whereas they are underdeveloped in federations (Benz 2017b). Interparliamentary conferences or organizations often provide services to the parliaments, but are not involved in multi-level policymaking. Nonetheless, members of parliaments can turn into "multi-arena players" (Auel and Neuhold 2017), which interact without being constrained by party politics or the policy preferences of their government and can play a mediating role in multilevel governance.

If they are not entrenched in loosely coupled structures, these processes turn disconnected or tightly coupled structures into loosely coupled constellations. They are essential to manage the role conflicts of actors in boundary-spanning positions, rule conflicts among linked institutions, or conflicts among policies determined in different arenas. Instead of having ties that are too strong or too weak, loosely coupled structures have institutional constraints that enable them to avoid these conflicts intensifying and to manage them. They provide opportunities for boundary-spanning processes and imply options for arriving at decisions on conflicting policies; they stimulate a recurrent interplay between inter- and intragovernmental politics and sequential policy-making, through which policies made in one arena can be adjusted to suit the policies in another; and they open ways for circumventing gridlock. Loose coupling establishes "redundant" connections (Landau 1973), creates an adaptive governance system (Bednar and Page 2016), and makes a federal democracy a dynamic system.

Characterizing federations as dynamic is a truism, and recent theoretical and empirical research has emphasized this aspect (Bednar 2009; Benz and Broschek 2013b; Broschek 2012). Scholars have pointed out that institutional legacies set a path of evolution. Moreover, they have considered changes in the party system and reconfigurations of cleavages in society as driving forces affecting the interplay of federalism and democracy. Yet what is more important for understanding the operation of federal democracies are the changes that result from policymaking and strategic interaction among heads of government, ministers, party leaders, or civil servants. These actors have boundary-spanning roles, and their position is decisive for linking democracy and multi-level governance in a federation, but they are also in an essential strategic position. They can shape policy agendas, modify processes, and initiate institutional change. The conflict-avoiding strategies described by Fritz W. Scharpf (1988) in his study on joint decision-making are one possible consequence, one that reduces dynamics to incremental change. Another would be the shift of negotiations from formal to informal meetings, from political leaders to the administration, or from generalists to specialists. Moreover, intergovernmental relations can turn out to be more inclusive and multilateral or exclusive and bilateral.

In parliamentary democracy, party leaders can avoid the high obstacles of governing with coalitions by forming minority governments. The dynamics of structures may result from institutional reform, which, for example, can aim to strengthen parliaments or institutionalize intergovernmental relations, introduce new modes of multi-level governance, or lead to a separation of powers. Yet they usually appear as the unintended consequences of actors' strategies for managing conflicts and coping with the interfering mechanisms of politics and policymaking. In consequence, the balance of federalism and democracy can be achieved, but not permanently – that is, it remains always at risk.

Balance or Domination

From a normative point of view, democratic federalism implies balancing the powers exerted in intragovernmental and intergovernmental arenas. Executives are accountable to their parliaments and citizens, while at the same time committed to dealing with external effects between jurisdictions in intergovernmental relations. What balance means, exactly, in this context is difficult to determine. There is neither an ideal relationship between federalism and democracy nor a standard generalizable to all federal systems. A meaningful definition refers to the opposite: a constellation of imbalance caused by a domination of either the logics of intergovernmental politics or politics in the democratic governments, with the effect that one of them cannot fulfil its function appropriately due to arbitrary interference from the other.

Executive federalism is usually an indication of the weak influence of parliaments or citizens in intergovernmental politics. However, domination would mean that executives neglect democratic processes, while making deals with other governments, and would, therefore, act irresponsibly and arbitrarily (see Fossum and Laycock, chap. 4). Usually, executive dominance is diagnosed during intergovernmental negotiations. But competitive federalism, which operates according to a market-like logic, can also undermine the power of parliaments, which may be forced to reduce taxes or support industry at the cost of other policies. On the other hand, in federal democracies, where party competition prevails in politics, negotiating agreements between governments or intergovernmental competition among policymakers for best practices can fail. The same situation occurs if executives are subject to the mandates of parliaments, which tie their hands in intergovernmental relations. In this case, the domination of parliamentary government, in a strict sense, with parliaments "keeping the government on a tight leash," hinders the flexibility and scope of manoeuvre necessary for intergovernmental coordination and cross-jurisdictional problem-solving. When parliaments assert their autonomy or claim sovereignty against intergovernmental agreements, a federation can be threatened with disintegration.

Presumably, some federations are more prone to imbalance than others. In the United States and in Canada, executive federalism has become an issue of concern among scholars observing the evolution of intergovernmental relations. In contrast, German scholars have emphasized the ineffectiveness of joint decision-making in their country's democracy, which was shaped by intense party competition and confrontation, at least before unification, although the democratic deficits of executive federalism are also a reason for their critique. Beyond that, balance or imbalance can be caused by particular situations. If governments face a crisis, power often shifts to the executive, whereas constitutional reforms require the agreement of parliaments, which can, in this case, become decisive arenas of deliberation and policymaking. Changes in the party system also affect the balance between federal and democratic institutions or among processes in these arenas. Finally, the strategic action of policymakers may alter the balance or imbalance of power.

The imbalance entrenched in structures is the most problematic and difficult to cope with. It may be reinforced by tight coupling or decoupling between federalism and democracy, whereas loosely coupled federal democracies are less rigid and allow structures to be modified without bringing in formal institutional reform. Nonetheless, these more flexible constellations do not guarantee a balanced system. Therefore, balance is always at stake, and it poses a constant challenge for actors in a federal democracy.

Conclusion

This framework tries to come to terms with the complexity of federal democracies. To a certain extent, theories of federalism reduce this complexity by presupposing a specific concept of democracy and highlighting the division of power or a plurality of communities as essential features of democratic federalism. Taking a realistic concept of federalism as a point of departure and then investigating its impact on the essential features of democracy appears to be a more promising approach.

Complexity poses an even greater challenge for empirical research. An appropriate analytical framework can serve to make complexity manageable. Yet, given the fact that federal democracies not only reveal differentiated structures and change over time but also vary in many respects and operate under different conditions, such a framework can provide only certain guidelines for research. This chapter has focused on basic categories that seem particularly relevant to understanding how federal democracies operate and how they can operate in accordance with a pragmatic idea of democratic federalism.

4 Out of Balance: Executive Dominance in Federal Settings

JOHN ERIK FOSSUM AND DAVID LAYCOCK

Modern democracies rely on a complex range of institutional and procedural arrangements for carrying out the people's will, however that is conceived and determined. Democratic governance presupposes authoritative institutions equipped with an organized capacity to make binding decisions and allocate resources as well as arrangements to enable citizens to jointly form opinions and hold power-holders accountable. To carry out and reconcile these different functions, democratic systems need an executive that can effectively and competently carry out political decisions – a strong *executive presence* – and representative bodies that control the executive and connect to the citizenry by rendering the political system responsive to their interests and concerns. Accordingly, modern democracies seek to *balance* governing effectiveness and societal responsiveness.

Federal democracies, as this book underlines, add a further balancing dimension, that of reconciling the requirements of federalism with those of democracy. Or, to put it differently, democratic efforts at balancing governing effectiveness with societal responsiveness must be reconciled with federal balancing of the interests and ambitions of communities at different levels of governing. These balancing acts are not easy, and imbalances often occur.

The purpose of this chapter is to shed light on a particular form of imbalance – namely, *executive dominance* in federal-type systems. The imbalance is two-dimensional. Executive dominance – in contrast to executive presence – represents a severe imbalance in executive-legislative relations. Further, federal systems add a particular – vertical – twist to executive dominance because, in federal systems, the power of executives rests to a considerable extent on intergovernmental relations. Systems for managing intergovernmental relations are necessary for effective governing in today's federal systems because of jurisdictional overlap and generally high levels of interdependence (along horizontal and vertical lines). At the same time, systems of intergovernmental relations can shelter executives from legislative control and oversight. The assumption that informs this chapter is that federal systems give a distinct twist to executive dominance.

We will argue that executive dominance is a particularly useful concept for examining legislative-executive relations, both within and across levels of governing. We draw on the neo-republican conception of democracy as non-domination to specify how a situation in which executives exceed their roles can qualify as executive dominance. Demonstrating this, moreover, sheds valuable theoretical light on the relationship between democracy and federalism.

We proceed in two steps. First, we spell out the core features of the neo-republican conception of democracy as non-domination, while acknowledging several other conceptualizations of non-domination. Revisiting this debate allows us to identify more precise criteria for (non-)domination. Second, we draw on these criteria to clarify three forms of executive dominance related to decision-making, intergovernmental relations, and constitutional and institutional design. We illustrate this with examples from Canada and the European Union (EU), whose structural features justify our particular attention.

Federalism and Democracy Defined and Coupled

Federal democracy is a coupling of two sets of principles – organizational arrangements and mechanisms – associated, respectively, with democracy and federalism. Both terms refer to practical governing arrangements, which are embedded in distinct normative principles. Democracy is rooted in the principle of self-governing community, whereas federalism is generally understood as self-rule combined with shared rule. Federalism can be seen as "a normative philosophy that recommends the use of federal principles" (McGarry and O'Leary 2007, 180). The principle of federalism places great weight on reconciling the multiple conceptions of community and communal rule of which a federation is made up,[1] whereas the principle of democracy is tailored to citizens' self-governing – strictly speaking, within the ambit of one community. Federal consociates are members of multiple communities with constitutionally entrenched rights to self-governing, while democratic citizens make up one democratic demos. Thus, federalism and democracy refer to different conceptions of community, different conceptions of governing and rule, and different conceptions of membership in the polity.

Any effort to couple federalism and democracy will exhibit tensions. We therefore need to explain what coupling is, the various forms it might take, and the federal and democratic implications we can discern from this. As Arthur Benz has underlined, federalism and democracy are not only two distinct principles; they also operate through different repertoires of mechanisms. Since modern democracies institutionally embed the democratic principle in variants of representative democracy, the requisite mechanisms are closely associated with forms of representation. In a similar vein, in today's world, the federal principle[2] – and federalism as a distinct political doctrine – is profoundly shaped by the statist notion of sovereignty and the statist institutional context wherein federalism is embedded.[3] Federal democracy, in turn, combines these features in a distinct manner, which we can see, for instance, in how they are coupled.

Benz (chap. 3) identifies three ways of coupling federalism and democracy: they may be tightly coupled; they may be loosely coupled; or they may be uncoupled. The implications for federalism and for democracy, respectively, vary with the type of coupling. In addition, our very understanding of coupling – and the shapes or forms that coupling can take – is affected by how we theorize democracy and federalism – in this case, through the lens of non-domination. With executive dominance, vertical and horizontal forms of imbalance cut across the different forms of coupling: there is no one-on-one relationship between executive dominance and a specific type of coupling of federalism and democracy.

In practice, in today's world of federations, the most relevant type is loose coupling. Modern federal-type systems are marked by overlapping jurisdictions and deeply implicated levels of governing. In loose coupling, "mechanisms influence each other, without having determining effects." This kind of linkage "depends on flexible institutional settings, which enable actors to adjust their strategies or policies in case they interfere with the rules or established patterns of politics in the other arena" (Benz, chap. 3). In the following, we first explain how non-domination assists our conceptualization of democracy and federalism, then discuss what we understand as executive dominance.

Democracy as Non-domination

The notion of democracy as non-domination has deep roots in republican thought. In recent years, this notion has been reinvigorated, especially through the works of Philip Pettit. As Pettit notes, non-domination is closely linked to freedom, but the two are far from synonymous. His conception of freedom is directly associated neither with negative freedom, as non-interference, nor with positive freedom, where freedom means self-mastery. It should instead be associated with a third form of freedom – freedom as non-domination: "as a condition under which a person is more or less immune, and more or less saliently immune, to interference on an arbitrary basis" (Pettit 1997, vii–viii). In contrast to the negative notion of freedom, non-domination is not concerned with interference as such, but rather the type(s) of interference involved. Some forms of interference do not compromise, but actually enhance, our freedom because they protect us against arbitrary uses of power. Pettit notes that "being unfree does not consist in being restrained; on the contrary, the restraint of a fair system of law – a non-arbitrary regime – does not make you unfree. Being unfree consists rather in … being subject to the potentially capricious will or potentially idiosyncratic judgement of another" (ibid., 5). Democracy as non-domination provides a justification for law as enabling and protecting persons and for government interventions to prevent arbitrary forms of power.[4] At the same time, and precisely because law figures as such an important constraint, the notion of democracy as non-domination places less emphasis on citizen participation than do most mainstream republican thinkers.

From this perspective, dominance is rule without justification, and it pertains to forms of unauthorized rule, absence of constitutional provisions, or absence of reciprocal power. The state and hierarchy are not synonymous with dominance. Hierarchies can engender dominance by excluding us from participating in decisions, forcing us to experience the rule or the system as unjust, and subjecting citizens to forms of rule that are non-transparent and generally inattentive to popular demands. Anarchy can also engender dominance if private actors press others into the service of an illegitimate purpose.

Pettit's version of democracy as non-domination places a strong onus on constitutionalism and counter-majoritarian institutions, including horizontal dispersal of power in specific institutions tasked with legislative, executive, and judicial functions, as well as dispersal of power along vertical lines. His strong emphasis on counter-majoritarian institutions has been criticized by Ian Shapiro (2012), who adopts a more explicitly political perspective on dominance, especially in terms of how to ensure non-domination. Shapiro underlines that dominance is relational and structural, but also that determining what constitutes dominance must consider subjective factors. Since not all forms of power constitute dominance, it is important to understand how those subject to power understand its exercise and effects. Shapiro argues, therefore, that to establish whether there is domination, one important source of information is insiders' knowledge. At the same time, insiders' knowledge may be an unreliable guide when people's basic interests are at stake. We therefore need to pay explicit attention to the basic interests of the actors involved (Shapiro 2016, 23).

Shapiro's conception of dominance has different implications from Pettit's for our thinking about how democracy and federalism are coupled, how we think about executive-legislative relations, and what constitutes executive dominance. He emphasizes political over legal institutions in countering domination; he also privileges majority rule in contrast to Pettit's emphasis on counter-majoritarian institutions. He notes that "the case of majority rule is that it minimizes the chances of domination when compared to the going alternatives, but this in no way precludes a majority from undoing what a different majority has done – whether in the recent or the distant past. Indeed, the possibility that new majorities might upset the status quo is part of what contributes to democratic stability" (Shapiro 2016, 44).

For Shapiro, then, majoritarian democracy provides the greatest institutional assurances against domination, but with the important proviso that this conclusion applies to the national, not the international, level. He envisages a more substantial role for the state and public institutions to combat forms of dominance that emanate from significant differences in material resources than does Pettit. He criticizes Pettit's account of public institutions as "a recipe for protecting the status quo, which could only be appealing from the point of view if one did not perceive it as heavily laden with domination" (Shapiro 2012, 331).

Finally, Pettit has been criticized by Erik Eriksen (2018, 992), who notes that "for Pettit, a decision is arbitrary and a source of un-freedom whenever it is taken or rejected without reference to the interests or opinions of those affected, for Kantians, the freedom of individuals should be protected regardless of their interests or opinions. In this latter perspective, non-arbitrary power is not foremost a matter of tracking the preferences of the affected, but rather of institutions securing the equal freedom of persons. Freedom can only be restricted for the sake of freedom itself. Political authority is based 'on the principle of it being possible to use external constraint that can coexist with the freedom of everyone in accordance with universal laws.'"[5] For Eriksen, the key issue is political status: legally protected autonomy is the best assurance for viable reciprocal relations.

To sum up thus far, the notion of democracy as non-domination posits that the core of dominance is subjection to arbitrariness. It operates at both interpersonal and institutional levels. Analysts disagree on how much emphasis should be placed on the subjective element of perceived dominance as opposed to relational and structural-institutional factors. That, in turn, renders the term well suited for assessing executive-legislative relations. Precisely how the notion of domination is to be applied hinges on which position one applies. Pettit's focus on law and counter-majoritarian institutions directs our attention to legal and procedural constraints through dispersion of power horizontally, across institutions, as well as vertically, from the central level to lower levels. His notion is biased in favour of constraints on majority rule that ensure minority protection, whereas Shapiro's notion places the onus on majority rule and democratic politics. Both theorists emphasize the need to track patterns of domination in relation to basic interests, with Shapiro being particularly concerned with the distribution of material resources. Eriksen's Kantian-inspired approach focuses on developing the right constitutional and institutional design.

These three positions on dominance are relevant when considering the specifics of executive dominance. Before we discuss the most relevant forms of executive dominance, we need to show how prominently federalism figures in the literature on non-domination.

Federalism and Non-domination

As a general assumption, the more weight we can attach to federalism as a means of countering domination, the less we should expect federalism to contribute to executive dominance. When we consider the different positions on non-domination presented above, we see that they offer quite different positions on federalism's role in deterring domination. Pettit's emphasis on constitutionalism and counter-majoritarian institutions is well attuned to federalism in the sense that he sees federalism as an important element in his broader scheme of power dispersion: "The republican rationale for dispersing power is, other things being equal, to increase the non-manipulability of the law and to guard against government exercising arbitrary sway over others … it is no accident that republicans have been traditionally partial to federations" (Pettit 1997, 178–9).

By contrast, Shapiro focuses on the conditions for majoritarian rule at the central level and does not place any emphasis on federalism. If anything, for him federalism would represent a constraint on majority rule. All the federations that emerged out of the British Empire – Canada, Australia, and India – combine majority rule with federalism. As such, they incorporate elements of Shapiro's and Pettit's preferred arrangements for combating domination. As we shall see when we unpack the notion of executive dominance, this combination, especially in Canada, is highly conducive to executive dominance.

The late Iris Marion Young saw non-domination as being intrinsic to federalism, but, in contrast to Pettit, she understood federalism more broadly and as a core element in the system of democratic governing. She labelled her approach to self-determination "non-domination" and contrasted that with the standard, sovereign-state notion of self-determination as non-interference. For Young, the latter is where "a self-determining people dwells together in a relatively large territory [that is] contiguous and bounded; the self-determining people exercise strong self-governing rights over this territory" (Young 2005, 139).

Young's notion of federalism has a bearing on how we think about coupling. A federation based on self-determination as non-interference would more or less uncouple federalism and democracy because there would be almost watertight compartments among units across horizontal and vertical lines. Young argues that this notion falls short, especially in circumstances where groups that seek self-government do not possess a contiguous territory and the necessary resources to ensure full independence. Her main example is Indigenous peoples' claims for self-determination. In these circumstances, systems based on self-determination as non-interference offer inadequate protections against domination because of patterns of interdependence and vulnerability. In addition, as we see in today's Europe, in particular, in cases of democratic backsliding, "A concept of self-determination that means primarily non-interference with the internal affairs of a sovereign government implicitly allows for domination within, to the extent that it forbids outsiders from interfering if they observe such domination" (Young 2005, 145).

In contrast to the model of self-determination as non-interference, Young introduces the notion of self-determination as non-domination. She notes that "this model of self-determination implies federalism as a mode of being together with other self-determining units" (Young 2005, 140). This model establishes a *presumption of non-interference*, coupled with institutions for joint decision-making capable of establishing the conditions under which intervention is needed to prevent domination. In relation to Benz's scheme, Young's notion of self-determination as non-domination presupposes an institutional structure wherein federalism and democracy are loosely coupled. The key normative standard that structures the relationship between federalism and democracy is non-domination.

In assessing Young's conception, Jacob Levy notes that "non-domination is an idea in the wrong register to fit fully a theory of federalism's foundations, because it defers decisions about jurisdiction until after deciding the merits of particular disputes. By contrast, non-interference, even if it is inferior to non-domination as a general account of freedom, is superior as a jurisdictional decision rule" (Levy 2008, 60–1). Levy agrees that non-domination should serve as the critical standard, but he finds that it fails to offer clear prescriptions if it is translated into a jurisdictional decision rule. The critical issue for him is that a decision structure that does not enable the involved parties to exit with reference to legally established rights and jurisdictional autonomy is vulnerable to undue interference and endless squabbles over *who* has legal rights and what the jurisdictional bounds should be.

The central issue is that we need to distinguish constitutive issues from questions of policy substance. If not, power asymmetries will matter too much to decision outcomes. Young's framework, Levy underlines, overextends the role of non-domination: it can and should serve as a critical standard for assessing power relations, but cannot directly serve as a decision rule. It should, however, operate as a critical standard by which to assess all decision rules. This discussion has implications for the conditions guiding loosely coupled federalism and democracy. One is that federalism and democracy must each be constitutionally recognized and institutionally embedded; without this, one principle will dominate, or one or both will wither (a process of de-federalization and de-democratization).

A second implication is that loose coupling requires some form of agreement on the requisite type of regime and mode of political community. Such basic agreement is important given the dilemma built into loose coupling: it can never be fixed in a constitution because it has to be open to adjustment. This very openness, in turn, provides little assurance of balance; hence, there will always be the prospect of imbalance, most likely through executive dominance. Nevertheless, the critical issue is that there need to be limits to the extent of imbalances. The literature on federalism operates with such limits, which is a point that none of the theorists on domination explicitly addresses.

We examine these limits by going back to Preston King's (1982) distinction between federalism and federation. The former refers to the values and principles – the federal spirit and notions of federalism as covenant, etc., while the latter refers to the political system's institutional make-up. King insisted that a federal structure that lacks an agreed-upon federalism falls short. From this perspective, a proper federation is based on agreement on the fundamentals of living together and on a sense of solidarity and spirit of cooperation. This is of direct relevance for the discussion of the EU as a federal-type entity. It has federal features, but there is no agreement on its federal vocation or on a viable European federal*ism* (Fossum 2017). We should expect instances lacking agreement on a viable federalism to couple federalism and democracy in distinct ways, which are particularly prone to imbalances.

A third implication is that loose coupling cannot be equated with self-determination as non-domination. This goes back to Levy's criticism of Young's scheme. There is no doubt that self-determination as non-domination lives very comfortably in loosely coupled systems, but it requires a federal system constitutionally structured (if not always practically operating) according to the precept of non-interference. The point is that loose coupling must somehow be made subject to legal-institutional and constitutional constraints as well as exit options. For systems of loose coupling to continue serving federalism and democracy, there has to be some element of constitutional and even institutional closure. Political systems that fail to reach viable constitutional and federal settlements will be quite prone to arbitrary domination.

Fourth, it is only under extreme conditions of uncoupling between levels of government that a federation will effectively operate according to the principle of self-determination as non-intervention. All modern federations have elements of shared and concurrent jurisdiction, and institutions for joint decision-making, because the wide range of tasks they perform are imbricated and thus very difficult to allocate to just one level.

Finally, as noted above, the literature on democracy as non-domination does not come up with a unified position on federalism's contribution to non-domination. We therefore need to disaggregate executive-legislative relations within federal settings. That is the task of the subsequent sections, which spell out three dimensions of executive dominance.

Unpacking Executive Dominance

Executive dominance exists when executives either lack proper democratic authorization or too easily escape meaningful accountability to the people through their popularly elected bodies. The sources of executive dominance may relate to the nature and actions of executives, but they cannot be confined to the executive. The nature and (in)action of relevant controlling agents also matters. For instance, parliaments may engender dominance if they increase arbitrariness (e.g., by compelling executives to strike informal deals[6] or by undermining or sidestepping minority rights and the role of courts[7]). Further, the basic structure within which executive-legislative relations unfold can engender executive dominance by heightening vulnerability to societal or other actors or increasing arbitrariness through inadequate institutional and legal-constitutional arrangements. In the following, we outline the core forms of executive dominance and discuss the conditions for achieving a *balance* between effective governance and democratic legitimacy.

In what sense might executives become dominant in a democratic setting? We have already seen that the notion of dominance in our analysis differs from the standard power-based notion of dominance, which is to convince someone to do something that the person would not otherwise have done. Our conception of dominance focuses not on power as such but on arbitrary interference. We have seen that, at the individual level, it involves some form of interference against which a person cannot protect himself or herself (Pettit 1997; Shapiro 1999). In an institutional system, by analogy, one element in the system interferes with or controls decisions affecting individuals (citizens), who lack the institutional capacity to articulate and defend their interests in a manner consistent with the underlying democratic rationale for the overall system. Where citizens' interests are represented through electoral processes, their representatives are unable to effectively represent their constituents' interests in relation to executive decisions, despite formal provisions for such representation in the system of governance. The characteristic of arbitrariness is important here since it helps to differentiate between executive presence and executive dominance: the former is about justified interference, whereas the latter is not. Justified interference is either subject to legal-constitutional provisions and controls (Pettit 1997) or is delimited by democratically inclusive and majoritarian procedures (Shapiro 1999).

In the following analysis, we spell out more precisely what we mean by executive dominance, with particular emphasis on how it manifests itself in executive-legislative relations. We highlight three key dimensions in relation to the notion of dominance. The point is to unpack the notion of executive dominance by uncovering its key institutional manifestations and find a way of comparing the degree of executive dominance in different political systems. We draw, in particular, on the Canadian and EU cases.

Executive dominance lies at the heart of the EU's democratic deficit (Curtin 2014; Fossum and Laycock 2013). With its roots in a system of states, the EU balances a quasi-parliamentary structure with a comprehensive system of intergovernmental summitry, steeped in the European Council and the Council of Ministers. How to render this system democratically accountable has been a central challenge for the EU for decades, and it has recently become far more acute with the

EU's related financial, social, and constitutional crises (Habermas 2012; Fossum and Menéndez 2014; Menéndez 2013). What is not well known in Europe is that Canada's federal state relies on analogous forms of intergovernmental summitry and has a comprehensive system of intergovernmental relations to regulate federal-provincial relations (Simeon 1972). This makes Canada a particularly apposite comparison with the EU on the issue of executive dominance. In contrast to the EU, however, Canada is a fully fledged parliamentary federation.

Executive Control of Decision-Making at the Same Level of Governing

This is the most obvious aspect of executive dominance. It refers to executive-legislative imbalance through a very high measure of executive control of decision-making. This involves the executive setting the agenda for the legislature, effectively formulating the set of policy option choices, directing or determining the legislature's choice among the alternatives specified, being in charge of implementing its selected policy options, and playing a central role in dealing with popular feedback. Thus, a system marked by executive dominance more or less reverses the parliamentary principle of formal executive responsibility to the legislature. This situation undermines the executive's accountability to elected representatives, and indirectly to voters, from which parliamentary government derives much of its democratic legitimacy. This first dimension of executive dominance highlights the horizontal dimension between governing bodies at one given level of governance. In updating his classic *Patterns of Democracy*, Arend Lijphart suggests that this dimension of executive dominance is particularly pronounced in the larger Westminster parliamentary systems of the United Kingdom, Australia, and Canada, but also notes its presence in the non-Westminster systems in Spain, Austria, and France (Lijphart 2012, 115–26).

When we think of this in relation to what was said above about domination, we see that this form of executive dominance can manifest itself in one, two, or all of the following: (a) legislatures incapable of reining in and holding the executive to account (because the legislature is weak or ill informed), (b) legislatures incapable of reining in and holding the executive to account because the executive dominates the party that controls the legislature, and (c) legislatures incapable of reining in and holding the executive to account because the executive shifts decisions to informal forums or arrangements and effectively shuts the legislature out of the decision-making process.

All three situations exhibit forms of imbalance that may amount to domination. Precisely how will hinge on the specific definition of domination that we adopt. With regard to (a) above, it matters whether a parliament is weak and ill informed for structural reasons, such as a lack of control of its own agenda and lack of informational capabilities to match executives and administrations, or whether it is ill informed because of particular circumstances that are amenable to change. From Pettit's perspective, the main issue would appear to be the presence or absence of legal and institutional provisions for parliaments to rein in runaway executives, whereas, for Shapiro, the main issue would appear to be the distribution of resources among actors within the decision-making system.

The European Parliament (EP), for instance, can only weakly hold the executive to account and suffers from deficiencies along both lines. One deficiency pertains to how the accountability relation is structured: it can approve or reject the European Council's suggestions for Commission president, but it cannot determine the Commission's composition (commissioners are proposed by the member states). It can, however, force the commissioners (as a collective) to resign.[8] Further, there is a clear gap between the tasks that executives conduct under the auspices of the EU and the EP's ability to hold the executives to account, especially given the EP's weak role in foreign and security policy. In terms of resources, the EP faces severe constraints, as will be spelled out in further detail below.

With regard to (b), we need additional information on political parties[9] to determine whether this condition is met. The third form, (c), manifests *arbitrary* domination most clearly because it provides executives with the greatest scope for escaping legal and parliamentary controls. The financial crisis demonstrated how vulnerable the EU was to external market shocks, and the caprice of financial markets, which can be construed as a source of arbitrary domination. The financial crisis served as a spur to increased executive dominance and reconfigured relations among institutions. Institutionally speaking, we see a relative strengthening of the European Council and an emphasis on handling the crisis through intergovernmental means (the so-called Union method), including fashioning intergovernmental treaties (e.g., the Treaty on Stability, Coordination and Governance in the Economic and Monetary Union), and striking informal intergovernmental bargains through extensive summitry (including bilateral meetings between Germany and France, which Montani (2012), for instance, criticized as a kind of *directoire*).[10]

Canada has frequently been held up as a case of executive dominance, and, as we shall see, it testifies to how majoritarian government can exacerbate executive dominance, not necessarily by increased arbitrariness but by creating a serious executive-legislative imbalance. In Canada, one major shortcoming derives from the single-member-plurality electoral system, which distorts the translation of votes into legislative representation primarily to the advantage of the first-place party. That facilitates artificial majority governments, in turn reducing the level of executive accountability to the legislatures to which they are formally responsible in this model of "responsible government." A further element of imbalance pertains to the practical strength of Parliament vis-à-vis the executive nominally "responsible" to Parliament.

Executives can exploit the structural imbalance by further circumventing parliaments – with increased arbitrariness as the result. Canada during the Harper era is a case in point. As prime minister from 2006 to 2015, Stephen Harper extended the power of the Prime Minister's Office (PMO), lessened the accountability of the federal executive and Parliament as a whole, and undermined deliberation within Parliament. He exercised unprecedented domination of Cabinet, his government caucus, and parliamentary committees (Docherty 2010; Aucoin, Jarvis, and Turnbull 2011; Morden, Hilderman, and Anderson 2018). However, Prime Minister Harper was only the most extreme manifestation of a long trend of increasing executive dominance at the federal level. Since the late 1960s, and certainly since 2015, under Justin Trudeau's direction, prime ministers have concentrated power in the PMO, the Privy Council Office, and the Department of Finance as well as with a small subset of trusted ministers and "courtiers." This has reduced most ministers, and all government backbenchers, to insignificance (Savoie 1999, 2008). Opposition MPs have few committee or other resources with which to effectively challenge the prime minister's policy agenda and are constrained by an unusually high level of party discipline (Bakvis and Wolinetz 2005; Morden, Hilderman, and Anderson 2018).

Stephen Harper's omnibus budget bills centralized even more power in the PMO and placed beyond debate the claim that the Canadian federal executive dominates its legislature more than any other Westminster system (Bakvis and Wolinetz 2005; O'Malley 2007). During its decade in power, the Harper government ignored opposition and media criticism of wholly unprecedented prorogations to avoid failed confidence votes. It manipulated parliamentary committees[11] and extended PMO control of Cabinet and senior bureaucratic behaviour as well as government information.

The EU has a parliament but is not based on a full-fledged system of parliamentary government; it is probably more apt to label it a kind of consensus democracy with numerous institutional controls on majoritarian rule. The EU-level executive is very fragmented (Curtin 2009), in sharp contrast to Canada, which saw a strengthened concentration of power in the central executive under Stephen Harper. The EU-level executive is situated in a range of institutions (European Commission, European Council, aspects of the Council, and the informal Eurozone Council) with an inordinately high level of control over decision-making. The representative-democratic structure fails to offer the measure of electoral accountability that we associate with representative government. There is no directly elected body at the EU level that can propose a law; everything has to go through the non-elected Commission. The ordinary legislative procedure (earlier labelled co-decision) is a complex procedure for forging consensus through inter-institutional deliberation and interaction. In practice, however, there is an increasing trend towards informal Commission, EP, and Council trialogues that effectively short-circuit parliamentary handling of legislative proposals – in the sense that deals are struck in secret among a limited number of actors (Farrell and Héritier 2003; Stie 2012). The increased use of trialogues shows how the executive-dominance virus infects the EP.

Executive dominance in the EU is amplified by the fact that the EU's Commission is not the only executive. The Council also carries executive functions, notably in foreign and security policy. Within this policy realm, the EP's role is merely consultative. The upshot is that, in the field of security and defence policy, issues are increasingly handled at the EU level, but the European-wide representative-body, the EP, is unable to influence and legislate on them.

These observations bear on the general question of the relative resources available to the different institutions. To what extent are parliaments dependent on executives or other actors for their functioning? There is much to suggest that, in this regard, the EP is in a rather vulnerable position. It is greatly hampered by the fact that it does not have taxing powers proper. This structural constraint arguably hits it much harder than the EU executive because the latter – especially the European Council and the Council of Ministers (not the Commission) – controls the sources of funds in the member states and the EU. This was readily apparent in the eurozone debt crisis, in which the German government (and parliament) played a central role as paymaster.

The EU example underlines the notion that inter-institutional relations and the terms of legislative-executive balancing are strongly affected by the relative resources available to the executive versus to the parliament. In addition, the EU example confirms that the terms of legislative-executive relations at any one level of governance are critically dependent on the resources available to that level of governance. Structurally speaking, weaker resource bases appear to entail weaker legislatures since the executive is more likely to have direct access to resources at other levels of governing.

Executive Dominance through Multi-level Intergovernmental Dynamics

The second dimension of executive dominance focuses more on the vertical dimension, or relations between the different levels of governance. It highlights the central role that executives occupy in multi-level governing systems structured as two-level games (cf. Putnam 1988), such as some federal systems[12] and the EU. A hallmark of executive dominance is that executives enjoy direct and privileged access to both main levels of governance, and they are able to play off other actors at both levels against each other; in this way, they evade responsibility to parliaments and citizens. Policymaking in these multi-level systems takes place in a densely organized system of executive interaction. The general assumption is that the more informal and the less subject to procedures such systems are, the greater their potential for arbitrariness. When that is matched by a significant executive-legislative imbalance, in structural and resource terms, executive dominance is further enhanced.

Two key features of executive dominance within this second dimension become apparent when we consider accountability. One aspect of accountability is about *making accounts*, and the other is about *holding to account*. It matters a lot to accountability relations *whose* accounts are used to structure the relations and *how* these accounts are framed. As a general assumption, the greater the emphasis on policy outputs, the more weight will be attributed to the executives' accounts. It is questionable whether that qualifies as executive dominance, however. Of more direct relevance would be executives' use of their privileged position in the intergovernmental realm to manipulate accountability, perhaps by denying that a given issue is relevant to the federal level or for lower-level parliaments. In situations of overlapping jurisdiction or unclear bounds, there is considerable scope for such manipulation by, and strategic advantage for, executive bodies.

The other feature of executive dominance under this second dimension pertains to holding to account. Legislative bodies at all relevant levels find themselves "one step behind" in such systems because their role is to respond to, or simply to ratify or reject, the bargains struck among the two levels' executive officials. This amplifies the accountability deficit incurred in the horizontal domain noted above. An important consideration here is whether such systems of intergovernmental relations are legally regulated, subject to transparency requirements, and generally complied with or whether they are less regulated, more informal, or even ad hoc. It is clear that the question of legal regulation has a bearing on both aspects of the accountability question: making accounts and holding to account. The less regulated such relations, the greater the scope for arbitrary domination, thus allowing executives exceptional powers both to frame the relationship and to escape the forms of representative accountability that such procedures might contain.

We can illustrate this problem with reference to Canada. In principle, executive dominance in the national government could be somewhat offset by meaningful provincial legislative control over premiers, their Cabinets, and provincial central agencies. However, over the past two decades, British Columbia, Alberta, and Ontario have developed "post-institutionalized," or premier-centred, Cabinet structures (Dunn 2002; G. White 2010; Marriott 2011; Thomas and Lewis 2018). This drift towards a "presidentialization" (Bakvis and Wolinetz 2005) of their representative institutions suggests that provincial governments do little to make up for the democratic legitimacy deficits generated at the national level.

The democratic legitimacy deficit in Canadian federalism displays both accountability and inclusion failures, and it involves a confusing welter of shared jurisdictions and agreements characteristic of executive federalism. Of the hundreds of intergovernmental agreements concluded between provincial and federal governments over the past several decades, only a tiny fraction have been discussed by either federal or provincial legislative committees (Simeon and Cameron 2008; J. Smith 2007; Simmons 2008; Graefe, Simmons, and White 2013). These typically bilateral agreements are presented to their legislatures as *faits accomplis* by federal and provincial governments on matters ranging from environmental regulation to federal social transfers to labour market mobility (DiGiacomo 2005).

Jennifer Smith suggests that "the closed processes of executive federalism can have the effect of immunizing controversies between the two levels of government from public debate, because the legislatures are excluded from these processes" (J. Smith 2007; see also Cameron 2001, 16). The record is not uniformly negative (Graefe, Simmons, and White 2013), but it suggests a serious problem with dominance as we understand it here.

The low levels of inclusion, justification, transparency, and accountability in "intergovernmental Canada" exacerbate national and provincial executive dominance. For citizens, this marginalization of elected officials attenuates any meaningful connections in, and accountability of, elective representation even further. As Cutler and Mendelsohn have shown, citizens have understandable difficulty holding federal and provincial politicians electorally accountable (Cutler 2004, 2008; Cutler and Mendelsohn 2005). Cutler suggests that "if politicians think voters lack motivation or the tools to accurately attribute responsibility, they may be able to shirk in their role as citizens' agents" (Cutler 2008, 651). Our point is that such shirking is now institutionally protected and seldom attended by political consequences. First ministers and their advisers constitute a small and enclosed loop of principal-agent interactions, in which Canadian citizens cease to be effective principals and are denied basic information that would allow them to identify the players or the strategies, let alone the scores, in this strategic game.

It could also be argued that it matters *how* parliaments might most effectively catch up with executives.[13] There are basically three options: (a) a single parliament can catch up with "its" executive at the same levels of governing (dimension one discussed above, the horizontal dimension between governing bodies at a given level of governance), (b) parliaments at the same governance level can cooperate to hold their executives to account, and (c) parliaments at all main governance levels can cooperate to hold executives to account.[14] The futility of many efforts to catch up at the first level, and the virtual non-existence of efficacious efforts at levels two and three, underscore the daunting challenges of developing viable executive-legislative balance in complex, multi-level federal systems.

Executive Constitution-Making or Change

The third dimension of executive dominance refers to constitution-making or change. The first aspect we are concerned with is about process and procedure; the other is about substance and institutional-constitutional design. With regard to process, the relevant scenario occurs when executives play a central role in constitutional amendment, while legislatures and direct popular input through referendums play limited roles, typically at the end of a complex process, thus limiting citizens' collective responses to either acceptance or rejection. This type of domination, while not constitutionally lacking foundations, gives executive officials a unique role in shaping the very nature of the polity. Again, it matters considerably whether the procedures are legally entrenched and complied with or whether they are more informal or ad hoc, with considerable executive leverage in their design and execution.

It is difficult to consider the issue of process as being entirely separate from substance, especially when it comes to core institutional and constitutional matters. In theory, executives could play a central role in establishing a constitutional-institutional structure that subsequently curtails their role. In practice, they establish structural arrangements that will ensure not just their roles as core "constitutional chaperones" but also their great leverage in doing so. The most pronounced instance of executive dominance would allow executives to continuously "set the terms of federal balancing as part of doing the balancing" (Fossum 2017). It is this role that the European Council effectively plays in the EU, in a complex system of interaction where the European Court of Justice also figures prominently.

These three dimensions provide a composite view of executive dominance, and they offer analytical leverage on the most democratically problematic elements of executive dominance, closely associated with arbitrary domination rather than with legally regulated procedures.

Conclusion

In this chapter, we took as our point of departure the neo-republican conception of democracy as non-domination to shed light on the relationship between democracy and federalism – in particular, how the phenomena that these terms signify are coupled, reconciled, and balanced. We placed particular emphasis on a specific form of imbalance – namely, executive dominance. We first presented a brief summary of the neo-republican conception of democracy as non-domination to specify under what conditions executive dominance could be defined as executives exceeding their role. The focus was on three sets of relations: executive-legislative relations at the same level of governing (a horizontal dimension), the system of intergovernmental relations (a vertical dimension), and executive dominance in constitution-making or change. We showed that the notion of dominance is a useful concept for examining legislative-executive relations within and across levels of governing and for shedding light on the relationship between federalism and democracy more broadly. The literature on dominance that we consulted differed considerably in terms of which institutional arrangements would most effectively deter domination. Pettit emphasized non-majoritarian systems with strong constitutional controls, including federal arrangements, whereas Shapiro emphasized majoritarian arrangements and did not place any emphasis on federal arrangements.

We provided empirical illustrations from Canada and the EU and found that both harbour significant elements of all three levels of executive dominance. Structurally speaking, and as could be expected from their different levels of systemic consolidation, executive dominance in the EU clearly dwarfs that in Canada. Nevertheless, as a parliamentary federation, Canada combines majority rule with federalism in a manner that yields a significant element of executive dominance. An interesting difference between Canada and the EU is in the strong centralization of power in the hands of relatively few executives in Canada compared to the far greater institutional fragmentation in Europe, extending well within the executive itself. By contrast, recent Canadian prime minister Harper amassed power in his well-staffed office and avoided political checks even over five years of minority government.

In principle, the strong scope for political centralization in Canada would suggest a greater range of institutional checks on power in Europe, even if parliaments are lagging behind. This expectation is not fulfilled, for several reasons. One pertains to the particularly strong EU executive presence in the realm of foreign and security power. Another, perhaps even more important, set of developments stems from the EU's handling of manifold recent crises, which have greatly increased executive dominance in Europe. Arguably, the most destructive feature of these crises is the greatly heightened arbitrariness, which has manifested in "emergency Europe" (J. White 2015) notions that are hard to leave behind.

The fact of emergency politics in Europe, as Jonathan White (2015) underlines, is associated with a fragmented, not a highly centralized, system of executive interaction. Arbitrary domination may ensue from strong leadership as well as from a lack of coherent leadership. The challenge facing Europe is to restore action capability while reining in executive dominance. The somewhat chastening Canadian example shows us that even established federations struggle to achieve this balance.

NOTES

1 There is an important distinction between *federalism* and *federation*: the former refers to a set of basic principles and the federal spirit, and the latter the system's institutional make-up (King 1982).

2 Federalism is about such values as respect, recognition, empathy, and toleration. The federal spirit, as Burgess (2012) underlines, is additionally and centrally imbued with liberal democratic constitutionalism.

3 "The oddness of all federal theory … is due to its having seized on the very concept (sovereignty) which it actually opposed … its oddity is due to federalism's having *defined* the autonomy of its territorial units in terms of sovereignty, whereas in fact it would have done better to try to *overturn* the idea of sovereignty; all efforts to divide what could only be conceived precisely in terms of total unity drew federal theory into constant paradox and contradiction" (Riley 1973, 88).

4 Pettit notes that "the commonwealth or republican position … sees the people as trustor, both individually and collectively, and sees the state as trustee; in particular, it sees the people as trusting the state to ensure a dispensation of non-arbitrary rule" (1997, 8).

5 The inserted quotation is drawn from Kant ([1785] 1996).

6 In the EU, the increased use of trialogues (inter-institutional agreements) at the early stages of legislation renders EU-level decision-making less transparent. This procedure is, however, not something that the European Parliament has compelled the other institutions to apply.

7 This latter point of sidestepping minority rights and the role of courts has figured as a concern in the EU, where executive-driven legislatures are actively undermining constitutional provisions, including minority rights, in, e.g., Hungary and Poland. In Canada, the issue has been raised in connection with the so-called notwithstanding clause in the Canadian Charter of Rights and Freedoms (s. 33), which permits legislatures to override certain provisions of the Charter. The Canadian situation is not comparable to the European one in the gravity of transgressions.

8 Through parliamentary hearings with incoming commissioners, the EP has also blocked several individuals.

9 See, e.g., Katz and Mair's (2009) contention that "cartelized parties" typically operate with the overwhelming pre-eminence of the "party in public office" over the "party on the ground" and the "party in central office." As Laycock (2014) argues, however, executive domination of the party organization is not only associated with cartelized party systems.

10 For an overview of types and frequency, see Dinan (2012).

11 In 2007, Harper's PMO distributed a 200-page guide to all Conservative House of Commons committee chairs "outlining methods to disrupt and delay committee hearings that were not going the government's way" (Docherty 2010, 83).

12 Not all federal systems behave in this way, as the Swiss and perhaps the Austrian systems attest. But even in federal systems, where divided executive and legislative branches reduce the degree of executive dominance operating on the first dimension, such as the American, there is still a tendency towards executive dominance on this dimension.

13 Arthur Benz (2015) developed a typology of possible multi-level parliamentary configurations and compared the EU with Germany and Canada to better understand the varieties and dynamics of multi-level parliamentary relations in these three entities as well as the broader issues of authorization and accountability that emanate from this.

14 This last version has been discussed in the EU context as a multi-level parliamentary field; see Crum and Fossum (2009, 2013).

5 Federalism and Democracy in the United States

TIMOTHY CONLAN

Modern federalism was born in the United States, as was a limited but promising form of representative democracy. Early on, both institutions – and the relationships between them – attracted great interest from scholars and observers such as Alexis de Tocqueville and John Stuart Mill. As the federal and democratic systems continued to evolve over the ensuing century and a half, the relationships between them became increasingly complex, but no less important.

In this chapter, I briefly examine how the relationship between federalism and democracy was conceptualized and understood when the US Constitution was written and how this relationship developed over the course of American history. Following that, I turn to empirical evidence on the nature of that relationship in contemporary American politics and address competing claims about the democratic character of American federalism, including from the normative perspectives developed in chapters 1 and 2 of this volume. The chapter then turns to an explicit assessment of the US case within the framework of institutional coupling developed in chapter 3. It pays particular attention to the changing role of checks and balances in a dual separation-of-powers system – both horizontal and vertical – when federal as well as executive-legislative relations are being stressed by partisan polarization. The chapter also addresses the role played by informal institutions linking federalism and democracy in the United States and the limitations of the competitive-federalism framework. Finally, the chapter turns to three significant trends that have significant implications for the federalism-democracy relationship in the United States: political nationalization, polarization, and delegitimation.

Federalism and Democracy in American History

The relationship between federalism and democracy has been a perennial concern in the United States. It was a prominent issue at the founding of the republic and evident throughout historical debates over slavery, civil rights, and political reform. It was also central to twentieth-century debates over the direct election of senators, state adoption of initiative and referendum processes, and expansion of the franchise as well as to discussions about the proper roles of the federal and state governments in social policy. It remains deeply relevant to contemporary debates about the strengths and weaknesses of third-party governance.

The Founding Era

Dissatisfaction with the first US Constitution – the Articles of Confederation – was based largely on practical concerns, but issues of democratic legitimacy also played a role in motivating constitutional change. Structurally, the Articles were deficient on matters of basic governance, including the central government's reliance on undependable states for funding and policy execution, the absence of an effective executive, and contentious and growing interstate rivalries. Advocates of a stronger union condemned this governance structure as "imbecilic," dangerous, and unworkable. At the same time, the confederal design of the Articles was conceptually dissonant with the revolutionary logic of republican liberty and popular sovereignty that had been expressed in the Declaration of Independence. The central government, in particular, suffered from a democratic deficit, even by the cramped standards of the day.

This question of democratic legitimacy became a central focus of debate at the constitutional convention and during ratification of the new federal Constitution of 1787. Although it contained many checks on direct popular government, the new Constitution expressly based its legitimacy on the principle of popular rather than state sovereignty. The Articles had established a "confederation ... between the states of New Hampshire, Massachusetts Bay, Rhode Island ... [and] South Carolina" in which "each state retains its sovereignty, freedom, and independence; and every power, jurisdiction, and right, which is not ... expressly delegated to the United States." The new Constitution, in contrast, created a much stronger central government, which was legitimized by "we the people" of the entire nation and empowered to deal directly with them in its areas of responsibility. The need for compromise (which generated, in James Madison's words, a framework that was "neither wholly [con]federal nor wholly national") and the framers' scepticism of direct democracy limited the majoritarian nature of the new government (Hamilton, Madison, and Jay [1787] 1938, 249). But majoritarian elements were clearly enhanced by the popular election of the House of Representatives, allocation of House seats and the Electoral College on the basis of population, and the creation of a template of representational federalism (Beer 1978).

Equally important, much of the ratification debate focused on competing visions of a federal republic. The Anti-Federalists, who opposed the much stronger national government established by the new Constitution, channelled the conventional wisdom of the era – that republican government could flourish only in a small and geographically limited polity (Beer 1992). This "small-republic" school of democracy reflected its advocates' experience with self-government in the former colonies and newly independent states, reinforced by Montesquieu's well-known argument in *The Spirit of the Laws*.

> It is natural for a republic to have only a small territory; otherwise it cannot long subsist. In an extensive republic ... the public good is sacrificed to a thousand private views. ... In a small one, the interest of the public is more obvious, better understood, and more within the reach of every citizen. (Montesquieu 1961, 395–6)

Against this philosophical argument, the advocates of the new Constitution needed to do more than argue that continued independence and effective governance required a more powerful central government, although they did this convincingly (see, e.g., *Federalist* nos. 8, 21, and 22; Hamilton, Madison, and Jay [1787] 1938). They needed to establish the democratic legitimacy of the new institutional design – its republican bona fides. In the wake of the American Revolution, the proposed federal structure could not be legitimized on the basis of federalism's merits alone, as Thomas O. Hueglin proposes in chapter 2 of this volume. The founders' ideology required a basis in republican principles, especially the principle of liberty. This, the framers understood, included both the absence of arbitrary constraint by government – negative liberty – as well as the positive expression of self-government and active consent (Beer 1978).

Thus, *The Federalist* legitimized the Constitution, in part, by emphasizing its strong framework of separated powers. The separate branches were intended to effectively check one another to prevent excessive concentrations of power and potential abuses. As Madison put it in *Federalist* no. 51, "Ambition must be made to counteract ambition" (Hamilton, Madison, and Jay [1787] 1938, 337). The federalist system was a core element of this overall design of structurally protected liberty: "A double security arises to the rights of the people. The different governments will control each other, at the same time that each will be controlled by itself" (ibid., 339).

More important, however, the authors of *The Federalist* explicitly emphasized the popular legitimacy of the new Constitution. As Hamilton stressed in *Federalist* no. 22,

> The fabric of American empire ought to rest on the solid basis of THE CONSENT OF THE GOVERNED. The streams of national power ought to flow immediately from that pure, original foundation of all legitimate authority. (Hamilton, Madison, and Jay [1787] 1938, 141)

Under the new Constitution, ultimate sovereignty was recognized to reside in the people, not the states, and in the demos, not the *demoï*. As Madison argued in *Federalist* no. 46, the different levels of government were instruments of the same sovereign authority.

> The federal and state governments are in fact but different agents and trustees of the people, constituted with different powers, and designed for different purposes. ... The ultimate authority ... resides in the people alone. (ibid., 304–5)

Finally, and most creatively, Madison turned the small-republic theory on its head. In *Federalist* no. 10, he argued that, along with other properly designed institutions, a large, continental-sized nation could better safeguard republican liberties than a small republic. Whereas popular representation could control abuses perpetrated by narrow interests (minority factions), only the scale of an extended republic could constrain intemperate majorities from oppressing minority interests and ensure, in the language of Fossum and Laycock (chap. 4), a more effective structure of non-domination. In Madison's words,

> The smaller the society ... and the smaller number of individuals composing a majority, the smaller the compass within which they are placed, the more easily they will concert and execute their plans of oppression. ... Extend the sphere and you take in a greater variety of parties and interests; you make it less probable that a majority of the whole will have a common motive to invade the rights of other citizens; or, if such common motive

> exists … to act in unison with each other. … In the extent and proper structure of the Union, therefore, we behold a republican remedy for the diseases most incident to republican government. (Hamilton, Madison, and Jay [1787] 1938, 60–1)

These early debates show that the relationship between federalism and democracy was a central concern at the very beginning of modern federalism. They also presaged many of the challenges of constructing modern democratic polities – with their complex combinations of majority rule, rule of law, protection of civil liberties, and respect for minority rights.

Federalism, Democracy, and Development

Democratic concerns have infused debates over federalism and politics ever since. Alexis de Tocqueville marvelled at the spirit of democracy in the new United States and attributed it in part to its federal structure. Local and state governments acted as training schools of democracy, he argued, inculcating democratic habits into the population.

> The strength of free peoples resides in the local community. Local institutions are to liberty what primary schools are to science; they put it within the people's reach; they teach people to appreciate its peaceful enjoyment and accustom them to make use of it. … In the restricted sphere within his scope, [the citizen] learns to rule society. (Tocqueville [1835–40] 1969, 63, 70)

Debates over the spread of slavery to western territories were fought out in terms of "popular sovereignty" – that is, allowing a majority vote in each newly admitted state to determine whether slavery would be legal there. Even anti-democratic, anti-majoritarian elements in society sought to couch their arguments in democratic rhetoric. John C. Calhoun ([1851] 2007) argued on behalf of "states' rights" and Southern slaveholding interests by developing his theory of the "concurrent majority." This concept required consent from all major economic and geographic elements of the (white) population in adopting major national policies. It thus envisioned a consensus-based, consociational approach to American federalism that provided explicit veto power to minorities – but in the name of the "majority" of interests.

Although Calhoun's vision was never fully accepted, elements became embedded in American political thought and politics, especially in the South. "States' rights" became the banner for defending first slavery and later Jim Crow laws and segregation in the South. If democracy failed to live up to its ideals in the United States and elsewhere, as Hueglin argues in chapter 2, American federalism also fell far short of the legitimating ideals of social solidarity and mutual responsibility that he elaborates. American federalism fell short by the standards of non-domination as well. Political deference to Southern whites within a framework of subsidiarity created a problem of minorities within minorities in American federalism. It led directly to the exploitation of the African American minority throughout the Southern region. Far from legitimating federalism in America, this toxic combination provoked William Riker's caustic observation that "if in the United States one approves of Southern white racists, then one approves of American federalism" (Riker 1964, 155).

Many twentieth-century debates melded issues of federalism and democracy as well. Progressive-era reforms designed to improve electoral processes were all state-focused, in recognition of state administration of elections and the federalist structure of election law. Reforms like the Australian ballot, primary elections to nominate candidates, instruments of direct democracy like the initiative and referendums were all fought over at the state level, and their uneven pattern of adoption reflects the federal character of the polity. Reforms requiring amendment of the Constitution – direct election of senators, women's suffrage, abolition of poll taxes and literacy tests for voting, lowering the voting age to eighteen – often began as movements at the state level and had to navigate the highly federalist amendment process (approval by three-quarters of the states).

The long arc of American politics – and federalism – has been towards more direct, majoritarian democracy; greater inclusiveness; and more equality. The direct election of senators, direct primaries for candidate nominations, increased civil rights protections for minorities, and the expansion of the franchise are all indicative of that. From a policy perspective, the expansion of the welfare state and the development of cooperative federalism are also consistent with these trends, especially when they established minimum national standards. But, as will be discussed in subsequent sections of this chapter, the continued tension between these majoritarian tendencies and the constraining, anti-majoritarian characteristics of US federalism – including equal state representation in the Senate, the electoral college, and the combination of state-local fiscal autonomy with uneven fiscal capacity – means that the anti-egalitarian character of US federalism, with its high tolerance for resource disparities and subnational policy differences, continues

(Peterson 1996). This is reinforced, as well, by the continued influence of small-republic ideology in American politics, which imposes further political constraints on equalizing policies and the welfare state (Conlan 1998; Robertson 2012).

Federalism and Democracy in the United States Today: Some Empirical Indicators

Empirical evidence is available on some of the arguments traditionally put forward regarding the relationship between federalism and democracy in the United States (Beam, Conlan, and Walker 1983). In particular, the small-republic idea that local and state governments function as more vibrant centres of democratic participation, deliberation, and representative decision-making lives on, and such arguments about the relationship between "size and democracy" can be explored empirically (Dahl and Tufte 1973).

For example, research has indicated that citizens' knowledge of state government lags behind that of the national government, which limits accountability (Fehrman 2016). One study found that slightly under 50 per cent of citizens could identify which party controlled their state legislature, compared with approximately 75 per cent who could do so correctly for Congress (Rodgers 2013). Political participation mirrors levels of knowledge. Although voter participation levels vary widely from state to state, participation rates in US elections are uniformly higher in presidential-election years. Voter participation drops about fifteen percentage points in gubernatorial elections held in non-presidential-election years, when they average only about 40 per cent of the voting-age population (Holbrook and LaRaja 2018, 86).

A similar pattern is seen in local elections, though with even lower levels of voter turnout. Contrary to the expectations of the small-republic theory, citizens' participation tends to be lowest in local races (Maciag 2014). The major exceptions involve more complex forms of political participation, where the accessibility of local government appears to permit more active participation. This includes campaigning on behalf of a candidate for office and having some contact from a campaign (McAtee and Wolak 2011).

American citizens do express more trust and confidence in state and local governments compared with the national government. Only about 20 per cent of the population expressed high levels of trust in the federal government in 2015 – numbers that have fallen sharply since the early 1960s (Pew Research Center 2015). Trust in state and local governments has remained higher and more consistent. Over 60 per cent of the public expressed a "great deal" or "fair amount" of confidence in their own state and local governments in 2014 (McCarthy 2016).

The ultimate test of representative government is coherence between citizens' preferences and the policy outputs of government. One of the principal democratic arguments on behalf of federalism is that it permits more accurate representation of the policy preferences of geographically distinct communities (Oates 1972). There is strong, consistent evidence that states perform this representative function in the United States. Wright, Erikson, and McIver (1987) measured public opinion in forty-eight of the fifty US states from the 1970s to the 1980s and found that citizens' ideological liberalism correlated strongly (R = 0.80) with an index of state policy outputs. States with more liberal citizens adopted more liberal policies, and states with conservative citizens adopted more conservative policies, on a consistent basis. This strong relationship between state public opinion and public policy outputs has been replicated in subsequent research (V. Gray 2018, 22).

Contemporary Federalism and the Extended Republic

In short, there is a mixed record of empirical support for contemporary attributes of the small-republic theory. Citizens tend to have less knowledge about state and local governments, and they participate less actively (as measured by voting, though not more robust forms of participation – attending meetings, talking about issues, etc.). But states and localities enjoy higher legitimacy (as measured by trust), and there is strong evidence of the representative nature of state governments.

But these dimensions of democratic governance do not tell the full story. Federalism is also implicated in issues related to Madison's concept of the extended republic. Madison feared that tyranny by majority factions would be the most severe dysfunction of republican government. The treatment of racial minorities throughout American history lends credence to that fear. States, in particular, have displayed a long history of discrimination against minority groups, including African Americans, Chinese and Japanese citizens and immigrants, Latinos, and Native Americans. The national government was hardly blameless when it came to discriminatory practices, but, as Madison predicted, rigid practices of discrimination were more difficult to construct at the national level. And the federal government was often an agent of reform and civil rights protections, from the 14th Amendment to the civil rights laws of the 1960s.

A similar dynamic of discrimination and mistreatment was also evident in social welfare policies. States – particularly Southern states – often insisted on maintaining a major state role as their price for accepting national welfare-policy expansions (Robertson 2012). That state role often extended beyond administrative implementation to include policy decisions over benefits and eligibility. The Social Security Act of 1935 provides an example. Old age pensions were designed as a national program, with uniform taxes, eligibility, and benefits nationwide and a national administrative structure. But unemployment insurance and cash welfare payments to the poor were created as intergovernmental programs, administered by the states. The latter program allowed the states to set benefit and eligibility standards, producing dramatic variations from state to state. Federal matching rates were ultimately adjusted so that poorer states received a more favourable match, but large disparities remain. And, according to one recent study, race continues to be a major factor in explaining these disparities: states with large African American populations continue to have the most restrictive welfare policies and payments (Hahn et al. 2017).

Ostensibly, a principal democratic goal of federalism is to combine the advantages of large and small republics. In the case of the United States, there is evidence that each level of government makes certain contributions to democracy in terms of participation, representation, and public policy, even as each level also displays weaknesses. Overall, there is public support for the resulting system of multiple governments with multiple avenues of public influence and involvement and multiple potential venues of service provision (Arceneaux 2005). Although both American federalism and American democracy fall well short of the ideals for each institution laid out by Hueglin, each has proved capable of reinforcing the other, in both positive and negative ways. Some of these institutional linkages are considered in the following section.

Institutional Linkages between Federalism and Democracy in the United States

The foregoing analysis of federalism and democracy in the United States illustrates some of the linkages between original and historical perspectives on these institutions and contemporary practice. However, the comparative framework developed in this book provides additional insight into this relationship in the United States and elsewhere. It effectively highlights many of the democratic tensions apparent in contemporary federalism, and it illuminates particular challenges that are often overlooked. For example, Benz and Sonnicksen have argued that the institutional structures of federalism and democracy are, in the framework developed in chapter 3, "decoupled" in the United States. The US system remains defined by a form of dual federalism: not in the strict separation of functions common in the nineteenth century, which has been altered by the rise of cooperative federalism, but by the continued "separation of policy-making at the two levels" and the "lack of interlocking institutional linkages between national and state governments" (Benz and Sonnicksen 2017).

This separation was widened by the passage of the 17th Amendment to the Constitution in 1913, which replaced state legislative election of US senators with direct popular election. At the state level, Benz and Sonnicksen argue that the United States is characterized by a "competitive federalism" model. The broad fiscal and policymaking autonomy afforded to states in the US model, combined with the mobility of individuals and capital, means that subnational governments "cannot escape competition with other governments" (Benz and Sonnicksen 2017, 11). This structure establishes an inherent tension with democracy in the United States: "The rationality of competition violates the principle of equality … [and the] autonomy of democratic institutions thus becomes offset or, at least, severely limited by the force of competition" (ibid.).

These tensions in the federal system are mirrored by weaknesses in democratic institutions, particularly the rise of presidentialism and executive federalism (Gais and Fossett 2005; Thompson, Wong, and Rabe 2020). The growing power of the president has unbalanced the horizontal separation of powers and increased the potential for executive dominance in American government. Moreover, the opaqueness of executive federalism corrodes democratic legitimacy. The complex, technocratic nature of modern intergovernmental relations – combined with the freewheeling nature of federal policy implementation using waivers – means that "the citizenry cannot wield influence over decisions coordinated between the various levels" (Benz and Sonnicksen 2017, 11).

Federalism and Institutional Change

These insights merit further analysis and elaboration. The following section explores the ways in which dual federalism has evolved in the United States, the extent and limits of competitive federalism in the US model, and the role of informal mechanisms of coupling in American federalism. Unlike many federal systems, much of the coupling occurs outside formal institutional channels, within the political party system, and through non-governmental entities like the intergovernmental lobby.

No institution in the United States has evolved more than the federal system over the course of American history. While state and local governments continue to enjoy an impressive degree of fiscal and policymaking autonomy when measured by comparative standards (Kim and Blöchliger 2015), the constraints imposed on that autonomy have grown dramatically. Traditional dual federalism, defined by the vertical separation of governmental functions, no longer exists. Today, there are over one thousand distinct federal grants-in-aid, which comprise over one-third of state budgets and one-sixth of the federal budget. With the Supreme Court's permission, these have eroded the separation of functional responsibilities among the different levels of government. The national government invests heavily in welfare, education, social services, law enforcement, health and safety, and other areas seemingly left to the states by the language of the Constitution. It imposes numerous federal regulations directly upon state and local governments and enlists them as implementers or co-regulators in many others (Posner 1998). Since the original federal-aid highway program in 1916, it has designed programs in such a way as to require state and local governments to professionalize their workforce and has altered the balance of power in state-local relationships (Derthick 1970). Intergovernmental linkages in implementing programs are so dense that they have inspired the metaphor of "picket-fence federalism," in which policy specialists and professionals at different levels of government form tight linkages and networks across governmental entities at each level.

This reality has reduced the degree of separation in policymaking among the levels of government (Benz and Sonnicksen 2017, 10). Many federal aid programs have been designed specifically to alter state and local decision making, providing strong fiscal incentives for the adoption of federal priorities. This may not be highly consultative, but it is distinguishable from policymaking separation. The choices made by state elected officials are structured and hemmed in by national standards and fiscal requirements in shared programs (Stoker 1991). By the same token, Congress needs to take state and local interests into account in order to assure that federal programs are effectively implemented. And it is subject to considerable state and local lobbying in the process. Thus, while certain forms of intergovernmental influence and consultation have diminished, as is certainly the case with the direct election of senators, other forms of mutual interaction and influence have grown (Beer 1976; Thompson 2013).

The Erosion of Informal Coupling

Absent formal mechanisms that couple federalism and democracy in the United States, informal means and institutions of coupling within the political and intergovernmental systems become more important.

This is particularly true of political parties, which play a central role in both modern democratic theory and the functioning of federal institutions. Political parties in the United States were traditionally highly decentralized organizations. The centre of power and influence lay at the state and local levels, and this power was often vested in the hands of mayors and governors. State and local party organizations were historically responsible for nominating and electing candidates for Congress, and they retained considerable influence over those candidates once they were in office (Riker 1964). The national parties, in contrast, were weak and loosely organized confederations of state parties whose primary purpose was to convene quadrennially to nominate a presidential candidate.

This historically decentralized structure of American political parties was, as Morton Grodzins (1966, 254) put it, "responsible for both the existence and form of the considerable measure of decentralization that exists in the United States." The parties, he wrote, "disperse power in favor of state and local governments" and served to make them "more influential in federal affairs than the federal government is in theirs" (Grodzins 1968, 9).

Since those passages were written, both the political and the intergovernmental systems have undergone dramatic changes. State and local party systems were already waning by the 1960s, due to the erosion of patronage politics, weakening party loyalties among the public, and changes in party rules and campaign financing (Hershey 2011). In contrast, the formerly weak national party organizations had grown much stronger, raising large sums of money, expanding staff and capacity, and recruiting, training, and providing a range of campaign services to candidates for national and state office. Nor are parties the only informal institutions of intergovernmental influence that have evolved over the past five decades. The so-called intergovernmental lobby – the National Governors Association (NGA), the United States Conference of Mayors, the National League of Cities, and others – was evolving as well. As mayors and governors lost power and control in the political party system, they sought to compensate by expanding their lobbying and policy advocacy activities in Washington.

The intergovernmental lobby is often considered one of the strongest interest groups in Washington (Haider 1974). James Martin, who lobbied for the NGA from the 1960s to the 1990s, argued: "When the governors get determined about something, there is no limit to their authority in Washington. … I think when two-thirds of the governors say that something ought to be done, that that becomes the law eventually" (Nugent 2009). Perhaps the best evidence of this came in 1972, when the nations' mayors and governors joined with the Nixon administration in muscling General Revenue Sharing through a reluctant Congress, overcoming fierce opposition by many of the most senior legislators in both chambers (Beer 1976). The governors also blocked Ronald Reagan's efforts to devolve federal welfare programs to the states, and they succeeded in achieving passage of state-friendly welfare-reform legislation in the 1990s.

This is not to overlook the challenges faced by the intergovernmental lobby. Its influence was easier to exert when the federal grant system was expanding and the remnants of state and local party influence were more apparent (Camissa 1995, 34). As federal budget stringency has become the norm and political parties have become more polarized, the unity among state and local officials that Martin spoke of is more difficult to maintain. Troy Smith has observed that incentives for individual states to go their own way and cut their own deals are ever present (T.E. Smith 2008). Still, studies of American interest groups in Washington have found the intergovernmental lobby to be among the most effective (Burch and Jones 2012). Along with political parties, the intergovernmental lobby illustrates the vital role played by non-governmental entities at the confluence of federalism and democracy.

The Extent and Limitations of Competitive Federalism in the United States

From a comparative perspective, the United States is often said to practise a form of competitive federalism. Compared with most other federal systems, it provides state and local governments with significant fiscal and policy autonomy, and it makes only modest efforts towards fiscal equalization. Moreover, some conservative economists have promoted competitive federalism as an ideal type that deserves emulation, arguing that it restrains the growth of the public sector and tames the governmental "leviathan" (Buchanan 1995).

But these characteristics can be exaggerated, and the system is less competitive than commonly perceived, on both the theoretical and the behavioural levels. A more accurate nomenclature may be "fend for yourself" federalism, coined by John Shannon of the Advisory Commission on Intergovernmental Relations, though even this involves a degree of analytical spin (Kim und Blöchliger 2015; Shannon 1987).

The theory originated with Charles Tiebout's 1956 article, "A Pure Theory of Local Expenditures." As the title suggests, this analysis focused on local governments, not states. It developed a concept of taxpayer mobility that fit the highly fragmented model of local government organization in many – but not all – US states. And it arguably applies in those metropolitan regions that spill over state boundaries, setting up a degree of state competition over tax rates, services, and local capital investment. New York, St. Louis, and Washington, DC, are prominent examples of multi-state metropolitan areas. But there are many exceptions to this pattern, such as Los Angeles, Seattle, Miami, and Denver. Fourteen of the twenty largest metropolitan areas in the United States are contained within the borders of a single state.

This is important because taxpayer mobility is far greater at the local and metropolitan levels than at the state level. It is much more common and feasible for people to move locally to a jurisdiction with lower taxes or better services than to relocate to a state in a different part of the country. Consequently, the empirical evidence of competitive federalism operating at the state level is fairly weak and inconsistent. The measurable effects of tax competition tend to be small in most studies (Gale, Krupkin, and Rueben 2015). Nor is there strong empirical evidence for the "race to the bottom" thesis when it comes to welfare services or state environmental policy (Potoski 2001; Schram and Soss 1998). For people, the barriers to migration are often high. For capital, factors other than state and local tax rates rank more highly in decisions about location.

However, there is no question that providing states with a high degree of fiscal and policy autonomy can have downsides. Given the economic and fiscal disparities across the states, a federal system that relies on states to raise a significant portion of their own revenues inevitably generates inequities. The absence of a major equalizing grant system in the United States exacerbates this problem. Some of the largest welfare-related grant programs do compensate for fiscal capacity, particularly Medicaid (health insurance for the poor and disabled) and nutrition grants, which together amount to over 65 per cent of all federal grant monies. Depending on the state, the federal government provides between 50 per cent and 78 per cent of total Medicaid dollars, with the rest coming from matching state contributions. Similarly, many states provide equalizing grants for education to local school districts. But, overall, the federal aid system is not equalizing. And the freedom that states enjoy to experiment and succeed with new policies implies the freedom to fail as well. States enjoy considerable freedom to enact bad policies as well as good ones. But if those policies enjoy broad public support, it is difficult to conclude that that is an undemocratic outcome, nor does it constitute competitive federalism.

Trends in Federalism and American Politics

Finally, when analysing the relationship between federalism and democracy in the United States today, it is helpful to take note of three important political trends that have significant implications for that relationship: the nationalization of parties and political campaigns, the polarization of the political system, and the eroding legitimacy of the federal government. Each trend has affected intergovernmental relations and policy in a variety of ways, from reshaping electoral politics to altering public opinion. Each deserves brief attention.

Nationalization of Parties and Politics

As noted earlier, the traditional party system in the United States was highly decentralized, and this both reflected and reinforced the decentralization of the federal system. State and local party organizations that lay at the heart of this decentralized system had greatly weakened by the late 1960s and 1970s, while the formerly weak national party organizations grew much stronger. They began raising large sums of money, expanded their staff, and became active in recruiting, training, and financing candidates for national and state office (Herrnson 2010).

This resulted in a power reversal between the national and state party committees. The national party committees were forced to launch major efforts to strengthen weak or moribund state and local party organizations, fundamentally changing the previous power dynamic. As Herrnson (2010, 253) describes it,

> National committee party-building programs have helped to strengthen, modernize, and professionalize many state and local party organizations. They also have altered the balance of power within the parties' organizational apparatuses. The national parties' ability to distribute or withhold money, party-building assistance, and other help gives them influence over the operations of state and local party committees. They, along with the national committee rule-making and enforcement functions, have [led to] … a flow of power downward from the national parties to state and local parties.

Partly as a result, elections for state and local offices are now often fought over national issues like marriage equality and health care (Fehrman 2016). Citizens increasingly vote straight party tickets for offices at all levels of government (Hopkins 2014), while efforts to insulate state and local politics from national forces now have limited effects. Outside money flows into crucial state and congressional elections, while candidates, activists, and voters are energized by national concerns.

All this has implications for intergovernmental policymaking. Locally bound members of Congress once routinely resisted presidents and party leaders in deference to parochial political leaders and interests. Locally driven electoral incentives biased the federal aid system towards narrow categorical grants (Mayhew 1974). National programs with significant implications for race relations at the state and local levels – such as welfare and unemployment insurance – were often left to state administration (Grodzins 1967; Robertson 2012). Today, in contrast, the vast majority of members now vote along partisan lines on the most important roll-call votes in Congress, regardless of local economic effects (Izadi 2014). Contemporary members of Congress believe that their elections are closely tied to those of their party at large, making "most politics … national" (Abramovitz and Webster 2016).

These developments have been registered in public policy. The propensity of Congress to enact federal mandates and pre-emptions that restrict the flexibility of state and local governments rose in the 1960s and 1970s in concert with the declining power of state and local party organizations (Posner 1998). As politics, issues, and communications have become more nationalized, intrusive federal policies have been adopted in even the most traditional of state and local responsibilities, including education, law enforcement, and fire protection. Policy proposals by the Trump administration – to mandate law-enforcement cooperation and threaten financial sanctions on so-called sanctuary cities, to make pre-emptive changes in the federal tax code, and to shift more infrastructure finance to the state and local levels – indicate that this trend is likely to continue.

Thus, the systemic bias in the structure of American politics has changed. It has shifted towards nationalization, not decentralization, and that has long-run implications for federalism, democracy, and informal coupling in the policymaking system. The insulation of state and local policy processes has been diminished, and a new, more vertical structure of politics and policymaking has become ascendant, often organized on a regionalized foundation of highly polarized red (Republican) and blue (Democratic) states. The following section explores this development in more detail.

Political Polarization and Coupling in American Federalism

Polarization has been called "the dominant theme of American politics over the past twenty years" (Baumer and Gold 2010, 1). It is increasingly pervasive among citizens, politicians, and the communications media. While much attention has been paid to its impact on elections and the behaviour of Congress, partisan polarization also affects the design and implementation of federal domestic programs as well as policymaking by the states themselves.

Geographically, the United States has increasingly become sorted into red states and blue states (Gelman 2008). The two major parties have become more ideologically coherent, distinct, and extreme, and citizens have followed suit. Polling by the Pew Research Center indicates that "Republicans and Democrats are more divided along ideological lines – and partisan antipathy is deeper and more extensive – than at any point in the last two decades" (Pew Research Center 2014). Partisan polarization is even more extreme in Congress (Mann and Ornstein 2016). Based on congressional roll-call votes, the 114th Congress (2015–16) was "the most polarized Congress since the early 20th Century and one where almost all issues have been drawn into the [left-right] dimension" (voteviewblog 2016).

High levels of partisan polarization in Congress have important intergovernmental policy implications. Under conditions of divided party government, they often lead to gridlock and stalemate (Binder 2003). Under conditions of unified party government, however, they can lead to major policy accomplishments, as seen during the first terms of the George W. Bush and Barack Obama presidencies. Intergovernmental policy initiatives such as No Child Left Behind, the USA Patriot Act, the American Recovery and Reinvestment Act, or ARRA (Obama's large stimulus program), the Affordable Care Act (ACA), and the Race to the Top education initiative are all prime examples. Such policy accomplishments under unified party government have long been viewed favourably from the perspective of democratic responsiveness, but the potential for strict party loyalty to undermine the independence of Congress and erode its ability to act as a check on the executive – a tendency that has become increasingly prominent during the Trump administration – underscores the potential for partisan polarization to contribute to executive dominance in American federalism (Thompson, Wong, and Rabe 2020).

Polarized party government is not confined to Washington. States across the nation have unified party governments at a much higher rate than in the past, and such states have passed an array of new policies – limiting abortion, welfare benefits, and public unions in conservative states and promoting green energy, minimum-wage hikes, and criminal justice reforms in many liberal states.

The intergovernmental lobby has been one casualty of this state-level partisan polarization. Whereas it was among the strongest interest groups in Washington as recently as the 1990s, it has come under pressure in the polarized era. Local government groups – whose members lean heavily Democratic – have little influence in a Republican Congress, while the effectiveness of the NGA is being limited by deep partisan divisions. Democratic and Republican governors so often go their separate ways that the NGA has difficulty taking positions on many critical issues of intergovernmental policy, including health care policy. As *Washington Post* reporter Dan Balz (2014) observes, the NGA has become "just another battlefield in the partisan wars that define American politics. … The states have turned, as Washington has turned, into camps of red and blue, pursuing different paths and speaking to, and for, two different Americas." Polarized federalism is intruding into intergovernmental administration as well. It challenges the established model of technocratic, picket-fence federalism with a new model of vertical partisan polarization. In Samuel Beer's (1978) terminology, the "topocrats" are deferring less to the technocrats and seeking to take power back – often on the basis of partisan ideology.

Traditionally, picket-fence federalism was the administrative manifestation of cooperative federalism. Professionals tend to share priorities and normative frameworks that often result in them having more in common with colleagues at other levels of government than with co-workers in their own jurisdiction. By the 1960s, this picket-fence structure was the most distinctive administrative feature of American intergovernmental relations (Walker 1995, 26). However, this technocratic system has increasingly come under pressure in an era of partisan polarization. This was evident throughout the Obama administration. Beginning with the ARRA in 2009, many Republican governors and state legislatures began to refuse federal assistance at rates far higher than in the past, often for explicitly political reasons (Nicholson-Crotty 2012). For example, several governors turned down additional federal funds for extending unemployment insurance benefits and high-speed rail.

A similar pattern emerged in the implementation of the ACA. Republican state attorneys general first sought to have the entire law declared unconstitutional. When this largely failed, Republican states resisted powerful fiscal incentives to implement the law. As of November 2018, fourteen Republican states still had not expanded Medicaid coverage under the ACA, depriving millions of citizens of health insurance coverage paid almost entirely by the national government. An additional group of mostly Republican states agreed to expand their Medicaid programs only under special Medicaid waivers, allowing them greater flexibility (KFF 2017). As for state participation in operating private health insurance exchanges under the law, twenty-eight states refused to set up and operate a health care marketplace, as envisioned by the legislation (ibid.).

This pattern of vertical polarization continues under President Trump, although the partisan roles between Washington and the states are reversed. Across a wide range of domestic issues, Democratic leaders at the state and local levels have mobilized to fight, block, or reverse initiatives from the Trump administration. This includes lawsuits initiated by states to block a number of its immigration policies (Tucker 2017; Yee 2017) and actions by a broad coalition of mostly Democratic state and local governments to continue following the carbon-reduction policies agreed to under the Paris climate accords (Baragona 2017).

Such processes of vertical polarization within the American intergovernmental system are thus restructuring forms of coupling in American federalism. Long-established mechanisms of intergovernmental cooperation in implementing and administering policy are eroding, and traditional avenues of intergovernmental consultation are losing influence. In their place, partisan channels of policy design, diffusion, and intergovernmental consultation are becoming institutionalized among and within all three levels of government (Rose and Goelzhauser 2018).

Delegitimation

A third trend with implications for democracy and American federalism is the delegitimation of the federal government. Over the past sixty years, public opinion surveys have registered significant declines in public trust in the national government. Only about 20 per cent of the population expressed high levels of trust in the federal government in 2015, compared with two-thirds in the early 1960s. There has also been a substantial increase in the percentage of the population that believes the federal government has "too much power" (Free and Cantril 1967; Kincaid and Cole 2011). In comparison, only 22 per cent of the public thought that states had too much power in 2009, and only 6 per cent of respondents thought local governments did.

There are a number of reasons why confidence in the federal government has diminished since the early 1960s, including the corrosive effects of the Vietnam War, scandals such as Watergate, and deepening partisan polarization. But one significant implication for federalism has been increased reliance by the federal government on "government by proxy" (Kettl 1988). Rather than rely on classic techniques of providing services directly by government employees, the federal government has increasingly turned to intermediaries and the tools of indirect governance, such as grants to states, private contracts, and tax expenditures (Light 1999). Delegitimation has been a significant factor driving this trend towards third-party governance. Policymakers seek to respond to public demands for services but are sensitive to public distrust of the federal government, and they have found that techniques of indirect government provide a tempting solution to the paradox (Derthick 2001).

Suzanne Mettler (2011) notes, however, that this can create a reinforcing cycle of distrust. Suspicion of the federal government, combined with greater trust in state and local governments, encourages Congress to rely on the tools of indirect government. But the resultant "submerged state" reinforces public suspicions of government and contributes to a downward cycle of cynicism and dissatisfaction. This is because indirect governance often obfuscates the positive contributions made by the national government, while being less efficient and less transparent to democratic accountability.

The implementation of Obama's massive stimulus program provides a recent case in point. On a systemic level, the ARRA of 2009 was largely deemed to be effective. It reduced unemployment and raised economic growth well above the levels projected without it (United States. Congressional Budget Office 2011). It won widespread approval from professional economists for its macroeconomic effects (Wolfers 2014). It kept states and localities from laying off hundreds of thousands of teachers and other government workers and maintained vital safety-net programs in a period of deep state budget cuts. And it produced a tiny fraction of the waste or fraud expected for a program of its size (Conlan, Posner, and Regan 2016, 3–4). Yet the ARRA generated tremendous public confusion and very little recognition of its positive impacts and contributions. Virtually no political credit redounded to the Obama administration or to Congress, despite spending $834 billion and successfully heading off a new economic depression.

Conclusion

The relationship between federalism and democracy in the United States is a complex and multifaceted one. It has been an issue of historic significance, but also one with contemporary relevance. Because the available data on this relationship is contradictory and incomplete, it is helpful to use the comparative framework developed in this book as an analytical tool for assessment. The mechanisms for coupling federalism and democracy are loose and informal, and they have grown more so over time. Partly as a result, the US system scores highly on subnational representation and institutional adaptability, but low on equality and intergovernmental transparency. All are intimately related to the federal design. All are likely to continue into the future.

6 Federalism and Direct Democracy in Switzerland: Competing or Complementary?

SEAN MUELLER

There are many reasons for the renewed interest in the relationship between federalism and democracy (see Benz 2016; Benz and Sonnicksen 2017; Burgess and Gagnon 2010; Detterbeck 2016; Fossum and Jachtenfuchs 2017). One is the increased variety of territorial arrangements at the nation state level, ranging from unitary decentralized through asymmetric and symmetric regionalization to outright federalization (see Hooghe et al. 2016). Are they all equally compatible with liberal democracy? Another reason is the increased centralization and pooling of sovereignty at the supranational level – which, in Europe, for example, is leading to an "ever closer Union" not just economically but also politically.[1] What insights can we glean from the interaction of federalism with democracy at the nation state level?

At the same time, democracy, or rather the expectations that citizens have of it, is undergoing transformation. Demands for more direct participation and/or deliberative venues to improve policymaking have slowly made their way beyond a small circle of supporters (see, e.g., Gerber and Mueller 2018). A case in point is the May 2018 constitutional referendum in Ireland, which followed the deliberations of a randomly selected citizen assembly. The European Union (EU), too, has launched a broad "consultation on the future of Europe," prepared by ninety-six citizens from twenty-seven member states.[2] Never before have global levels of participatory and deliberative democracy been as high as in the last decade (Coppedge et al. 2018). Yet the various territorial reference points remain intact. Thus, as both the extent and the variation of democracy increase, the need to understand its interaction with federal institutions is ever more pressing.

This renewed interest in the relationship between federalism and democracy essentially stems from two fundamental political transformations. One is rescaling – that is, the (de)centralization within nation states, the pooling of sovereignty at the supranational level, the rise of regional authority, and the increasing interdependence and interaction among levels of government (see, e.g., Hooghe et al. 2016). The other is the populist demand for new forms of, and opportunities for, citizen participation in protest against presumed elitist and executive-dominated policymaking (Gerber and Mueller 2018; see also Fossum and Laycock, chap. 4). Both transformations are visible in the Swiss polity, which, in the comparative literature, is often praised for both its strong federalism and its high quality of democracy (Benz and Sonnicksen 2017; Burgess and Gagnon 2010).

In the interaction of federalism with democracy, profound theoretical issues are at stake. Accepting, for the moment, that the two can be placed on an equal level (see, however, Hueglin, chap. 2) – namely, as two related but different logics of organizing collectively binding decisions – federalism and democracy can either complement each other or clash. Both provide for some kind of political participation and define specific decision-making thresholds, even if one works through territory and the other through citizenship. Both strive to maximize legitimacy and efficiency, yet one divides power vertically and the other horizontally. At least, such is the undisputed understanding of both concepts in Switzerland, the country studied in depth in this contribution: both federalism and democracy, especially direct democracy, operate as safeguards against the domination of a single cultural group, a political party, or even one or all representative institutions.

But the question of the relationship between federalism and (direct) democracy is of relevance well beyond the Swiss case, given the observations made before: what happens if governance spreads over ever more territorial levels *and* citizens are more and more directly involved *at the same time*? Since, in Switzerland, both democracy and federalism have emerged and developed more or less in parallel,[3] with one neither fully dominating nor operating in total isolation from the other, insights from this case might provide at least some answers. Indeed, perhaps the greatest Swiss paradox – and presumably the key to the system's stability – lies in mutual reinforcement: federalism provides for a division of labour *and* cooperation among democratic communities, while direct democracy serves to regularly question, adjust, and ultimately affirm this "federal spirit" (Burgess 2012).

The remainder of this chapter proceeds as follows. The next section defines both federalism and democracy and discusses how they relate to the analytical framework that structures this book. The third section introduces the basic features of the Swiss political system, paying particular attention to its democratic and federal institutions. Their basic logics of operation are analysed in the fourth section in the form of four arguments: direct democracy enabling federalism, direct democracy obstructing federalism, federalism obstructing direct democracy, and federalism enabling direct democracy. The concluding section summarizes and provides an overall assessment of the Swiss system in general and its complex links between federalism and democracy in particular.

Definitions

Federalism and democracy resemble first cousins: while they share an important stock of basic features, others differ markedly. Table 6.1 lists one commonality and three important differences.

Both federalism and democracy belong to the family of institutions that *divide political power*. Theorists of both principles regard the division of power as a means to achieve accountability, prevent tyranny, protect liberty, and ensure the legitimacy of the overall political system. *Federalist* No. 51 nicely articulates this parallelism:

> The power surrendered by the people is first divided between two distinct governments, and then the portion allotted to each subdivided among distinct and separate departments. Hence a double security arises to the rights of the people. The different governments will control each other, at the same time that each will be controlled by itself. (Hamilton, Madison, and Jay [1787] 2003)

However, while federalism does so *vertically*, dividing power among political entities situated at different territorial echelons, democracy achieves the same result *horizontally*, dividing power among governmental branches located at the same territorial level. Presidential democracies are the clearest example of a strict division of powers between the legislative and executive branches, with the members of each popularly elected and their survival mutually independent (Shugart and Carey 1992). The corresponding manifestation of this in the federal universe is dualism, whereby governments at different levels are responsible for entire policy areas, including legislation, administration, and financing (Dardanelli et al. 2019; Hueglin and Fenna 2015).

By contrast, while parliamentary democracy builds on the fusion of powers between government and parliamentary majority, overall power remains divided *within* parliament between the majority and minority parties. Analogous to this, administrative federations separate functions rather than policies – for example, the federal government may legislate on environmental protection, but the rules are

Table 6.1. Democracy and federalism

Feature	Democracy	Federalism
1. Commonality	Division of power	
2. Dimension of dividing power	Horizontal (intragovernmental)	Vertical (intergovernmental)
3. Basis of rule	People	Territory
4. Constituent political communities	One	Many

implemented by the bureaucracies of the constituent units. Thus, for all their differences, both presidential and parliamentary systems provide for a division of power: between president and parliament or between majority and minority. Federalism, too, is unthinkable without at least some functions and/or policy areas being allocated to a higher, and others to a lower, level. Yet while democracy divides power at the same level, federalism empowers different levels.

A second major distinction concerns the basis of rule. Democracy is founded on rule by *the people*, either directly (e.g., in citizen assemblies) or indirectly (through elections), or by combining the two ("semi-direct democracy"; Linder and Mueller 2017, 295). In this way, it makes perfect sense for democracies to allow even citizens living abroad to vote because personal linkage (citizenship) trumps territory (residence). The credo "one person, one vote" is agnostic about location. For federalism, however, it is *territory* that gives meaning to and legitimizes the exercise of rule. Not individual citizens but entire political communities receive the right to participate in decision-making – provided they are territorially bounded and their area is recognized as a federal unit. Territorial participation typically happens through second chambers (see Hooghe et al. 2016). Here seats are typically allocated regardless of the population of the federal units (Stepan 1999) for the only thing that matters is to be a federal unit. When regions are of varying demographic size – which is almost always the case – this corporatist principle of "one region, one vote" puts federalism on a direct collision course with individualist democracy (cf. Kymlicka 1995). While democracy treats all citizens alike, no matter their region, federalism treats all regions alike, no matter how many citizens.

Last, democracy conceives of its citizens as members of a single, constituent political community – the demos. This demos delegates its power to smaller, highly specialized groups of people: law-making is delegated to parliament, execution to Cabinet, implementation to civil servants, and adjudication to the courts. Even the most direct form of democracy, a citizen assembly with supreme and final decision-making capacity, remains dependent on an elected or appointed body to prepare its agenda, steer deliberative debates, and adjudicate close votes and, later, on a bureaucracy and the courts to implement decisions and rule on appeals (see Schaub 2016). Also, since the people are conceptualized as a single political community, there can be only one majority, of either voting citizens or all those eligible to vote.

In federal thinking, by contrast, there are always *several* constituent political communities. Citizens are, at the very least, members of both the federal and at least one regional demos (see Benz, chap. 3). Whereas democracy describes a path towards finding the will of "the" majority, federalism aspires to protect the freedom from interference of these separate communities. It is for this reason, among others, that territorial autonomy comes into play: only with at least some power over legislation, implementation, and/or finances do the separate communities acquire or retain real meaning (Braun 2000; Dardanelli et al. 2019). Largely, then, democracy is built on delegating political power within a single community, whereas federalism operates by protecting the different communities both from each other and from the larger, overall demos. This aspect of federalism, also called self-rule, is as essential to a federal political system as its twin sister, shared rule, which denotes the participation of lower levels of government in decision-making at a higher level (see Watts 1998, 7; cf. Elazar 1987; Hooghe et al. 2016; Mueller 2014).

Where do these admittedly schematic definitions of our two key concepts leave us in terms of coupling? Imported into the research on federalism by Benz and Sonnicksen (2017) and Benz (chap. 3) are three possible connections between federalism and democracy: decoupling, tight coupling, and loose coupling. As we will see, the Swiss case is an almost ideal case of loose coupling between federalism and democracy. At heart, the Swiss are quite anarchic, which translates into extreme forms of both democratic and federal separation of powers – within governments, between the legislative and executive branches, and between levels of government.

At the same time, though, parties in parliament and their representatives in the executives as well as federal, cantonal, and local governments are motivated to negotiate agreements because they act in the shadow of *popular* rule. Both parties and executives accept that the ultimate arbiter of disputes should be the people directly, in binding referendums. Even the cantons themselves are empowered to launch a facultative referendum and, thus, challenge any act of the federal parliament. Moreover, federal constitutional amendments need a double majority of voters and cantons and therefore require that governmental and societal actors find agreement to assure the assent of both the (Swiss) people and the (cantonal) peoples. All this assures non-domination by any single political actor (see also Fossum and Laycock, chap. 4).

In turn, when it comes to the differences between democracy and federalism, tolerance and (in)difference abound, meaning that frictions arise only occasionally, and, when they do, they are dealt with pragmatically and as consensually as possible. The main reason for this is the still very much non-centralized character of Swiss federalism (cf. Elazar 1987, 64). Even the competences that the central state has acquired over the past 170 years are generally implemented subnationally (Dardanelli and Mueller 2019). A good example of Swiss politics is the fact that the right to levy both the federal direct tax as well as the value-added tax is only temporary, needing the renewed approval of citizens and cantons every fifteen years (Art. 128 and Transitional Provision 13 of the Federal Constitution, or FC). The Swiss state is much more a fiduciary entity than a Leviathan. Popular rule counteracts both executive dominance, which, in other federations, tends to undermine democracy, and party politics, which can hamper how interdependence is managed in a federal system because of its focus on electoral mobilization and problems rather than solutions. But direct democracy also comes with its own challenges to federalism, as the subsequent discussion will reveal.

Federalism and Democracy in Switzerland: Overview

Switzerland is an interesting case for studying the interplay of federalism and democracy because it usually receives high scores on rankings pertaining to both dimensions. Thus, indexes of democratic quality consistently rank Switzerland in the top-five (see, e.g., Democracy Barometer 2016; Freedom House 2017; Hasenöhr, Pölzlbauer, and Campbell 2016; Polity IV 2014) or at least top-ten countries (see SGI 2018). At the same time, indexes of federalism and regional authority equally rank the Swiss system among the most decentralized, federal, or both (see Lijphart 2012, 178; Dardanelli et al. 2019; Hooghe et al. 2016). However, in each dimension, one institutional peculiarity stands out that is not usually captured by such indexes: direct democracy on the one hand and subregional – that is, local – autonomy on the other (see, however, Coppedge et al. 2018; Ladner, Keuffer, and Baldersheim 2016). In the following sections, these two peculiarities will be contextualized along with the operation of "standard" democratic and federal institutions for both, in their own way, considerably affect the interplay between democracy and federalism.

Democracy

Swiss democracy is probably as close as it comes to ideal-type power-sharing (Lijphart 2012; Bernauer and Vatter 2019). At the national level, power is divided among three main institutions: government, parliament, and the Federal Supreme Court (functional division of powers); within parliament between two equally powerful chambers (bicameralism); within government among seven coequal ministers (collegialism); and, finally, between the representative institutions and the people through frequently held referendums (direct democracy). The presence of extensive forms and use of direct democracy alongside "normal" representative institutions make Switzerland a particularly consensus-oriented political system (Vatter 2018a, 563).

All the representative institutions are renewed regularly: both parliamentary chambers (National Council and Council of States) are elected in direct elections every four years; the Swiss government (Federal Council) is elected every four years by the two chambers in joint session (United Federal Assembly); and the Federal Supreme Court is elected by parliament every six years. Once the government is elected, it cannot be dismissed by parliament – nor can it, for its part, dissolve the latter and call early elections. Nevertheless, re-election of acting ministers is customary: since the founding of modern Switzerland in 1848, on only four occasions has a member of government seeking a consecutive term not been re-elected (Giudici and Stojanović 2016).

Elections to the National Council (two hundred seats) take place using proportionality. Voters have as many votes as there are seats in their constituency. They can vote for a fixed party list, mix candidates from different parties, delete or double up individual candidates, or even create their own list (Mueller and Gerber 2016). However, because each of the twenty-six cantons is an undivided constituency, and because seats are distributed to cantons in proportion to the number of their inhabitants, elections in the smaller cantons are highly disproportionate. In fact, six cantons have only one national councillor and de facto apply the plurality system. Moreover, if we consider – as did the Federal Supreme Court when it ruled on cantonal electoral systems (Mueller and Bernauer 2016) – that an effective threshold of 10 per cent or higher violates the principles of proportionality, elections to the National Council are "undemocratic" in the nineteen cantons with eight or fewer seats (Linder and Mueller 2017, 117). In other words, only 64 per cent of the seats in the National Council are filled using "actual" proportionality. Matching the electoral districts onto cantons was a democratic concession to federalism when proportionality was introduced in 1918–19.

Elections to the Council of States (forty-six seats) take place according to cantonal rules. Although the cantons are free to adopt any kind of direct or indirect electoral system, all have introduced popular elections over time (Vatter 2018a). Again, cantons are undivided constituencies, but, in this case, seats are distributed to them regardless of size: each canton is represented by two councillors of state (or senators, to simplify). The six former "half-cantons" are entitled to only one senator each. In autumn 2019, twenty-three cantons used a two-round majority-plurality system, two cantons (Jura and Neuchâtel) used proportionality, while the voters of the (half-)canton of Appenzell Inner-Rhodes had already elected their only representative at the annual citizen assembly in April that year (cf. Mueller and Gerber 2016).

Turning to direct democracy, at the national level three main institutions exist. First, every change to the Federal Constitution needs to be approved in a binding, nationwide referendum (*obligatory referendum*). A simple majority of voting citizens and a majority of cantons need to consent to the amendment. The vote of each canton is determined by its popular majority, no matter how slim the margin. In other words, each voter's preference is counted twice: first as part of the national demos and then as part of one of twenty-six cantonal *demoï*. Citizens living abroad can vote and are allocated to their last canton of residence. In determining the majority of a canton, all cantons weigh equally, but the "decisions" of the half-cantons are weighted by half, so that the majority is calculated from a total of 20 + (6 × 0.5) = 23 – that is, 12. A tie of 11.5.–11.5, which is possible if at least two half-cantons end up on opposing sides, leads to an amendment being rejected – no matter how great the overall popular majority approving it or how slim the margins in individual cantons. (Cases of diverging popular and cantonal majorities are shown in table 6.2 later in this chapter.)

The second instrument of importance is the *facultative referendum*, which is a sort of suspensive veto against a piece of legislation. It is suspensive because it carries over an act approved by parliament into a nationwide popular vote, when a simple majority of the voting electorate has the final say. No cantonal majority is necessary to approve or reject an act since the underlying constitutional article must already have received its federal blessing through the obligatory referendum. A facultative referendum can be demanded by at least fifty thousand citizens within one hundred days of the publication of the act – or by eight cantons within the same time frame. Of all 181 facultative referendums voted on between 1874 and 2016 (Linder and Mueller 2017, 305), only one was called by the cantons. However, on that one occasion, they were successful; as a result, from their perspective they have achieved a 100 per cent success rate (Schnabel and Mueller 2017).

The third and final direct-democratic instrument of political importance is the *popular initiative*. A minimum of one hundred thousand citizens can propose a constitutional amendment, provided that their signatures are collected within eighteen months of its official announcement. Unlike at the EU level, citizens do not need to come from a minimum number of cantons in specific numbers, nor do they have to represent the different languages or other communities – although such is the practice. Once the signatures have been collected and validated, the proposal is debated by both the government and parliament. However, neither can block the initiative from being put to a nationwide, binding referendum.[4] Since it pertains to the Federal Constitution, such an initiative, like the obligatory referendum, requires approval by majorities of both people and cantons.

The obligatory referendum has existed since 1848. Until 2016, of 195 government proposals to change the Federal Constitution, only 49 (25 per cent) were rejected (Linder and Mueller 2017, 303). The facultative referendum has existed since 1874, and, until summer 2016, despite a total of 2,862 pieces of legislation, a referendum was successfully called on only 181 occasions (6 per cent). However, once challenged, laws were eventually rejected in 43 per cent of the cases (3 per cent of all acts; ibid., 305). The popular initiative, in existence since 1891, led to 211 referendums up until June 2018. Only 22 (10 per cent) mustered the required double majority (Switzerland. Bundeskanzlei 2018c). Cantons and municipalities have their own instruments of direct democracy (see below).

Federalism

The Swiss federation consists of three levels of government with, on aggregate, roughly equal powers. Each level has its own source of income (mainly indirect taxation and excise duties nationally, mainly direct taxes subnationally), participates in revenue sharing with other levels, has certain policy domains for which it is chiefly or even exclusively responsible (e.g., defence and currency at the national, education at the cantonal, and housing at the local level), and possesses its own legislative, executive, administrative, and judicial organs. The overall federal model is one of administrative or cooperative federalism (see Hueglin and Fenna 2015), with the cantons implementing both their own and federal decisions (Dardanelli and Mueller 2019).

At the lowest level of government, there are approximately 2,200 communes or municipalities. Formally, they are subordinate to the twenty-six cantons; in practice, however, political dynamics are very much bottom-up, so actual autonomy varies from canton to canton (Mueller 2015). Figure 6.1 displays the three levels of government and their main political entities (it excludes the courts) and how they relate to each other.

There are three subnational deviations from the federal system of government described above: all cantons have unicameral parliaments as well as popularly elected government; and most communes, especially the smaller and German-speaking ones, have citizen assemblies in lieu of elected parliaments (Ladner 2016). The rather small and German-speaking cantons of Glarus and Appenzell Inner-Rhodes also still hold the *Landsgemeinde*, an annual citizen assembly with final decision-making power in all cantonal matters (see Schaub 2016). *Landsgemeinden* operate next to and together with the cantonal government (whose president directs the assembly proceedings) and the cantonal parliament (whose decisions become law unless overturned or modified at the assembly). In other words, the lower the level of governance and the smaller the political community, the more direct the influence citizens have over policymaking.

Figure 6.1 also shows the average sizes of the electorates at each level. With only 2,300 eligible voters, on average, the Swiss local government landscape is very small scale (Ladner, Keuffer, and Baldersheim 2016). In fact, half of all municipalities have less than one thousand voters. The cantons, too, are very small – the average of 205,600 voters hides the fact that, apart from Zurich (920,000) and Bern (730,000), no canton has more than half a million voters. While this makes for numerous and very small political communities, cantonal borders do not generally reflect the political cleavages of either the past or the present (see also Bochsler 2017).

A final noteworthy feature of the Swiss Confederation concerns inter-cantonal cooperation. Cantons cooperate formally and informally, in government conferences and through treaties, bilaterally and multilaterally, regionally and nationwide, and politically as well as on individual policies. By the last count (Arens et al. 2017; Schnabel and Mueller 2017), some fifty conferences transpired and approximately eight hundred treaties were in force. While horizontal coordination can be interpreted as a result of cantonal autonomy – cantons are free to negotiate and enter into binding agreements with whomever they desire (see also Hueglin, chap. 2) – the downside of cooperation is that it is often driven by necessity (e.g., lack of funds or insufficient administrative capacity) and not always by opportunity (e.g., to create economies of scale). Since one of the main critiques of inter-cantonal cooperation relates precisely to its interaction with democracy, it is discussed below.

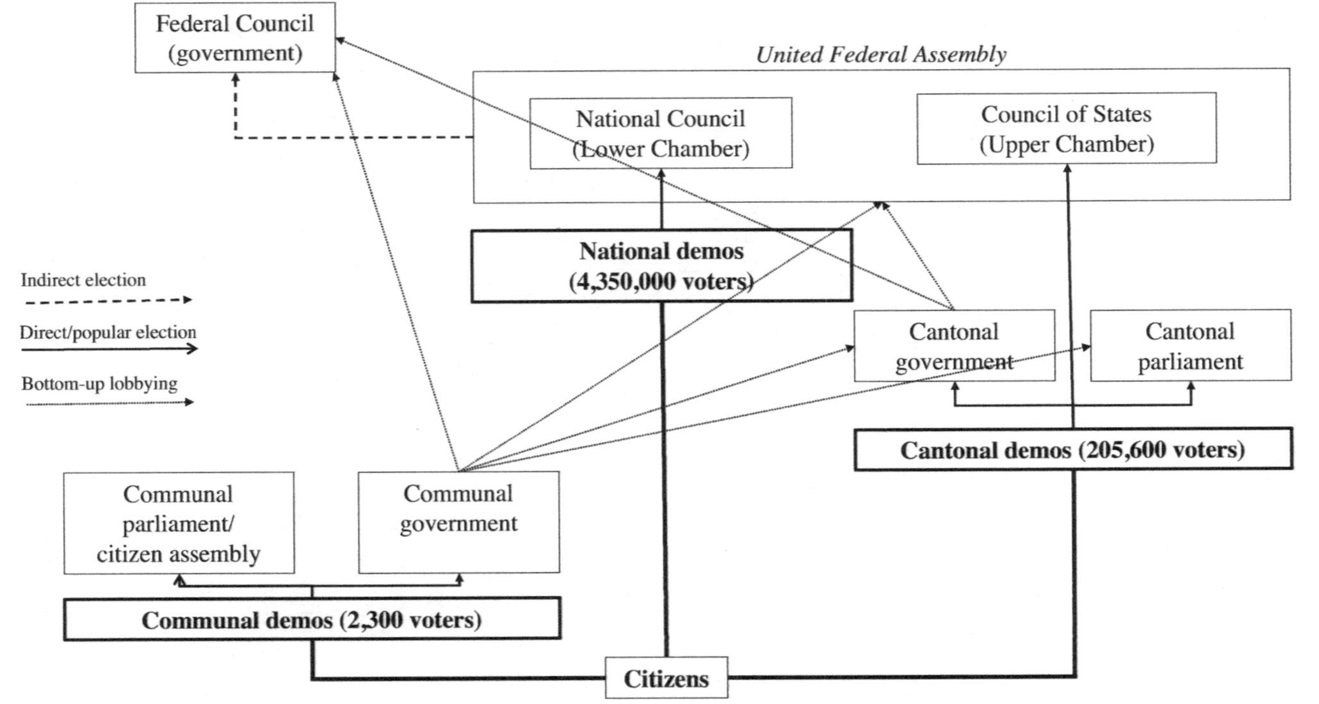

Figure 6.1. Swiss multi-level democracy

Source: Author's concept; electorate sizes are based on the referendum of 12 February 2017 (Switzerland, BFS 2017).

Interactions

This section assesses the relationship between federalism and (direct) democracy through four analytical prisms, which concern the enabling and obstructing effects of one on the other and vice versa. While the overall pattern is one of mutual reinforcement due to only loose coupling, tensions emerge, notably whenever the two principles pull in opposite directions and cannot advance without the other (tight coupling).

Democracy Enabling Federalism

What evidence is there to support the assumption that democracy enables federalism? At the most abstract level, some basic tenets of liberal democracy – rule of law, proportionality, necessity, and legality – also help consolidate the Swiss federal order. What is more, the democratic principle of *popular sovereignty* – that the people should decide – extends to the protection of the very existence of cantons as political entities. All twenty-six cantons are named in the Federal Constitution (Art. 1). Hence, both abolishing one and merging even just two of them would require changing the Federal Constitution, which, as seen above, requires a double majority (see also "Federalism Obstructing Democracy" below). Strictly speaking, this democratic protection of the existing federal order might be seen as violating the federal principle since it is the cantonal peoples (in their multitude), and not the cantonal authorities, who must approve federal constitutional change. However, federalism is primarily about the protection of territorial *communities*, not their political authorities. If this can be achieved by letting the members of those communities decide directly, without having to rely on bodies elected by them, then that goal is even better realized than under conditions of representative democracy.

Of course, it is still possible that the Swiss demos and majorities in the electorates of twenty-four cantons could decide to merge two cantons against their will. However, two other democratic principles come to the rescue: *proportionality* and *necessity*. The latter means that the state should interfere only when absolutely necessary, the former that the extent of its actions should be proportionate to its goals. Thus, both principles express scepticism towards public interference at *any* level – the burden of proof lies with the public, not the private, sphere. Translated into a territorial logic, this situation strongly resembles the federal principle of subsidiarity (see also Hueglin, chap. 2). In Switzerland, subsidiarity means that a canton assumes a task only once its local governments cannot deliver it anymore and that the Confederation assumes a task only once the cantons cannot do it anymore (Dardanelli and Mueller 2019; Mueller 2015). Subsidiarity is equivalent to a bottom-up logic of power delegation, and proportionality and necessity are its democratic bulwarks. Since 2004, subsidiarity even has its own article (5a) in the Federal Constitution.

Finally, the existence of the *rule of law* – the element that makes a democracy a liberal democracy (Albertazzi and Mueller 2013) – guarantees that there is an umpire in the form of the Federal Supreme Court. While the court does not have the power to review federal legislation to determine its constitutionality, it does have the capacity to review all cantonal legislation, including cantonal constitutions (Lienhard et al. 2017, 417). The result of this is twofold: on the one hand, the court can bring a canton's legislation in line with national guarantees. This is undoubtedly an infringement on cantonal autonomy and, thus, a democratic danger for federalism (see the following section). On the other hand, federalism also implies at least some unity and centralization, not just diversity and non-centralization. When federal units consent to centralization, they do so because their interests are best served by an agent defending them on their behalf. In turn, cantons and even municipalities can themselves appeal to the court to defend non-centralization and territorial autonomy (Art. 189 FC).

Thus, the Supreme Court is the arbiter that adjudicates inter-territorial disputes. Lacking such an arbiter could push the federal order into endless quarrels (as in Belgium) or drifting apart (as in Bosnia). In other words, the kind of "umpire" provided by liberal democracy is demanded by federalism itself (Burgess 2012, 271; Watts 1998, 8).

Democracy Obstructing Federalism

Nonetheless, some democratic principles clearly work against federalism. Chief among them is the core value of both electoral and direct democracy: one person, one vote. This rules out inter-territorial equality. The National Council is the most obvious example of this: because seats are distributed to cantons in proportion to their population, larger cantons have a bigger say than smaller ones. In fact, the combined weight of MPs from the five biggest cantons would be enough for an absolute majority of 53 per cent. At the same time, citizens residing in larger cantons have more votes (e.g., thirty-five in Zurich) than those living in smaller ones (e.g., one in each of the six smallest cantons), and the effective threshold for parties is correspondingly lower. In National Council elections, it is even possible for candidates to reside in one canton but be elected in another. In both 2015 and

2019, this was achieved by Magdalena Martullo Blocher (daughter of Christoph Blocher) of the Swiss People's Party. Nothing could more clearly contradict the federal principle of the centrality and integrity of territorial borders.

When it comes to federal referendums, the meaning of cantonal borders varies from unimportant to decisive. Territoriality is irrelevant for the facultative referendum: since only a simple, popular majority across Switzerland is required, how the different cantons vote is of only statistical interest. (However, at least eight cantons can *call* for a facultative referendum; see "Democracy" above.) By contrast, cantonal borders play a decisive role for obligatory referendums and popular initiatives since, for them to be accepted, a cantonal majority is required as well as a simple popular one. Thus, a majority of cantons can retain the status quo by blocking constitutional change, but, to move ahead, the cantons need the people. In this way, federalism (in the form of a cantonal majority) and democracy (simple popular majority) each has a veto over constitutional change (see the two sections below).

The Federal Constitution also mandates cantons to have a democratic constitution of their own, approved direct-democratically and subject to change if demanded by its citizens (Art. 51.1 FC). But, while the political rights of citizens in national affairs must be guaranteed without reservation, cantons can vary in the access they allow to political rights regarding cantonal and local affairs. In the canton of Glarus, for example, the right to vote on cantonal matters, which includes the right to participate in the cantonal citizen assembly, has been lowered to sixteen years of age; in the canton of Schaffhausen, voting is mandatory; and quite a few cantons and communes permit foreign residents to participate too.

However, since 2002, the Federal Supreme Court has begun to rule on the constitutionality of various cantonal electoral laws, deciding that wherever parties need more than 10 per cent of the valid votes cast to be guaranteed a seat (effective threshold), the nationally guaranteed *democratic* principle of the equality of votes is violated (Mueller and Bernauer 2016). As a result, many cantons have modified their electoral systems, notably by introducing the "double proportional system" developed by Augsburg mathematician Friedrich Pukelsheim. Nevertheless, in 2014, two cantons (Uri and Zug) petitioned the federal parliament to change the Federal Constitution and "restore cantonal sovereignty in electoral matters" (SPK 2017). By December 2018, however, the National Council had rejected the idea.[5]

A final manifestation of the anti-federal potential of democracy can be found in the rules governing the composition of the Federal Council. Not only are the large cantons ahead by far in the number of "their" members compared with smaller cantons (Giudici and Stojanović 2016), but also, until 1999, no more than one member could come from the same canton. This ensured a more even balance of representatives. Since then, it has happened twice that two members have come from the same canton (ibid.), leaving even fewer seats for the other cantons. More generally, the Federal Council risks losing its federal character to the extent that democratic, non-territorial criteria such as age, party, and gender take precedence over territorial criteria such as religion, language, region, and the canton itself. However, it should also be noted that because federal councillors are elected by both chambers sitting in common session, the Upper Chamber is not fully deprived of a say over the composition of the executive, as has occurred in parliamentary democracies such as Germany and Spain. Nevertheless, with only forty-six members facing two hundred national councillors, the weight given to the Upper Chamber is roughly a quarter of that of the Lower Chamber, and a government minister needs only a simple majority of valid votes to be (re-)elected.

Federalism Obstructing Democracy

For Stepan (1999), three elements matter in assessing the degree to which federalism in a country is "demos-constraining": the overrepresentation of constituent units in the Senate or Upper Chamber, that chamber's power vis-à-vis the popular, Lower Chamber, and the degree of decentralization. In principle, then, Switzerland is almost an ideal case of demos-constraining federalism:

1. In the Council of States, all cantons are represented equally, regardless of size. The only exceptions relate to the former half-cantons, but, even here, all six are given one seat, although they, too, differ markedly in size: Basel Countryside has 290,000 inhabitants, Appenzell Inner-Rhodes 16,000 – a ratio of 18:1.
2. The two chambers have exactly the same powers. Only the influence over the election of the federal executive and judges is reduced, in actual practice, by holding joint sessions.
3. Policymaking powers are divided roughly equally among the federal, cantonal, and local levels, meaning that two-thirds of state activity is located at the subnational level. This further decreases the powers of the Swiss demos, whether exercised directly or through its national authorities.

There is, however, an even more blatant disregard for nationwide democracy emanating from Swiss federalism: the already mentioned

Table 6.2. Conflicting popular and cantonal majorities, 1848–2019

Year	Issue	Type	People yes (%)	Cantons yes*	
				No.	%
1866	Weights and measures	OR	50.4	9.5	43.2
1910	Proportionality for National Council	PI	47.5	12	52.2
1955	Consumer protection	PI	50.2	7	31.8
1957	Civil service	OR	48.1	14	63.6
1970	Federal finances	OR	55.4	9	40.9
1973	Education	OR	52.8	10.5	47.7
1975	Proactive economic policy	OR	52.8	11	50.0
1983	Renewable energy policy	OR	50.9	11	47.8
1994	Simplified naturalization	OR	52.8	10	43.5
1994	Cultural subsidies	OR	51.0	11	47.8
2002	Against asylum abuse	PI	49.9	12.5	54.3
2013	Family subsidies	OR	54.3	10	43.5
2016	"Against marriage punishment"†	PI	49.2	16.5	71.7

Source: Switzerland. Bundeskanzlei (2018b).

* Total number of cantonal votes up to 1978: 22; since 1979: 23.

† Result later annulled by the Federal Supreme Court, but initiative subsequently withdrawn. The winning minorities – people or cantons – are highlighted in grey.

Key: OR = obligatory referendum; PI = popular initiative.

double-majority requirement to effect constitutional change. Table 6.2 lists the thirteen instances – from 1848 to 2019 – when popular and cantonal majorities diverged. Almost half these cases took place in the last thirty-five years, and two in the past five years, so there seems to have been an increase in conflicts of this type. Popular majorities in favour of change were thwarted by a cantonal majority against on nine occasions. Cantonal majorities in favour of change were blocked by a popular majority against only four times. Finally, three of the four "popular victories" concern popular initiatives – that is, extra-parliamentary demands, which, almost by design, are more extreme in character – but rejecting them can still lead to change in the medium term. By contrast, eight of the nine "cantonal victories" relate to the obligatory referendum – that is, proposals by the federal authorities. Rejecting them deals a more severe blow to representative democracy than rejecting popular initiatives, so federalism comes out as the stronger opponent of democracy than the other way around.

Federalism is even more clearly anti-democratic in substance when it allows non-democratic regimes or elements at the cantonal level to be maintained. The chief example here is the denial of women's right to vote in Appenzell Inner-Rhodes until 1990–1. Political rights in cantonal matters are regulated by cantonal law, and a majority of men in that canton had decided against extending the right to vote to female citizens, even after they had been given full political rights at the national level in February 1971. Other, more recent examples include the attempt to introduce degressive tax rates in Obwalden, approved in a cantonal referendum, but rejected by the Federal Supreme Court in 2007 as contradicting the Federal Constitution (NZZ 2007), and a ban on burqas, introduced in Ticino and St. Gallen in 2013 and 2018, respectively (NZZ 2015, 2018).

While the anti-democratic and anti-liberal character of the last two examples is subject to debate, denying half its citizens the right to vote purely on gender grounds is hardly justifiable using democratic arguments. And yet federalism, or rather the extensive political autonomy accorded to cantons coupled with *their own* democratic legitimacy, was at least co-responsible for the late introduction of universal suffrage. However, to the extent that all three examples are fully democratic from a *procedural* point of view, direct democracy, or rather the anti-democratic, anti-liberal electorates in these three cantons, are to blame, not federalism.

Finally, federalism has the potential to obstruct national democracy through inter-cantonal coordination (Arens et al. 2017). As at the international level, treaties and coordination among polities take place primarily between executives (see also Fossum and Laycock, chap. 4). For some, this amounts to a "democratic deficit" (Moeckli 2009, 7). Thus, instead of citizens having a chance to vote on a cantonal or federal law prepared by their respective parliament, rejecting a treaty – if, in fact, a vote does take place – leads to complicated renegotiations. Schwaller (2003, 14), in turn, regards this as a price to pay for maintaining a healthy and forceful federalism since even "a cantonal parliament would prefer to accept or reject – after having previously been informed and possibly consulted – an inter-cantonal treaty, rather than having to accept a federal solution without being asked at all."

The point here is that what is good for federalism (cantonal autonomy) is not necessarily good for democracy (accountability and citizen influence). Noteworthy from the point of view of coupling is the fact that national democracy (i.e., the federal government, parliament, and the electorate) generally abstains from interfering in horizontal federalism. For example, the federal government is merely "invited" to attend the meetings of the Conference of Cantonal Governments.[6]

However, democracy – and especially direct democracy – is forceful enough to strike back, or at least to attempt to, as two examples from the education sector show. Primary education is the one policy area where cantons have remained the most autonomous regarding both legislation and implementation (Dardanelli and Mueller 2019). It is also the area with the most extensive inter-cantonal coordination. On the one hand, there is HarmoS, an inter-cantonal treaty to harmonize mandatory education (EDK 2018; Schnabel and Mueller 2017). As of October 2018, fifteen cantons were members of HarmoS, while all seven cantons that refused to join did so through a cantonal referendum (EDK 2018). What is more, in 2016, the electorate of St. Gallen clearly rejected an initiative that would have forced it to leave HarmoS (NZZ 2016). On the other hand, since 2004, the twenty-one cantons with a German-speaking majority or minority have developed a common study plan, called Lehrplan 21 (D-EDK 2018). The plan has been challenged no less than eleven times through instruments of direct democracy – yet cantonal electorates have approved it each time (IFF 2018a, 2018b; SRF 2018).

Federalism Enabling Democracy

Turning now to the last point of the contrast between federalism and democracy, the main mechanism through which federalism enables and even strengthens Swiss democracy is *size* and *multiplication* (cf. Scott 2011). The fact that the national electorate is divided into twenty-six cantonal composites and then further into some 2,200 local polities not only triples the opportunities for citizens to participate but also tailors them to specific problems occurring at specific levels. This situation enhances the standing of each layer: communal politics for local matters; the cantonal arena for larger, but still not too large, questions such as hospitals and higher education; and federal influence over national problems such as border control, defence, and foreign policy. Invigorating all three federal levels in this way enhances the democratic quality of each and, thus, of the whole system.

Moreover, the importance of a single vote and, therefore, the chance to cast the decisive vote increase in smaller electorates. A citizen of a municipality with an electorate of only 2,300 voters, half of whom do not even turn out to vote, has a bigger say than the same citizen at the cantonal level, with an average of 205,600 voters (see also figure 6.1). But the real key to understanding the democratic potential of federalism is that the various mechanisms exist *alongside* one another: citizens vote at the local, cantonal, and federal levels. What is more, not only representative but also direct democracy exist at all three levels: in fact, most cantons and many communes go beyond this in the degree to which citizens directly influence policymaking – for example, through the financial referendum (whereby spending decisions beyond a fixed sum are automatically put to a popular vote) or, in the city of Bern, a mandatory popular vote on the budget *every year* (Linder and Mueller 2017, 192, 330-1). Without federalism as non-centralization, subnational arenas for citizen participation would be less meaningful, and, without federalism as centralization, participation at the national level (as a citizen of Switzerland and resident of any one canton) would be equally redundant.

A smaller size has further benefits, such as a more homogeneous composition of the electorate and better possibilities of popular oversight due to proximity and closer scrutiny. Since local decisions pertain to local affairs, they can be more directly assessed than national decisions relating to national domains: whether the sidewalk in front of the bakery was fixed is easily verifiable, whereas the Swiss human rights dialogue with China is a much more elusive affair. Regarding cultural homogeneity, linguistic and religious fragmentation is lower in the cantons than in Switzerland overall. No canton has as many effective language groups as Switzerland as a whole – in fact, all but three (Valais, Fribourg, and Grisons) are basically monolingual. Also, only four cantons are more fragmented religiously than Switzerland as a whole, with most cantons ranked clearly lower. Thus, to the extent that citizens prefer living in culturally homogeneous democracies, for example, canton Uri (94 per cent German, 79 per cent Catholic) trumps Switzerland (64 per cent German, 37 per cent Catholic) as a democratic arena.

Federalism as non-centralization gives meaning to these microcosms. At the same time, however, it enables democracy at the national level to thrive. The cantonal electorates choose all members of the federal parliament directly; parties are built in a bottom-up fashion, with cantonal parties confederating nationally; and, equally, cantonal authorities can avail themselves of democratic channels (such as petitions, initiatives, and referendums; participation in expert groups and consultation procedures; or territorial lobbying) to make their voices heard. As important actors in national democratic processes, cantons make sure that different points of view are heard. This not only ensures democratic pluralism and furthers legitimacy but also contributes to greater effectiveness since cantons themselves are often – and increasingly – the ones later implementing federal legislation (see, e.g., Dardanelli and Mueller 2019).

Yet Swiss federalism makes an even more profound contribution to democracy. Switzerland is divided between rural and urban; Catholic and Protestant; German-speaking and French-, Italian-, and Romansh-speaking citizens. These different groups are also territorially concentrated. That this recipe for disaster has, instead, become one for success has to do with its cross-cutting nature: the different cleavages cut across and thus weaken, rather than overlap and thereby reinforce each other (see Bächtiger and Steiner 2004). This has helped avoid the country breaking up along religious or linguistic frontiers and contributed to it becoming a civic nation. For not only was there never a single culture behind which one could rally, but also every group defined by one cleavage (e.g., German speakers) is split by others (e.g., urban and rural, Catholic and Protestant German speakers). The notion of *Willensnation*, captured so well in Schiller's rendering of the fellowship oath in his play *Wilhelm Tell* ([1804] 1998), perfectly expresses the attempt to build a common Swiss identity on political and voluntary, not ethnic and deterministic, grounds.

But creating this *Willensnation* without the cantons would have been impossible. The origins of the Swiss federation lie in the thirteenth and fourteenth centuries, in defence and arbitration treaties among the cantons. These were similar to each other culturally – rural, German-speaking, and Catholic – but divided politically. Until today, most cantons have remained non-ethnic, civic creatures. There is, for example, not one canton for all French-speaking Swiss, and even Italian speakers have historically been present in both Ticino and parts of Grisons. Cantons also have their own history, their own contemporary political institutions, and their own visions of the future, to paraphrase Renan (1882). Cantonal autonomy in culturally sensitive areas such as education, culture, religion, and language has also meant that there has been less demand for further protection of cultural groups as such. The civic character of the Swiss cantons further enhances the direct-democratic side of Swiss nationalism: regular referendums at all three levels of government underline the character of Switzerland as a visible, tangible, and desired (ibid.) democratic community of democratic communities.

Conclusion

This chapter has studied the relationship between federalism and (direct) democracy in Switzerland. While democracy obstructs federalism whenever the idea of the single demos trumps territorial differentiation, liberal-democratic principles such as the rule of law, proportionality, necessity, and legality help consolidate the Swiss federation. An umpire in the form of an independent arbiter is necessary even by federal standards, and the Council of States is involved in selecting federal judges.

Moreover, both democracy and federalism rely on the same basic source of legitimacy: explicitly and regularly expressed consent based on the premise that the people(s) have the final say through referendums. At all three levels, therefore, citizens can approve, challenge, and modify the rules governing the different communities they form.

Nevertheless, the equal representation of cantons in the Council of States and in intergovernmental relations contradicts the democratic principle of one person, one vote – most clearly when cantonal and popular majorities regarding constitutional change collide. Although this is a rare event, it happens; and when it happens, cantonal majorities against change are more often victorious than popular ones in favour. The broad autonomy accorded to cantons can also damage democracy *within* cantons, as seen most clearly in the case of women's right to vote. At times, cantonal autonomy preserves and protects regional non-democracy from the fundamental rights guaranteed at the national level.

However, when it comes to daily as opposed to constitutional politics, federalism provides numerous opportunities for meaningful popular participation at the cantonal and local levels. Dividing the national polity into twenty-six smaller and 2,200 even smaller units increases the influence of individuals by reducing the number of competing votes and increasing homogeneity. Federalism strengthens democracy in the form of parliamentary and governmental elections, direct-democratic instruments at both the cantonal and local levels, and national semi-direct democracy. Furthermore, both Swiss federalism and Swiss democracy build on a civic understanding of nationhood, for which the division of power is key. At this most basic level, federalism plays as important a role for consociational democracy nationally as direct democracy does for and within the cantonal polities.

Overall, then, there is more harmony and complementarity between Swiss federalism and democracy than clash and mutual obstruction. While the one includes the different territorial communities in national decision-making, the other provides citizens as individuals with both initiating and blocking opportunities. At the same time, while the cantons cooperate with each other in a confederal manner – through treaties and conferences – contentious treaties (e.g., regarding primary education) can be challenged by parliaments and/or become the subject of a binding referendum. If they are approved (direct-)democratically in this way, the results of (con)federal cooperation are strengthened even further.

Of course, no system of rule is devoid of exceptions and flaws, and Switzerland has experienced its own frictions between federalism and democracy. But the system is usually creative enough to fix itself. The coping mechanism it has developed to deal with these frictions is this: let the people decide since the people constitute both the cantons and Swiss democracy overall. Therefore, because both federalism and democracy emphasize autonomy and self-rule in some areas and shared rule (participation and co-decision) in others, there is complementarity in their one common feature – the extensive distribution of power in both governmental dimensions – while each is, in its own way, linked to direct democracy. If in doubt as to where power should lie, a popular vote will decide.

In turn, the multiple linkages to the people(s) through principles and practices of direct democracy compound to generate an overarching pattern of loose coupling between Swiss federalism and democracy regarding its three main differences: horizontal vs. vertical power-sharing, citizens vs. territories, and one vs. many polities. Cantonal parliaments can veto inter-cantonal treaty-making, but cantonal governments also possess their own democratic legitimacy; citizens can challenge and approve or reject, in binding referendums, policy proposals at all three levels of governance; and Swiss welfare, cohesion, and solidarity greatly depend on the civic character of the cantons.

The fact that branches and levels of government do not continuously wind up entangled in frictions and deadlocks, or revert to competition, fragmentation, and "going it alone," despite such a wide range of veto powers distributed in the horizontal and vertical dimensions of government, points to the balance that the loosely coupled Swiss federal democracy has managed to achieve. Ironically, it is precisely *because* there are so many actors, each with their own democratic legitimacy and occasional popular majorities, that negotiations are a daily feature in political Switzerland.

NOTES

1 "An ever closer Union" is first mentioned in the 1957 Treaty of Rome, establishing what later became the European Union (EU). It also served as one of the targets of Prime Minister David Cameron's efforts to negotiate a better EU membership deal for the United Kingdom; see, e.g., https://fullfact.org/europe/explaining-eu-deal-ever-closer-union/, accessed 29 October 2020.

2 At https://ec.europa.eu/commission/future-europe/consultation-future-europe_en, accessed 29 October 2020.

3 It is no coincidence that the founding myth of Switzerland is an oath sworn by representatives of three separate valley communities to help each other. Until today, this German *Eidgenossenschaft* (oath fellowship) forms part of the official name of the country and several of its institutions (e.g., the Eidgenössische Technische Hochschule Zürich).

4 Parliament can declare a proposal invalid. However, it is usually reluctant to do so: only four popular initiatives have been invalidated in full since 1891, and a single sentence of a fifth one was declared invalid in 2015 (Switzerland. Bundeskanzlei 2018a).

5 See Swiss Parliament, https://www.parlament.ch/de/ratsbetrieb/suche-curia-vista/geschaeft?AffairId=20140307.

6 See Art. 3 of the convention establishing the Conference of Cantonal Governments of 1993, amended as of 2006, accessed 28 December 2018: https://kdk.ch/de/die-kdk/grundlagen/.

7 Germany: How Federalism Has Shaped Consensus Democracy

SABINE KROPP

Contrary to the promises of normative theories (Hamilton, Madison, and Jay [1787] 1989; see also Hueglin, chap. 2), federalism forms an ambivalent relationship with democracy (see Benz, chap. 3; Benz and Sonnicksen 2015, 2017; Benz and Kropp 2014; Lane and Ersson 2005). Referring to the basic considerations of historical institutionalism (Benz and Broschek 2013c; Mahoney, Kimball, and Koivu 2009; Mahoney and Thelen 2010, 15–17; Pierson 2004, 156), recent studies have suggested that federalism and democracy represent interacting institutional layers, which do not always align. Rather, compound, multidimensional institutional settings may embody incompatible logics and create permanent pressure for adjustment (Behnke and Kropp 2016, 587). Changes in one institutional layer affect the functioning of the other and give rise to (un)intended dynamics. It has remained a difficult task to unravel this complicated relation among the different layers because each federal model is unique and can be combined with various manifestations of democracy.

The German model of federalism, which is the subject of this chapter, provides an especially intriguing case in this respect. It is often interpreted as the prototype of cooperative federalism, which is shaped by the principle that shared rule outweighs the forces of self-rule. At the central level, German federalism is combined with a strict representative model of parliamentary democracy. In sharp contrast with de facto existing regional disparities and economic asymmetries, which further increased after reunification in 1990, the Constitution (also called the Basic Law) aims to guarantee "equivalent" living conditions across the country (Jeffery and Pamphilis 2016, 176).[1] This provision – which is a rather vague legal term, open to interpretation – is obviously at odds with the principle of federal variety that underlies the self-conception of other federations, such as Switzerland, the United States, and Canada.

German federalism has long been viewed as rather "unitary" in character (Hesse 1962) and has even been claimed to resemble a "cryptic unitary state" (Abromeit 1992). The unitary character of federalism, again, is bolstered by a corresponding federal culture that gives preference to unity, federal comity, and loyalty.[2]

Sceptical analyses have elucidated the democracy-subverting character of German federalism, which is fundamentally shaped by *mandatory* cooperation and *intertwined* responsibilities. Since federal entities plan, finance, decide, and implement programs jointly, processes become opaque, and responsibilities are widely obscured. Joint decision-making[3] not only affects input legitimacy but also tends to decrease output legitimacy because decisions are typically made at the level of the lowest common denominator or based on problematic package deals (Scharpf, Reissert, and Schnabel 1976, 20–58). Since actors cannot exit negotiations without obstructing a common solution, the status quo will persist if no agreement can be achieved. Moreover, negotiations in federations are typically led by governments and administrations – a characteristic that is believed to be prone to elite capture – that is, the ability of elites to further their own interest instead of representing the interest of their electorate. As a corollary, the dominance of executives diminishes the power of parliaments and creates agency and accountability problems (see also Fossum and Laycock, chap. 4). Parliamentary majorities, which are formed in parliamentary systems to support their governments, are unable to reject package deals or compromises without precipitating gridlock and inflicting damage on their governments.

The German case is particularly instructive for studying the interplay between federalism and democracy. Cooperative federalism, which is marked by negotiations and unanimous rule, is tightly coupled with the parliamentary arena, whose distinctive characteristics are party competition and simple majority rule. This tight coupling has frequently been the object of critical debates because changes in one institutional dimension often cause frictions in the other. These circumstances have been blamed for impairing the "true" nature of German federalism, rendering efficient solutions impossible, and they have been criticized as running contrary to the fundamental requirements of democracy.

The analysis provided in this chapter describes how this contentious relationship has changed in Germany over the last two decades. It argues that conflicting trends within and between the tightly coupled institutional layers can be observed. First, it focuses on how the shifts in the party system and coalition politics on both levels have affected the functioning of federalism, thereby exploring why the strong interlocking of federalism and party competition has shifted Germany towards consensus democracy (see also Lijphart 1999b, 178) and what side effects this creates. The next section examines the effects of the sequential federalism reform (2004–17). It places special emphasis on the question why this inconsistent reform package revitalizes the criticized "democracy-diminishing" character of German federalism and what causes the observed trend to defederalization. The third section concerns the effects of administrative federalism and its inherent agency problems. Moreover, it examines to what extent the interlinkage between the party-federal and administrative-federal arenas has made decision-making processes more flexible and how the recent federalism reform impacts this flexibility. In the concluding discussion, the results of this analysis are critically assessed vis-à-vis normative theories. Thus, the normative yardsticks themselves become the object of analysis.

The Effects of Tightly Coupled Parliamentary and Federal Arenas: Enforcement of Consensus Democracy

In Germany, the tight coupling of the parliamentary and federal arenas is predominantly a result of the specific role of the German Bundesrat[4] in drafting federal legislation. Throughout German post-war history, about 40 to 60 per cent of all federal laws have been so-called consent laws (*Zustimmungsgesetze*), which must be approved by the Bundesrat. In the remaining cases (*Einspruchsgesetze*), the "Länder chamber" can apply only a suspensive veto, which can subsequently be overridden by a majority of the MPs in the Bundestag.[5] This institutional setting has often been criticized because it creates strong veto points and slows down policy change. Because each Land government must cast its votes as a bloc (Art. 51(3) Basic Law), the Länder coalition governments need to reach consensus on how to vote before a federal bill is passed on to the Bundesrat. Hence, Länder governments usually determine in their coalition agreements that they will abstain from voting if the parties in government cannot agree on a common position. Abstentions, however, count de facto negatively since the Bundesrat's majority is required for the adoption of bills requiring its consent.

The consequences of this institutional architecture have been criticized as a friction that leads to serious drawbacks affecting both legitimacy and efficiency (Lehmbruch 1976, 2000). This view is predicated on an ideal-typical distinction between competing parties on the one hand and the federal units destined to negotiate on the other: whereas competition and simple majority rule are considered the dominant rules in parliament, where parties are guided by *programmatic* positions, federalism is attributed to negotiations driven by *territorial* interests.

Significantly, this perspective reflects the approach of some of the Basic Law's founding fathers and mothers, who wanted to keep party politics out of the Bundesrat negotiations.[6] But, at the same time, it disregards that fact that the Länder governments are formed from regional elections, which themselves follow the logics of party competition (see Detterbeck 2016, 647–53).

Depending on the given majority, a "structural divide" (Lehmbruch 1976, 7) inherent in German federalism was predicted. This friction seems to become especially problematic in situations in which Länder governments are composed of parties that are in opposition in the Bundestag but, at the same time, command a majority of votes in the Bundesrat. Under the conditions of countervailing majorities, this situation imposes the logic of party competition on the Bundesrat. This scenario has been assessed sceptically because it hinders actors from pursuing genuinely "territorial" interests, impairs competition among regional "best practices," and, in the end, inhibits federal learning ("yardstick competition"; Benz 2012). Taking the converse perspective, the logic of cooperation is transmitted to the parliamentary arena in times of diverging majorities because the government is forced to bargain with "oppositional" Länder governments. Under such circumstances, party competition, which is principally supposed to create alternative political solutions, is diluted.

This particular understanding of German federalism has not gone unchallenged (see Sturm 1999). To explore the real effects of the Bundesrat's strong veto position more precisely, it is crucial to evaluate how majorities in the Bundesrat are composed and how parties in government determine their strategies in light of their respective composition. Using the so-called R-O-M-scheme as a navigational tool enables us to distinguish the various types of Länder coalition.[7] By sorting governments according to their party composition, it becomes apparent that Länder governments made up of the same party (or parties) as the federal government (R-Länder governments) have been more an exception than the rule in German post-war history (see figure 7.1).

The opposition camp, for its part, was able to form compact majorities in the Bundesrat principally between 1972 and 1982. Consisting of governments dominated by the Christian Democratic Union (CDU) and Christian Social Union (CSU), it deployed its majority to block or renegotiate major reform bills introduced by the federal coalition of the Social Democratic Party of Germany (SPD) and Free Democratic Party (FDP). This constellation further substantiated critical assessments of the Bundesrat's veto potential (Lehmbruch 1976). Conversely, the SPD camp used its – albeit relative – strength in the Länder to present itself

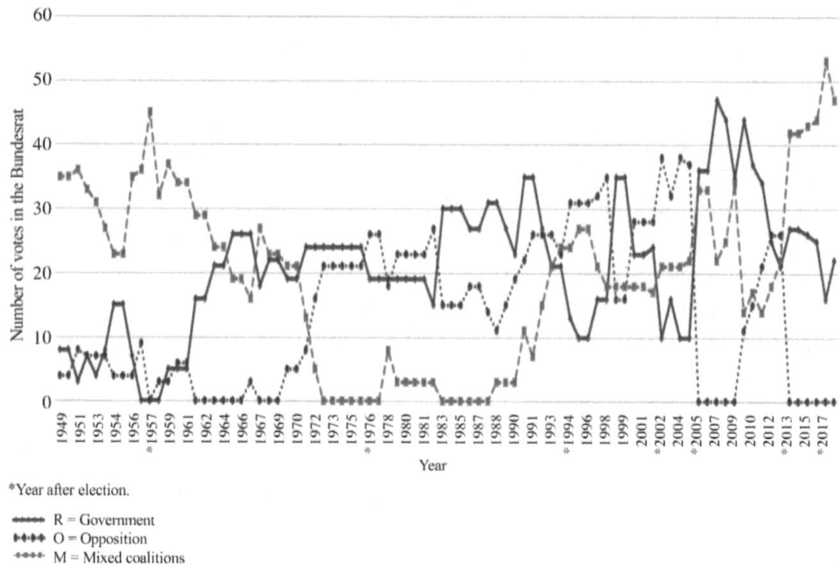

Figure 7.1. Party composition of the German Bundesrat

as an alternative to the government of Helmut Kohl (1982–98) and to gradually "upload" its growing power from the Länder to the federal level in the 1990s. Correspondingly, SPD-led Länder coalitions frankly vowed in their coalition agreements to be a "counterweight" to the federal government (Kropp and Sturm 1998, 195–6). Most of the time, however, mixed Länder coalitions (M-Länder) held a remarkably strong position or even a relative majority in the Bundesrat, as figure 7.1 shows.

As the diversity of Länder coalitions has grown since reunification, mixed coalitions have regained a strong role in drafting federal legislation. To cite a recent example, the third grand coalition of CDU/CSU and SPD in post-war history, led by chancellor Angela Merkel (2013–17), united about 80 per cent of the seats in the federal parliament, but relied on the cooperation of the Green Party throughout that eighteenth session. The Green Party was, at times, a partner in up to ten Länder governments: without negotiations with the "green Länder camp" – which, for its part, consolidated itself as a bloc of G-Länder[8] in the Bundesrat – no law subject to Bundesrat consent would have passed. Yet it is striking that out of the 553 bills debated in the Bundesrat during that session, only one did not pass. This finding reveals the remarkable and unexpected flexibility of intertwined federalism. Throughout German post-war history, no more than 3.2 per cent (a relatively high rate, achieved in the eighth session, 1976–80) of all bills introduced during a session have been rejected by the Bundesrat after being reviewed by the Conciliation Committee (Vermittlungsausschuss). However, these figures reveal nothing about how the Bundesrat's veto potential impacts negotiations *before* a final decision is made.

Responding to this complexity, the federal government is compelled to adjust its strategies to the respective party constellation (Burkhart and Manow 2006). First of all, it should be noted that parties in Länder governments adjust their voting behaviour in the Bundesrat by weighing a mix of overlapping interests, which can ideal-typically be distinguished as territorial, electoral, and party motives (Detterbeck 2016, 647–8; see also Toubeau and Massetti 2013). Party positions are just one of several motives and do not necessarily prevail. They become relevant if issues are polarized and exhibit conflicts of value; but, even then, the programmatic positions of the federal party and its Länder branches as well as among the Länder may diverge. Moreover, because the Länder governments often trade off polarized issues against other interests, contested policies may become part of comprehensive package deals and side payments. This enables parties to come to agreement even in situations of great polarization. By contrast, if fiscal and tax issues or distributive programs are on the agenda, Länder governments predominantly advocate "egoistic" Länder interests ("territorial logics"; Heinemann et al. 2015, 680). By giving specific regional considerations priority over party loyalty, R-Länder often put pressure on the – equally composed – federal government (Renzsch 2000).

This observation is firmly in line with other findings, which suggest a remarkable decentralization within the party organizations. Although vertically integrated, German federalized parties have never been able to simply "download" their will to their respective Länder branches and establish strict intra-party hierarchies (Weichlein 2019, 133–40). Rather, they perform as the major agents undertaking the "coupling" of the various institutional layers (Riker 1964; Detterbeck 2016, 647). In fact, party candidates are predominantly selected "from below," meaning that local and regional nomination bodies within a party have the final say. German parties are loosely coupled systems, which often have difficulty balancing multiple positions and conflicting intra-party groups.

In the past few years, the parallel development of intra-party decentralization has been further boosted by growing regional asymmetries and the ongoing diversification of the coalition landscape. In their electoral campaigns, Länder party branches often distance themselves from their federal organization, especially to avoid being held responsible for unpopular policies pursued by the federal government.[9] Correspondingly, both federal and Länder issues are represented in citizens' voting decisions in Länder elections (Völkl 2016, 249, 260). This goes hand in hand with the increasing importance of the territorial logic in German federalism, which seems to give the Länder party branches more autonomy. As a side effect, this tendency may help to further loosen the tight coupling between the federal arena and party competition in the Bundestag. Beyond that, however, one should be aware that, in light of remarkable economic and fiscal asymmetries, "territorial" conflicts are not necessarily less complicated and may also generate a high level of dispute.

To manage these cross-cutting conflicts, the federal government needs to adjust its bargaining strategy vis-à-vis the Bundesrat in advance. In this process, three basic scenarios are thinkable: First, if it has no realistic chance of forming a majority in the Länder governments, the federal government can tailor its bills to the positions of those Länder with which it can probably find common ground. If actors follow such a strategy of "self-restraint" under these conditions of divided government (Manow and Burkhart 2007), gridlock can be avoided. As a corollary, however, this is more likely to result in incremental policies and "muddling through" than actual reforms: solutions may be politically conducive, but remain "suboptimal" with respect to the efficiency criterion.

Second, if the federal government is faced with a narrow majority consisting of M- and O-Länder, it is apt to offer incentives and benefits that serve the territorial interests of pivotal Länder governments to break up the cohesion of formative party camps. Third, if counter-majorities in the Bundesrat are insurmountable, the government may accept the fact that policy issues need to be negotiated within the Conciliation Committee. There, however, bills become part of comprehensive package deals so that their initial intention often becomes blurred. Hence, this procedure is rarely followed because it runs counter to the preferences of the ministries and the corresponding "policy experts" in the parliamentary party groups, who tend to insist on "appropriate" solutions. One other possibility is that bills can be split into one part that requires the Bundesrat's approval and another that can pass with a simple majority in the Bundestag after the Bundesrat has claimed a suspensive veto.

In most of these outlined constellations, party conflicts shift immediately from the federal level to the respective Länder coalitions, which themselves need to balance their voting behaviour in the Bundesrat with other issues and agree on complex package deals. Which arena – the Bundesrat or the Länder government – is considered the primary one in such "nested games" (Tsebelis 1991) does not follow a general rule; rather, parties in Länder governments weigh the options and consequences of such "arena shifts" from case to case.

Due to the increased fragmentation of the party systems in the Länder, the coalition landscape has become remarkably diverse. At the beginning of the nineteenth, and latest, session in September 2017, six parties in thirteen differently composed Länder governments were represented in the Bundesrat. Since 2013, no O-Länder governments have been formed. In 2018, the Länder minister-presidents (i.e., the premiers) belonged to five parties – in other words, no longer just to the three main parties: CDU, CSU, and SPD. Before the 2017 federal elections, which generated a seven-party system in the Bundestag, no plausible scenario was conceivable that could have created an "R-majority" in the Bundesrat. Instead, each constellation would have been confronted with a relative majority of mixed coalitions.

The different phases in German post-war history indicate that the pendulum has swung several times, from decades in which the federal government could not rely on a majority of its own in the Bundesrat back to periods in which more coherent party blocs could be formed. Since 1949, in terms of democratic theory, the political system has oscillated between more majoritarian and more consensual periods. This can be seen as an advantage since the institutional setting could retain remarkable dynamics. If M- and O-Länder hold a majority in the Bundesrat, the German federal government finds itself in a constellation that is similar to that of a minority government.

This constellation partially solves the problems of tight coupling because it opens up the parliamentary arena for negotiations. Currently, in about 40 per cent of all legislative procedures (i.e., when consent laws are to be decided on), the federal government is forced to negotiate with parties that are not part of the federal government, but at the same time operate as coalition partners in Länder governments. Under such circumstances, the power-sharing character of the institutional setting is strengthened, and consensus democracy is invigorated. This trend is further reinforced by federal grand coalitions, which also absorb party competition to a certain degree.[10] Due to the tight coupling of the parliamentary and federal dimensions, some decisions are even based on informal, all-party coalitions. In these situations, one can expect incremental policy change to be the dominant pattern.

Contrary to this prediction, however, the last few decades have seen far-reaching reforms being adopted (see Rüb 2014), including reforms to family issues, gender equality, defence policy, and the social welfare system. But they were not so much the result of federalism gaining more flexibility (see below) as the relevant parties adopting centrist positions in the policy space and, thus, being able to compromise. While the SPD moved slightly to the right after it came to power in 1998 and implemented contested social welfare reforms (*Hartz IV*), the CDU gave up a number of its conservative positions after 2005. Both parties included green issues in their programs, while the Green Party adopted more centrist positions on socio-economic issues. A common approach to explaining such policy change is veto player theory (Tsebelis 2002, 28, 31): partisan players could be "absorbed" and the "unanimity core" enlarged, while, at the same time, parties in (the federal and Länder) governments moved away from their former status quo. Federalism has not hampered this change; in fact, it has served as a testing ground for new parties, a repositioning of established parties, and novel coalitions.

New parties usually move into Länder parliaments before they succeed on the federal level. In the past few years, however, the right-wing, populist Alternative für Deutschland (AfD), which started out as a party sceptical of the European Union (EU), but adopted anti-Islam and xenophobic positions during the 2015 refugee crisis, has gained representation in all sixteen Länder parliaments. In 2015, all parties except the AfD gradually adopted more leftist positions, leaving space for the AfD to fill this "representation gap."[11] In 2017, the party also surpassed the 5 per cent threshold[12] in the federal elections (winning 12.6 per cent), and it is currently the strongest opposition party in the Bundestag. Still, the party has not been accepted as a coalition partner and, thus, has had no immediate impact on federal negotiations. But it affects the federal system indirectly in that party systems on both the federal and the Länder levels have become more segmented, thereby restricting the number of realistic coalition options. For example, as of December 2019, eight Länder coalitions, as well as the federal grand coalition, consist of three parties, a situation that can produce a considerable range of sometimes incongruent policy positions. Since the federal elections held in 2017, polarization among the established parties has been increasing; growing policy distances exert pressure on consensus democracy.

The Effects of Federalism Reform: Defederalization and Recurrence of Joint Decision-Making

Although German federalism had undoubtedly allowed for flexible solutions in the past, a comprehensive reform of federalism ranked high on the political agenda after reunification (Behnke and Kropp 2016;

Burkhart 2009; Burkhart, Manow, and Ziblatt 2008; Scharpf 2009). In line with the basic objective of "disentanglement," the Bundestag and Bundesrat adopted incremental constitutional reform between 2006 and 2017. In 2006, responsibilities were more clearly assigned to the various territorial levels. Three years later, the law on public debt was reformed. Finally, the fiscal equalization scheme was reconfigured in 2017. In comparative perspective, German federalism reform is an especially intriguing case because it was divided into three distinct steps, which followed various ideas, contradicted each other, and, finally, had undesirable effects. During the reform decade, different institutional layers were asynchronously the object of change. Because policy change was first and foremost achieved by a – more or less coincidental – programmatic repositioning of the parties, it was intended to make decision-making more predictable by changing the rules of the game. The reform package was qualified as the "mother of reforms," meaning that subsequent policy reforms could more easily be enforced after a comprehensive reform of federalism had been adopted. It is not an exaggeration to conclude that this attempt has partially failed. It is symptomatic that decision makers are currently reanimating joint decision-making, centralizing responsibilities, and reversing former decisions (Benz and Sonnicksen 2018; Kropp and Behnke 2016, 669). In effect, a remarkable defederalization is taking place, while the democratic deficits resulting from joint decision-making are being revived.

A basic argument derived from this new institutionalism is that ideas and beliefs are central ingredients of reform (Schmidt 2008, 306–9; W. Scott 2014, 66–70). Strikingly, the sequence of German federalism reform was inspired by different, not to mention opposite, ideas. Whereas the first step was guided by the notion of dual federalism and disentanglement, the principle of austerity and budgetary consolidation directed the second. The third step, again, revived the idea of solidarity, while the other already existing concepts have retained some importance.

Before 2006, a forceful discourse coalition had pursued the competitive model of federalism. The main actors were the financially strong Länder, such as Bavaria, Hesse, and Baden-Württemberg, which wanted to gain better-defined responsibilities and concomitantly reduce their contribution to horizontal fiscal equalization. They were supported by the presidents of the Länder parliaments, who wanted to regain parliamentary power; economists; and some neo-liberal think tanks. The primary goal was to make decision-making more flexible and less opaque, and the process was intended to dissolve areas of joint decision-making. The re-parliamentarization of *executive federalism* (as a way to make federalism more democratic) was also a basic objective of the reform, although the notion of creating more effective institutions ranked higher on the agenda. The first reform attempt, in 2004, failed because the federal government had tried to play a role in education policy (Welsh 2014), normally a jurisdiction of the Länder, and which the Länder would not agree to. The grand coalition built in 2005 adopted the reform in 2006, after all actors had realized that they could not afford this endeavour to be a complete failure.

The reform was effective in that it reduced the number of consent laws from nearly 60 per cent to less than 40 per cent (Stecker 2016, 623).[13] This allowed the federal and parliamentary arenas to be gradually decoupled, and responsibilities were more clearly assigned to either the federal or the Länder level (Dose and Reus 2016, 632–40; Jeffery et al. 2014). Moreover, federalism was made more flexible because deviation rights were introduced in some policy domains, even though it is symptomatic of the overarching unitary culture that the Länder rarely make use of them. As a result of the reform, German federalism now combines various federal models (Jeffery and Pamphilis 2016). However, the measures have received mixed reviews. They have been criticized from the point of view that the desired disentanglement gave rise to zero-sum games, in which benefits accruing to the Länder turned into defeats at the federal level and vice versa. Essentially, the first round of reform omitted the battleground of fiscal equalization, which mirrors all problems inherent in joint decision-making. An all-encompassing reform was considered too complex to be finalized within the narrow time frame.

The second reform step of 2009 was clouded by the financial crisis and economic depression. The high national debt was regarded as a major problem to be solved and thus avoid future crises. To cope with this challenge, new debt rules were implemented in the Constitution (Art. 109(3), Art. 115, Art. 143d Basic Law), and, as of 2020, these rules prohibit the Länder from financing their budgets with new debt (see Korioth 2016, 688–91). For its part, the federal government has been required to run balanced budgets since 2016, although it has some leeway: its net new indebtedness must not exceed 0.35 per cent of the nominal GDP in the respective year. In addition, a Stability Council, comprising the federal and Länder ministers of finance as well as the federal minister of economic affairs, was established to supervise public budgets. The council, whose main instruments are based on the principle of "naming and shaming" and giving financial advice, is established in the Constitution (Art. 109a). It is a clear embodiment of joint decision-making.

With respect to both federalism *and* democracy, proper sequencing is a key variable for understanding the outcome of comprehensive reform packages (Kropp and Behnke 2016, 673; Falleti 2005, 328–32). If administrative reforms that transfer responsibilities to lower territorial levels are realized *after* fiscal decentralization is accomplished, reforms will be relatively stable because subnational governments are principally able to fulfil their tasks. By contrast, if fiscal decentralization is delayed and tasks have been devolved to the lower levels, sub-federal governments will be unable to take over full responsibility. Instead, they will be tempted to shirk their responsibility and shift the burden onto other federal entities. The federal government, again, can point to the devolved competences of the lower levels to relieve itself of responsibility. In such constellations, accountability as a basic democratic principle is partially invalidated. Moreover, actors are inclined to (re)centralize tasks to rebalance fiscal and administrative responsibilities. Any attempt to strengthen parliaments remains half-hearted as long as they command responsibilities but lack the necessary fiscal resources to fulfil their tasks.

Looking back on the sequential reform of federalism in Germany, this was exactly the mechanism that was at work. In the end, the various elements of the reform were out of step. Most obviously, the inability of the Länder to finance their budgets with new debt thwarted the basic objective of re-parliamentarization in that it restricted their parliaments' budgetary rights. It exacerbated fiscal scarcity because they were not given autonomous powers of taxation to finance their additional tasks (Korioth 2016, 701).

After lengthy negotiations between the Länder and the federal government, an agreement to reconstruct the fiscal equalization scheme was finally adopted in July 2017 as the third stage of federalism reform. There had been tremendous conflicts among the Länder because their local and regional tax base – which was the yardstick for raising taxes (*örtliches Aufkommen*) before the horizontal and vertical fiscal equalization was accomplished – was extremely diverse. Some of the "new" (former East German) Länder still account for less than 70 per cent of the average tax base and are strongly reliant on fiscal support (Wieland 2013, 17, 20). In contrast, the wealthy Länder in the south, mainly Bavaria, strove to gain more tax autonomy and substantially diminish horizontal equalization (Heinemann et al. 2015). Due to the immense financial disparities among the Länder, just four or five out of sixteen had been net-donor states, with Bavaria paying the lion's share.

Considering this imbalance, the public as well as the federal government were surprised that the minister-presidents of the Länder were able to agree on a common negotiating position. Since territorial interests prevailed in this argument, party conflicts remained subordinate. The solution negotiated among the Länder introduced a distinct "verticalization" of the equalization scheme. By shifting the fiscal burden mainly to the federal budget, the redistributive conflict was (partially) transformed into a distributive one; the Länder that would receive additional tax money (albeit in differing amounts)[14] were able to transform the complex situation into a positive-sum game. Unsurprisingly, the federal government, which went rather blindly into this situation, demanded compensation with some delay. It claimed responsibility for a couple of policy issues: among others, traffic infrastructure, the digitization of public administration, and improvements in school infrastructure in financially weak localities.

This approach coincides with public demands to further dismantle the exclusive responsibilities of the Länder. The prevailing arguments are that complex tasks can neither be satisfyingly fulfilled nor coordinated within narrow, regional borders (due to external effects or insufficient administrative capacities), nor can they be financed exclusively by the beleaguered state budgets. The financially weak Länder are particularly willing to let the federal government buy their genuine responsibilities because they eschew being punished by their electorates for failures in policy.

At first glance, this mechanism seems to denote "centralization by exchange": the Länder accept an upward shift of responsibilities in exchange for fiscal resources, while the federal government gains additional competences in return. In the German context, this trade-off has a special twist because it enables the Länder governments to participate even more in drafting federal legislation. Since reforms themselves take place within the consensus-demanding frame of joint decision-making, the Länder governments usually know how to secure their vested veto rights. This development should not be equated with simple centralization; rather, it yields a hierarchical pattern of joint decision-making (see Benz 2017a). As such, it reproduces the democratic deficits caused by mandatory cooperation, such as lack of accountability, transparency, and de-parliamentarization. Moreover, it tightens the criticized coupling between the parliamentary arena and the Bundesrat – a result that is diametrically opposed to the goals of the first reform step. In a nutshell, the trend has launched a creeping process of defederalization. It enables the Länder to shirk responsibility and avoid blame, while allowing the federal government to encroach into the genuine jurisdiction of the Länder (Bednar 2009, 10).

The Effects of Administrative Federalism: Containment of Party Polarization and Agency Problems?

Another lens through which German federalism is frequently analysed is associated with the term "administrative federalism" (Hueglin and Fenna 2015). This label stresses that the federal level is predominantly responsible for passing legislation, while the Länder implement federal legislation that falls within their own areas of responsibility and at their own cost (*Verwaltungskonnexität*). This specific division of labour dates to the nineteenth century, when the Länder developed into states with a fully established administration and when, as of 1871, the Bundesrat, designed as the assembly of the Länder representatives, fulfilled legislative as well as executive responsibilities in the newly established German Empire (Frotscher and Pieroth 2018, 212–14). As an embodiment of the authoritarian state, the Bundesrat was a counterweight to the Länder parliaments' increasing demands for participation. After controversial debates in the parliamentary council (Parlamentarischer Rat), which drafted the Basic Law in 1948–9, the executive character of the Bundesrat was reaffirmed (Weichlein 2012, 121–4).

With the democratization of the Länder constitutions, however, the Länder governments became fully legitimized by their parliaments. Since the Länder had existed before the Federal Republic was founded in 1949, the minister-presidents became strong figures in the early postwar era. The ministerial administrations of the Länder had already begun to launch horizontal cooperation in carrying out various policies and establishing patterns of cooperative federalism. With respect to output legitimacy, federal law-making was professionalized by including the expertise of the Länder bureaucracies in drafting federal legislation at an early stage of policymaking. Yet, although administrative federalism has undoubtedly had positive effects, it has also had democracy-diminishing consequences.

A dense network of intergovernmental committees and councils exists in all policy areas, thereby achieving continuous, horizontal coordination among the Länder as well as between the federal government and the Länder (vertical coordination). These bodies exist at all ministerial levels, ranging from the heads of division to the ministerial conferences at the top of the coordination pyramid (see Hegele and Behnke 2017). The committees of the Bundesrat, again, are composed of bureaucrats specialized in an issue to be negotiated in the respective Länder ministries. This finely tuned, inter-administrative cooperation has undoubtedly improved the quality of law-making, but it has also strengthened the executives and concomitantly diminished the scrutinizing function of parliaments. Parliaments have difficulty monitoring governments in inter-parliamentary bodies due to their size and party fragmentation. In addition, inter-administrative processes are not transparent and, thus, not conducive to public deliberation.

In short, administrative federalism reinforces output legitimacy because it enhances expertise and issue-driven politics, but, at the same time, it affects input legitimacy (see Hueglin, chap. 2; Fossum and Laycock, chap. 4). From the point of view of principal-agent theory, one might ask whether the bureaucratic logic shaping German federalism has become so predominant that it subverts the responsibility of elected representatives.

Empirical findings draw a sophisticated picture here. Surveys suggest that German civil servants define their role as representatives of the state, but they reject being perceived as party delegates (Bogumil, Ebinger, and Jochheim 2012, 164–6; Jochheim and Ebinger 2009, 338; Schwanke and Ebinger 2006, 243). They consider themselves to be mainly experts and, in accordance with the Weberian legalistic tradition, advocates who secure the rule-bound implementation of law. In sharing these role definitions, they also often share a similar understanding of the problems to be solved.

Europeanization has further strengthened the administrative character of German federalism. Continuous coordinate activities within policy areas have created vertical "professional brotherhoods" (Wagener 1979), which comprise the various federal entities and reach the EU level. Hence, it seems plausible that when routine politics is being negotiated, inter-administrative coordination keeps party polarization in check.[15] Territorial, multi-level, and professional aspects are given precedence over party positions.

Some findings even indicate that a growing number of political bureaucrats are inclined to prioritize their expertise over the political preferences of the (politically accountable) minister (Bogumil, Ebinger, and Jochheim 2012, 166–8) – a trend that would cause serious agency problems. But because this result was generated immediately after the government turnover in 2005, it is unclear whether this trend persists. However, it would be a gross exaggeration to state that bureaucratic logic prevails or even undermines party competition and ministerial accountability. Since *political* bureaucrats[16] in the higher ministerial ranks usually anticipate the political objectives of their respective minister – to whom they are responsible – and strongly appreciate the political character of their tasks, ministers are principally able to enforce their will. Recent findings support this view because they reveal that civil servants are appointed according to the criteria of expertise *and* party loyalty, which do not necessarily conflict (see John and Poguntke 2012). In other words, administrative federalism does not entirely absorb party conflicts; agency problems are not rampant. Therefore, it should not be considered an anti-democratic element, although more empirical, in-depth studies are needed. This assessment is further supported by recent studies, which emphasize that structural and party differences among the Länder are not coordinated away (Hildebrandt and Wolf 2016; Jeffery et al. 2014, 1361).

Overall, regardless of historical idiosyncrasies, it becomes clear that German federalism is shaped by a complex interplay between party-based federal cooperation and administrative-federal cooperation. Actors' strategies usually stretch over various, sometimes conflicting, arenas that constitute the multidimensional setting. As a result, they are basically able to change their principle arena and redefine policy issues if they consider it necessary or appropriate (Tsebelis 1991). The minister-presidents of the Länder, for instance, can give genuinely "regional" interests precedence over party loyalty; by shifting a problem to the intergovernmental (inter-administrative) arena, they can contain the effects of party competition in federal negotiations. The opportunity to undertake such strategic arena shifts has kept the multilayered order flexible. However, maintaining this flexibility presupposes that neither the federal government nor the Länder are able to dominate administrative networks. But considering the recurrence of hierarchical, joint decision-making and the observed trend to centralize administrative tasks, one can expect such flexible arena shifts to become more complicated in the future.

Concluding Discussion

Taking the complexity of German federalism into account, it is unsurprising that the above analysis does not yield a single, distinct result. In the multilayered system, interacting, sometimes even conflicting, dynamics emerge. The analysis showed, first, that the tight coupling of both institutional dimensions – the federal and parliamentary arenas – has strengthened consensus democracy at the cost of party competition, simple majority rule, and the provision of clear-cut alternatives. Since the 1980s, the increasing fragmentation and segmentation of the party systems on both territorial levels have reinforced decentralization within party organizations and, at the same time, sustained the territorial logic at the cost of strict party discipline – a development that softens the criticized tight coupling.

Second, due to the awkward sequential federalism reform, the recurrence of joint decision-making revived well-known democratic deficits. Moreover, the reform package caused a creeping defederalization by weakening the autonomy of the Länder governments. Third, the administrative logic inherent in the German federal system increases the quality of lawmaking and enhances output legitimacy. At the same time, it neither invalidates party competition and political accountability nor makes regional differences obsolete. The interlinkage of the administrative-federal and party-federal arenas has allowed actors to undertake flexible arena shifts, but this flexibility is endangered by the centralizing effects resulting from the federalism reform.

In institutionally complex systems, it is unlikely that simultaneous or sequential changes in different layers completely harmonize. To date, it is difficult to evaluate exactly how these trends will integrate in the future. Yet there is good reason to conclude that German federalism is not in good shape. While it seems beyond dispute that the trend is towards defederalization, it is more difficult to come to a unanimous conclusion about how the dynamics outlined in this chapter will influence democracy.

At the outset of this study, it was highlighted that normative theories suggest a need for a critical assessment of German federalism. The bulk of the analyses of its democratic quality refer to the majoritarian model of democracy as their basic yardstick. From this theoretical angle, joint decision-making affects transparency, reduces parliamentary scrutiny, and diminishes the innovative potential of both federalism and parliamentary democracy. These findings certainly hit the mark, but, at the same time, they reveal only half the truth. It is important to note that consensus-enforcing institutions are not simply a second-best solution; they also respond strongly to the ideas of representativeness and social consciousness (Lijphart 1999b, 274, 287). They are able to include a broader variety of policy positions and societal demands, protect minorities, and curtail abundant power, and they are more sustainable on the output side. In fragmented societies, for instance, it is nearly impossible to apply simple majority rule without provoking destabilization.

Although it might be disputed that Germany still represents a rather homogeneous society, cooperative federalism has undoubtedly had its merits (see Hueglin, chap. 2). Arguing on an abstract level, it warrants noting that actors are forced to play iterated games and need to consider the interests of their counterparts before finalizing their strategies. This makes decisions more sustainable and contributes to political stability. Leaving this abstract terrain and turning to a concrete historical example, we see that cooperative federalism was conducive to accommodating the East German Länder during transition. Thus, the federal system was clearly democracy-supporting; joint decision-making did not allow for a "big leap." The political, economic, and social transformations could not have been managed by simultaneously adopting a huge, single reform package. Instead, problems had to be processed step by step. In such ongoing processes, mandatory federal cooperation enables the Länder as well as the federal government to consistently negotiate their interests: in an institutional setting shaped by joint decision-making, supported by parties that, in themselves, work as federal negotiation platforms, problems can be accommodated in a continuing discourse (Hueglin 2000, 2013a, 2013b; Kropp and Behnke 2016, 682).

However, as the polarization and segmentation of the party system increase, the consensus model of democracy, which has worked rather smoothly over the past decades, is coming under pressure. Considering the change in the German party system, it seems debatable whether the institutional setting can preserve its former flexibility and further oscillate between consensus and majoritarian democracy. The most disadvantageous scenario would be that formal institutions, shaped by strong veto points and tight coupling, force increasingly polarized partisan actors into cooperation at the cost of government stability, institutional flexibility, and efficiency. So far, distributive politics has been conducive to absorbing party conflicts because negotiations can be transformed into positive-sum games.

The crucial question is what happens when redistributive issues are back on the agenda and whether polarized parties are then able to agree on a common solution. In a more optimistic scenario, the established parties will retain their ideological flexibility while cooperating, but this would probably come at the cost of clear-cut political alternatives. Reflecting on a third possible option, a loosening of the tight coupling between the federal and parliamentary arenas might be suitable: the Länder would gain more autonomy, receive sufficient fiscal resources, *and* have the political ambition to fulfil their tasks. However, since the federalism reform has failed in this respect, it seems rather implausible that this last scenario will become reality in the near future.

NOTES

1 Before the reform of 1994, the Basic Law even stipulated "uniform" living conditions.

2 Most importantly, federalism forms a tense relationship with the constitutional principle of the "social state clause" (Art. 20(1) and 28(1) Basic Law). This rather fuzzy clause has been substantiated step by step by the Federal Constitutional Court and social courts, emphasizing that the state *must* provide equal or at least equivalent social benefits to all its citizens. See the rulings of the German Federal Constitutional Court BVerfGE 22: 180, 204; BVerfGE 45: 376, 387.

3 In the German system, joint decision-making is a result of the functional division of labour: the federal government and its parliamentary majority are predominantly responsible for legislation, while the Länder

implement federal laws and co-decide in the Bundesrat. In addition, joint decision-making is legally prescribed for various policy issues and mixed financing. It was originally regarded as an adequate instrument, enabling cross-regional planning while avoiding the negative sides of simple centralization.

4 The Bundesrat consists of the Länder governments. Depending on the number of their inhabitants, the Länder command between three and six votes each.

5 This is the lower house. However, if the Bundesrat applies a suspensive veto with a two-thirds majority, the Bundestag can override it, but only with a congruent – that is, at least two-thirds – majority; see, e.g., Art. 77(4) Basic Law.

6 It was mainly the Christian Democratic Union (CDU) that preferred the Bundesrat model, whereas the Social Democratic Party (SPD) favoured a Senate model. From the SPD's point of view, the Senate model would have allowed a "social majority democracy" to be established, able to achieve encompassing social and political reforms in the post-war era. See Niclauß (1998).

7 *R* stands for *Regierung* (government); R-Länder governments are composed of the same parties as the Bundestag (or one of its parties). *O* means *opposition*: O-Länder governments comprise the same party (or parties) as the opposition in the Bundestag. *M* (*mixed*) coalitions consist of Länder parties that form part of both the government majority and the opposition in the Bundestag.

8 Traditionally, Länder governments led by the SPD organize as A-Länder; CDU/CSU–headed governments are labelled B-Länder. As a result of the increasing strength of the Green Party in the Bundesrat, that party's centre of power was temporarily relocated from the Bundestag parliamentary party group into the Länder parties' G-bloc in the eighteenth session.

9 The effects of this tight coupling became especially apparent in 2005. After a series of elections to Länder parliaments in which his SPD lost power, chancellor Gerhard Schröder asked for a vote of confidence to dissolve the Bundestag. His basic argument was that the federal government had lost support for its reforms and was confronted with an overwhelming majority of O- and M-Länder in the Bundesrat. (See figure 7.1.)

10 As an effect of ongoing party fragmentation, however, the current grand coalition, built in 2018, is supported by just 56 per cent of all seats in the Bundestag; thus, it appears to be a rather average, minimal winning coalition.

11 See Infratest dimap, ARD-Deutschlandtrend, November 2015, accessed 21 May 2018: https://www.infratest-dimap.de/fileadmin/user_upload/dt1511_bericht.pdf.

12 This refers to the rule that parties must win at least 5 per cent of the vote in national elections in order to be represented in the Bundestag.

13 According to the reformulated Art. 84(1) Basic Law, the Länder execute federal laws in their own right and, thus, must regulate their administrative procedures. Meanwhile, they may enact deviating regulations; explicit approval by a majority of votes in the Bundesrat is no longer necessary. A recent evaluation of the Bundesrat's role in federal legislation concluded that, while before 2006 about 40 per cent of all approval duties were covered by Art. 84(1), this number dropped to less than 10 per cent after the reform (Stecker 2016).

14 The reform of 2017 abolishes explicit equalization among the Länder. As a result, Bavaria, North Rhine–Westphalia, and the former East German Länder receive the highest amounts, while the federal government is, as of 2020, obliged to distribute among the Länder transfers of about 10 billion euro a year.

15 Recent research reveals moderate party politicization within the Bundesrat's committees, which consist of Länder bureaucrats and are a crucial element of administrative federalism; see Finke and Souris (2017).

16 There is a thin layer of political bureaucrats in top positions, and they can be dismissed by the minister and sent into early retirement without the need to give substantive reasons.

8 Between Co-evolution and Intercurrence: How Democracy Has Shaped Federalism in Canada

JÖRG BROSCHEK

The relationship between federalism and democracy is complex and contingent. Federalism, for example, can strengthen input democracy as it opens up an additional arena for participation. At the same time, it can be "demos-constraining" (Stepan 1999, 21) and, therefore, pose a problem for input legitimacy on the federal level. Likewise, federalism can strengthen output legitimacy by affording territorial minorities with protection from the interests of majority groups or simply by fostering policy innovation. At the same time, it can have the opposite effect by producing deadlock and stalemate. Democracy, for its part, can contribute to a healthy federal balance between self-rule and shared rule, but it can also undermine the federal system. In Germany, for example, a highly integrated and polarized party system has distorted, at least temporarily, the articulation of territorial conflicts in the Bundesrat (Lehmbruch 2000).

While earlier scholarship in the field has tended to either embrace the benefits of federalism for democracy or cast doubt on whether it has any effect at all, recent scholarship seems to be much more cautious and nuanced in its assessment of how federalism affects democracy and vice versa (Benz 2009; Benz and Sonnicksen 2017; Hueglin 2013a; see also Hueglin, chap. 2). Identifying a universal, healthy balance between federalism and democracy is obviously impossible. Rather, addressing this question requires acknowledging the idiosyncrasies of individual cases. They pertain to, for instance, the specific configuration of democracy and federalism, the variants of coupling between them, and the demands raised by collective actors representing the centre and various peripheries as well as non-territorial minority groups within a given polity.

This chapter uses the example of Canada to examine the problems and dynamics resulting from a specific combination of democracy and federalism, a combination based on loose coupling. The chapter builds on concepts developed in the literature on American political development (APD) to analytically frame the discussion, with a particular focus on the Canadian case. APD scholarship suggests disaggregating a given polity into its main components to gain a deeper understanding of how they interact in and over time, and how this interaction results in a "durable shift of governing authority" (Orren and Skowronek 2004, 123). An important assumption underlying this approach is that, more often than not, individual components do not neatly align. Rather, they embody different logics and temporalities, which animate dynamic patterns of institutional adjustment over time. The concept of *intercurrence* captures this distinct historical-institutionalist approach to the study of institutional development, highlighting "multiple-orders-in-action" (ibid., 113; see also Sheingate 2014, 471–3). Intercurrence interprets a polity as being composed of historically constructed authority relations, whose simultaneous operation and interaction impose constraints and serve as "repositories of purposeful political action" (Orren and Skowronek 2004, 18).

Building on this conceptual framework, this chapter examines the configuration and consequences of intercurrent authority relationships between democracy and federalism in Canada. It argues that the loosely coupled co-evolution of democracy and federalism has generated frictions between them. At the same time, however, this situation has opened up a pathway of institutional change that has allowed political actors to respond in different ways to ongoing, open-ended conflicts. More specifically, this contribution reconstructs, first, how the power-concentrating effects of Westminster democracy have perpetuated the self-rule orientation of Canadian federalism, with the effect that the degree of coupling has become even weaker over time. Second, it discusses how Westminster democracy has influenced intergovernmental dynamics by generating cyclical swings between unilateralism and cooperation.

Federalism and Democracy

Federalism and Democracy as Ordering Principles

Federalism and democracy are two foundational ordering principles, each embodying its own normative ideas, organization, and behavioural logics as well as legitimate resources. To assess how both principles co-evolve and interact, it is necessary to clarify some of their general characteristics. Adopting two distinct perspectives – one static, the other dynamic – offers a useful point of entry.

First, one analytical approach to federalism and democracy is to identify their core elements from a *static perspective*. Most generally, federalism as an idea (and the federation as its institutional manifestation) represents an organizational principle of the modern state that establishes constitutionalized authority relationships between constituent units and the federal level. As an ordering principle that allows for the expression of territorial politics on a constitutionally entrenched basis, federalism is rooted, on the macro-historical level, in centre-periphery conflicts. Regardless of whether territorial cleavages become weaker over time or continue to persist, they leave their imprint on the institutional architecture of the state. Through federalization, the state formally adopts a mechanism to accommodate centre-periphery conflicts that creates at least two equipotent governmental tiers, each constitutionally endowed with primary law-making authority (Barrios-Suvelza 2014). In this way, federations variously balance autonomy and interdependence (Bolleyer and Thorlakson 2012; Broschek 2015a, 2015b; Rocher 2009).

The relative degree of autonomy that either level of government enjoys depends on the strength of self-rule mechanisms. Self-rule mechanisms concentrate authority within territorial units, allowing them to act rather independently from each other. For example, competences and fiscal resources can be allocated dualistically, allowing intergovernmental cooperation and the representation of sublevel units at the federal level to be kept at a minimum so as to increase the scope for autonomous action. Shared-rule mechanisms, in contrast, distribute authority in such a way that requires both governmental tiers to collaborate. Examples include an integrated allocation of competences, whereby one level legislates, while the other level is responsible for the implementation; a strongly institutionalized system of intergovernmental relations; and a powerful second chamber, which, along with the first, can limit the scope for autonomous action of each governmental tier and create interdependences.[1]

If we view federalism and democracy through a static lens, we can also identify core principles underlying the notion of democracy. At its heart, democracy captures the idea of self-government. It presupposes the existence of a political community that, regardless of how diverse it is, exercises political authority through collective action to establish a general consensus on and to pursue a common good.[2] But this minimal definition can be only a starting point. Authors such as Thomas Marshall (1950), C.B. Macpherson (1977), and David Held (1996) have emphasized how different, sometimes conflicting, goals create an ongoing tension inherent in democratic governance. This tension results from at least three irreducible goals: democracy as a means of participation, protection, and inclusion.

The first goal points to what is commonly referred to as input legitimacy (Scharpf 1970, 1993). Self-determination is based on the premise that citizens are provided with meaningful opportunities to partake in collective decision-making (primarily through elections). Majoritarian, Westminster-style democracies correspond most closely to this ideal by ensuring that elected governments respond to the preferences of a large proportion of the electorate. Moreover, political participation not only influences the direction of policy change but is also an ongoing process of political community building and community reinforcement. The act of collective participation, therefore, in itself sets into motion a sometimes implicit, but deeper, process of deliberation, through which citizens perceive and see themselves as part of a larger demos (Habermas 1992).[3]

At the same time, however, democracy requires mechanisms to ensure that the integrity of the polity itself, or certain (minority) groups within the political community, are effectively shielded from the potentially harmful or discriminatory effects of collective decision-making. In addition, the political community is always a sharing community (Banting and Boadway 2004). Without regulative and redistributive mechanisms that establish a certain degree of socio-economic equality, the right to participate, or minority rights, remain rather meaningless, and the democratic polity, by today's standards, incomplete. In other words, mechanisms that generate input legitimacy must always be complemented by mechanisms generating output legitimacy.

A second analytical approach to federalism and democracy is that they are *dynamic*. The architecture of federal democracies varies. Historically, the contingencies of state formation furnish individual polities with certain idiosyncratic features. But this initial configuration is not set in stone. The changing nature of a federal society, along with ideational change in the normative order surrounding a polity, creates an ongoing tension between and among the constitutive elements of federalism and democracy, and this tension, from time to time, results in an increased demand for their institutional recalibration. Regardless of the concrete nature of the problems addressed in reform discourses in federal systems, on a deeper level they always revolve around demands to readjust the relative weight of self-rule and shared rule within the federal architecture (Broschek 2015a).

Likewise, discourses on democratic reform, in essence, result from demands to better align the three core elements with their changing socio-economic and sociocultural environments. As Thomas Marshall

(1950) showed for the British case, democratization exhibited a sequential pattern of mostly incremental reforms. Spanning an extended period of almost three centuries, the democratic citizenship regime continuously expanded, from entrenched, protective civil rights; over participatory political rights; to inclusive social rights. In a similar vein, APD scholarship has conceptualized democratization as an ongoing developmental process, which, at times, has been caught in a "democratization trap" (Lieberman 2009). An important driving force behind democratization in the United States was the gap between the early establishment of universal democratic norms, on the one hand, and the simultaneous violation of these norms due to their limited and highly selective application on the other hand (King and Lieberman 2009). These democratic norms afforded change-seeking actors with a powerful ideational "weapon" (Blyth 2002, 39) to challenge the status quo from within. At the same time, such efforts encountered resistance from those privileged groups endowed with democratic rights, who often, directly or indirectly, benefited from the uneven distribution of rights.

If viewed through a broad historical lens, the democratization trap is not an American peculiarity, but a persistent feature that presents itself in contextual variations. As German historian Paul Nolte (2012, 17–19) has argued, democratization, past and present, can be understood as a history of unfulfilled promises, manifested in the gap between ambitious, progressive goals and their deficient implementation in practice (*Erfüllungsgeschichte*); as a quest for new ideas and forms in an open, contingent historical process (*Suchbewegung*); and as a history of crisis (*Krisengeschichte*): as a form of authority *and* a form of living (Friedrich 1959), democracy is inevitably conflict-laden. Democratization, therefore, not only involves contestation about how much relative weight the three constitutive elements should have within a given polity, but also their scope – that is, the boundaries of the political community. Input and output legitimacy, in other words, create a permanent tension that needs to be readjusted from time to time.

Co-evolution and Intercurrence

On the one hand, federalism and democracy are two distinct, separate arenas of a polity. Often, they originate in different historical periods. While democratization and nation building have been intertwined with state-building, the institutionalization of arenas has usually occurred through sequential developments (Benz 2013). As a consequence, they embody asynchronous, temporal dynamics and may create conflicting imperatives for those actors who operate within them. In the language of APD scholarship, they represent distinct "sites" of political authority; that means "a prior political ground of practices, rules, leaders, and ideas, all of which are up and running" (Orren and Skowronek 2004, 20; see Olsen 2009 for a similar approach applied to the European Union [EU]). Accordingly, both arenas are demarcated by institutional boundaries and, as such, co-evolve within a polity through time.

On the other hand, the federal and democratic arenas are variously intertwined, and the boundaries between them permeable, sometimes even overlapping. From an institutional point of view, democracy and federalism are constitutive elements of the larger constitutional architecture, simultaneously engaging in the production of binding decisions and the exercise of political authority through collective action. From a social point of view, a federal democracy splits the demos into different regional or national political communities and, at the same time, seeks to reinforce its reaggregation on the federal level. Finally, from an actor-centred perspective, both arenas are variously connected, primarily through political parties and the party system, with the former being more or less vertically integrated and the latter being more or less congruent (i.e., the characteristics of the party system at both levels of government have a high degree of similarity).

Investigating the simultaneous operation of political arenas in and over time, and its consequences for institutional dynamics, lies at the heart of APD scholarship (Orren and Skowronek 1994, 2004; Sheingate 2014). APD conceptualizes reciprocal interactions among multiple orders as intercurrence. Intercurrence highlights how collective action in one arena is shaped by the presence and activities of actors in other arenas. Implied here is the notion of path dependency: "snapshot views" of intercurrent patterns must be understood within their broader historical trajectory. In other words, the co-evolution and interaction of arenas at any given point in time occur in a historically constructed political order.

An example of intercurrence between the federal and democratic arenas is presented in Edward Gibson's (2013) book, *Boundary Control*. Using three case studies – the American Solid South, Argentina, and Mexico – Gibson systematically examines how local elites deploy different strategies of boundary control to sustain authoritarian enclaves within federal democracies. The persistence of these enclaves demonstrates how contradictory imperatives are built into a polity, in varying degrees, through the existence of multiple orders and how they represent an important source for endogenous institutional change. More generally, if political arenas display a high degree of alignment, institutional continuity is expected to predominate change. The reverse can also be true: different logics and temporalities can create multiple tensions and frictions between and among arenas, generating pressure for institutional change (Lieberman 2002).

The question of when and how intercurrence produces frictions depends on rather contingent contextual conditions. It is, in other words, difficult, if not impossible, to identify universal propositions about how democracy and federalism align in a way that either disrupts or stabilizes a balanced relationship between the two arenas. In Germany, for example, the debate over the disruptive potential of federalism for democratic governance was limited to academic circles until the early 1990s. This changed, however, in the wake of reunification and intensified Europeanization. Since the early 1990s, we have observed a broader public discussion on the need to modernize the federal system. In this debate, there is a general agreement that various forms of joint decision-making – the strongest form of shared rule – is detrimental to input and output legitimacy. In the case of the former, compulsory negotiations between executives from the federal level and the Länder (states) are blamed for the ongoing disempowerment of the Land legislatures, the potential for opposition parties to obstruct the federal government's policy agenda through the Bundesrat, blurred responsibilities, and an incentive to entertain strategies of blame avoidance and, eventually, a trend towards depoliticization. As for output legitimacy, most observers agree that there is an inherent tendency to generate ineffective policy solutions, recurrent episodes of stalemate, and a limited scope for policy innovation (Schultze 1999; Scharpf 2009).

This discourse is very different from the one in Canada. As will be shown in the next section, the concentration of power in the democratic arena has proved to be detrimental to the representation of regional interests on the federal level, especially for those who have perceived themselves as marginalized or peripheral. Efforts to entrench institutional checks to contain the disturbing "outward-reaching" effects of Westminster-style democracy have failed. This, in turn, has opened the door for unilateral transgression of institutional boundaries in the federal arena, a pattern that, for some observers – in particular, from Quebec and the West – represents what Fossum and Laycock (chap. 4) consider arbitrary and unauthorized executive dominance, violating the federal principle of self-rule. The friction resulting from such disturbances has been addressed within a loosely coupled institutional framework, which has not led to stalemate, but generated cyclical shifts between unilateral and cooperative interaction over time.

Intercurrence between Federalism and Democracy in Canada

The configuration of federalism and democracy in Canada is almost unique in the way it places emphasis on the concentration of power within each constitutive component of the political order. While most federal democracies exhibit a more balanced institutional calibration between shared rule and self-rule in the federal arena on the one hand, and between input and output legitimacy in the democratic arena on the other, Canada tilts heavily towards one extreme in each dimension. The main pillars of the federal institutional architecture create strong incentives to reinforce the principle of self-rule rather than shared rule. First, and most important, the British North America Act (BNA Act) established a federal system built on the premise that the federal level and the provinces enjoy exclusive jurisdiction related to matters coming within the classes of subjects enumerated in ss. 91 and 92. The formulation "exclusive" in the preamble of s. 92, which lists the subjects of provincial legislation, is crucial here. Despite a general agreement among a majority of the Fathers of Confederation to establish a strong federal government, the notion of exclusive authority indicates constitutional limits to federal interventions, a fact that even John A. Macdonald acknowledged during the Confederation debates (Vipond 1985, 272).

Thus, the dual allocation of competences aligned federalism institutionally with the principle of self-rule (for both governmental tiers). At the same time, the weak second chamber, the Senate, and the weakly institutionalized system of intergovernmental relations offer only limited institutional counterweights for rebalancing the federation towards the shared-rule pole. Moreover, the principle of Westminster democracy perpetuates the power-concentrating effect of federalism. Although the doctrine of parliamentary supremacy has been limited throughout Canadian history, most notably by British imperial supremacy, constitutional conventions, and, since 1982, the Canadian Charter of Rights and Freedoms, it has promoted the evolution of highly centralized, strong executives on the federal and provincial levels. Accordingly, not only the federal order but also the democratic order in Canada lean towards one pole as they emphasize input legitimacy.

This basic configuration has systematically engendered a number of reoccurring governance problems since 1867. Two forms of intercurrence between democracy and federalism appear to be of particular importance. First, Westminster democracy has reinforced the pronounced self-rule character of Canada's federal order and undermined efforts to strengthen shared rule. Second, Westminster democracy has promoted cyclical swings between unilateralism and cooperation within the intergovernmental arena.

Intercurrence I: Westminster Democracy and Institutional Drift towards Self-Rule

In 1978, Richard Simeon observed in his "Opening Statement to the Special Committee on the Constitution" that "national political institutions are unable to serve as the central arena for reconciling regional and national interests. I do not believe these failures are the effects of any one government or party" (Simeon 1978, 6). Simeon echoed a problem that has – implicitly, at least – persisted for decades, but that surfaced more explicitly in the discourses surrounding Canadian intergovernmental relations in the early 1970s. In his article "The Structural Problem of Canadian Federalism," published in 1971, Donald Smiley was first to systematically discuss the lack of responsiveness of federal political institutions to minority regional interests in Canada. Adopting a historical perspective, Smiley argued that the original Confederation scheme had established a fairly balanced configuration of interstate and intra-state mechanisms. Most notably, intra-state controls were entrenched through the Senate, which was, in his view, considered to be an important body ensuring the representation of regional interests at the federal level. Moreover, he pointed to the federal spirit within the Cabinet, where regional notables enjoyed considerable power vis-à-vis the prime minister, along with a patronage-based federal bureaucracy that could recruit civil servants on the basis of regional origin rather than on merit (Smiley 1971, 335–8; see also Cairns 1979a).

Smiley's assessment of the importance of intra-state mechanisms in the original Confederation settlement – especially the role of the Senate – is not undisputed. The work of Jennifer Smith (1988) and Robert Vipond (1985, 1989) suggests that the BNA Act had never envisaged a strong role for intra-state federalism, but overemphasized interstate mechanisms from the very beginning. Regardless of these differences, however, there is general agreement that the representation of regional interests at the federal level has declined over time and that the principle of Westminster democracy has largely contributed to this development.

The first reason is, as Alan Cairns (1968) has argued, that the first-past-the-post electoral system has exacerbated regionalism and hampered efforts to resolve these conflicts. On the one hand, the electoral system has promoted the emergence of third parties with strong regional support and led to a fragmentation of the party system. In his words, it "has consistently exaggerated the significance of cleavages demarcated by sectional/provincial boundaries and has thus tended to transform contests between parties into contests between sections/provinces" (ibid., 62). These territorial (rather than partisan) conflicts have reinforced the interstate framework of federalism through "province-building" (Black and Cairns 1966, 40) dynamics during the twentieth century. Second, and more important, the electoral system has strengthened party discipline in the House of Commons and encouraged the transformation from Cabinet to prime ministerial government, which, in turn, has weakened incentives to accommodate regional interests within federal political institutions. As Cairns summarized in 1979, the electoral system

> makes the parliamentary representation of political parties far less representative of the territorial particularism of Canada than is their actual voter support. ... The Conservatives are pushed in the direction of being an English Canadian party and the Liberals in the direction of being a Quebec party with negligible prairie representation. ... The prairie provinces are effectively frozen out of any position of adequate influence in the governing councils of the Liberal party, while the province of Quebec is likely to be excessively weak in any Conservative government elected in the near future. (Cairns 1979a, 8)

Political institutions are, as Orren and Skowronek (1994, 2004) put it, outward reaching. What they mean by this is that actors working within one institutional component of a political order attempt to control the behaviour of persons working within a different institutional component. In Canada, Westminster democracy has contributed to a decline of intra-state mechanisms (or shared rule between the provincial and the federal levels), with the result that it has become increasingly difficult for peripheral regions to effectively control, or at least influence in a meaningful way, the political process on the federal level. This, in turn, has produced frictions between democracy and federalism. The input side of democracy has become increasingly perceived as deficient because the electoral system and party politics have turned out to be insufficiently capable of reflecting regional diversity in the federal political arena. Simultaneously, the weakness of the mechanisms generating output legitimacy, by protecting minorities from the detrimental effects of majority rule, have further perpetuated this dynamic.

Francophone Canadians were among the first to experience the lack of responsiveness of federal institutions, at the end of the nineteenth century. They could neither prevent the execution of Louis Riel in 1885 through interventions in the federal Cabinet nor effectively protect francophone minorities outside Quebec in the wake of the New Brunswick and Manitoba school questions in 1871 and 1890, respectively. Throughout the twentieth century, moreover, various protest movements and parties in the west expressed discontent about the distorting effects of majority rule and ongoing centralization within the House of Commons and the federal executive. During the first decades of the twentieth century, agrarian protest movements like the Progressives and political parties like Social Credit considered majority rule and party discipline to be tools of central Canadian (economic) interests, used to subordinate peripheral regions. In the 1990s, this ongoing tension found its expression in the Reform Party's battle cry, "The West Wants In!"

It was not until the 1970s, however, that this problem and potential institutional remedies found resonance in a broader reform discourse. According to Cairns (1979a, 3), the necessity of strengthening intra-state federalism to tackle the "crisis in intergovernmental relations" and the "apparent decline in the legitimacy and effectiveness of the central government" became "almost a new conventional wisdom" (ibid., 2). Numerous parliamentary reports dealt with different facets of the problems, and, in 1985, Donald Smiley and Ronald Watts compiled a comprehensive report for the Royal Commission on the Economic Union and Development Prospects for Canada (Smiley and Watts 1985). Presumably, the most prominent proposals envisaged a reform of the electoral system and the second chamber. As for the former, one common theme during the 1970s and 1980s was the idea of strengthening intra-organ controls by adding "provincial seats" to the House of Commons, according to which a certain number of seats in the House would not be filled by regular single-member constituencies, but through a different method aimed at ensuring provincial representation. Advocates of this proposal expected a greater degree of proportionality between the distribution of seats won by each party in a region on the one hand and their respective share of the popular vote on the other. As for Senate reform, one prominent solution was to replace the Senate with a German-style Bundesrat.

Since the mid-1990s, after the failure of the Charlottetown Accord in 1992[4] and the re-election of the Liberals under Prime Minister Jean Chrétien, the reform discourse on intra-state federalism in Canada has shown signs of abating. On a deeper level, this appears to reflect a trend towards greater disconnection of democratic and federal reform discourses. As substantial reforms towards intra-state federalism have never materialized, while, at the same time, both governmental tiers have become even more independent of each other than in the past, peripheral actors increasingly seem to have lost interest in entrenching mechanisms to control the political process on the federal level. Instead, the provincial realm has re-emerged as their primary political domain. Using the language of APD scholarship, friction-generating intercurrence between the two arenas has become weaker as they realign themselves on a more co-evolving trajectory. Or, using the concept of coupling introduced by Arthur Benz (chap. 3): while the two arenas are not entirely "decoupled," the degree of coupling between them has become looser.

A number of developments point in this direction. For example, the debate over democratic reform in Canada has been concerned with problems inherent in Westminster-style democracy, but, unlike in the past, it barely captures the territorial dimension of these problems. At the heart of this debate has been the issue of electoral reform. Several initiatives to replace the first-past-the-post system have taken place in British Columbia, Ontario, New Brunswick, Quebec, and Prince Edward Island. In almost total isolation from these provincial efforts, the issue of electoral reform has also regularly emerged on the federal level. Opponents of the first-past-the-post system, however, no longer problematize the exacerbation of regional conflicts. Instead, they raise concerns about the lack of fairness towards smaller parties, most notably the Green Party and the New Democratic Party. Democratic reform is conceived as being either a provincial or a federal matter.

Another indicator for this trend is the west's shifting priorities in questions concerning institutional change. To be sure, gaining better access to, and control of, federal institutions is still an element in the reform repertoire of many core actors representing the interests of western Canada. But the ambitious reform agenda of the 1970s and 1980s has largely boiled down to the issue of Senate reform. The western-based, populist Reform Party, which entered the House of Commons in 1993 and formed the Official Opposition, focused almost exclusively on Senate reform as a means of strengthening intra-state federalism, while other dimensions of reform, most notably electoral reform, largely disappeared from the agenda. Moreover, instead of the Bundesrat model, the so-called Triple-E Senate – that is, *elected* directly, *equal* in representing the provinces, and *effective* with significant powers – had already emerged as the template for reform in the Charlottetown Accord.

As a Senate-based model, this reform option would have offered a weaker basis for the representation of territorial interests than the direct representation of provincial executives in a model akin to the German Bundesrat. And even after the new Conservative Party of Canada came to power under Stephen Harper in 2006, the reform discourse did not gain the momentum it had had in the late 1970s and 1980s. When the Conservatives were able to win their first majority government in 2011 (after two consecutive minority governments in 2006 and 2008), the founder of the Reform Party and close Harper ally Preston Manning applauded with, "Thank you, people of the West! Thank you, Canada! The West is In!" (quoted in Berdahl 2014, 45). The Harper government, however, did not attempt to engage in major institutional reforms to strengthen intra-state federalism. Instead, it sought to continue its lukewarm effort to gradually change the selection mode and tenure of senators.

The main leitmotif for federalism reforms under Harper was not intra-state federalism, but his concept of "open federalism." At the heart of open federalism lies the idea that the federal level refrain from any interventions into provincial jurisdiction as much as possible and refocus its activities on exclusive federal competences. Rather than strengthening shared rule by entrenching participation rights for provinces at the federal level, therefore, the idea of open federalism was sought to bolster self-rule for each governmental tier and to decouple both as far as possible. On the level of political rhetoric, this shifting stance from "voice to exit" (Broschek 2020) had already surfaced in the famous "Firewall Letter," an open letter to Alberta's then premier Ralph Klein, published in the *National Post* in 2001. In this letter, Harper and other prominent conservatives from Alberta encouraged Klein to better protect the province from what the signatories considered illegitimate federal intrusions into provincial autonomy – for example, by replacing the Royal Canadian Mounted Police with a provincial police force, creating an Alberta Pension Plan, and collecting personal income taxes through the province instead of the federal Canada Revenue Agency.

Intercurrence II: Westminster Democracy, Unilateralism, and Cooperation – A Cyclical Pattern

Canada's inability to improve the capacity of federal institutions to better reflect territorial diversity was identified by Donald Smiley (1971) as "the" structural problem of Canadian federalism. Eight years later, Alan Cairns (1979b) published a landmark contribution on a different malfunction in the institutional structure of Canadian federalism, with the title "The Other Crisis of Canadian Federalism." His starting point is – similar to that of the landmark study on joint decision-making in Germany by Scharpf, Reissert, and Schnabel (1976) – a "declining capacity for the effective use of the authority of government for the attainment

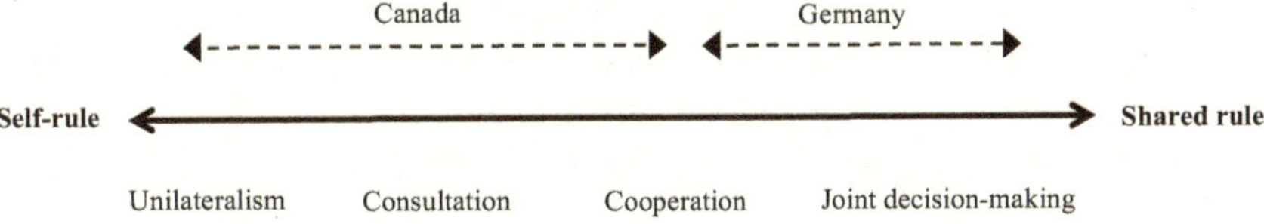

Figure 8.1. Modes of intergovernmental relations

Source: Author's concept, based on Bakvis and Skogstad (2012, 5).

of public goals" (ibid., 175). Unlike in Germany, however, governance problems in Canada do not result primarily from compulsory negotiations between the federal level and constituent units.[5] On the contrary, Cairns identifies "self-defeating competition" and a "destructive struggle" driven by the "conflicting, overlapping, and discordant ambitions" of federal and provincial actors as the main reason for ineffective policy outcomes:

> The federalism of contemporary big government at both levels can best be understood in terms of the tendency of each government to seek to minimize the policy contradictions in its own jurisdiction and reduce the environmental uncertainty emanating from the conduct of other governments. ... Each government, in brief, strains, to exaggerate somewhat, to attain and exercise the power of a unitary state. (Cairns 1979b, 191–2)

The problem Cairns examines in his article is essentially a consequence of the predominance of unilateralism as a mode of intergovernmental relations. While this mode is almost absent in Germany, in Canada it tends to fluctuate between episodes of unilateralism and episodes during which cooperation between both tiers of government predominates (see figure 8.1).

Not all forms of unilateralism are harmful (see also Fossum and Laycock's discussion of different forms of executive dominance in chapter 4). In fact, unilateralism is a very broad category. Certain forms of unilateralism are often even regarded as having a potentially beneficial impact on policy outcomes, as in the case of mutual adjustment, yardstick competition (Benz 2012), or governmental self-restraint through "negative coordination" (Scharpf 1997). Other sub-modes, most notably regulatory competition, "thrust and riposte" (Leslie 1987, 66), and encroachment (Bednar 2009) are considered to pose a threat to a healthy federal balance as well as to efficient and effective governance. Again, using Orren and Skowronek's (1994, 2004) analytical lens, it is the outward-reaching character of institutional components that can become a problem. If the activities of the federal government control political activities taking place within provincial boundaries (or vice versa) in an illegitimate way, frictions are likely to arise.

Two main factors facilitate the periodic prevalence of unilateralism in Canada. First, the dual allocation of competences is highly ambiguous (Vipond 1985, 1989). Although the Fathers of Confederation sought to exclusively assign individual competences to each governmental tier through ss. 91 and 92 of the BNA Act, in practice it turned out to be impossible to exactly demarcate the boundaries of individual jurisdictions. During the first decades after 1867, the (British) Judicial Committee of the Privy Council (JCPC) had to resolve numerous conflicts arising from the institutional ambiguity embedded in the BNA Act – often, but not always, favouring the provinces. These early developments had two long-term consequences, both encouraging unilateralism in the intergovernmental arena: for one thing, the cumulative effect of the JCPC's decisions enlarged the provincial site of political authority vis-à-vis the federal level by giving the provinces' institutional boundaries a wide interpretation. At the same time, as the Canadian state on both levels assumed more functions during the twentieth century, and as interdependences increased, the boundaries between the federal and provincial levels became more permeable.

While this – first – factor stems from the dual nature of Canadian federalism, the second factor is more directly a consequence of Westminster-style democracy and, more specifically, the principle of parliamentary sovereignty. In a highly ambiguous institutional environment like Canada, it is difficult to clearly specify the limits of this principle. The problem is further complicated as the doctrine applies not only to the federal parliament but also to provincial legislatures. As the JCPC stated in *Hodge v. The Queen* in 1883, provincial legislatures are, within the constitutional limits of s. 92 of the BNA Act, "supreme, and [have] the same authority as the Imperial Parliament, or the Parliament of the Dominion."[6] Accordingly, as long as a legislative measure of either the federal level or a province does not clearly violate the constitutional limitations of parliamentary sovereignty, it is intra vires, even if it has negative implications for other jurisdictions.

Historically, the federal level has more directly encroached upon provincial jurisdictions, while the unilateral behaviour of the provinces has only indirectly constrained the federal government. Until the early twentieth century, the federal government frequently used the power of disallowance to nullify provincial legislation. While this power fell into disuse, it was replaced by an even more important and functionally equivalent tool: the federal spending power. Former prime minister Pierre Trudeau defined the spending power as "the power of Parliament to make payments to people or institutions or governments for purposes on which it ... does not necessarily have the power to legislate."[7] While this power is not mentioned explicitly anywhere in the Constitution, federal governments have referred to several provisions – such as ss. 91(1A), 91(3), 102, and 106 – to develop this doctrine (see also Telford 2003). More often than not, the federal spending power has been contested because the federal government has either unilaterally imposed conditions on how transfers have to be spent or bypassed the provinces altogether by initiating programs directed at persons or institutions that fall into exclusively provincial jurisdictions.

The provinces, for their part, have been able to undermine exclusive federal competences by exercising their authority to legislate unilaterally in matters that formally fall within their sphere, but negatively affect the federal level. A recent example is internal and external trade policy. The Constitution suggests a general competence for the federal level in both sectors. S. 91(2) assigns to the federal level the responsibility for the regulation of trade between Canada and other countries, and s. 121 seeks to establish a framework for the Canadian economic union by prohibiting explicit trade barriers among the provinces (Berdahl 2013). However, regarding internal trade, non-tariff barriers have been an ongoing issue in Canadian politics. The federal government is, in effect, unable to enforce the harmonization of standards among the provinces or to prevent them from using their monopolies to restrict dairy, wine, and beer imports from other provinces. Similarly, it is almost impossible for the federal government to negotiate encompassing trade agreements such as the Comprehensive Economic and Trade Agreement between Canada and the EU without ensuring prior provincial compliance because many provisions affect provincial jurisdiction.

Although unilateralism poses a permanent threat to the federal balance in Canada, this mode has not always predominated the system of intergovernmental relations. Rather, it resurfaces from time to time, punctuated by episodes during which cooperation becomes more prevalent. This cyclical pattern has reproduced itself with remarkable regularity (see table 8.1). The approach of Prime Minister Pierre Trudeau, for example, was very different from the one adopted by his son, current Prime Minister Justin Trudeau. Pierre Trudeau held the view that only a strong federal government could effectively counter centrifugal dynamics within the federation. Only reluctantly did he involve the federal government in negotiations with the provinces, if necessary; he preferred to act unilaterally, especially during his last term

Table 8.1. Cyclical pattern in intergovernmental relations: Between unilateralism and cooperation

In office	1980–4	1984–93	1993–2003	2003–6	2006–15	2015–
Party	Liberal	Progressive Conservative	Liberal	Liberal	Conservative	Liberal
Prime minister	Pierre Trudeau	Brian Mulroney	Jean Chretien	Paul Martin	Stephen Harper	Justin Trudeau
Approach	Unilateral	Cooperative	Unilateral	Cooperative	Unilateral	Cooperative
Example	Proposal for unilateral patriation of Constitution and Canadian Charter of Rights and Freedoms (1980) National Energy Program (1980)	Negotiation of constitutional amendments (Meech Lake and Charlottetown Accords)	Unilateral reform of Canada Health and Social Transfer system and unemployment insurance (1995–6) New unilateral spending initiatives in provincial jurisdictions after 1998	Attempt to create a pan-Canadian system for early childhood development and care Health Accord 2004	Attempt to unilaterally reform the Senate Open federalism	Pan-Canadian Framework on Clean Growth and Climate Change

as prime minister, between 1980 and 1984. Justin Trudeau, by contrast, championed a new approach to cooperative federalism throughout his electoral campaign in the summer of 2015. He clearly distanced himself from Stephen Harper's concept of open federalism, instead promising to invite the provinces to work together on common goals like climate change and other issues.

In short, prime ministers seem to be inclined to adopt a different approach to intergovernmental relations than their predecessor. Although there has always been a gap between political rhetoric and political practice, it is possible to find evidence for how this approach is reflected in certain developments. For example, while Stephen Harper held only two First Ministers' Meetings during his nine-year tenure as prime minister, in the wake of the financial crisis in 2008 and in early 2009, Justin Trudeau has met with the provincial and territorial premiers in First Ministers' Meetings six times since November 2015 (as of this writing).

Again, Westminster-style democracy contributes to this dynamic pattern because it creates a strong incentive for incumbents and aspiring candidates to distinguish themselves by developing distinct political leadership styles. As Lawrence LeDuc and Jon Pammett (2016) have shown, this leadership pattern requires formulating credible responses to three main challenges in Canadian politics: party leaders must position themselves well on questions of economic prosperity, national integration, and the welfare state. Given the importance of federalism, this leadership challenge inevitably demands that a leader indicates an appropriate approach to meeting these goals within the federal institutional framework.

Conclusion

Canada represents a typical case of a loosely coupled federal democracy. From both a historical and a comparative point of view, therefore, it contrasts sharply with the German case, where federal and democratic arenas have always been tightly coupled. But it also contrasts with other federal democracies that display a more balanced configuration of self- and shared rule as well as input and output democracy, such as the United States and Switzerland.

A comparatively loose degree of coupling was already inherent in the original constitutional scheme that was hammered out between 1864 and 1867. The BNA Act placed strong emphasis on self-rule, while mechanisms of shared rule were of minor significance. Accordingly, the constitutional framework established a political order in which power and authority were concentrated in the institutional arenas of federalism and democracy, rather than shared between them. This original setting has become amplified over time, with the result that the linkages between federalism and democracy are even weaker today. To be sure, a combination of other factors – societal, ideational, and institutional – have also contributed to this long-term outcome. Most notably, three discrete political communities have struggled for recognition as *demoï*: English Canada, French Canada, and Indigenous peoples. What is more, it has also been impossible for all three demoï to agree that they belong to a single "people," the demos that constitutes the federal framework of Canadian democracy (Russell 2004). While these societal and ideational factors are important, this chapter has argued that the principle of Westminster democracy itself has had a profound impact on the development of federalism in Canada.

The dynamic pattern revealed displays both continuity and change. More specifically, using Orren and Skowronek's (2004, 12) terminology, federal dynamics feature "persistent," "emergent," and "cyclical" patterns. First, the direction of institutional change has remained persistent insofar as the electoral system, the dynamics of party competition, and prime ministerial government have reinforced the power-concentrating effect of a federal system based on self-rule rather than shared-rule mechanisms. By contrast, efforts to readjust the institutional framework by strengthening shared rule within federal institutions, most notably through electoral and Senate reform, have failed. As a result, within the universe of the six "classic" Western federations,[8] Canada is unique in the way its institutional architecture is geared towards self-rule.

Second, emergent institutional change, most notably through the introduction of the Canadian Charter of Rights and Freedoms in 1982, has rectified this imbalance to a certain extent. The Charter has empowered the Supreme Court to be an actor adjudicating conflicts that result from frictions between the democratic and federal arenas. Institutional ambiguity regarding the constitutional division of power, along with the "layering" of new individual and collective Charter rights onto the existing political order, has furnished the Supreme Court with significant power to specify the scope and boundaries of federal and provincial authority, and to reshape the constitutional relationships between territorial and emerging non-territorial political communities in Canada. In this regard, the Charter has constrained the principle of Westminster democracy on the federal and provincial levels and strengthened output legitimacy by further entrenching the constitutional rights of Indigenous peoples, women, ethnocultural minorities, and the LGBTQ community (Cairns 1992).

Third, the combination of self-rule federalism and Westminster democracy concentrates power within individual arenas. Under the condition of institutional ambiguity, this can create an incentive for unilateral behaviour. As this chapter has shown, in Canada this configuration has promoted a cyclical pattern in the system of intergovernmental relations: periods of time in which unilateral behaviour is paramount have alternated with periods during which federal and provincial governments are more willing to cooperate.

As a loosely coupled federal democracy, the Canadian case tends to exhibit a number of systemic problems related to input and output legitimacy that are very different from those usually identified in more tightly coupled federations. Cyclical shifts between unilateralism and cooperation in the intergovernmental arena, for example, barely occur in Germany, where varieties of joint decision-making represent a persistent mode of interaction (Benz, Detemple, and Heinz 2016; Kropp 2010; Scharpf 2009). Accordingly, reform discourses in Germany's tightly coupled system have revolved around specific, recurring problems for input and output legitimacy. Regarding the former, the disempowerment of the Länder legislatures; the obstruction of a federal government's agenda through the second chamber, the Bundesrat; and blurred responsibilities tend to undermine responsible and accountable government. Regarding the latter, half-baked policy solutions, muddling through, or even stalemate tend to erode governmental capacity for effective governance and policy change.

In Canada, such problems are a rather rare exception and largely limited to processes of formal constitutional change, as was the case during the era of "mega-constitutional politics" between the 1970s and 1992.[9] The loose coupling of arenas in Canada usually preserves democratic accountability and responsible government because exit options remain available (Schultze 1982, 1999): provincial governments can often withdraw from negotiations, while the German Länder governments agree to the inevitability of outcomes that they actually do not support. While it is true that, in Canada, as in other federations, negotiations take place behind closed doors and the concentration of power in the executive at both levels of government tends to weaken the role of legislatures in intergovernmental relations (see Fossum and Laycock, chap. 4), provincial and federal governments still need to justify why they support an agreement instead of "going it alone."

This does not mean, however, that loosely coupled systems are immune from problems of input and output legitimacy. The main challenge resulting from the concentration of power in both arenas in Canada is the latent threat of harmful unilateral action. This potential can pose a problem for input legitimacy when one level of government transgresses and encroaches on the boundaries of another level (Bednar 2009). If, for example, the federal government decides to deploy its spending power to launch new programs in areas of exclusive provincial responsibility, provinces perceive it as an illegitimate constraint on their capacity for political self-determination within their jurisdictions. Moreover, output legitimacy may suffer not only from ineffective competence duplication and overlap but also from unpredictable and highly contingent policy shifts and reversals.

At the same time, Canada has survived as a federal democracy for more than 150 years. From a historical perspective, the basic configuration of federalism and democracy has made it possible to sustain a country "based on incomplete conquests" (Russell 2017). According to Peter Russell, Canada has emerged as a multinational federal democracy constituted by three foundational pillars: English Canada, French Canada, and Aboriginal Canada. Great Britain did not completely conquer the French-speaking, Catholic population in what later became the province of Quebec, and neither did the British and French colonial powers – or the Canadian state, for that matter – succeed in assimilating the Indigenous peoples. This historical legacy confronts federalism and democracy with an ongoing, fundamental challenge because all three foundational pillars coexist and interact without being able to form one, single demos.

As the painful experience with mega-constitutional politics during the 1980s and early 1990s showed, tight coupling exacerbated inherent tensions – to an extent that almost led to the break-up of the country. While intercurrence between the democratic and federal arenas through loose coupling has always carried a disruptive potential, it has acted simultaneously – seemingly paradoxically – as a prerequisite for addressing frictions because it promotes change rather than stalemate. In light of this, the peril of latent unilateralism appears all the more to be a necessary evil within an otherwise suitable, federal-democratic institutional framework.

NOTES

1 The distinction between self-rule and shared rule has become increasingly popular in comparative federalism and multi-level governance scholarship. It is often associated with Daniel Elazar's work (1987) and has been variously used more recently (see Behnke and Kropp 2016; Hooghe, Marks, and Schakel 2010; Hooghe and Marks 2016; Mueller 2014). I refer

here to my earlier work (Broschek 2015a, 2015b, 2016), which suggests that a combination of the two types of mechanism variously underpin the institutional architecture of federal systems. Self-rule and shared rule, therefore, need to be conceived as spanning a continuum within which federal systems can be located, leaning more or less towards either pole.

2 Here understood as resulting a posteriori from ongoing deliberation among the members of the political community.

3 For Schmidt and others, this process should be considered an analytically distinct dimension of democracy – that is, "throughput" legitimacy (V.A. Schmidt 2013; Hueglin, chap. 2).

4 The Charlottetown Accord was a major proposal to amend the constitution that was defeated in a nationwide referendum.

5 Joint decision-making as an intergovernmental mode is of minor importance in Canada. It is largely limited to constitutional politics. Another notable exception is the Canada Pension Plan. Changes to this social insurance–based program are subject to a similar formula (Banting 2005).

6 Judicial Committee of the Privy Council, *Hodge v. The Queen* (Canada) [1883] UKPC 59.

7 Pierre Elliot Trudeau, quoted in Karine Richer, "The Federal Spending Power," PRB 07–36E (Ottawa: Library of Parliament, Law and Government Division, 22 September 2011), 1.

8 The United States, Canada, Switzerland, Germany, Australia, and Austria.

9 Constitutional amendments, for the most part, require the consent of both Houses of Parliament and two-thirds of the provincial legislatures representing at least 50 per cent of the population.

9 Party Federalism in Australia

ANDREW BANFIELD AND ANTHONY SAYERS

Australian democracy has always meant party democracy. The presence of a robust Labor Party in the colonies before federation in 1901, and as the major pole around which electoral politics continues to revolve in every state and territory as well as nationally, has shaped the character of the federation and its democratic politics (Sharman and Sayers 1998).[1] The need to coordinate a response to its organizational and electoral success across the federation defined much of the development of parties on the right of politics across the twentieth century (Brett 2003; Crisp 1978; Loveday, Martin, and Parker 1977). The development of tightly coupled party organizations controlled by state and territory-based branches has profoundly shaped representative democracy in Australia.[2] These parties prosecute election campaigns in their own jurisdictions and dictate the personnel and organizational character of their national counterparts. The reproduction of the patterns of competition between Labor and non-Labor across the federation has given form to the competition for government among elites that is central to modern democracy (Schattschneider 1960) and has been essential to the development of the institutions of intergovernmental relations.

Strong, nationwide parties at both the state and the federal levels, short electoral cycles, and a formation of government that alternates between parties of the centre-left and centre-right have encouraged a shared social liberalism, expressed in a utilitarian view of the state as the provider of public goods and services (Castles 1985; Collins 1985; Deeming 2013; Hancock 1931; Sawer 2003).[3] Formal organizational linkages between the national and state branches within the major parties strengthen this effect. Politicians are enmeshed in a web of federal and state policy concerns within their own party, while governments must negotiate with their partisan opponents in other jurisdictions to achieve major policy objectives. These goals are achieved without appeal to strident ideology or the pursuit of deep constitutional reform, thereby cementing a pragmatic view of institutional politics (Hollander and Patapan 2007; Phillimore and Harwood 2015). State and national politicians of all partisan stripes have largely accepted the growing fiscal authority of the federal government to operate through the states as the major mechanism for achieving policy goals.

Despite the centralizing form of Australian fiscal politics, the states remain relatively autonomous, as measured by net regional authority (Hooghe et al. 2016, 292; although see Fenna 2019, 38). They retain the constitutional and administrative capacity required to implement nearly all major public policies. The dual, legalistic character of Australian federalism offers politicians a range of possible institutional mechanisms for bringing federal fiscal power to bear through the states to achieve jointly constructed policy objectives. This, along with increasingly powerful bicameral legislatures, ensures institutional complexity, along with the redundancy and multiple veto points this implies (Bednar 2009; Landau 1973). Adversarial and cooperative approaches among the states and between the states and the federal government continue to occur, often side by side, at a steady rate (Painter 1997). The result is a regular recoupling of federal institutions as partisan politicians search for practical fixes to both political and policy challenges, short of engaging in uncertain constitutional reform (Benz and Sonnicksen 2017).

The institutions of intergovernmental relations in Australia exhibit a cyclical character: tightly coupled for periods when the federal government uses its fiscal powers to purchase state buy-in in search of near-term policy objectives, with periods of abeyance when the value of contestation is outweighed by its costs, resulting in a loosening of institutional coupling. Pragmatic, non-constitutional adaptation exposes voters and politicians alike to the contingent character of intergovernmental relations as governments negotiate policy outcomes (Behnke and Benz 2009; Broschek 2015b). The latter part of the twentieth and early period of the twenty-first centuries have introduced new dynamics into this traditional approach. The loosening of institutional coupling between the Upper and Lower Houses of bicameral state and Commonwealth parliaments threatens the power of first ministers in bicameral parliaments to make intergovernmental agreements.[4] At the same time, the introduction of the Goods and Services Tax (GST) in 2000 has politicized formerly bureaucratized federal fiscal relations, encouraging first ministers to compete for funds. They must also manage regionalized intra-party dynamics as states and territories governed by the same party pursue distinct policy directions. This suggests that intergovernmental bargaining is likely to be increasingly uncertain and contested.

Three case studies help us to explore the interaction of parties, intergovernmental relations, and democracy. The first is the introduction of compulsory voting around 1920. The second is the introduction of proportional representation for electing the Senate in 1949. The third is the modification of the electoral and legislative functions of the state Upper Houses in the late twentieth century. Each had both intended and unintended effects on parties, democracy, and the operation of federalism. Together, they highlight some of the distinctive characteristics of federal institutional arrangements in Australia. We use the insights from these case studies to consider the increasingly contentious politics associated with distributing funds generated by the GST, which has become central to fiscal federalism in Australia. Competition over this distribution, combined with the relatively tight institutional coupling of more than two decades of Council of Australian Governments (COAG) negotiations in search of economic reform, now threatens to turn "tensions into frictions because actors are subject to contradictory logics of action when they are compelled to cooperate" (Benz, chap. 3). Openness and uncertainty, along with the unintended consequences of complex institutional relations, are important elements of federalism's contribution to democracy and the character of institutional coupling in Australia.

Federated Political Parties

In creating multiple arenas for party competition and government formation, federalism provides opportunities for variation within and among parties, party systems, and legislatures (Aldrich 1995; Chhibber and Kollman 2004; Riker 1964; Sharman 1990; Thorlakson 2007).[5] Party systems encourage stability by channelling the expression of political demands to and among political elites. They help define which issues are important, the acceptable mechanisms for solving problems, and the issues that are too disruptive to be brought into politics (Filippov, Ordeshook, and Shvetsova 2004, 38–9; Mair 1997, 953). The redundancy offered by the multiple points of access to political power that are embedded in federated parties and party systems is a key source of resilience in federal arrangements, but also unpredictability given that bargains among elites are always imperfect (Landau 1973, 188; Bednar 2009, chap. 7; Schattschneider 1960, 38).

The introduction of compulsory voting in Australia is an example of the unpredictability of institutional reform that flows from such bargaining. While supported and resisted by the left and right at different times, it is now an accepted element of Australian politics and one that the major parties use to enhance their electoral fortunes. It has also encouraged the replication of partisan dynamics across the federation, which, in combination with the power of state branches in the major parties, has embedded a federal dynamic in their integrated structures.

The development of the Australian party systems was heavily shaped by the existence of Labor parties (or their precursors) in the colonies that came together to form the Commonwealth of Australia on 1 January 1901 (Reid and Forrest 1989, 14; Loveday, Martin, and Parker 1977). Colonial labour organizations coordinated the selection of delegates, favouring greater national (Commonwealth) governmental powers, to attend the 1897 pre-federation Constitutional Convention (Crisp 1978). These Labor parties came to anchor the developing state and federal party systems after federation (Strangio 2009). Labor entered national politics with a federated structure that reflected the coordination of the several existing colonial parties.

Although Labor was present in early Commonwealth parliaments, politics was mainly driven by disagreement over federal tariff policy, with the major divisions occurring between protectionists and free-traders (Crisp 1978). The tariff question was largely settled by 1910, and the party system reorganized around competition between Labor and the emergent Liberal Party, which was the result of a merger of protectionists and free-traders (Godbout and Smaz 2016; Strangio 2009). In general, right-wing governments are formed by a coalition of two parties, the Liberals and a smaller party, currently the Nationals, and are referred to as *the coalition*. While ideological and organizational schisms within the major parties occurred throughout the twentieth century, Labor versus a single or coalition of parties on the right remains the most powerful coordinating force in all Australian parliaments (Loveday, Martin, and Parker 1977), an outcome facilitated by the adoption of compulsory voting.

Compulsory Voting

The introduction of compulsory voting in Queensland in 1915 and the Commonwealth in 1924 (eventually followed by all other jurisdictions) was initially favoured by right-wing parties as a means of blunting the perceived organizational superiority of what had become the Australian Labor Party, which was thought to have an unmatched capacity to mobilize its voters (Evans 2006; Hirst 2002). Over time, evidence suggested that working-class voters – Labor supporters – were disproportionately likely to be non-voters, making Labor the major beneficiary of compulsory voting (Mackerras and McAllister 1999; Miller and Dassonneville 2016).[6] After its initial hostility to the regulation, Labor came to embrace it as a means of protecting its vote share and stabilizing its presence in every Australian jurisdiction (Sharman and Sayers 1998). The effects of compulsory voting spread in other unpredictable ways across the federal landscape. Most importantly, the inclusion of more working-class voters and a party of labour in each jurisdiction strengthened the view that class was more important than federalism as an organizing force in Australian politics, and it bent public policy debates in all jurisdictions towards Labor's interventionist approach (Fowler 2013).

The introduction of compulsory voting also had profound effects on party organization. As with the introduction of per-vote public subsidies in the 1980s, compulsory voting strengthened the parties in some ways, but reduced the importance of voter mobilization. Public subsidies protected large, existing parties from smaller, insurgent parties, thereby strengthening their electoral position and encouraging an inward-looking organizational politics. Parties became less focused on mass membership and increasingly professional, offering reliable career paths for some members and running sophisticated election campaigns. Seeking to enhance their influence and careers, members came increasingly to focus on internal party dynamics, such as policymaking and personnel selection rooted in the state-based party organizations. This led to the development of internal party factions, which competed for control of these functions (McAllister 1991; Parkin 1983; Parkin and Warhurst 1983). The contest to control state branches is a central driver of party vigour and a major source of federal dynamics within the major national parties.

State branches control membership, the selection of delegates to policy conventions, candidate selection for state and federal elections, and the prosecution of election campaigns for both the local and the federal branches of their party (Koop and Sharman 2015; Leigh 2000; Victorian Labor 2020). They control access to both state and federal caucuses, which retain a pre-eminent role in the selection and dismissal of party leaders. Those wishing to shape policy debates, candidate selection, or leadership outcomes must understand and be able to influence the state branches to attract enough votes to be successful (Aroney and Sharman 2018). The intense competition for control of the state branches has contributed to the factionalization of parties, particularly the Labor Party, which has formalized factions, further multiplying the routes to power available to political elites (Leigh 2000; McAllister 1991).

The branch structure of parties, and the over-representation of smaller states due to equivalency in the number of senators, entrench state concerns in national party caucuses, thereby strengthening this federalizing effect. Moreover, senators now widely see themselves as democratic equals to their Lower House counterparts and are increasingly powerful actors within party forums (Sharman 1990, 1999). In sum, compulsory voting evidences the capacity for federalism to refract the effects of institutional reform. On the one hand, the reproduction of battle lines and class-based politics across the federation has generated a common set of policy concerns and an apparent reduction of federal diversity. On the other, it and other reforms have created powerful, state-based, highly federalized national party organizations that exhibit distinct dynamics from one jurisdiction to the next (Aroney and Sharman 2018; Smiley 1972).

While party organizations and the competitive dynamics of each of the seven party systems across the country vary, a key role for Labor in each one results in the replication of ideological battle lines (Sharman and Sayers 1998).[7] This provides a series of comparable test beds in which parties face similar policy challenges and institutional arrangements, encouraging experimentation and learning across jurisdictional boundaries. This was evident as Labor pursued reform of the Upper Houses in the seven Australian legislatures, six of which remain bicameral. Each was grounded in idiosyncratic circumstances, resulting in unique outcomes. Yet all resulted in reduced institutional coupling between the Upper and Lower Houses in the local parliament.

Reform of Senate Elections and State Upper Houses

National bicameralism is a corollary of federalism: it provides a chamber that gives the voters or governments in each region a special role in the construction of federal legislation. In Australia, five of six state parliaments also have two chambers, a remnant of colonial arrangements. Like the Senate, the state Upper Houses provide additional access points to the legislative process for under-represented interests, while imposing additional veto points, a situation that complicates governmental agendas (see Stone 2005). The rise of the Labor Party across the first half of the twentieth century produced a confrontation between its preference for majoritarian politics and the consensus-seeking nature of federalism and bicameralism. Yet federal Labor's hostility to federalism waned across the twentieth century, and, by the 1970s, the party was making efforts to accommodate non-majoritarian politics, partly in response to demands from the state parties (Grattan 1973, 399; Parkin and Marshall 1994, 28).

This was also encouraged by the unexpected benefits that Labor received from making a politically expedient modification to the electoral system of the Senate in the 1940s. Kept out of government for twenty-three years until the 1970s, it learned to use the newly legitimized, non-majoritarian Senate to challenge coalition governments (Bach 2003). At the state level, Labor spent much of the latter part of the twentieth century trying to reform the powerful Upper Houses in the five states that retain a second chamber.[8] Labor had been systematically under-represented in these chambers due to skewed electoral systems, so the chambers were dominated by non-Labor parties that could vote to prevent reform (Stone 2002). Once again, Labor had to come to terms with the non-majoritarian effects of bicameralism: democratizing these legislative councils threatened to legitimize their counter-majoritarian character, placing constraints on executive authority.

The Senate was largely excluded from a central role in legislative politics for the first half of the twentieth century. Although a formally powerful chamber, it was held to be functionally subordinate to the House of Representatives. Its electoral system tended to reproduce the result found in the Lower House, giving it a governmental majority. As a result, it usually rubber-stamped legislation coming to it from the House. Marking its subordinate role, parties often rewarded stalwarts who had done good service – rather than exhibiting strong abilities – with a Senate seat (Miragliotta and Sharman 2017). Fearing an electoral rout under the existing rules, the Labor government introduced proportional representation for Senate elections in 1948. While Labor achieved its short-term goal, the new rules also enhanced the democratic legitimacy of the Senate, while making it more difficult for the party or parties forming government in the Lower House to win a majority of seats in the chamber.

This increased legitimacy and increased say for non-governmental parties profoundly altered the functioning of the Senate. It attracted good candidates and began to make use of its substantial powers to reshape the legislative processes of the federal parliament (Bach 2003). Across the 1960s and 1970s, it developed internal mechanisms, such as committees that allowed it to question ministers, and a newfound willingness to reject or amend legislation – including budgets – coming to it from the House of Representatives. Ironically, the balanced partisanship of the Senate and its enhanced role in the parliament that flowed from the 1948 changes were central to the constitutional crisis that saw a Labor government with a majority in the House of Representatives removed from office in 1975. The opposition-controlled Senate used its powers to delay the passage of supply bills (appropriating the money required to keep government functioning) long enough to precipitate a crisis, which ended when the governor general dismissed the Whitlam Labor government. The opposition Liberal Party easily won the subsequent election. The matter remains a source of popular and academic controversy (Kelly and Bramston 2015).

The success of governmental legislative agendas, and even their survivability, now depends on how they manage Senate business, while senators enjoy an enhanced role within the parliament and their parties. Given governments' limited success in winning the Senate, they rely on senior senators – usually members of Cabinet – to negotiate the passage of legislation through the chamber, which often requires compromises with either the other major party or minor parties and independents (Sayers and Banfield 2013). A study in unintended consequences, institutional reform aimed at a short-term concern has restructured the operation of the Commonwealth parliament and political parties. The Senate is among the most powerful upper chambers in the democratic world, and its role in overseeing executive action is a central element of Australian politics (Bach 2003, 111; Lijphart 1999a; Taflaga 2018).

At the state level, Upper Houses were particularly vexing for Labor in that their methods of election favoured conservative parties, and Labor won its first state Upper House majority in Victoria in 1952 (Stone 2002). Since reform often spanned more than one election, this all but guaranteed that non-Labor members would be required to accept any change that abolished or modified their chamber. Towards the end of the twentieth century, Labor governments came to realize that enhancing the democratic credentials of the Upper Houses was one route to reform. It helped them gain public support and was difficult for non-labour parties to oppose (Sayers 1986). The price, however, was the enhancing of the powers of these non-majoritarian chambers, a price Labor paid across five decades and five states from the 1950s on (Stone 2002, 274–8). Labor's democratization of the legislative councils through the introduction of proportional representation has enhanced their legitimacy and, by extension, their capacity to restrain executives formed in the state Lower Houses.

Against its majoritarian instincts, the Labor Party has been central to the strengthening of core non-majoritarian institutions of Australian federalism. While the Senate had long possessed the formal authority to act as a brake on the executive formed in the House, it won that power only after having its authority enhanced by Labor's 1948 electoral reform (Sharman 1990). Labor's pragmatic compromise between its philosophical and political preferences has resulted in a similar outcome in the states. The Upper Houses are more democratically constructed, express greater representative diversity, and enjoy enhanced legitimacy and the power to restrain executives formed in the Lower House (Costar 1992; Costar and Gardiner 2003; Stone 2002, 2005). Some have labelled this strong bicameralism "semi-parliamentary" because they see Upper House oversight of executives formed in the popular Lower House as being at odds with parliamentary government (Ganghof, Eppner, and Pörschke 2018; R. Smith 2018; Taflaga 2018; but see Weale 2018).[9]

Excluding Queensland and the territories, Australian parliaments are now composed of powerful upper chambers elected differently than their Lower House counterparts, resulting in idiosyncratic patterns of partisan competition. Upper Houses are now more directly involved in representation, policy, legislation, and governmental survivability. The non-majoritarian logic of second chambers provides additional access and veto points – thereby opening up, democratizing, but also complicating government. This situation provides ample opportunity for disagreement over legislation both within and across the two Houses and reduces the likelihood that a government formed in the Lower House – and its first minister – can guarantee passage of legislation through both chambers. Legislative success requires negotiation and compromise within at least one House and usually across the bicameral divide. Given the opportunity for disagreement between the Houses, the relative decoupling – or loose coupling – of Australian bicameralism is now an entrenched part of its federal democracy.

Intergovernmental Relations

The growing fiscal power of the Commonwealth across the twentieth century, combined with the continued constitutional authority and administrative capacity of the states, drives intergovernmental negotiations in Australia. Fiscal relations have progressed through four stages since federation, each with distinctive dynamics shaped by the changing character of Australian democracy. The result is a hybrid system that mixes highly bureaucratized institutions, which manage regularized fiscal relations among governments, with more volatile arrangements, which manage political and democratic realities. The two systems interact episodically, forcing patterns of institutional coupling to respond to democratic impulses. In the most recent period, the establishment of COAG and the introduction of the GST, along with reduced governmental control of the legislative dynamics of the state and Commonwealth parliaments, have remade intergovernmental relations and brought greater democracy and unpredictability to these arrangements.

Intergovernmental relations in the period after federation were dominated by Premiers' Conferences as governments negotiated the new Constitution and its emerging democratic traditions. The 1920s saw the beginning of a century of High Court activism that greatly expanded the constitutional reach of the Commonwealth, although not matched by an equal reduction in state powers. It also saw the institutionalization of federal fiscal relations, driven by periodic fiscal crises. The Australian Loan Council (ALC) and the Commonwealth Grants Commission (CGC) were developed to manage financial relations between the Commonwealth and state governments. An example of the confluence of crisis and federal fiscal capacity, the ALC was established with membership from all governments following the First World War to coordinate state and Commonwealth debt servicing and to prevent borrowing rates from being bid up. The CGC was established in May 1933 as a commission separate from government to allow the Commonwealth to use its fiscal powers to assist Western Australia after more than two-thirds of voters in that state had supported secession at a referendum in April of that year (Musgrave 2003; Coleman, Cornish, and Hagger 2006, 152). Its initial aim was to partially equalize the fiscal resources available to the states, although this expanded in the late twentieth century. For much of the twentieth century, the major components of intergovernmental fiscal relations – money market loans by state and federal governments and grants to states from an increasingly wealthy Commonwealth – were governed by the ALC and the arm's-length CGC, which applied ad hoc solutions to the horizontal inequalities highlighted by the first ministers at Premiers' Conferences.

During and following the Second World War, these institutions were variously used to greatly expand the fiscal reach of the Commonwealth, making use of conditional or tied grants to try and shape policy outcomes. By the late 1960s, increased professionalism within the CGC and state treasuries had led to the resolution of the horizontal fiscal imbalances among states that had been identified in the 1920s and 1930s. The 1970s saw the Whitlam Labor government's expansion into higher education and health care and various attempts to skirt state authority in other areas. This was then followed by the unwinding of some of these changes by the Fraser coalition government and a failed attempt to shift more revenue collection to the states. With the CGC's equalization role made all but redundant, the first ministers agreed in 1977 to give it an expanded role in overseeing the growing size and number of federal grants to the states.

COAG, which includes the president of the Australian Local Government Association, became the peak body for intergovernmental discussions in 1992, replacing the Premiers' Conferences. COAG was an outflow of the economic reform agenda of Prime Ministers Hawke and Keating in the 1990s. As Painter (1998, 10) notes, "Hawke's New Federalism was born of pragmatism rather than principle: his political agenda required the states' cooperation." COAG was instrumental in shaping the introduction of the GST in 2000 under Liberal Prime Minister Howard. The states and territories formed the Council for the Australian Federation in 2006 to better coordinate their response to the Commonwealth. COAG incorporated and regularized intergovernmental agreements and subcommittees dealing with fiscal relations, economic reform, pressing policy issues, and the traditional areas of ministerial-level interaction. Its Council on Federal Fiscal Relations oversees the Intergovernmental Agreement on Federal Financial Relations (formed in 2009), which is now the central mechanism for transferring monies through the federation. The COAG Reform Council drove a second wave of economic reform from 2010 to 2014.[10]

The introduction of the GST in 2000 has remade intergovernmental relations. It replaced financial assistance grants and various state taxes with an automatic transfer calculated by the CGC, removing the role of the Commonwealth from determining the level of general revenue grants to the states each year. There is now a central administrative formula for distributing funds that has become a bone of serious political contention. As with all such mechanisms, there are features of the GST redistribution calculation that produce apparently perverse outcomes. For instance, after the collapse of the resource boom in Western Australia in 2014, calculations based on the previous good years resulted in the Commonwealth returning to the state only about thirty cents in every dollar of GST raised there (Maxwell 2018, 166). Liberal and Labor politicians in Western Australia used this to successfully politicize fiscal relations, winning major concessions from the federal government that increased and enhanced the predictability of funding, but further reduced the role of the Commonwealth in determining the general revenue enjoyed by the states (see Commonwealth of Australia 2018). This has only encouraged all first ministers to search for opportunities to claim that their state is unfairly treated by the GST formula, thus exposing the work of the CGC to the forces of popular politics.

These calculations are further complicated by the integrated character of Australian parties, the reproduction of patterns of competition across the federation, and the loosely coupled character of Australian parliaments. The contrast with Canada is instructive. Like Australia, Canada melds federalism with a British parliamentary tradition. Yet, unlike Canadian first ministers, who dominate their legislatures, six of the nine Australian first ministers cannot guarantee the passage of enabling legislation that might flow from intergovernmental agreements (Sayers and Banfield 2013). Instead, they must negotiate it through parliaments with Upper Houses in which they may not hold a majority, requiring them to take account of the concerns of opposition parties and those that support them. In addition, and again unlike Canada, where parties are not usually linked across the federal divide (Thorlakson 2007), the integrated nature of political parties in Australia involves politicians in a web of policy and electoral obligations outside their own jurisdiction. Intergovernmental policy may be assessed, in part, through its effect on the fortunes of partisans or opponents in other jurisdictions, seen clearly in recent efforts to renegotiate the distribution of GST revenues, in which politicians have used the dispute to attack partisan opponents in other jurisdictions (Burrell 2010).

The demands of practical politics also constrain the power of the Commonwealth in other ways. While fiscally powerful, it must bear the cost of imposing taxes, while the states benefit from spending the revenue it transfers to them. Should it challenge a state's spending priorities, the party in power at the federal level and its state partisan colleagues risk an electoral backlash from state voters in both state and national elections. This effect is heightened by the short, three-year federal election cycle, which limits opportunities for the federal government to both audit and control state spending (Sayers and Banfield 2013). While it is able to achieve its reform objectives through pragmatic fiscal policy, the Commonwealth has not pursued extensive constitutional or institutional reform that might reshape the distribution of political authority, thus leaving the constitutional authority of the states largely protected (Phillimore and Harwood 2015). Intergovernmental relations continue to be dominated by relatively short-term, pragmatic policy concerns and episodic engagement (Hollander and Patapan 2007).

Surveys of public opinion as to the preferred distribution of power in the federation suggest that voters are also driven by recent political events. In 1979, when the question was first asked, two-thirds thought that the federal government had enough power and that the balance was about right. In 1997, there was a move to empower the states. By 2008, there had been a significant shift to the Commonwealth, with 40 per cent of respondents suggesting that the states should give more power to the federal level. By 2014, public opinion had swung back to 1997 levels: 54 per cent of people thought that the federal government had enough power (McAllister 2014, 10).

There is a similar view of financial relations between governments. In 1979, 49 per cent of people thought that the Commonwealth should give more money to the states, and, by 2008, that number had dropped to 37 per cent. By 2014, that number had rebounded to almost 1979 levels, with 43 per cent of people saying that the Commonwealth should provide more money to the states. Interestingly, young people "are almost twice as likely to endorse the states against the federal government" compared to the oldest group (McAllister 2014, 11). In a recent comparative survey of four federations, only in Australia were young people clearly more in favour of decentralism than older voters (Deem 2018, 158).

The institutions of intergovernmental relations in Australia reveal the changing democratic conditions within the federation. Across the twentieth century, federal governments were content to mostly manage intergovernmental relations through their strengthened fiscal position rather than through a restructuring of constitutional authority. The development of the ALC after the First World War was an equal partnering between the federal and state governments. Just over a decade later, the CGC revealed the growing sense, captured by Hancock (1931), that the federal government had an instrumental interest in moving controversial matters to quasi-governmental bodies that it controlled and using its fiscal power to direct politics. By the late 1960s, the CGC had all but achieved its objectives, with no claimant states remaining. Its ambit was expanded to cover all federal government grants to the states in the late 1970s as the Commonwealth sought greater input into policy outcomes. The pursuit of economic reforms since the 1990s has required federal governments of both the left and the right to use COAG to negotiate agreements with the states, which retain the lion's share of constitutional and administrative capacity. The episodic and changing character of intergovernmental arrangements is in sharp contrast with other models, such as the German joint-decision system.

The opportunity for first ministers to contest the distribution of GST funds has resulted in greater politicization of intergovernmental relations. Challenging a formula is not the same thing as attacking another government, and it is much easier than if the federal government were formed by the same party as that of the state leader or if the effects of changes had implications for partisans in other jurisdictions. The power relationship – the character of federal coupling – is not as straightforward as it might seem if one considers only the fiscal dominance of the Commonwealth. The way this dominance is now expressed – distributing GST funds through a formula open to modification – has altered these dynamics. It is tempting to conclude that the relative slowdown in COAG interaction reflects the difficulties posed by an institution designed for relatively tight coupling becoming a forum for contestation. Yet this cannot be avoided for long. The ongoing legislative and administrative competence of the state governments requires intergovernmental agreement for any major policy changes. Despite the apparent continuity of COAG, intergovernmental institutional arrangements will continue to be pragmatic, mainly ad hoc responses to the particular constellation of forces at work, at any one time, that have dominated Australian intergovernmental relations for a century (Phillimore and Harwood 2015).

Discussion and Conclusion

Our three case studies go some way to exploring the interaction of partisan politics, parliamentary reform, and federal dynamics. Once initiated, the complexities associated with distributed power tend to refract the effects of reform in unpredictable ways. The result, party federalism, reveals the interaction of a set of repeated patterns of electoral competition across multiple jurisdictions by integrated parties competing across short electoral cycles for control of increasingly independent parliaments. Labor's role in anchoring these party systems and its ideological preference for national programs – in areas as diverse as control of industrial relations to health care – has been critical in driving partisan engagement within the federation. Parties of the right have also favoured centralization when it facilitates major policy objectives and, at times, to forestall Labor's electoral success. This bipartisanship can be seen most clearly in centralizing the responses to major external pressures, such as the First and Second World Wars, and, in particular, changing local and global social and economic conditions towards the end of the twentieth century (Moon and Sayers 1999; Sayers and Moon 2002). This model of Australian federal democracy has generated, over a century of successful policy "throughput," a central requirement for success and legitimacy (Hueglin, chap. 2).

Commonwealth governments have introduced major reforms and policy change using flexible intergovernmental arrangements that leave the expansive constitutional authority of the states largely intact. The character of institutional coupling has produced episodes of innovation and reform, driven by short-term political or policy objects and the politicians involved in the negotiations (Phillimore and Harwood 2015). The pragmatic, episodic nature of major engagements between partisan politics and the federal dynamics helps to explain the continued vitality of federalism in Australia. With perhaps a few minor exceptions, no party has shown much interest in pursuing a formal remaking of the balance of federal powers. Despite the myth of centralization, it is largely limited to fiscal politics, with the states enjoying expansive constitutional power and the core administrative capacity required to implement locally sensible policies consistent with the principle of subsidiarity (Hueglin, chap. 2).

The democratization of the Senate and state Upper Houses over the last seventy years has been largely achieved by Labor governments caught on the horns of a dilemma. They could alter an electoral bias against them to improve their access to power (a short-run issue in the case of the Senate), but, in so doing, empower a chamber that might restrain future Labor governments formed in the Lower House. This nicely captures the complexity of power dispersal in a federation with bicameral legislatures. Reformers must attempt to internalize the logic of divided power in proposing change, yet change generates unintended consequences and new veto points. Some now argue that in forgoing overwhelming powerful Lower Houses, Australian legislatures are semi-parliamentary in form (Ganghof, Eppner, and Pörschke 2018). Limiting executive dominance and invigorating parliaments is consistent with the democratic advantages of neo-republicanism noted by Fossum and Laycock (chap. 4).

The practical advantages of having states deliver goods and services and maintaining infrastructure with federal monies, while short-term policy goals are met through negotiations rather than major institutional reform, has been highly effective in Australia. This can be seen in the episodic creation of intergovernmental mechanisms and agreements across the last century. Federalism and bicameralism continue to offer numerous points of contact, at which politicians and leaders can shape political outcomes. Repeated patterns of partisan competition, short electoral cycles, and organizationally integrated major parties provide governments with many ways of coupling and decoupling institutions in pursuit of policy objectives. The growing power of six Upper Houses, often controlled by non-governmental parties, is likely to add uncertainty to this situation and further suppress the appeal of major constitutional change.

The consensus-building logic of most of its parliaments is now central to Australian politics and intergovernmental relations. Negotiations among first ministers will increasingly reflect the diverse political agendas of divided chambers and growing uncertainty as to whether executives can guarantee the passage of legislation. The intersection of this and the heightened politicization of fiscal relations through a mutable GST formula has set the stage for a new era of intergovernmental relations. Given Australia's history, we are likely to see institutional innovation that takes account of the more contested character of fiscal relations by pursuing institutions that allow looser coupling between the governments of the federation.[11]

NOTES

1 The Queensland Labor Party briefly formed the first elected socialist government in the world in Queensland in 1899.

2 The party system dynamics of Labor versus non-Labor noted in this chapter hold true for all parliaments, including those of the Northern Territory and the Australian Capital Territory. However, the limited constitutional status of the territories – they are formally administrative units of the Commonwealth – limit the applicability of the constitutional dynamics discussed below. As well, unicameral territory legislatures are not subjected to the bicameral politics found in all other parliaments save unicameral Queensland (see note 8 below).

3 National elections are required every three years, although, in practice, they usually occur before this; state elections are generally held every four years, but again, sometimes earlier.

4 This effect is not found in unicameral parliaments such as Queensland and the Territories.

5 Electoral rules set the conditions under which party organizations and system-wide competition develop. Parties in any one system, as well as across jurisdictions, may display distinctive mechanisms for selecting candidates and leaders as well as deciding policy. Internal linkages across jurisdictions, where they exist, can vary in form and intensity. The structure of state and national party systems, both in constituent parties and in their relative levels of support and resulting patterns of governmental formation, may vary.

6 Although not the discussion of mixed results as the effect of compulsory voting in Fowler (2013, 160).

7 We will leave the unicameral territories aside for most of the discussion.

8 Queensland's Legislative Council was abolished through legislation introduced by the Theodore-led Labor government in 1922.

9 The dominance of independents in the Tasmanian Legislative Council has made its development distinctive (see Kellow 2003).

10 These subcommittees are currently called councils and consist of Federal Financial Relations; Disability Reform; Transport and Infrastructure; Energy, Industry and Skills; Attorneys-General; Education; Health; Closing the Gap; and Australian Data and Digital.

11 On 29 May 2020, Prime Minister Scott Morrison announced the dissolution of COAG and its replacement by the National Federation Reform Council (NFRC). The National Cabinet, a meeting of all first ministers, would be formed to deal with the coronavirus crisis of 2020 as the NFRC's central deliberative and decision-making body (see Council of Australian Governments 2020).

10 Belgium: The Democratic State of the Federation

PETRA MEIER AND PETER BURSENS

The question we address in this chapter is how the efforts to translate the initially unitary Belgian state into a federal one is beneficial to democracy. Belgium has been a parliamentary democracy since its inception in 1830, while it has been a federation only since 1993. It is a typical example of a unitary state that has gradually downloaded competences to the substate level, so that it now qualifies as a federation. The basics of the Belgian federal state architecture were set up during the first state reform of 1970. Since that date, six state reforms have taken place. While the first four (1970, 1980, 1988–9, 1993) laid down the foundations of the current federal system, the last two (2001, 2011) fine-tuned that system. In other words, federalism was superimposed on parliamentary democracy and not the other way around. It is this chronology that invites us to examine what the evolution towards a federation has meant for the democratic nature of the Belgian state.

Interestingly, and in contrast to a rich literature (see Hueglin, chap. 2), the impact of federalism on democracy has not been a very salient issue, either for Belgian political actors or for scholars of Belgian federalism. For example, it has never been a direct concern in the setting up of the federal state architecture and the struggle for an increased downloading of competences. Over the last few decades, political scientists, legal scholars, journalists, observers, and even politicians themselves have dealt with the case without paying much attention to the issue of democracy beyond the general understanding that federalism is good for democracy. The rationale underlying the restructuring of the Belgian state has been to appease the divergent aspirations of the two main ethnolinguistic communities (the Flemish and the French). The downloading of competences reflects their diverse interests (Van Dyck 1996) and is an attempt to pacify the (never particularly violent) tensions and antagonisms between the Dutch-speaking and French-speaking elites.

At least initially, there was no shared aim of turning the Belgian unitary state into a fully fledged federation (Deschouwer 2012). Belgian federalism has also not been evaluated extensively in this respect, either by academics or by political elites. Even more fundamentally, "There has never been a clear agreement on what the end point of the reforms should be. Every reform came about in an attempt to keep the system going" (Deschouwer 2006, 903). "There has been no blue print of the current Belgium, and there is no blue print of the future Belgium. ... The Belgian state is unfinished and open ended" (Deschouwer and Reuchamps 2013, 263). Only recently have a few scholars started to reflect upon the democratic nature of the Belgian federation, more particularly in terms of input legitimacy (De Grauwe and Van Parijs 2009, Popelier et al. 2012, 2014; van Haute and Deschouwer 2018) and in terms of social federalism and the organization of the welfare state (De Grauwe and Van Parijs 2011; Popelier and Cantillon 2013). Against this backdrop, it is time to examine the Belgian case of federalism from a more comprehensive, democratic perspective.

Our aim in this chapter is, thus, to look back and reflect upon what democratic benefits the federal system caused the Belgian polity to win and lose. To begin, we define *democracy*, very simply and in accordance with Benz and Sonnicksen's introduction (chap. 1), as government by the people, without it being necessarily directly exercised by the people. In a democracy, the supreme power is vested in the people. Thus, with respect to Benz's articulation of democratic legitimacy in a federation (chap. 3), we consider the representation of both the demos and the *demoï* characterizing Belgian society. Also in accordance with the introduction to this volume, we define a *federal system* as integrating diverse communities of citizens.

In the first section, we describe the foundations of the Belgian political system as a consensus democracy; in the second section, its traits as a federation. In the remainder of the chapter, we discuss what is at stake from the point of view of democracy. In their introduction to this volume, Benz and Sonnicksen emphasize that, for a federal system to be democratic, there needs to be balance. When it comes to democracy, balance concerns the decision-making relations within a level of government, the balance between input and output legitimacy. However, when it comes to federalism, balance concerns the relations between the governments in a federation, whereby one power – that is, the executive – should not be able to take advantage of the other – the legislature – using the organization of interactions between the different state levels of the federation.

To evaluate these instances of balance in the Belgian case, we follow Fossum and Laycock's identification (chap. 4) of a balance within each level of government and a balance across levels of government. To this end, we unpack two focuses of domination, reflecting the prevalence of a federal over a democratic logic in the Belgian federal state architecture and functioning. The first focus analyses the extent to which federalization has contributed to a dominance of executive over legislative power, both within and between governments. The second focus deals with the dominance of the demoï over the demos – that is, examining to what extent the demoï cover all groups of the demos. Both features stem from the transformation of a unitary state into a federation. We will develop these focuses of domination in the third and the fourth sections, respectively. In the conclusion, we wrap up the main findings of the chapter and reflect on what the Belgian case can contribute to the articulation of the tensions between democracy and federalism in general.

Belgium as a Consensus Democracy

Belgium has been a constitutional or parliamentary monarchy, qualified as an archetype of Lijphart's (1999b, 2012) consensus democracy, long before it took its first steps to becoming a federation. It showcases the characteristics that Lijphart attributes to this type of democracy; it actually even fits perfectly into his initial definition of a consociational democracy (Lijphart 1977). Consensus democracies, according to Lijphart, are typical for – or, rather, suit – divided societies. Belgium introduced an extreme form of proportional-list electoral system very early, in 1899, and has applied it across all electoral levels ever since. The initial two-party system – the Liberals (founded in 1846) and the Catholics (founded in 1884) – evolved into an extreme multiparty system, as Sartori (1976) would define it. In addition to the three traditional political families (adding the Socialists to the two mentioned above), green parties, extreme-right parties, and nationalist or regionalist parties came into being, while, more recently, the extreme left has become prominent again. The three traditional parties split into Dutch-speaking and French-speaking components, while the newer ones were set up as separate parties from the beginning. To this should be added the parties in the German-speaking part of Belgium (Delwit, van Haute, and Pilet 2011). Depending on the electoral level, up to twelve parties now compete for votes, especially in the bilingual Brussels Capital Region and its municipalities, resulting in coalition governments of up to seven parties.

The tendency to forge coalition governments has been instrumental in securing cooperation agreements. The prime example is the formation of governments of national unity, triggered by the two world wars (Witte, Craeybeckx, and Meynen 2010). Similarly, early state reforms stimulated the formation of grand coalitions to enable the next steps in the federalization process. First, each state reform required a two-thirds majority in parliament. Second, and, as mentioned earlier, federalization – among other factors – stimulated the fragmentation of the party system. With no really large parties (although there are temporary exceptions, such as the Dutch-speaking regionalist party N-VA among the Dutch-speaking parties over the last decade), governments require an increasing number of coalition partners. Third, in the absence of federal parties, whenever parties of both ethnolinguistic groups are involved, such as at the federal level and in the case of the Brussels Capital Region, leading coalition parties often include their ideological counterpart from the other ethnolinguistic group. Fourth, and for the same reason, parties tend to avoid governing at one electoral level when they are in opposition at another electoral level. All these factors make not only for complex coalition negotiations but also for oversized coalitions.

The Belgian parliament is bicameral, another typical feature of consensus democracies – although, as we will discuss later, the Senate lost much of its power in the latest state reform. Consensus democracies also tend to be characterized by a balance between government and parliament; however, as in most Western democracies, the executive has come to dominate the legislative branch over the last few decades. This process was stimulated not only by the increasing complexity of public policymaking and the capacity of large political Cabinets at the disposal of government ministers but also, as we will discuss later, by the federalization of the Belgian state architecture (Fiers 2006). Important agreements tend to be negotiated among coalition party leaders and their entourage, while coalition agreements, especially those comprising state reforms, are excessively detailed. Combined with the government's majority in parliament and the two-thirds majority needed to pass state reforms, parliament has little room to manoeuvre (Van Aelst and Louwerse 2014, 477). Furthermore, several concertation, conflict-preventing, and conflict-resolving tools have been integrated into the workings of the federal system, and they favour and give the initiative to government rather than parliament. These rules and procedures will be explained in more detail in the next section.

Finally, Belgium shares other features of consensus democracies, such as a neo- corporatist system of social dialogue (granting a major role for employers and trade unions in the formulation and implementation of social and economic policies), a rigid constitution (notwithstanding the six state reforms brought in over the last half-century), a judicial review of constitutionality by an independent court, and, finally, its federal state architecture.

Belgium as a Centrifugal Federation

In the wake of the fourth state reform (1993), Swenden and Jans (2006) characterized Belgium as a federation with a set of distinctive characteristics. They pointed to the double constituent-unit structure and argued that the Belgian federation was an asymmetrical one, supplemented by increasing political asymmetry and incongruence. There is extensive constituent-unit political autonomy but limited fiscal autonomy,[1] and there are largely exclusive, but no coherent, packages of policy competences. All this is embedded in a de facto, bipolar, federal context (Dutch-speaking versus French-speaking) with a centrifugal tendency. Finally, intergovernmental relations are organized along inter-executive and inter-party lines. These features are still present today. We discuss those that are particularly relevant for the purpose of this chapter.

Given its double-constituent-unit structure, Belgium is an atypical federation, the foundations of which were laid during the first state reform in 1970. While not concretely elaborating anything in that respect, that reform stipulated that Belgium would comprise regions and communities (Deschouwer 2012). The Belgian territory is divided into three regions: the Flemish Region, Walloon Region, and Brussels Capital Region, in charge of territory-related policy competences. There are also three communities: the Flemish Community, the Federation Wallonia-Brussels (formerly the French Community), and the German-speaking Community, which represent the three language groups and oversee cultural and "personalized matters." While this is a non-territorial form of federalism, limits are set on the communities' jurisdiction. The institutions of the German-speaking Community maintain jurisdiction over the members of their community living in the Eastern Cantons of the Walloon Region; those of the Federation Wallonia-Brussels deal with the remaining citizens of Wallonia and the French-speaking citizens in the Brussels Capital Region; and those of the Flemish Community deal with citizens in Flanders and the Dutch-speaking citizens of the Brussels Capital Region. Hence, a French-speaking citizen living in Flanders still falls within the jurisdiction of the institutions of the Flemish Community and vice versa.

While one territorial level is officially not prioritized over another, there is, at least on the Dutch-speaking side, a tendency to emphasize the existence of the two (ethnolinguistic) communities (the Dutch-speaking and the French-speaking) – or three, if one includes the German-speaking Community – rather than the territorially organized regions. This dominance of the ethnolinguistic identity is also manifested in the Belgian federal state architecture and in different respects (Celis and Meier 2017, 418). The Flemish Region and Community have merged their institutions under the label Flemish Community. On the French-speaking side, region and community have not merged, but efforts are being made to increase the linkages between the French speakers in the Brussels Capital Region and those in Wallonia, not least by renaming the former French Community the Federation Wallonia-Brussels. Similarly, the German-speaking Community has steadily extended its competences in regional matters. In addition, the federal Senate is a Senate of the communities.

Both at the federal level and in the Brussels Capital Region, the smaller ethnolinguistic group enjoys guaranteed representation, both in parliament and in government (Pilet and Pauwels 2010). Similarly, each ethnolinguistic group has mechanisms to protect against the violation of its interests. We have already mentioned that political parties have been divided along linguistic lines since the 1960s and 1970s. Employer organizations, trade unions, and the rest of civil society also have Dutch-speaking and French-speaking branches. The prevalence of the community logic has led to compromises that benefit the three communities to the detriment of the federal level. Competences that are treated differently by different communities (education, culture) and regions (economy, environment, agriculture) have been devolved to the constituent units (see, e.g., Hooghe [2012] on how the system functioned in the absence of a federal government). At the same time, however, the federal level is in charge of other policies, such as large parts of the budget, infrastructure, and social security, which also greatly affect the communities and regions.

The underlying logic of the federalization of Belgium was never to foster cooperation between the regions and communities or between the constituent units and the federal level. On the contrary, any form of cooperation was generally avoided because downloading was meant to reduce existing conflicts. Competences were downloaded to pacify conflicting interests (Deschouwer 2012), leading to constituting entities that, to a large extent, function independently from one another. Smoothing over the antagonism and tension between the ethnolinguistic groups has resulted in not only an ethno-federal but also a competitive state architecture, with a centrifugal dynamic dismantling the centre (Popelier and Cantillon 2013, 628–30).

One mechanism built into the system that allows for competition is the existence of largely exclusive policy competences. In some cases, downloading competences required cooperation agreements, such as in the case of the regionalization of public transport, and these agreements are also required when it comes to uploading and downloading European Union (EU) policies. But, all in all, cooperation agreements are rather the exception: relied upon when required, but not the rule of spontaneous political cooperation between policy levels.

In the past, the most efficient system for ensuring cooperation was the contact among the party elites, within the political family and beyond. Contacts within the political family were maintained in the first decades after the formerly unitary parties split into linguistic parts, and the generation of politicians who had been socialized in a pre-federal Belgium still served as mediators. Contacts were further sustained by the fact that some traditional sister parties kept their headquarters in the same or adjacent building(s). This asset eroded over time, however, as these headquarters became geographically separate.

This situation became apparent in 2007, when the older generation of politicians was brought in to make the political dialogue work after the impasse of the elections that year; however, they and the new generation of politicians operated in two separate worlds, did not know each other, and, in some cases, had never even spoken to each other. Finally, over the last decade, contacts among party elites beyond the political family have partly eroded. The Dutch-speaking nationalist N-VA, especially, does not respect the logic of fair play that underlies a consensus democracy, an attitude facilitated by the fact that it is the dominant player not only in Flanders but also in Belgium as a whole and that it has no French-speaking sister party.

Nevertheless, some form of cooperation has developed over time. The federal Concertation Committee,[2] set up in the wake of the third state reform in 1998–9 (at the same time as the cooperation agreements), meets once a month. Its aim is to avoid conflicts of competences (such as the ongoing dispute over the noise standards in the Brussels Capital Region in relation to the national airport of Zaventem, just outside the city). It took the Concertation Committee a long time to become effective. This might be explained by a certain coming of age of the constituting entities of the Belgian federation, which are now mature enough to deal with each other. It might also have to do with these entities recognizing the need for some form of cooperation, a need more strongly felt since their privileged ties with their sister party across the language border have eroded. Or it might just be a pragmatic answer to the need to organize some policy competences in a joint effort now that they realize that federalization has gone too far to be effective.

A major illustration of the latter is the mobilization of the Concertation Committee in 2020 to ensure coordinated efforts to fight the coronavirus pandemic.

In addition, while the uploading of competences has been discussed here and there very recently, it has no real support, so cooperation is the only way forward. Also, and, as mentioned earlier, the different jurisdictions are compelled to follow a cooperative form of federalism in regard to EU policies. The EU encourages cooperation – namely, in those matters in which Belgium has only one voice but several governments in charge of a particular policy (Beyers and Bursens 2006, 2013). Agriculture is an example of such a policy area (education is an exception). All such cooperation is at the executive level and thus almost exclusively intergovernmental.

Nonetheless, most mechanisms of cooperation and dialogue focus on solving problems, and especially on protecting minorities, not on (proactive) cooperation. Such rules and procedures regulate conflicts of interest (dealt with by the Concertation Committee) and conflicts of competence (dealt with by the Constitutional Court[3]), and they allow for both the alarm bell procedure[4] (dealt with by the federal government) and – in specific cases – double majorities (requiring not only a two-thirds majority overall but also a simple majority within each language group). Because all these rules and procedures (except for the double-majority requirement) are agreed to by consensus, both language groups have substantial veto powers. While such mechanisms could serve cooperative purposes, they do not. Indeed, and again, the rationale was not to build cooperative institutions, but to appease or solve conflicts.

Federalism and Democracy in Belgium

If we now consider this description of the Belgian state from the perspective set out in the introduction to this volume (chap. 1), we can detect two focuses of domination. The first focus concerns the relation between the executive and the legislative branches of power. The second relates to a negation of the existence of a demos to the advantage of the demoï. We will explain both and what they mean, in terms of the relation between federalism and democracy, in more detail in the following sections.

First Focus of Domination: The (Parties of the) Executive over the Legislative Branch

From the description of Belgium as a consensus democracy and of its main features as a federation emanates a clear domination of executive over legislative power. As stated earlier, this stems partly from the general tendency for – within each governance level separately – the executive to be strong compared to the legislature. In this respect, Belgium is a textbook example of what Fossum and Laycock (chap. 4) identify as the manifestation of executive dominance: a weak and ill-informed parliament and parties that dominate the executive as well as the legislature. However, this domination of the executive has been further strengthened by the way the federal system and its rules and procedures of interaction among the constituting entities have been designed. It involves a domination of the executive both within and between the government levels. In addition, due to the strong position of (the leaders of) the political parties, this executive domination can be more accurately described as domination of the executives' majority parties than as simply a domination of the executive *tout court*.

Unlike many other countries, Belgium has been governed almost exclusively by coalition governments based on agreements that are jealously guarded by all coalition partners. Having respect for a coalition agreement, and the pressure on all sides to do so, stems from a lack of trust among the governing parties – particularly when critical issues are on the agenda. Party support is even more pressing when (at the federal level or the level of the Brussels Capital Region) issues are at stake that concern the language groups and double majorities are required. Coalition governments at both the federal level and that of the constituent units can be stable only if they can rely on the continuous support of the majority parties in the respective parliaments. Hence, in a system of coalition governments, parliamentary discipline is crucial to ensure that enough representatives of all majority parties continuously support government policies.

Furthermore, in Belgium, it is party leadership, not parliamentary group leadership, that controls individual members of parliament (MPs). This means that power is not in the hands of the leading MPs, not even in the hands of the federal or regional executive leaders, but in the hands of the parties and, in particular, of the (majority) party leaders. The latter are different from the parliamentary group leaders. They usually, but not necessarily, hold a seat in one of the legislatures (or even executives), but exercise control over all parliamentary groups of all assemblies. This powerful position of the political parties is not new. At the beginning of the federalization process, and even before, the Belgian system was considered a textbook example of a partitocracy. The federal structure has only strengthened this phenomenon. Not only have parties been able to copy their powers to all the constituent units, the dominance of executives in the system has also given parties a crucial role in intergovernmental relations. The fact that grand agreements (such as state reforms) are negotiated by party leaders and their staff is a prime example of their central position. More systemically, as the existing parties simply split up in the wake of federalization and in the absence of federal parties, party headquarters feel an urgent need to coordinate their members in the parliaments – and eventually governments – of the different levels (De Winter and Dumont 2006; De Winter and Van Wynsberghe 2015; Pilet and Meier 2018). This strengthens the party leaders' position as central brokers in Belgian politics because they are not only pivotal actors but also the best informed. The most open and intense lines of communication across political levels go through them.

Like any other federal system, Belgium has installed some intergovernmental relations between the governmental levels to prevent and overcome the externalities of the individual policies of any one of them. This has become crucial because consecutive state reforms have increasingly created unclear divisions of competences, creating fertile ground for externalities. It is close to impossible for the constituent units to exercise their competences without interfering with those of the federal level (Verrijdt 2014). However, whether informal or formal, Belgian parliaments are rarely involved beyond their own jurisdiction. They are not even constitutionally entitled to set up cooperation agreements. And while the Senate was transformed into a Senate of the communities during the fourth state reform of 1993, a profile refined during the latest state reform in 2011, it was simultaneously stripped of all policymaking and even policy-initiating capacity and saw its level of activity reduced to nine meetings a year.

While in some federal states the Senate has a pacifying role, in Belgium it has never been imbued with the power to act as conciliator or broker of cooperation between the levels of government. Belgian parliaments are not one of the formal tools available to solve or at least mitigate externalities: the Constitutional Court deals with conflicts about competences, and the Concertation Committee and the alarm bell procedure handle conflicts of interest. In addition, it is not the parliaments but the governments that bring cases before the Constitutional Court and negotiate in the Concertation Committee. And while the alarm bell procedure can be triggered by any parliament, it is the governments that deal with whatever problem is on the table. In short, informal relations between levels are close to non-existent, but the formal ones are exclusively in the hands of the executives.

The executive dominance of intergovernmental relations reveals another concern. While regional jurisdictions are accountable for them (through regional elections) and the federal government is partially accountable for them (through the split federal elections; see the next section), no jurisdiction is directly accountable for them. Parliaments are absent from inter-regional relations, even to the extent that they find it hard to control their own executives when they engage in intergovernmental negotiations. They also lack any collective channels of parliamentary scrutiny. Just as the federal and regional parliaments barely cooperate or even inform each other with respect to their mandate for the Belgian negotiators in the Council of Ministers of the EU (Bursens, Maes, and Vileyn 2015), they do not collectively oversee domestic intergovernmental relations.

In short, the domination of executive power over legislative power makes Belgium a clear case of executive federalism, albeit a very politicized type of executive federalism, because majority parties also dominate the administrative areas of the executives. This tendency is strengthened by the way the federation and its rules and procedures were designed. There is a substantial imbalance because one type of actor – the (majority parties of) the executives – profits from the interactions within and across multiple levels of government. The high level of policymaking power and subsequent political autonomy both within and across governmental levels point to the uncoupled nature of the Belgian political system, as Benz and Sonnicksen argue (chap. 13). When the governments of the constituent units aim to enact policies that please the electorate in their respective constituencies exclusively, tensions can arise. The conciliatory mechanisms that are activated to deal with these tensions are dominated by the leadership of the majority parties, and the agreements they reach are maintained by each party through the executives they are part of. The parliaments do not monitor whether the agreements among the executives are upheld.

Second Focus of Domination: Demoï over Demos

The second focus of domination emanates less clearly from the description of the Belgian political system but is even more present: the domination of the demoï over the encompassing demos and the almost utter lack of any formal recognition of the latter in political processes. While establishing federalism aims to protect minority rights, one could pose the question whether, within a federal demos, minorities are overprotected and therefore the majority not well enough respected. The Belgian system has instituted very strong constitutional protections of the French-speaking minority at the federal level and the Dutch-speaking minority in the Brussels Capital Region. But these measures, including language parity in governments, have guaranteed representation of the language groups in the legislatures, and double-majority requirements (Pilet and Pauwels 2010) are arguably disproportionate, thus threatening proportional representation. Sottiaux (2014) argues that protection of minority rights creates a situation in which one of the constituting demoï, reflecting the majority of the population, is unable to influence redistributive and tax policies because it is found mainly at the federal level, where the minority is overprotected.

What is more concerning, however, is the fact that many institutions and mechanisms that have been instituted by federal systems to compensate for the effects of granting autonomy to the constituent units are underdeveloped in the Belgian case. First, with respect to political institutions, the latest constitutional reform has weakened the country's bicameralism, which is one of the crucial channels that the demoï of the respective constituent units have to participate in federal decision-making. The reformed Senate is conceived as a chamber that not only represents the (parliaments of the) constituent units but also grants them participation in federal decision-making. However, as already described, and parallel with this new composition, it has seen its power substantially reduced: its legislating and controlling powers were eliminated in the sixth state reform in 2011 (Deschouwer 2012). The reason for this reform was that some regionalist political actors sought to eliminate the second chamber altogether in an attempt to move to a confederal system, in which the two main communities would govern the country without federal policies needing Senate approval.

However, it is not so much the de facto abolishment of the Senate that is important in the Belgian case as the fact that the House of Representatives is built upon the logic of representing and protecting the demoï rather than the demos. The quasi-abolition, or at least full decommissioning, of the Senate does not affect the demoï because the two main demoï meet in the House of Representatives. This chamber, due to the electoral system and the protection of minority rights, is composed of and run by the constituent entities of the country, which enjoy substantial veto powers. Both the already discussed alarm bell procedure and the double-majority rule apply to the House, and members are elected through monolingual lists composed by parties operating within and in interaction with a single language group. Members are sworn in, in one language.

As a result, the federal demos is not represented anywhere. A similar situation exists in the Brussels Capital Region. While it is officially bilingual, sub-nationalities do not officially exist at the level of the individual citizen, and while voters can decide whether to vote for Flemish or French-speaking parties and candidates in each election, the representatives of the people have what is called a linguistic identity – which is permanent. Like the federal Parliament, the bilingual character of the Brussels Capital Region is not represented at the legislative level.

This absence of any representation of the demos in the Belgian federal system means that the federal and regional governments are not actually accountable to their citizens. In addition, the state reforms have turned politics into a far more complex issue, one that is difficult for the average citizen to understand. For instance, voters do not fully distinguish between the levels of government when voting (Dandoy 2013; Deschouwer et al. 2015; van Haute and Deschouwer 2018). It is challenging for them to cast their ballot for the correct level of parliamentary assembly, making it hard to define the Belgian system as a "substantive democracy" (Schattschneider 1960). Taking a top-down perspective, it is relevant to ask, "Who is accountable to whom?"

While the situation at the level of the constituent units is clear in terms of electoral districts, the federal level suffers from an accountability deficit because there is no federal electoral district, and no federal parties, and because the electoral colleges are organized by language group (Deschouwer and Van Parijs 2007; Lacey 2017; Pilet and Pauwels 2010; Sottiaux 2011). Citizens can hold only part of the federal government accountable: the ministers who belong to the political parties of the language group in the governing majority that the citizens have been able to vote for. From a formal point of view, this means that "there are no federal political elites accountable to the Belgian population" (Deschouwer 2006, 908). But from a political perspective too, the implications are substantial. Political parties campaign exclusively within, and make promises to, their own language group. Because they do not need the citizens of the other language group to vote for them, they have no incentive to defend their interests.

However, to form a federal government, the winning parties of both language groups (most likely those who have excelled at claiming to defend their groups' respective interests) need to compromise. This creates a problem: they cannot fully answer to their voters because the federal majority also needs to answer to the voters of the other electoral district, who may have been promised much different solutions to major policy and institutional issues. Deschouwer and Reuchamps (2013, 264) call this "post-electoral obligation to cooperate without pre-electoral incentives to moderate." The obligation to govern together is difficult because it implies losing face before the electorate.

Another complication is the fact that when voters disagree with federal policies, they can vote out of office only the federal ministers of their own language group. Party families have decreasing contacts across the language barrier, and federal governments are sometimes composed asymmetrically, in part because historically different types of parties dominate in the different language groups (Delwit, van Haute, and Pilet 2011; De Winter, Swyngedouw, and Dumont 2006); thus, there is hardly any way to sanction ministers or parties from the other language group. In fact, the Belgian federation hosts two party systems in one state. This negative effect of the split party system is aggravated by the crucial position of the political parties in the system, as was discussed in the previous section.

The Belgian interest-representation system is also mostly split (Heylen and Willems 2019, 868). The organization of interests follows the allocation of competences so that a large number of interest groups has split or established decentralized branches. The constituent units have largely copied the neo-corporatist style of interest representation in their respective territories, enabling similar access at the lower level as at the higher level. However, advocacy at the federal level is complicated for those groups whose interests run across the linguistic divide. For example, social policies are established federally, while being advocated by decentralized or even split interest groups like trade unions, the LGBTQ community, and the women's movement in its struggle to defend the needs of women living in poverty (Celis and Meier 2017).

While some may wonder to what extent there has ever been a demos in Belgium, the federalization of the Belgian state has institutionalized the demoï within the federal state architecture, turning the country into an ethno-federation in which the demos is constrained by the demoï. The federation is characterized by the strong domination of one actor (the demoï) over the other (the demos) because the system is tailored to recognize the interests and needs of the demoï – mainly two of the three demoï because the German-speaking Community tends to be neglected in the interplay of the demoï at the federal level.

Conclusion: The Democratic State of the Belgian Federation

Although the Belgian federal structure has clear advantages by bringing policies closer to the respective demoï and, thus, addressing their divergent needs, we see several issues that undermine rather than support the democratic nature of the federation. These issues can be summarized as the dominance of executive over legislative power and the dominance of the demoï over the encompassing demos. While the former puts constraints on the quality of democratic government at each level, the latter hinders the interlinkages between the levels and thus the democratic character of intergovernmental relations between them.

Moreover, the combination of the two types of dominance endangers democracy in the Belgian federation.

The common denominator in all this is the organization and strength of the political parties. While they are crucial actors in any type of representative democracy, they can also be detrimental for democracy when they become too powerful. Both the formal organization of the Belgian party system and the de facto position of the parties within and between the levels of government are problematic. Within the federal and constituent-unit levels, parties dominate both the executive and legislative branches. Party leaders negotiate and guard the implementation of government agreements, decide on candidates for elections, and determine the voting behaviour of their MPs. Because only regional parties exist, there is at least congruence between jurisdiction and party organization on the constituent-unit level. However, considering its (redistributing) competences, the legitimacy of the federal level seems to be even more undermined in the absence of federal political parties and the related absence of federal media and public opinion.

The non-existence of truly federal elections and, therefore, the absence of equality in the electoral sense is highly problematic for the legitimacy of the federal government: there is too much emphasis on the representation of the constituent demoï and too little on the representation of the demos. In addition, the dominant role of the political parties vis-à-vis both legislative and executive actors results in domestic intergovernmental negotiations and agreements that are not truly accountable to the people. The constitutionally established legislative federalism points to an absolute separation between the two levels of policymaking. Constituent units enjoy a very high level of autonomy and do not interfere in each other's competences; even foreign policy powers are, according to the principle *in foro interno, in foro externo* (foreign policies are carried out by the government levels that hold the competences internally), allocated to the constituent units. This means that democratic governments at all levels and intergovernmental relations between the levels operate separately. Neither the federal level nor the constituent units show much consideration for any externalities that their respective policies may cause.

Moreover, intergovernmental relations formally involve only executive actors. Again, political parties pop up as crucial actors because they seem to be the only ones that connect the different levels through strong party leadership. However, a closer look at the party system shows it to be even more uncoupled because neither federal parties nor a federal electoral district exists. Parties (and party leaders) may be the only substantial link between the levels, but since the parties are separate, this is only a very weak and partial link, one that functions mainly to their advantage – and eventually to that of the language group they belong to. The only situation in which party leaders are strongly connected (or tightly coupled) is when state reform is being negotiated, and this occurs in overly politicized, joint decision-making settings. As the editors of this volume rightly point out (chaps. 1, 13), such a tight coupling risks creating severe tensions because party leaders need to reach an agreement based on completely different ideas and electoral interests.

The tension between federalism and democracy is not a salient issue for most Belgian political elites. As we have argued, the constitutional reforms that have turned Belgium into a federal state were not triggered by the ambition to make the system more democratic. The dominant rationale was to address conflicts among the language groups, with the objective of preserving the Belgian state. This logic explains why the reforms not only decentralized competences but also instituted several tools to manage conflicts that could arise from decentralization. We have discussed the double majority necessary for constitutional changes; the Constitutional Court, which rules in cases of conflict over competences; and the Concertation Committee and alarm bell procedure, which deal with conflicts of interest. In addition, conflicts over constitutional change itself are resolved within the national government by a small number of elites. Except for the judicial treatment of conflicts over competences, the political treatment of all types of conflict is firmly in the hands of the parties and, above all, the party leadership. This is not a very uplifting analysis because the feature that has been identified as aggravating the democratic failure is the same feature that is supposed to fix it – political parties – a fact that is crucial to understanding Belgian politics.

On a larger scale, Sottiaux (2011) offers a bold solution for enhancing democracy in Belgium: either restore the federal political space or decentralize it even further. Comparisons between the EU and Belgium, treating both as instances of federal polities, come to a similar conclusion (Sinardet and Bursens 2014; Rummens and Sottiaux 2014). Restoring the federal political space implies turning back many of the measures that were brought in by consecutive state reforms, such as upgrading the legislative and control functions of the Senate, introducing a federal electoral district, and ensuring parliamentary scrutiny of intergovernmental relations. However, all this assumes the presence of federal political parties, a federal public sphere, and mutual trust among the language communities. One may, understandably, have serious doubts about these preconditions and, therefore, about the feasibility of this option.

The latter solution would mean further decentralizing the political architecture in the direction of a confederation. All collective Belgian policies would then take the form of intergovernmental agreements among the constituent units, placing the locus of democracy squarely within the constituent units. Obviously, evaluating the democratic character of such a confederation would need quite different benchmarks than the ones used in this article. However, like the first solution, the confederal scenario is not very likely to happen because it would mean breaking up the Belgian state into two independent states. And neither the "re-federalization" nor the "confederalization" scenario enjoys sufficient support among the political parties. Thus, some institutional re-engineering of the current arrangement is the only feasible way to reconcile democracy and federalism in Belgium. The diagnosis presented in this chapter may help identify at least some partial remedies.

NOTES

1 While communities still do not have fiscal autonomy, and will not because Belgium does not recognize sub-identities, the fiscal autonomy of the regions increased tremendously with the sixth state reform of 2011 (Decoster and Sas 2012).

2 Composed of the prime minister, the minister-presidents of all the constituent-unit governments (it includes the minister-president of the government of the German-speaking Community only when the issue concerns that community), five ministers from the federal government, and one minister each from the Flemish government and the government of the Brussels Capital Region, but from the other language group than that of the minister-president.

3 Also composed of an equal number of Dutch-speaking and French-speaking judges, half of them former politicians.

4 This procedure allows three-quarters of the members of a language group of the House of Representatives (and of the Parliament of the Brussels Capital Region) to introduce a motion whenever they think that their interests are not being taken into account.

11 Democracy and Federalism in Spain: Interactions, Tensions, and Compatibilities

CÉSAR COLINO

Introduction: Debates on Democracy and Federalism in Spain

In Spain's current federal system, the principles of liberal, representative democracy, or parliamentarianism, and those of autonomy, or decentralization, have historically been conceived as positive and mutually reinforcing elements: to exist, they need each other (Juliá 2019, 306–9). Thus, relations between democracy and federalism have rarely been problematized. They have been considered, mostly from a normative point of view, to be two compatible principles. However, less attention has been paid in political or academic discourse to a number of possible interactions or even tensions, usually discussed in other, similar federal countries, between these two principles, regimes, or arenas of the political system. Moreover, until very recently, the Spanish system was regarded as having worked reasonably well in these two arenas, and a predominantly positive vision has prevailed concerning the relations of both principles as well as the quality of democracy in Spain.

Recently, however, a growing debate has emerged on the quality of Spanish democracy, and the negative or positive consequences of the Spanish model of federalism for the workings and quality of democracy have featured prominently (see Colino 2014). For most observers – even if they are aware of some of the problems with the distribution of powers and the design of the Senate (Arroyo Gil 2018) – Spain's territorial institutions have paved the way for a growing balance of power between governments, such as through the vertical and horizontal division of powers (Tudela 2016; Castellà 2018). They have also enabled a high degree of integration: many parties and groups participate in their regional executives, influence public policy at both levels of government, and act as a check on other governments – for example, through multi-level coalition politics (Alonso 2011). This would have occurred even without significant problems of governance, as attested by Spain's so-called economic miracle, the development of an advanced welfare state, and the overall high rating that democracy in Spain has achieved on all the usual comparative indicators of democratic quality.

Recent developments in parliamentary politics, particularly since 2015, clearly related to the political and electoral consequences of the financial crisis, have led minority central governments to encounter unprecedented difficulties in forming government and winning approval for their budgets or other necessary reforms of the economy or education. This is reflected not least in four national elections between 2015 and 2019. Recent years have also seen a deadlock in constitutional and financial reforms to the territorial model, thereby impeding, for example, any solution to, or even negotiation of, the demands that have led to a serious constitutional crisis in Catalonia or to deficits of fiscal federalism and shared-rule institutions. This has intensified political and academic debate in the wake of the fortieth anniversary of the Spanish Constitution. We have thus witnessed numerous discussions about Spanish democracy and its alleged manifold economic, political, territorial, and institutional crises (Bosco 2018). Among them is what is considered the most serious conflict of the Spanish territorial model thus far: the secessionist crisis in Catalonia and its relationship with the alleged crisis of Spanish democracy.

At this critical national juncture, and with some exceptions (see Blanco Valdés 2018), mostly pessimistic assessments abound. Pundits and academics rush to criticize the parliamentary or representative sphere of Spanish democracy and the quality of its institutions and its leadership, generally blaming the Transition of the 1970s. They see in it the origin of most of the problems of excessive executive and partisan dominance, of both the administration and the judiciary (Colomer 2010; Jiménez Asensio 2016); the inability to deal with political inclusion, multinationalism, and diversity (Requejo 2010; Fishman 2019); and even the current tendency towards democratic deconsolidation and stalemate (Colomer 2018a; Olmeda 2019). Some have criticized what they see as the damaging consequences of the peculiar territorial institutions and workings of Spanish democracy, regarded as a democratic anomaly, mainly due to the role of regional nationalism and its influence on its central representative institutions (Martínez-Tapia 2016; Blanco Valdés 2018; Arias Maldonado 2019).

Others have criticized how parliamentary democracy has evolved, how its adversarial nature, among other things, has played a role in Spain's failure to achieve the original goals of the territorial system and led to the current impasse and conflict situation (Vallès 2016). Still others have emphasized the problems in both the parliamentary arena (its majoritarianism, minority governments, and polarization) and the territorial one (its allegedly absent multi-level cooperation and regional participation) as being key historical deficiencies of Spanish democracy. Thus, they denounce it for not resembling other democracies more closely, such as Germany, with its consensual governments and cooperative federalism (Colomer 2018b; see also Kropp, chap. 7), arguing that this fateful and historical failure explains the current crisis of Spanish democracy and its inability to reform itself.

Looking at the trajectory of Spanish democracy over the last forty years, there is some truth to these criticisms; however, it seems clear that most are overly pessimistic or simply exaggerated, responding to a hypercritical and derogatory mood that is characteristic of Spanish intellectuals during major national crises. Some of these assessments are merely normatively oriented, making reference to unsubstantiated standards abroad. Others lean towards some sort of Spanish exceptionalism, idealize or ignore other federal democracies, or simply fail to explain why Spanish democracy has been able to reach, in practice, a relatively high degree of success after forty years. With the same legacy, institutions, and actors that are now projected in the past as the roots of the disaster, Spanish democracy showed, until recently, a high degree of legitimacy, stability, and relatively good performance of governance (Blanco Valdés 2018). In other words, most of the above-mentioned accounts lack analytical consistency and tend to ignore similar crises or stalemates in other countries; they are unable to put Spain's performance in comparative perspective or to acknowledge some of its recent intergovernmental successes, such as an impressive fiscal consolidation process and economic recovery (Colino and Hombrado 2014). They seem unable to understand how Spain has been able to adapt and cope reasonably well, until very recently, with the tensions that are typical of parliamentary federations with a complex and diverse social make-up.

More balanced and comparatively oriented accounts are therefore needed (see Molina 2020). The current "perfect storm" cannot be completely explained by the same factors that used to account for Spain's democratic achievements, such as its consensual Transition, its integrative and flexible territorial model, and its solid and stable parliamentary system. To account for its recent malfunction and the governance and legitimacy problems that the Spanish democracy is currently experiencing, we need to better understand not just the new context and exogenous changes but also how the two policymaking arenas constituting the Spanish democracy – the parliamentary and the intergovernmental – have empirically interacted and what tensions they have been subject to until now. We need to look at the role of its institutions, and its relations with civil society and the strategies of political actors, to explain why some of the traditional tensions of the system have become frictions and conflicts, which have led to decisional deadlock in some areas.

With few exceptions – some having to do with relations between parliamentary representation and party systems and the intergovernmental arena in Spain (see Grau Creus 2000; Pallarés, Astudillo, and Verge 2015; León 2017; Gray 2020) – there have not been many attempts to problematize and empirically study the interactions, both tensions and compatibilities, of the two arenas of political decision-making. Nor do we know much about how exogenous changes in both the regional and the national party systems (e.g., the unfreezing of the Catalan party system) or the economy and public opinion have changed the interaction between the two decisional arenas. The questions to address in this chapter, then, even if only in an exploratory fashion, are, How has the interrelation between the two principles and arenas of parliamentary democracy and intergovernmental relations and their logics evolved in Spain, and why? What are the implications for the functioning, efficiency, stability, legitimacy, and quality of democracy and balance of power in Spain? In other words, how has it worked in terms of integration and governance, or input and output democracy, and why?

Using the analytical framework put forward by Benz and Sonnicksen (chap. 1; see also Benz, chap. 3) and elsewhere (Benz and Sonnicksen 2017), I seek to show how the majoritarian, executive-dominated, and polarized parliamentary arena has been mostly loosely coupled with a largely cooperative and vertically oriented but flexible intergovernmental arena and how, despite tensions that have intensified during times of majority government, the system has coped with them through several informal mechanisms, such as integrated parties, shifting of arenas, and other mechanisms of multi-level political exchange. These institutions and mechanisms avoided, until most recently, decisional deadlock and disintegrative tendencies. Periods of absolute majority in the central parliament created tensions by decoupling the two arenas and creating politicization, conflict, and deadlock in intergovernmental relations. Periods of minority governments in the central parliament, combined with the influence of regional parties as pivotal actors, produced their own tensions, which were circumvented through informal mechanisms that made a looser coupling of both arenas possible. Recently, the increasing polarization and fragmentation of parliament, the loss of the multi-level coalition potential of some regional parties, the competitive or even defiant strategies of some regional leaders and parties, and the ensuing judicialization of conflicts have led to deadlocks and a crisis of legitimacy at the centre.

The chapter proceeds as follows: In the next section, it briefly addresses the historical origins of the current system, looking at the parallel processes of democratization and federalization and their effects on the current functioning of Spanish democracy. It then reviews the main institutional characteristics and the empirical logics of both parliamentary democracy and intergovernmental relations in the Spanish case. It goes on to apply this analytical framework to explain the mutual relations, tensions, and compatibilities of both arenas as well as the changing degree of coupling and its determinants. It concludes with some comments on the implications of this for the quality of democracy in Spain.

The Legacy of the Parallel Process of Democratization and Federalization on the Workings of Democracy

When searching for the near-antecedents of the current Spanish federal democracy, we should look at the Second Republic of the 1930s, a unicameral parliamentary system with an advanced democratic constitution in terms of citizens' rights. It allowed the system to be decentralized and the new urban middle classes and workers to be integrated into it. As in other periods, and as a reaction to the centralism and authoritarianism of previous regimes, democracy at that time was identified with territorial autonomy and cultural recognition, and the forces that sustained the republic came mainly from the left but also from substate nationalist movements and small, centre-republican parties (Townson 2001). The republic was, in fact, a shaky liberal democracy supported by a weak social foundation. The fragmentation and polarization of its party system, and its enemies on the left and the right, made it vulnerable to another military intervention (Álvarez Tardío 2005). The coup in 1936 provoked a civil war, which was the prelude to the Second World War in the rest of Europe and eventually large parts of the world, and it extinguished liberal democracy during the long dictatorship of Francisco Franco, which lasted from 1939 to 1976 (see Colino and del Pino 2010).

The transition to democracy in 1977 and its consolidation in the early 1980s required the action of elites and civil society combined with a skilful leadership to forge a process of "crystallization" of institutions and new patterns of behaviour, which had originated during the economic and cultural modernization phase of the 1960s. It also meant the conscious willingness to avoid the mistakes considered to have led to the demise of democracy and to civil war during the Second Republic and the willingness of all leaders and parties to act consensually in favour of democracy (Günther, Montero, and Botella 2004; Encarnación 2004). The design of new institutions, together with the moderation and demobilization of the social movements and the support of parties on the left and right as well as regional nationalists, was a necessary condition for the successful negotiation and accommodation among the elites of a new constitution, which "refounded" Spanish democracy and the Spanish state (Powell 2001; Tusell 2007; Radcliff 2017; Moreno, Colino, and Hombrado 2019).

The new 1978 Spanish Constitution embraced democracy, rule of law, cultural pluralism, and the welfare state as its main values (Ferreres 2013). Its founders intended it to promote political stability and prevent conflict and polarization. Issues on which complete agreement could not be reached, such as the territorial model, were dealt with through ambiguous formulas, to be resolved when democracy had been fully consolidated. Nevertheless, the Constitution restructured the traditional Spanish state by identifying democracy with regional and local autonomy, thus forming the basis of new, constitutionally protected, local self-government and regional democracies. By recognizing nationalities and regions throughout the Spanish territory, it responded to old aspirations of autonomy, not just in those territories with nationalist movements but in all of them.

At the same time, the process followed the old, familiar Spanish pattern of constitutional pacts with local territorial elites. For example, a new pact was made with the nationalist elites of the Basque Country, which recognized certain pre-constitutional, historical rights and granted special fiscal powers to their region in return for their acceptance of the Constitution and relinquishment of political violence. It was the first Constitution to gain substantial popular support and legitimacy and the only one to allow a true, liberal democracy to flourish in Spain (Colino and del Pino 2011; Colino and Kölling 2020).

Regarding the parliamentary arena, given the Transition's consensus-building requirements and the historical experience of instability and political violence during and after the Second Republic, the founders agreed during the constituent legislature in 1977–8 on a sort of rationalized parliamentarianism, a model that was less interested in controlling the government or empowering citizens than in guaranteeing the stability of the executives and strengthening the new, emerging parties by fusing their powers in the majority group in parliament. It also chose to reinforce party groups as opposed to individual members of parliament (MPs). In addition, despite the first drafts of the Constitution, which intended to create a more perfect bicameralism, the final text gave the Congress of Deputies pre-eminence over the Senate in the legislative process (Castellà 2006, 2008). In practice, the most important powers of the Spanish parliament are over the budget and scrutiny of government policies. And, as in other parliamentary or Westminster systems, a clear dominance of the executive over parliament to carry out the legislative agenda emerged, regardless of the number of seats won by the majority party in parliament.

At the same time, decisions made during the Transition about the institutional design of the electoral system and party funding regulations were intent on reinforcing the political parties (Colomer 2010, 2018a). The electoral system, predetermined by the 1977 electoral law before the Constitution was written, and mostly adopted by the constitutional rules, is theoretically proportional. It has had clear, majoritarian effects due to the small size of most constituencies – half of which work like a purely majoritarian system – and has favoured a largely bipolar and highly stable party system. This has reduced competition and partisan fragmentation and favoured the right-leaning parties of central Spain. And, until very recently, it has impeded the rise of other statewide parties that could act as coalition partners in any minority government in the central parliament.

In the intergovernmental arena, several historical precedents and several decisions made during the Transition also explain a number of the current features of Spanish democracy. The Constitution did not completely regulate the decentralization, or federalization, process. Devolution was inspired by the principle of choice or voluntariness, inherited from the republican decentralization experience in the 1930s. This meant that the initiative to accede to devolution was left to the very territorial entities that would benefit from it, and it had to be negotiated with the central parliament. The Constitution offered several routes to regional autonomy that the regions could pursue. It allowed them to draft their own statutes of autonomy, the main aspects of which were their policy responsibilities and internal organization. These statutes had to be drafted within the framework of certain exclusive central powers and had to respect the basic constitutional principles of unity, equality, and solidarity.

At this time, several critical events occurred that shaped the path of institutional reform in the following years. For example, the pre-autonomy regimes for thirteen regions were approved in 1977, before the Constitution was finalized, and, in 1980, Andalusia signalled its willingness to fast-track decentralization, alongside so-called Nationalities. This event determined the evolution and current form of the political system by mobilizing the territorial elites, and it was the impetus for the multilateral decentralization, the resymmetrization of the originally asymmetrical allocation of competences in favour of autonomous communities (ACs) with Nationalities, and the evolution of a more cooperative and vertical federal system (Novo Arbona and Pérez Castaños 2018).

This method of federalizing the system, by disaggregation or asymmetrical devolution, using bilateral commissions to negotiate the transfer of powers from the central government to each of the subunits, is one of the main determinants of the workings of current intergovernmental institutional arrangements. But it created weak institutional mechanisms with which the constituent units could control the power of the centre since the centre controlled the decentralization process, its sequence, and its contents, and it determined the pace and scope of the transfer of its own power. At the same time, as in other, similar cases, this devolutionary form of federalization created a structure with a pre-eminent first chamber, which represents all citizens, and a second chamber, which represents the territories but has rather weak territorial representation and power.

In addition, this devolution produced a largely functional distribution of competences, whereby the central level predominantly enacts legislation or tries to share this power and the units are in charge of executing it. The originally asymmetrical development of the Spanish model also accounts for the excessive importance of national framework legislation, the survival of bilateral mechanisms of intergovernmental relations, and the underdevelopment of horizontal coordination mechanisms among the ACs, which, having different powers and interests from the beginning, had little incentive to coordinate. All these factors account for the traditional focus of the Spanish model on self-rule rather than shared-rule mechanisms and for the type of horizontal relations among the constituent governments, which have remained relatively underdeveloped (Colino 2020).

The Logics of Parliamentary Democracy in Spain

We could say that Spanish democracy shows, at least in its formal arrangements, predominantly majoritarian features in Lijphart's (2012) famous executive-parties dimension. In this dimension, all features are clearly majoritarian except the interest-group system, which shows punctuated periods of corporatist concertation during the transition years and later. If we look at its other characteristics, Spanish democracy shows a clear concentration of executive power in single-party majority

Cabinets. Even in the case of a minority government, the most frequent situation in the Spanish parliament, central governments have both political and constitutional resources at their disposal, which enable them to govern as if they had a majority (Ajenjo and Molina 2009). The executive, particularly the prime minister, shows a clear dominance in the three dimensions of executive dominance analysed by Fossum and Laycock (see chap. 4). It is dominant in its horizontal relationships with the legislature, in the vertical system of intergovernmental relations, and, informally at least, in constitution-making or change. This has produced comparatively stable governments and a loss of influence of parliament. Several factors account for this dominance: the discretion of the prime minister to appoint members of Cabinet, a process that is not accountable to parliament; the rules governing parliamentary groups, which promote strict party discipline; and the constructive vote of no confidence, adopted from the German Constitution, which requires an absolute majority and the simultaneous vote for a new prime minister. In other words, before ousting a prime minister, both the governing party and all opposition groups have to agree to support an alternative candidate (van Biezen and Hopkin 2005; Field and Hamann 2008a; Colomer 2010). This happened only once, in 2018.

Several institutional arrangements and procedural rules, such as party regulations and the electoral system, have systematically favoured a two-party system with clear pluralities or majorities and highly disciplined parties in parliament. At the same time, the national parliament has always featured a number of non-statewide party groups (nationalists and regionalists) sitting in both Houses. Moreover, in its forty years of operation and thirteen parliamentary terms, the Spanish parliament experienced no coalition government until January 2020, when the Spanish Socialist Workers' Party (PSOE) and Unidas Podemos agreed to form a minority coalition. Single-party executives, often supported by informal parliamentary coalitions with non-statewide parties, have displayed important degrees of authority to set and pursue their political and policy agendas.

The Cortes Generales is the legislature of Spain, established by the 1978 Constitution. It is a bicameral parliament consisting of the Congress of Deputies (350 MPs), regarded as the lower chamber, and the Senate, considered the Upper House. The procedural regulation of the organization of the Congress (committees, initiatives, debates) promotes disciplined parliamentary groups to the detriment of individual MPs (see Field and Gray 2019). Opposition groups do not have a great deal of influence on policy due to the sustained fragmentation of the Lower House and to a substantial need for coordination among ideologically quite different party groups. Nevertheless, in some cases, and in some policy areas, a large amount of legislation is passed through consensus and cooperation between the government and the opposition, while, in many other instances, consensus and cooperation are achieved with the minority regionalist or nationalist groups (Field 2014, 2015; Palau and Muñoz 2018).

This Spanish form of majoritarianism is occasionally tempered by several informal practices. These are the informal parliamentary coalitions with small or non-statewide parties, certain conventions that favour territorial minorities in the business of parliament, and partisan proportionality in the election or appointment of members of constitutional bodies, such as the traditional nomination by parliament of some judges of the Constitutional Court or some members of the Judiciary Board sympathetic or ideologically close to Catalan or Basque nationalists. All groups in parliament tend to collaborate to pass legislation on basic institutional rules, although not so much on sector-specific policies (Günther, Montero, and Botella 2004; Field and Hamann 2008b; Chaqués Bonafont, Palau, and Baumgartner 2015).

In Congress, statewide parties have, on only five occasions, won less than 90 per cent of the popular vote in elections (1989, 2011, 2015, 2016, and 2019) and more than that in five elections (1986, 1993, 1996, 2000, and 2004), 92 per cent in two elections (1977 and 1979) and 93 per cent in the other two (1982 and 2008) (Blanco Valdés 2014). This clear hegemony of the statewide parties, which the electoral system amplifies by converting it into parliamentary seats in the Lower House, has occurred in parallel with two phenomena that have strengthened the weight of substate nationalist options in the Spanish political system. The first is that, since 1977, there has been a strong territorial concentration of the regional nationalist vote, which has enabled two nationalist parties – the Catalan Convergence and Union (CiU) and the Basque Nationalist Party (PNV), along with the Canarian Coalition – to serve as potential coalition partners with the statewide parties when they are in a minority position and to affect, despite their small share of seats in the central parliament, the normal functioning of the parliamentary system and the institutional and territorial policies of the central government (Tudela 2016).

The second phenomenon occurred during the periods 1979–2003 and 2004–11 in Catalonia and 1979–2009 in the Basque Country, when these nationalist allies of the central government ruling party were also ruling parties in their respective territories. This increased the pressure for decentralization. In the current central parliament, elected in December 2019, fragmentation increased, with six statewide parties and eleven non-statewide parties winning seats. The latter represent altogether 11 per cent of the national vote.

Article 69 of the 1978 Spanish Constitution establishes a mixed composition in the Senate, characterized by two types of senator: those who are elected in their constituency by direct, universal suffrage through a majoritarian formula (three out of four senators) and those who are regionally appointed (one out of four). The latter are appointed by the ACs, usually nominated by their regional parliaments through procedures regulated by their statutes of autonomy (on the Senate, see Castellá 2006; Vírgala 2013; López-Basaguren 2018). Apart from its constitutional role as a co-legislative power and its prerogative over scrutiny and control, the Senate's formal powers include some that are equal to those of the Lower House on selected regional issues, on which it may deliver its opinion before the other House does. These issues are the authorization of cooperation agreements among the ACs, the regulation of the Interterritorial Compensation Fund, the assessment of the need to issue harmonizing laws, and the eventual implementation of measures to force regional governments to comply with their constitutional obligations. This is the now famous Article 155, used for the first time in 2017 to apply direct rule in Catalonia. Since then, the use of this article has been upheld by the Constitutional Court; thus, it remains to be seen whether it can acquire new meaning and represent a practical increase in the powers of the Senate.

The Senate also intervenes in the reform of the regional statutes of autonomy and hosts a debate (in theory every year, but, in reality, only in 1994, 1997, and 2005) on the state of the State of Autonomies, in which all the regional presidents take part and symbolically use their co-official languages. Lately, the Senate has also hosted the meetings of the Conference of Presidents. In practice, the Senate has little legislative influence since it has only suspensive veto power. From 2004 to 2011, the party composition of the Upper House differed from that in the Congress of Deputies, and the opposition parties (e.g., People's Party and Catalan nationalists) allied against the PSOE government, repeatedly vetoing legislation passed by the lower chamber. In fact, the Senate vetoed and returned the national budget bill to the Congress in 2004, 2007, and 2008. Even in these cases, the Congress has been able to override the veto, negotiating a majority vote.

As a result, in most cases, the role of representing regional interests in national legislation and policies has been taken on by the parliamentary groups of nationalist or regionalist parties in the Congress, through their control and legislative initiatives, and their weight as necessary voting partners for the government group (Castellà 2008; Grau Creus

2010). Another consequence is that statewide parties have adapted to decentralization and their electoral competition with regional parties. They have changed their organizations accordingly, with their regional branches gaining more influence within the party organizations and leadership (Rodríguez, Harguindéguy, and Sánchez 2019). Regional party groups have also gained clear influence in the main statewide parties' parliamentary groups (Sáenz 2012).

Regarding parliamentary democracy at the regional level, most governments have developed into presidential systems in practice, although almost a third of them have operated as coalition governments (Garmendia 2019). Regional presidents have achieved a heightened relevance and have usually acted as "regional barons" of statewide parties. They are the main representatives of their territories' interests in Madrid, especially when their party is not in office in the central government, and have increased their influence within their national party organizations (Barrio, Colomé, and Garcia 2018).

Until 2015, before Podemos and Ciudadanos arrived on the political scene, statewide third parties at the national level were virtually absent. Now, with the emergence of Podemos, Ciudadanos, and Vox as well as a spin-off of Podemos, Más País, four new parties have entered parliament (Rama 2016; González 2017; Blanco Valdés 2017; Bosco 2018). Furthermore, despite the consensus-seeking behaviour and moderation of elites typical of the first years of the Transition, party politics and competition since the mid-1990s have been moving towards the adversarial politics and polarization between the two main statewide parties that are typical of other majoritarian democracies. The polarization of the media, the conscious negativism of campaign strategies, and the personalization of politics have reinforced this trend.

This polarized and adversarial climate was introduced in the mid-2000s mainly by the parties of the right, when they were in opposition, out of electoral and/or ideological interests (see Colino and Cotarelo 2012; Bosco 2018). It has coincided with the polarization and party politicization of several institutional policies or issues, especially territorial reforms, regional language policies, devolution, and anti-terrorist policies (which were once typically bipartisan matters). They have been used to attack the government, and any pact the government has made with regional nationalist parties, depicted as a betrayal of the country (see Chaqués Bonafont, Palau, and Baumgartner 2015). This divisive climate around the issue of further devolution or the establishment of new, shared-rule institutions has in the last few years blocked any attempt at constitutional reform (e.g., of the Senate) with the required two-thirds majority of the Spanish legislature or of the territorial funding system (Vallès 2016; Harguindéguy, Coller, and Cole 2017).

The further fragmentation of the parliament and the conversion to secessionism of the mainstream nationalist parties in Catalonia that are represented in the Spanish legislature has worsened the situation by impeding the creation of majorities, not just to adopt reforms but even to approve a viable budget in the last two parliamentary sessions. In 2018, however, regional, including secessionist, parties were instrumental in winning a motion of no confidence against the conservative Partido Popular government, bringing the PSOE to power and intensifying polarization and accusations of betrayal by the now-right opposition parties. New elections had to be called after both the opposition parties on the right and the regional Catalan parties refused to support the socialist budget. After two repeated elections in April and November 2019, the new government, an unprecedented minority coalition of PSOE and Podemos, seems bound to be dependent again on the support of non-statewide parties.

Intergovernmental "Logics" in Spanish Democracy

When we come to the federal-unitary dimension, in Lijphart's terms (2012), we find that Spain has more similarities with consensual democracies: features of federal and decentralized government; a rigid Constitution, which can be changed only by supermajorities and two consecutive legislatures; strong, judicial review of constitutionality by the courts and the Constitutional Court; and an independent central bank typical of the consensus model. Spain's second chamber, the Senate, which, although clearly not powerful, exercises some scrutiny and control. Due to the necessary ambiguity of the constitutional pact, the territorial model has displayed a high degree of flexibility and openness.

Gradually, through several developments in its regional constitutions or charters (the statutes of autonomy) and the increasing homogenization of regional institutions and legal interpretation of the territorial system, the Spanish model has developed from a regionalized into a federalized system. The guarantee of autonomy for ACs in the Constitution, like that of other federal systems, has gradually become a basic principle of the Spanish state, implemented through constitutional safeguards reflected in mechanisms of constitutional rigidity and through the protection of the Constitutional Court. Spain also has a constitutionally entrenched division of powers, the main tenets of which are outlined in the Constitution and whose details were developed in the regional statutes of autonomy.

Neither the regions' autonomy nor the division of powers may be rescinded or withdrawn unilaterally by the central parliament. The statutes of autonomy are quasi-constitutional and have equal constitutional status. Although ACs do not have a direct role in constitutional reform, their parliaments play a role, along with the Spanish parliament, in amending their regional charters, and in some of them, their population has to approve these changes in a referendum. In addition, ACs can participate in the reform of the Constitution through the Senate, whose assent is required to approve any constitutional reform, in that a tenth of the senators (half the senators appointed by the regional parliaments) may put any constitutional reform that they deem to go against regional autonomy to a national referendum (Aja and Colino 2014; Colino and Hombrado 2017).

As mentioned, the Senate has failed to act as a territorial chamber, one that represents the interests of the ACs in national policymaking. Rather, this role has been mostly assumed by the Congress of Deputies, the lower chamber, where the parliamentary groups of nationalist or regionalist parties have defended, through their scrutiny and legislative initiatives, the interest of their (or all) ACs in national legislation (Grau Creus 2010). The relationship between governments, and the participation of the regional level at the centre, has evolved into a less formalized model than the German collaboration model. It is more like the Canadian model, although with less control than the provincial legislatures, and is characterized by a medium level of articulation and institutionalization (see León and Ferrín Pereira 2011; Colino 2013; Sáenz 2013). Some ministerial conferences (approximately twenty have been effective) and other second-level, intergovernmental commissions or working groups of high-ranking officials (about one thousand) have evolved as the machinery of intergovernmental decision-making in Spain (see Aja and Colino 2014).

Bilateral, vertical relations between the ACs and the central government are carried out at the level of executives, and they have been increasingly formalized in the statutes of autonomy and national administrative regulations. The bilateral cooperation commissions bring together the central and each of the regional governments individually. They emerged naturally, as a continuation of the bilateral commissions established for the devolution of services, to address the problems that appeared to the new regional administrations and the conflicts between the central government and some ACs. Although many intergovernmental cooperation or coordination bodies are regulated, and despite the Conference of Presidents, a rather hierarchical approach to cooperation has prevailed. With some exceptions, such as long-term care, rural development, and the fiscal cooperation bodies, there has been no predominance of compulsory joint decision-making, as in Germany; most intergovernmental bodies are merely consultative. Their agreements are voluntary, based on unanimity rules, and binding only on those subscribing to them.

As has been pointed out, Spanish intergovernmental institutions, combined with the mostly majoritarian and single-party parliamentary conditions at both levels of government, have promoted self-rule to the detriment of shared rule (Blanco Valdés 2014). A decisive factor in the evolution of intergovernmental relations arrangements may have been the initial willingness of the ACs to assert themselves rather than establish cooperation mechanisms. For some time, they failed to perceive the usefulness of cooperating with each other, concentrating instead on negotiating and cooperating with the central government – if possible, bilaterally – an approach that gave them more visible benefits (García Morales 2013).

The increasing federalization and the deepening of self-government implied by the homogenization of competences and resources led to the need for more shared government through new multilateral bodies, in both the national and the European arenas. This was one of the drivers of the reform of the regional statutes of autonomy in the 2000s, which sought to establish new mechanisms for regions to participate in central decisions (Elías Méndez 2009). Given the lack of incentives at the beginning and the absence of horizontal forums to discuss them, the ACs only slowly realized the benefits of horizontal cooperation, a realization that was sometimes forced on them by the demands of their citizens.

In the 2000s, horizontal mechanisms of collaboration began to develop, but they were interrupted by the economic crisis and the change in most regional governments to conservative parties and the conservative nationalists in Catalonia (Colino 2010; Matia Portilla 2011; Tajadura Tejada 2013). Some reforms were also introduced, with mixed results, that allowed the ACs to select, through the Senate, some of the justices of the Constitutional Court (Sánchez Barrilao 2009). This process demonstrates how different parties, leaders, or prime ministers espouse different attitudes towards intergovernmental collaboration. Socialist governments at the central level seem to be more favourable to promoting intergovernmental collaboration and shared-rule institutions, especially if they are in a minority position in the central parliament.

The interlocked and ambiguous distribution of responsibilities in the Constitution has generated a high degree of jurisdictional conflict between the levels of government. This has been largely the result of prior rulings by the Constitutional Court and lack of party congruence at the two levels of government, especially in Catalonia, which accounts for a third of all conflicts that are brought before the court (Rodríguez, Harguindéguy, and Sánchez 2019). The court has been criticized recently for allowing too many central cross-cutting competences to revert to the central state that had been designed in the Constitution to be regional. The role of the court when adjudicating political conflicts about the model of decentralization and the possibility of integrating some of the demands of recognition and further devolution has also been highly influential, such as its 2010 ruling on the 2006 Regional Statute of Catalonia and several judgments on the secessionist bid by the Catalan parliament and executive.

Regarding the results or capacity of the intergovernmental system, over the years the Spanish federal system has developed the capacity to coordinate and collaborate between governments through the evolution of the aforementioned network of intergovernmental bodies. Here the central government has sought to promote joint decision-making and coordination in those areas where the ACs have concurrent jurisdiction, such as industry, telecommunications, energy or technology policy, and international trade. Contrary to other cooperative systems, and because of Spain's unique mixture of institutional arrangements and division of powers, decision-making has not been plagued by pathologies more typical of joint decision-making arrangements, such as decisions being blocked in the second chamber or by veto actors in intergovernmental bodies. The country has achieved some success in coordinating national plans and strategies for climate change, stability and fiscal consolidation, modernization policies, high-speed public transportation, the organ transplant system, and the promotion of Spanish companies abroad. In other policies, however, problems and failures have been identified, including in transportation planning, infrastructure planning (Romero and Farinós 2006), and long-term care, where cooperative relations and intergovernmental bodies have been politicized or deactivated by the conservative central government during the recent economic crisis (Baron 2017).

In recent times, for instance, vertical intergovernmental relations and implementation of central public policies have been increasingly politicized by the main opposition party, which has used intergovernmental bodies and regional governments to block or impede the implementation of some central or shared policies for ideological or simply electoral reasons. This occurred during the 2000s, for example, with long-term care programs, anti-tobacco laws, the introduction of civic education in schools, and some centralized regulations on abortion. During the recent secessionist crisis, regions governed by the main opposition party, such as Andalucía and the Basque Country, or by nationalist parties, such as Catalonia, were also acting against the central government in intergovernmental bodies, such as those coordinating fiscal consolidation efforts.

Finally, most attempts at institutional reform or adaptation of intergovernmental arrangements have occurred without constitutional reform, mainly through reforms of the regional statutes of autonomy traditionally agreed upon at the national level by the two main statewide parties. More recent reforms have been occasionally demanded or initiated by regional nationalist parties or by regionalist parties and the branches of statewide parties in other regions. The Catalan and other regional parties used the last round of reforms in the mid-2000s as an alternative to constitutional reform, and they pursued a bottom-up reinterpretation of the Constitution to achieve more accommodation and resources. This reinterpretation, agreed to by most national and Catalan parties in the national parliament, was rejected by the Constitutional Court.

Regarding the reform of the funding system, clear coalitions of regional governments seem to stand in the way of more than just gradual change, without producing clear losers. Currently, as a result of the recent secessionist bid by the Catalan government, negotiations on any territorial reform have come to an impasse, and the traditional parameters of intergovernmental constitutional negotiations in the Spanish model seem to be blocked or have altered. This has complicated the usual accommodating strategies and instruments of intergovernmental actors and the necessary mutual trust (authority or policy concessions, fiscal appeasement, or further devolution, which seem to be no longer effective) (Colino 2020).

Linkages and Tensions or Frictions between the Parliamentary and Intergovernmental Arenas

Let us turn to mutual effects and coupling between the principles and logics of parliamentary democracy and federalism in Spain. Given the institutions typical of a parliamentary system, as described, as well as the integrated parties and the party systems that give an important role to the regional parties in the central parliament, we would expect a considerable degree of coupling between the two arenas. This degree of coupling does not need to be permanent, but seems to be contingent on other circumstances, and its different implications vary over time and create various tensions or frictions, depending on several processes and the strategies of the actors involved. In other words, the two principles seem to affect each other negatively, through an excessive coupling, but only in specific circumstances of polarization and partisan constellation at the central and regional levels.

The minority situation of the central government and the partisan congruence between the levels of government affect the degree of coupling and mutual influence between the two principles and, therefore, the outcomes of increased input or output democracy in the system. Some tensions are also contingent on the constellation of the parliamentary majority or the congruence of parties between the levels. For example, experience since the 1990s has shown that majority governments on the right with strong congruence on both levels is the constellation most prone to provoke many of these tensions – such as certain centralizing tendencies, for ideological or adaptive reasons such as an economic crisis, that have brought about counter-tendencies and demands in several ACs for more autonomy and institutional reforms. Somewhat paradoxically, minority governments and lack of party congruence at both levels promote collaboration and centripetal tendencies, not only because of the need for multi-level party agreements and reduced polarization but also because of increased accommodation of regional demands. This constellation tends to promote improved input democracy.

Some coping mechanisms have been used as a typical escape from tensions. Examples are negotiations within multi-level coalitions, negotiations within parties, shifting problematic decisions to the administrative level of the intergovernmental system (León 2017), or simply the judicialization of conflicts in the intergovernmental and parliamentary arenas (Harguindéguy, Sola, and Cruz 2018). Until recently, these mechanisms had avoided deadlock.

Since the recent economic and secessionist crises, there has been an upheaval in the party system, and it has brought about several clear changes in the relationship between federalism and democracy in Spain (Bosco 2018). As mentioned above, for the first time, new, small statewide parties are gaining a meaningful role in the central parliament. However, at the same time, both democracy and federalism could be said to be in bad shape (executive dominance, loss of influence and fragmentation of parliament, the judicialization of politics, stagnating intergovernmental cooperation, and the secession crisis). Institutional design, such as government formation rules and the rigidity of constitutional amendment requirements, is not the only factor to blame for the lack of functional adjustment or the inability to deal with new demands. Also responsible for the current situation are external social and economic crises, which may lead some citizens to vote differently or seek alternative political methods, resulting in delegitimation and tensions. For example, the recent fiscal crisis, the increasing interregional, distributive conflicts, and the radicalization of competing party elites at the regional or national level have exacerbated political tensions and reduced legitimacy and citizens' trust.

By exacerbating existing political tensions and redistributive conflicts, a constitutional crisis and a public questioning of the Spanish decentralization system have emerged. For example, one could argue that the economic crisis, the reduction of regional governments' policy discretion and political autonomy, and a competition for sovereigntist votes are among the main drivers of the increasing separatist sentiment and grievances within the Catalan population as well as the recent conversion of the ruling mainstream nationalist party in Catalonia to secessionism.

The way in which the intergovernmental arena has evolved in Spain has had various effects on the parliamentary arena, which have sometimes benefited output democracy. For some observers, this tighter coupling produces tensions: for example, the relevance of substate nationalist parties, along with the electoral system and the openness of power distribution, have combined to prevent statewide parties from playing any pivotal role in cases of minority governments. This has given the regional nationalist parties the capacity to exchange policies or governability for power and resources with central governments, thereby distorting representation in parliament (Blanco Valdés 2014). Three nationalist parties (CiU, PNV, and the Canarian Coalition) have long dominated the governments of their respective regions, and they have been able to disproportionately affect the normal functioning of the parliamentary system in Spain and everyday politics. In other cases, the existence of these different parties and multidimensional competition may complicate decision-making and agreement, even government formation, but may, at the same time, facilitate governability and coordination when the goals of different statewide and regional parties are compatible. This may also help foster diversity and reduce intergovernmental conflict, thereby promoting support, legitimacy, and innovative policy or institutional solutions.

For example, Field (2016) has shown how it is precisely because of the existence of these different parties and multidimensional competition, with their different goals and logics, and the compatibility between the goals of the statewide and regional parties, that a comparatively high degree of governability and governing capacity has been possible in Spain despite minority governments. She shows that relations between the governing party in the central parliament and the substate nationalist parties during periods of national minority governments is quite cooperative, though with some variation. For example, cooperation between the Catalan nationalist party, CiU and the statewide governing parties declined in the 2000s, while cooperation between the Basque PNV and the governing party remained relatively constant.

Field also presents evidence that majority governments in the central parliament make cooperative relations less likely. At the same time, decentralizing stances in the nationalist parties' manifestos do not explain patterns of party competition since substate nationalist parties can espouse a more significant redefinition of centre-periphery relations, while engaging in cooperative-alliance behaviour in the central parliament. Their behaviour is associated, in part, with opportunities to influence policy and with inter-party competition in their respective regions (Field 2015). Having coalition governments in the regions, likely to be more frequent in the near future, also creates multi-level links of mutual dependence, thereby offering new incentives to strengthen the relationship between the parties. This situation tends to occur when a statewide party is part of a regional coalition and at the same time has formed a minority government at the central level and needs parliamentary support (León 2017).

On the other hand, regarding the effect of parliamentary politics on the intergovernmental arena, other authors have described the main tension as being between the parliamentary dynamics of majoritarianism and polarization and the need for cooperation in the intergovernmental arena. Adversarial politics and polarization in the parliamentary arena, together with the use by the right-wing parties of territorial issues as issues of party-political and electoral contention against the other parties, have prevented the necessary cooperation and impeded or blocked highly needed reforms in constitutional areas (Vallès 2016). This politicization has also contaminated or blocked other sectoral bodies from intergovernmental cooperation.

Still other authors believe that the majoritarian culture and stance of governments at both levels impede agreements and give leaders incentives for competition rather than intergovernmental collaboration; this attitude has impeded, for instance, any resolution of the Catalan secessionist conflict (Colomer 2017; Mueller 2018). In the last year, some of the traditional, substate nationalist parties have lost (sometimes voluntarily) their role as possible coalition partners; this has impeded the potentially benign influence of federalism on parliamentary democracy and may reinforce majoritarianism in the next few years.

Now that the new minority coalition government of the PSOE and Podemos has come to power, party congruence is high, and the coupling of the parliamentary and intergovernmental arenas has been tightened through the parliamentary support of the regional parties and the enhanced significance of territorial issues as bargaining chips for the minority parties. Thus, it remains to be seen how the relation between federalism and democracy will play out in the next few years and how the actors cope with the tensions and frictions that are expected to arise.

Conclusion

In Spain, the two principles of democracy and federalism appear to be coupled and have a clear mutual influence. This has had some positive impact on the quality and the input and output legitimacy of Spanish democracy. Intergovernmental logics seem to have promoted, at times, more consensualism in central decision-making. The presence and strong influence of substate nationalist and/or regionalist parties in the lower chamber have positively affected the functioning of parliament, albeit sometimes distorting the equality of representation. But the intergovernmental workings of the *Estado autonómico* (State of Autonomies) may temper the tendency to majoritarianism and lack of accountability, thereby forcing informal coalitions, cooperation, and participation and improving control of the executive by parliament and its responsiveness to territorial demands. At the same time, federalism has changed the structure of the main national parties, through internal federalization and by giving regional organizations and leaders a role in national decisions, while potentially eroding party discipline. Deputies are increasingly faithful to their regional party branches along with their parliamentary group.

The logic of Spanish parliamentarianism seems to have affected, at times tempering and at times aggravating, the more centrifugal and competitive tendencies of Spanish federalism. In times of tighter coupling of the two principles, it has promoted coping mechanisms such as greater negotiation and joint decision-making. It has helped integrate substate nationalist actors into central decisions and promoted recognition, coordination, and shared rule, but it has also promoted centralization and hierarchical solutions, or unilateralism.

12 Democracy and Federalism in India: Mutually Reinforcing?

WILFRIED SWENDEN AND KATHARINE ADENEY

Understanding the Indian Demos and Its Implications for Federalism and Democracy

India is a fascinating test case for exploring the complex relationship between federalism and democracy. There are important sociological and historical factors that pushed it into embracing a multilayered state format. Given its immense size and demography as well as the extent of its religious, linguistic, and territorial diversity, it would be difficult to imagine India being governed democratically in a unitary way. Its history also prepared it for a federal structure of government post-independence. The state that India inherited and created after Partition and independence was "put together" (Stepan, Linz, and Yadav 2011, 120–3) by merging seventeen provinces with more than 550 princely states (representing about 28 per cent of its population but 48 per cent of its territory). Unlike the manner in which it governed the provinces, the British exercised only indirect rule over the princely states (which were headed by princely rulers). The colonizers also left India with the Government of India Act (1935), which served as its (and Pakistan's) interim Constitution until a new Constitution was promulgated in January 1950. In it, the provinces were given a limited degree of self-rule based on provincial assemblies, which were elected on a limited franchise. (Around 12 per cent of the adult Indian population could vote in the provincial elections of 1937 and 1946.)

Respect for autonomy for the erstwhile provinces, cemented by regional elections, secured their continuation as important institutions (now referred to as *states*) in the Constitution. However, the princely states ceased to exist and were – sometimes forcefully – incorporated into the Indian state, often by merging them with the erstwhile provinces. India, within its current territorial boundaries, was a new state, one that had not existed as a self-governing entity before. Therefore, the birth of India was accompanied by a process of state- and nation building. There were strong undercurrents that, at the time of independence, at least, pushed the Indian state to construct a partially *integrationist* notion of the demos, or nation, rather than an *accommodationist* one that fully reflected all the territorial, linguistic, and religious diversity of the newly born state.

First, out of the long struggle against British colonialism emerged a broad-based, grass-roots liberation-movement-turned-party, the Indian National Congress, which was already well established across most of what became India's post-independent territory (Adeney and Wyatt 2004, 9–11; Tudor 2013, 100–24). This movement demonstrated its widespread support in the provincial elections of 1937 and 1946. In the 1937 elections, at least, it also amassed a good deal of support among the Muslim community, capturing most seats in the North-West Frontier Province, a Muslim-majority state, and twenty-six out of the fifty-eight seats reserved for Muslims overall (Bates 2007, 150). Congress projected itself as a religiously inclusive party, aimed at giving voice to all Indians (a promise that it did not always keep once it came to govern most of the Indian Hindu-majority provinces after the 1937 elections).

Prominent leaders such as Jawaharlal Nehru supported the formation of India as a union state – that is, a territorially diverse state, but with the most important legislative and fiscal powers residing at the centre and with emergency powers enabling the centre to suspend state autonomy (Adeney 2007, 115–17). Furthermore, there were strong currents within the Congress Party, especially pushed by Mahatma Gandhi, to promote Hindustani (the common, spoken form of Hindi and Urdu) as the national language of India, in spite of the party's decision in 1920 to redraw the boundaries of its subnational branches along vernacular lines – that is, to make them congruent with areas in which regional languages were spoken.

The accommodation of territorial, linguistic, and religious diversity to which Congress had – often reluctantly – agreed in the build-up to independence came under pressure as a result of Partition, the second and more intense undercurrent pushing India towards integration. British India was divided on the basis of religion. Partition in 1947 into India and Pakistan was accompanied by severe communal violence, led to the displacement of the millions of people who had ended up at the "wrong side" of the border, and caused at least one million deaths. Two of India's most significant provinces, Punjab and Bengal, were also partitioned in the process (Talbot and Singh 2009, 7–8). Partition pushed the minds of more of India's Constituent Assembly members in an integrationist direction.

In territorial terms, India opted for a centralized union strong enough to ward off secessionist threats. The Constitution retained a number of emergency provisions from the Government of India Act – most notably, the ability to suspend the autonomy of states (so-called President's Rule – see further below) and the right of the national parliament to legislate in state competences when deemed "in the national interest." Further centralizing features related to the right of the Indian state alone to determine citizenship, the inclusion of a long list of competences in which the centre holds exclusive or concurrent powers (in the case of the latter, central paramountcy), and the attribution of a large set of fiscal powers to the centre, making the states reliant on central grants and allocations for part of their income.

In terms of linguistic accommodation, India sought to push through Hindi as the national language, and it initially refused to redraw the boundaries of its provinces with non-Hindi-speaking majorities along linguistic lines (although it did allow the provinces to choose the language in which they operated). As we will show, democratic pressures from below enabled linguistic federalism to be implemented and English to be retained as an associate official language alongside Hindi as an official (not national) language. Yet, while the Indian state sanctioned multilingualism shortly after independence, it has found it much harder to accommodate religious diversity.

With the size of the Muslim minority reduced to around 10 per cent of the population at the time of independence and the subcontinent divided along religious lines, Congress elites argued that India should adopt secularism and a composite understanding of the demos, perhaps best expressed through the notion of "unity in diversity" (Adeney 2007, 92; Stuligross and Varshney 2002, 432–7; Swenden 2018, 109–12). Although reserved seats for Muslims in parliament were controversially abolished, the state lent equal support to all religious communities (e.g., in education) and allowed Christians and Muslims to practise their own personal laws on issues such as marriage, divorce, and inheritance. However, although the Constituent Assembly of India was almost entirely made up of politicians belonging to the Congress Party, a significant minority propagated the alternative view that while Muslims could retain the right to practise their religion, they should no longer be entitled to their own personal laws (Austin 1966; Bajpai 2011, 47–63). P.S. Deshmuk, a senior Congress delegate, even suggested an ethnonational understanding of citizenship tied to religious (Hindu-Sikh) belonging (Shani 2010, 154). In this view, the truncated Indian state and identity should be built around the notion of Hindu majoritarianism, which had been a significant force in civil society since the late nineteenth century.

Thus, the compromises that were reached on the relationship between state and religion were unsettled. Congress, which constituted a vast majority in the Constituent Assembly, did not seek to impose a uniform civil code governing the personal law of all religious communities, but inserted it into the Constitution as a principle of intent (or so-called directive – i.e., non-justiciable – principle) (Lerner 2011, 136). The compromises reached in the Constituent Assembly have been challenged over time, most notably by the Hindu nationalist Bharatiya Janata Party (BJP), which is in government at the national level at the time of writing.

The variable understandings of the demos across time, party, and territory have affected the operation of Indian federalism and its relationship with democracy in several ways. The subsequent three sections seek to make sense of this relationship. The first sets out in more detail the multilayered but centralized structure of the state. This centralized structure implies that Indian federalism does not suffer from certain costs, which some theorists of democracy have frequently levelled against federal systems (e.g., Hueglin, chap. 2) – most notably, the inability to project the "will of the people" (majority rule), the risk of judicial overreach. Conversely, the ease with which parliamentary majorities can assert their hierarchical power (as during the single-party Congress and BJP majorities in the past and present) and undermine the autonomy of the states is a threat not just to Indian federalism but also to the characterization of India as a *liberal* democracy. This is especially so at the time of writing (November 2020) because the centre is controlled by a polity-wide party that seeks to turn India into a Hindu Rashtra (or Hindu nation).

Second, we demonstrate that, in this centralized, federal structure, the parties and the party system have played a significant role in coupling the federal and democratic attributes of India's political system and making its multi-level democracy *more or less* federal and linguistically inclusive (Benz and Sonnicksen 2017). Within Indian parties, power is typically concentrated. The powerful leaders of parties in office tend to reside in the executive. Thus, it follows that centre-state relations in India are also, first and foremost, inter-executive relations. This opens up federalism in India to a critique of executive dominance, as Fossum and Laycock assert (chap. 4). However, given that such dominance is established across levels, it is difficult to hold federalism responsible for this. Rather, we attribute a larger share of the blame to the strict party discipline that parties have imposed on their legislative representatives, facilitated by provisions such as the "anti-defection law," according to which a federal member of parliament or member of a state legislative assembly cannot normally defy (abstain or vote against) the party whip without losing her seat in the legislature concerned.

In the third and final section, we show that a partially integrationist understanding of the nation is not the same as a multicultural or accommodationist one, which takes territorial and non-territorial group differences as the basis for territorial or cultural autonomy and asymmetry. India's partially integrationist identity has found it difficult to accommodate (territorial and non-territorial) demands based on minority religions (Adeney 2007, 120). In this regard, even the integrationist vision of the demos by the Congress Party (in contrast to the majoritarian view of the BJP) has often promoted the disproportionate use of central force against groups that have been perceived to threaten India's territorial integrity. Therefore, the centre has been less willing to accommodate the demands of those states with a non-Hindu majority.

This is illustrated by its delay in conceding demands for the creation of a Punjabi-speaking state (which would have created a Sikh-majority state) or its decision in August 2019 to demote (and bifurcate) India's only Muslim-majority state, Jammu and Kashmir, into two union territories, an administrative level below a state that is administered directly from the centre. In addition, although no government willingly allows the dissolution of its territory, as Steven Wilkinson (2002, 23) has argued, "The Indian state exercise(s) more caution in repressing identities that it feels are mainstream," such as Hindu, than those that are not. This has undermined democracy in several peripheral regions. Despite this approach, a multilayered Indian identity coexists with, and has been promoted by, the federal structures that have been developed.

The Origins and Features of a Centralized Federation

The Constituent Assembly adopted a multilayered democracy, which, for the reasons outlined above, it referred to as a union, not a federation. Furthermore, the need to develop India's economy added to its centralization. India inherited a largely agricultural economy, with limited industrialization, low life expectancy, low economic growth, and extreme rates of poverty. To develop the country, Congress adopted an ambitious development agenda in the form of a state-led, or planned, economy. A para-constitutional (statutory) Planning Commission subsumed under the Prime Minister's Office (PMO) was tasked with overseeing the central and state spending specified in five-year economic plans (and annual state plans). The Planning Commission also had to consent to state expenditure on infrastructure or development, even in areas of exclusive state competence. The centralized steering of the economy was in line with the leading ideology among developing countries of the time. In some sense, it emulated the five-year planning cycles of the then Soviet economy, although India's economy was more mixed than its Soviet counterpart and played out against the backdrop of recurrent democratic elections at the level of the centre and the states.

India also inherited a parliamentary system of government, elected by a majoritarian, simple-plurality electoral system. This majoritarian electoral system is likely to generate single-party government and, therefore, wholesale government alternation. Indeed, India experienced single-party Congress majority governments at the centre until 1989 (with a brief exception between 1977 and 1980), even though the party's vote share never exceeded 48 per cent (its historic high in 1984). Although India had minority and/or coalition governments most of the time between 1989 and 2014, single-party control of the centre has returned, with the election of a BJP-majority government in 2014, albeit with the support of seat-sharing arrangements with party-political allies. Combined with a parliamentary system that concentrates power within the parliamentary executive and a centralized federal constitution, the recurrence of single-party dominance at the central level has amplified the centralized tendencies in India's democracy (see third section below).

Even so, there are a number of ways in which the Indian Constitution envisaged an important role for the states. The states are relatively well protected through a number of constitutional or "federal" safeguards, which cannot easily be lifted without constitutional amendment. First, as in other *functional* federations such as Germany or even Switzerland, while most legislative powers (exclusive, concurrent, and residual) reside in the centre, the states hold important competences in a number of areas. In India, these relate to land, water, power, agriculture, health, policing, and education. The centre may not be entirely absent from these fields (especially if, as in the case of education, a power is constitutionally listed as concurrent), but it often relies on the states to implement its legislation. Consequently, the states vastly outspend the centre in social services (education, health, family welfare, and other welfare schemes), agriculture, power, irrigation and flood control, and even transport and communications (Rao 2007, 159).

Second, although the founders placed most fiscal powers with the centre, they left decisions about the base rate and collection of most indirect taxes with the states. Hence, the states acquired control over sales tax, state excise duties, tax on land and agricultural income, stamp duties, and registration fees. Yet, with the exception of sales tax, these state taxes generated relatively small revenues. In contrast, the centre was given control over most direct taxation (personal and corporate income tax) as well as customs taxes, union excise duty, and taxes on services. Although these central taxes generate around 60 per cent of all tax revenue, the founders subsumed most of them into the "divisible pool of revenue" – that is, these taxes had to be *shared* among the centre and the states. Neither the central Ministry of Finance nor the central and state finance ministers were put in charge of this distribution. Instead, that task was delegated to a Finance Commission, a constitutionally listed expert body whose members are appointed for a five-year, non-renewable term by the president of India. The Finance Commission (unlike its Australian counterpart) decides not only on how interstate (horizontal) shared tax revenue is distributed but also on how shared tax revenue needs to be carved up between the centre and the states.

Third, although India is seen to be a union, unlike the union of Great Britain and Northern Ireland it has a supreme Constitution, most provisions of which (except for the list of directive principles, as set out above) are subject to judicial review by the Supreme Court.

In sum, one could argue that the important role that the states acquired in the *delivery* of key social services as well as law and order have turned them into important players within India's multi-level system. That importance is also recognized by citizens, who in time not only have turned out in higher numbers in state than in general elections but also express a strong attachment to their state. A survey carried out by the Centre for the Study of Developing Societies in 2004 found that 53 per cent of respondents were in full agreement with the statement, "We should be loyal to our region (state) first and then to the country" and that only 15 per cent fully disagreed[1] (CSDS Data Unit 2004).

However, at the same time, this feeling of state loyalty coincides with a strong sense of "pride in being Indian." Overall, 89 per cent of respondents to a national survey on the state of democracy expressed being very proud (60 per cent) or proud (29 per cent) to be Indian, whereas only 3 per cent of respondents claimed to be not proud (2 per cent) or not proud at all (1 per cent) (Lokniti Programme for Comparative Democracy 2008, 258). There are small differences among the regions of India, but the overall pattern is the same. Indian identity is thus multi-layered: most Indians hold strong attachments to both the state in which they reside *and* the wider country to which they belong. The federal structure and its linguistic accommodation have promoted these dual loyalties well, even if there is, as Wilkinson (2015, 440), has pointed out, a misunderstanding about which level of government is responsible for delivering which services.

Centre-State Coordination and the Shadow of Hierarchy

As in many other parliamentary federations (e.g., Canada), the mechanisms of intra-state federalism (the explicit incorporation of regional interests into political institutions at the centre) are poorly developed in India. Intergovernmental relations take place across several forums, but either they are weakly institutionalized (Bolleyer 2009, 1–28) or they contain an inbuilt centralist bias. In this sense, intergovernmental relations operate mostly under the shadow of hierarchy.

Intergovernmental relations in India, also as in most parliamentary federations, are primarily inter-executive relations, thus further strengthening executive dominance (Fossum and Laycock, chap. 4). There are relatively few forums in which key state executive leaders (chief ministers and their state ministers) and federal executive leaders (prime minister and their union ministers) meet on a regular basis. The National Development Council of the erstwhile Planning Commission, and the Governing Council of the National Institution for Transforming India (NITI) Aayog, which replaced the commission in 2015, are the foremost examples. Following a constitutional amendment in 1990, the Inter-State Council (ISC) was created as the key organ of intergovernmental relations and dispute resolution envisaged by the Constitution. The ISC brings together the prime minister, six union Cabinet ministers, and the chief ministers of all the regions and union territories, but it met only eleven times between 1990 and July 2018 (Tillin 2019, 96).

In fact, intergovernmental disputes are more often resolved through ad hoc meetings of party or state leaders or, when central and state governments are controlled by the same party (or parties), through mechanisms of intra-party coordination. Thus, coordination within and among parties across multiple levels provides the most important mechanism for resolving intergovernmental strife. However, coordination is always subject to the shadow of hierarchy, given the centralized blueprint of the Indian federation and the agenda-setting prerogative of the union government in national development overall (see further below). Furthermore, in polity-wide parties (Congress and the BJP), the most seminal party leaders reside at the federal level, not the state level, especially when the party is in government at the federal level.

Despite the infrequency of structured intergovernmental negotiations at the highest ministerial level, meetings, negotiations, and agreements at the level of (senior) civil servants are more recurrent. In the day-to-day coordination of centre-state relations, these take the form of statutory national council meetings in policy fields such as health, rural employment, and local self-government (Saxena 2013, 81). The presence of senior civil servants helps to streamline these intergovernmental relations. Members of the Indian Administrative Services (IAS), Indian Police Service, and Indian Forest Service are recruited nationally after having passed competitive entry exams. Once admitted, however, they go through intensive training sessions and are aligned with a particular state cadre. The camaraderie and esprit de corps, especially among "batch mates" – civil servants who were recruited and trained in the same year – can facilitate the coordination of intergovernmental programs. Typically, half the members of a cadre originate from the state in which they serve; the other half are outsiders. Most civil servants serve at the level of the state (either in the state capital or, more likely, in the districts).

District magistrates provide an especially important link between front-line or "last-mile" bureaucrats, clients, and higher-level (administrative and political) offices. IAS officers can also serve in the national government (on deputation from the state in which they are encadred). Therefore, they can build up expertise across multiple levels of the state, and, while this may facilitate a more uniform application of the law across the country (and thus centralization), such administrative linkages can help to iron out centre-state differences of opinion or prevent disagreements from turning into intergovernmental disputes (Potter 1996; Radin 2007).

However, in the end, civil servants are accountable to elected officers. Although the central level organizes their recruitment, salary, and pensions, they are accountable to the government of the region associated with their cadre. A regional government cannot dismiss civil servants, but it can transfer them to less desirable outposts or functions should it believe that they obstruct its political agenda. Similarly, the central government can "return" an IAS officer to the region in which she is encadred if it is of the view that her services are no longer required. Thus, democratic politicians can undermine the effective operation of intergovernmental federalism, especially in cases where parties or levels are pitted against each other in policies that have gained great political salience.

The specific nature of executive federalism in India raises two issues: one related to democracy, the other to federalism. From the viewpoint of democratic theory, intergovernmental relations that take the form of inter-executive agreements or memoranda of understanding can raise issues of accountability. Such agreements, which are common in India (Singh and Saxena 2013), are typically not widely published, and Indian legislatures have played a particularly weak role in scrutinizing them. In fact, Indian legislatures, especially state assemblies, hold very short sessions. The record of annual sitting days is even worse for legislative assemblies (Jensenius and Suryanarayan 2015, 864–70; PRS Legislative Research 2014).[2] Between 2012 and 2016, the legislative assemblies of Haryana, Goa, and Gujarat sat for twelve, twenty-seven, and thirty-one days, respectively (PRS Legislative Research 2017). Several legislative assemblies also lack select committees that can scrutinize their executives, let alone the intergovernmental arrangements in which they engage.

In this context, it can be noted that the Rajya Sabha, as the national House of States, or second chamber, is also not well equipped to represent the legislative interests of the states. Not only are the regions represented according to population, but its legislative powers (especially in fiscal matters) are also inferior to the powers of the Lok Sabha (Lower House). Members of the Rajya Sabha need not reside in the region that they "represent," and many come from different parts of India. Furthermore, their indirect election by regional legislators has opened the door to centralized candidate nominations, especially for candidates proposed by polity-wide parties such as Congress and the BJP (Shastri 2006, 599–609).

The second issue, related to federalism, is that intergovernmental relations appear to take place under the shadow of hierarchy. The NITI Aayog is subsumed under the PMO, as was, until 2015, the former Planning Commission. The Home Ministry oversees the ISC. Under centralized planning (1952–2014), regional governments were not systematically involved in making the binding five-year economic plans, and they had no direct representation on the commission. Instead, chief ministers had the ability to voice their dissent or concerns in annual meetings of the National Development Council. In contrast, the NITI Aayog under Narendra Modi has developed a forum in which chief ministers can influence policy earlier on in the policy cycle. Subgroups of chief ministers can debate proposed changes to central schemes, which the centre and states co-fund in so-called regional councils. However, their appointment is at the discretion of the NITI and prime minister, as is the selection of themes that the NITI should consider for assessment (though, in principle, on the advice of the Governing Council, in which the federal government, all chief ministers, and the governors of union territories are represented) (Swenden and Saxena 2017, 57). Furthermore, the advice of the regional councils is frequently ignored by the central ministries, including the Ministry of Finance (Swenden 2019, 30).

The constitutional provisions governing territorial finance do a better job of protecting state interests, perhaps because decision-making in this area is partially outsourced to technocrats. By convention, Finance Commission reports have been implemented by the federal government, even when – as in the case of the most recent report (2015–20) – they proposed an increase in the regional share of the net proceeds of shared tax revenue from 32 per cent (2010–15) to 42 per cent (2015–20) (Sharma and Swenden 2018, 66).

Similarly, the constitutional allocation of tax sources to different levels of government implies that changes cannot be made easily without obtaining the explicit consent of the states. Constitutional amendments in this field require the consent of the central parliament, with a special majority *and* a majority of the state legislatures. For example, this provided the states with a collective veto in negotiating the Goods and Services Tax (GST) constitutional amendment, which was finally passed in 2016 after protracted delay. In doing so, the states gave up their entitlement to the state sales tax, their most important source of revenue. Economists have long argued that the ability to vary sales tax rates by state has prevented India from functioning as a harmonized market.

The states ultimately agreed to replace their (and a number of central) indirect taxes with a GST, but demanded that any decisions on its design be subject to the consent of an intergovernmental GST Council. On this GST Council, representatives of the federal government hold one-third of the votes, while the combined vote share of the states makes up the remaining two-thirds. Proposed alterations to the GST rate structure can be blocked if they encounter the resistance of at least twelve states, or, conversely, they are approved when they meet with the consent of at least nineteen states. However, the federal government alone can block any proposal of the states, even should the latter unanimously endorse a proposed amendment (Sharma 2020).

Centre-Regional Coordination as Inter- and Intra-party Coordination

Given the relative weakness of institutional mechanisms to represent state interests, we argue that the extent to which the Indian polity adopts a more (de)centralist direction hinges largely on the nature of the party system and the existing coordination mechanisms *within and among* political parties. Until 1967, Congress ruled the national and nearly all the state governments; therefore, intergovernmental relations were conducted primarily as intra-party relations. Under the leadership of Nehru, the party system was characterized as a "Congress system" (Kothari 1964), in which Congress accommodated smaller parties of pressure at the margins and tolerated a certain level of dissent within. Although quite centralized, party organizational positions within the central and state party branches were contested, and Nehru communicated with his chief ministers regularly. Generally, centre-state relations were cordial. However, the election of a Communist government in Kerala in 1957 resulted in the imposition of President's Rule – a constitutional provision that permits the governor of a state (in the event that the state government is unable to function effectively) to recommend to the president that the state machinery be controlled directly by the central government.

Following Nehru's death, and especially in the wake of Congress's defeats in more than half the state governments in the 1967 elections, the party moved in a centralizing direction under the leadership of Indira Gandhi, Nehru's daughter. Congress dominated national politics until 1989 (except for a brief period between 1977 and 1980), but its national dominance coincided with the increasing presence of opposition-ruled states, especially during the 1980s. Hierarchical control replaced intra-party mediation as the dominant mode of decision-making in relation to Congress-ruled states. Intra-party elections for functions at lower echelons (including candidates for state legislative elections and state party office) were abolished, and their selection was made subject to the consent of the central party leadership instead.

Centralized and dynastic politics reduced the level of state party agency – in fact, Indira Gandhi imposed President's Rule against chief ministers of her own party or recurrently changed party chief ministers to prevent them from building up a strong power base of their own (Kochanek 1976; Swenden and Toubeau 2013, 267–8). The party also adopted a centralist and confrontational approach to state governments headed by non-Congress parties. During the 1970s and 1980s, these states revolted against the rise of discretionary grants and the inflation of centrally sponsored schemes, which the centre used to placate Congress-led governments (Sharma 2017, 27–31). States such as Tamil Nadu, West Bengal, and Punjab were at the forefront of movements seeking a strengthening of regional autonomy (Wyatt 2009).

The result of this confrontationist strategy was a hollowing out of democracy *and* federalism. Between June 1975 and March 1977, Gandhi's Congress Party even put India under a national emergency, curtailing civil rights and suspending all elections. Aside from a national emergency, Congress (and the Janata coalition, which displaced it between 1977 and 1980) used President's Rule to rid itself of state governments controlled by opposition parties. As table 12.1 demonstrates, of 128 occurrences of President's Rule between 1950 and 2018, 70 (55 per cent) took place between 1970 and 1990, and it was imposed for a longer period of time.

Table 12.1. Frequency and average duration of President's Rule (1950–2018)

Decade	No. of uses	No. of days
1950–60	6	234
1960–70	14	239
1970–80	47	197 + 636 days of National Emergency
1980–90	23	251
1990–2000	22	165
2000–18	16	182 + Jammu and Kashmir

Source: Adeney (2007, 185–9); for updates up until 2015: Swenden (2016, 500–1).

The dynamics of centre-state relations changed fundamentally with the emergence of minority or coalition governments at the centre, linked to the gradual demise of the Congress Party as the predominant Indian party. Although Congress lost its majority in 1989, it would take until the late 1990s for the party system to stabilize around two competing alliances, with Congress and the Hindu nationalist BJP as the node of each. Both nodal parties required parties with a more regional following to build national legislative majorities (Adeney and Sáez 2005; Ruperalia 2015; Ziegfeld 2016). This pluralization of the Indian party system changed the dynamics of centre-state relations and the quality of Indian democracy. However, in terms of centre-state relations, few changes were made to the constitutional architecture of Indian federalism (Singh 2019). The position of the polity-wide parties with a more centralized outlook was simply too strong.

Furthermore, some regional parties, especially from North India (Bihar and Uttar Pradesh), represented caste-based rather than regionalist interests. Thus, they sought access to central executive power to honour their caste-specific demands and pursue programs to further their social justice agenda. Finally, regionalist parties whose claims were more directly linked to issues of regional identity or substate nationalism articulated conflicting demands on issues such as territorial finance or national welfare. Regionalist parties from relatively high-income states such as Tamil Nadu often sought a larger share of tax revenue, on the basis of economic performance, or more state autonomy in social welfare. In contrast, regionalist parties from a low-income state such as Assam sought to secure more federal financial assistance or a larger contribution of the centre in national welfare. Thus, mobilizing these states on issues that were linked to territorial finance or national development was difficult, all the more so since constitutional amendments affecting the distribution of powers require the consent of parliament with special majorities and that of a majority of state legislative assemblies.

However, the inability of one national party to monopolize its grip on central power strengthened respect for subnational democracy. The number of instances of President's Rule has declined sharply since 1990, as table 12.1 shows, a situation that also reflects, in part, the approach of the Indian Supreme Court, which adopted a more activist stance in policing its imposition.[3] Furthermore, a change in economic ideology (the gradual replacement of the planned economy with one more liberalized and increasingly globalized) happened around the same time. This change reinforced the scope for state agency since economic investments at the state level no longer required central planning or central ministerial consent.

Despite the "decentralizing phase" in Indian politics between 1989 and 2014, the unexpected return of one-party government in 2014, this time led by the Hindu nationalist BJP, and its actions when in power, have exposed the centralist imprint of the Indian Constitution once again. The centralist impulse has been felt in how intergovernmental programs are managed (whereby direct cash transfers tied to national development schemes credit the central government with "ownership" of such schemes instead of following a more traditional system of in-kind benefits that rely on state or local intermediaries [Tillin and Pereira 2017, 341–4]); in attempts to organize central and state elections concurrently; in the centring of electoral campaigns around Premier Modi (and the BJP's unwillingness to identify chief ministerial candidates before state elections); and in the heavy-handed approach of the BJP in relation to Jammu and Kashmir, which in August 2019 was demoted and bifurcated from one state into two union territories without the explicit consent of its state legislative assembly (see below). However, the BJP implemented the state-favourable recommendations of the XIV Finance Commission and has also encouraged state benchmarking and "competition" (albeit using centrally determined parameters). Interstate economic competition does not undermine the Hindu nationalist orientation of the BJP at the centre in the same way as the special autonomy of Kashmir did (Sharma and Swenden 2018, 61–4).

Likewise, notwithstanding the return of one-party dominance, the Supreme Court held on to its more restrictive tolerance for the application of President's Rule. For instance, in 2016 it invalidated the attempt by the BJP to apply it to Uttarkhand and Arunachal Pradesh, and it even reinstated both ousted Congress governments until they were defeated in subsequent state assembly elections (Swenden and Saxena 2021). However, even Supreme Court justices do not operate in a "democratic" or political vacuum, and when pressure builds to enforce a more centralized or majoritarian reading of the Constitution, the court may fall into line. For instance, the Supreme Court did not stop the imposition of a National Emergency in 1975, nor did it halt the widespread abuse of President's Rule until 1994. More recently, and less than four years after the return of single-party government in 2014, four senior justices thought it necessary to warn of undue interference of the central government in determining which cases would be heard and by which justices (*Hindu* [Chennai], 13 January 2018). Fourteen months after the centre unilaterally moved to bifurcate and demote Jammu and Kashmir (August 2019), the Supreme Court has yet to pronounce judgment on the matter. Thus, more effective decentralizing pressures have come through the ballots of Indians, voting for multiple parties.

Integration and the Limits of Subnational Democracy

In some sense, the federal structure has been able to preserve democracy where it was challenged in territories holding locally dominant linguistic groups. But it has been less successful at doing so with locally dominant tribal and religious groups. Paradoxically, at times the centralized nature of the Indian Constitution has enabled territorial accommodation: although it resisted at first, Congress was forced into conceding "linguistic federalism" between 1953 and 1966. "Rightsizing" (O'Leary, Lustick, and Callaghy 2001) the state or redrawing internal state boundaries, unlike in coming-together federations such as the United States and Switzerland, does not require the explicit consent of the states: Article 3 requires only a parliamentary majority (Tillin 2013, 32–4; Tillin, Deshpande, and Kailash 2015).

Yet, despite the top-down procedure, the incentives have been primarily bottom-up and democratic (Hausing 2018, 450–4). As one of the authors of this chapter has previously argued, "The belated acceptance of linguistic reorganization [and the retention of English] was an outcome produced by the danger of internal party dissent as well as external protest" (Adeney 2007, 77). Concerns have been raised by regional leaders about the inability of regional units to effectively represent the "people" without such reorganization and the need for effective self-government. The States Reorganization Commission (SRC) has made specific reference to increasing the quality of democratic governance through this reorganization process by operating in the language of the people.

However, the SRC of 1955 did not accept the legitimacy of all the demands for reorganization. It rejected the bifurcation of the Bombay

Presidency along linguistic lines on the grounds that other thorny issues required resolution (in this case, the status of the multilingual city of Bombay). It rejected others because of a conflict between the nation-building rationale of the union (based on secularism) and the religious nature of the demands (in this case, the creation of a Sikh region out of Punjab). Both these demands were eventually conceded, as were many others. (India now has twenty-eight states, the most recent created in 2014.) Yet the formation of Punjab was formally granted on linguistic (Punjabi), not religious (Sikh), lines (Brass 1974), and even though it created a predominantly Sikh state, Sikhs were in a bare majority within the revised borders. More widely, a study of the debates leading to state formation illustrates different interpretations of the demos: some tie in with substate identities in the main (and, thus, endorse a more multicultural understanding of the demos, as set out in the introduction (chap. 1), and some seem to imagine the Indian nation as a whole (thus emphasizing the need for an overarching identity, bolstered by a national language, dominant religion, and strong centre).

Federalism has worked to bolster the inclusion of its diverse population in the Indian state and has enhanced its democratic credentials as a result. The language compromises of the 1952–70 era were important elements in bringing democracy closer to the people. This structure has reinforced the multilayered sense of the Indian identity and facilitated the accommodation of multiple *demoï*. It has also contributed to a rise in regional and regionalist parties and the gradual regionalization of the party system. In turn, and notwithstanding centralization, regional policies have diverged across a range of areas, reflecting interstate differences in party competition, social mobilization, and caste and class structures. For instance, in Tamil Nadu and Kerala, health care provisions are more universal and public than in other parts of India. Some authors have argued that this ties in with the ability of citizens in these states to forge stronger bonds based on a shared substate identity (Singh 2019); others have emphasized the social origins of such policies, reflecting the relatively small cohort of upper-caste citizens (Brahmins and Kshatriyas) in comparison with the Hindi Belt states of the north. Yet others have stressed the significance of competitive populism in the party system or the colonial path dependencies – in particular, more radical land reform and the stronger footprint of missionaries in the southern states (Tillin, Deshpande, and Kailash 2015).

Thus, the expression of regional variations in policy preferences has led to regionally divergent policies. Occasionally, these variations have also informed federal policy. (The federal government's largest flagship program – MGNREGA – which offers one hundred days of employment to the rurally unemployed, was first tried out in Maharashtra; midday meals for school children were first piloted in Tamil Nadu.)

However, the central insistence on integration (aside from along linguistic lines) has often undermined the successful management of ethnonational tensions, especially when they are expressed in border regions with religious minorities (such as Jammu and Kashmir, Punjab, and some states in the northeast, especially Nagaland, Meghalaya, and Mizoram). In the process, both subnational autonomy (federalism) and democracy have been put on ice. The Constitution contains an anti-secession clause, and political parties can be condemned (and outlawed) for their "anti-national" behaviour if they campaign on secessionist platforms. Where a secessionist threat (was believed to have) exist(ed), as in the aforementioned states, the centre has applied a strategy of military repression and suspended or sometimes manipulated ("rigged") regional democracy (Adeney 2017, 139; Swenden 2016, 503–8).

Despite the distinct constitutional status of Jammu and Kashmir (Art. 370, Art. 35), which entitled the state to its own constitution, flag, and prime minister, the repeated outlawing of state parties and rigging of state elections from the 1950s onward has worked to hollow out the state's distinctive status and to undermine the trust of its citizens in democracy (Bose 1997). In August 2019, the BJP, emboldened by its decisive election victory in the April–May 2019 general elections, not only implemented its long-held election promise of abrogating Article 35A of the Indian Constitution and making Article 370 inoperative, but also went two steps further by bifurcating the state (into Ladakh and Jammu and Kashmir) and demoting them to the status of union territories. (Only Jammu and Kashmir has a – proposed – directly elected legislative assembly.) The Kashmir valley continues to house several hundred thousand soldiers (for a population of barely seven million people), and its citizens are subject to "anti-terror laws," which institutionalize censorship and enable detention without due process.

Similar "illiberal" practices have been observed in the northeast of India, despite the presence of special laws and (substate) legislative bodies that protect the traditional rights and customs of their tribal citizens. As Lacina (2009, 2017, 168–88) has observed, the central government has been all too often complicit in trading stability (a commitment of the centrally sponsored, local elites to uphold the integrity of the Indian state) for democracy. Many state or substate governments have actively worked to undermine their political opponents and the interests of rival tribal groups, even where – as in the case of Bodoland – these groups constitute a demographic majority (Bhattacharyya and Mukherjee 2018, 471). Occasionally, the crackdowns have been followed by territorial accommodation and the restoration of democracy, sometimes with the implicit support of formerly insurgent parties if they have been willing to renounce their formerly secessionist claims. But the centre has not always been successful in restoring the federal and democratic features of a state.

Conversely, the centre has not necessarily acted effectively against state majorities that seek to impose their view of the "state demos" against locally repressed minorities. This illustrates the point made by Benz (chap. 3) that there can be challenges to democracy where federalism appears to exempt majorities from having to respect the rights of citizens who do not share the characteristics of a majority population within a state, be it on the basis of language or religion. For example, constitutionally promised linguistic-minority rights are not observed since many states simply do not file a return to the Commissioner for Linguistic Minorities, and reports from several states document the recurrent failure of their governments to publish documents in minority languages or make provisions for using them (India. Commissioner for Linguistic Minorities 2014). The tension between group and individual rights is clear.

Similarly, in many regions of India there has been tension between the provision of the Constitution allowing the propagation of religion (Art. 25) and High Court judgments prohibiting propagation within a particular state. Twenty-four of India's twenty-eight states have passed laws that apply Hindu dietary customs (banning the consumption of beef) to communities that do not share these restrictions (Jaffrelot 2017, 55–7). These provisions have hit religious minorities (such as Muslims) hard but also other communities, such as the former Untouchables, now known as Dalits, who are likely to be employed in the tannery trade and also rely on beef as a cheap source of protein. This example illustrates differences in the effective citizenship of religious minorities and the inability of successive central governments – but especially those led by the BJP – to sanction a multireligious understanding of the Indian demos.

This was revealed in the pogrom of 2002 in Gujarat, when up to two thousand people, mainly Muslims, were massacred and many more thousands displaced in what Human Rights Watch termed a "state-abetted pogrom" (Human Rights Watch 2002). Law and order is a state subject in India, and the police in Gujarat were criticized for their role in the violence, often aiding the perpetrators in some cases and failing to prevent attacks in others. Although the breakdown of law and order would have provided sufficient ground for the centre to recommend President's Rule, this was infamously *not* applied in this case. The

BJP-led coalition at the centre did not want to impose it against a state headed by one of its own: Narendra Modi. However, regional political parties in the governing coalition were also worried that applying pressure on the central government to use it to protect religious minorities could lead future central administrations to use it, out of revenge, to dismiss their own governments.

Conclusion: Balancing Federalism and Democracy

It is difficult to see how India could survive as a democracy without some form of federalism. The country is simply too diverse, and the identification of its citizens with levels of government other than the Indian state is too strong. In other words, the long-term survival of the Indian demos as an imagined Indian community encompassing India's current state boundaries presumes the recognition of multiple demoï within.

However, our analysis has shown that there has not always been a clear fit between the structures of the state and this reality of India as a composite culture. It is difficult to argue that federalism in India has provided a watertight dam against the will of the people or fostered a *gouvernement des juges* (judicial activism). On the contrary, the urge to build a strong centre, capable of holding and sometimes forcing India together, has threatened its federal credentials. Occasionally, this urge has also threatened the survival of India as a democracy, as, for example, during the National Emergency between 1975 and 1977. There is growing consensus that, since 2014, following the election of a Hindu majoritarian government at the centre with an absolute parliamentary majority, the space for debate has been shrinking and (state-tolerated) violence against religious minorities (especially Muslims) has been rising (Saldanha 2017). India is still democratic in the sense that elections are held on a regular basis and determine who composes the national, regional, and local governments, but the polity is now "less liberal," and concerns have been raised about the "fairness" of the electoral process itself (Kapur and Vaishnav 2018; Mahmood and Ganguli 2017; V-Dem 2018). The top-down decision to demote and bifurcate Jammu and Kashmir, and recent changes to the national citizenship law (which fast-track Indian citizenship to non-Muslim – in practice, predominantly Hindu – refugees from neighbouring countries but preclude such rights to Muslims), appear to relegate Muslims to second-class citizens within India (Adeney 2020).

Whether this crisis of democracy has also diluted federalism remains an open question, in part because the BJP has been able to spread its wings into the government of more than half the Indian states. However, there is evidence of political and administrative centralization, and, while there is strong fiscal centralization, the spending autonomy of the states is less open to further centralization due to constitutional guarantees and technocratic decision-making (Sharma and Swenden 2018).

Federal systems can, of course, be quite centralized, but the Indian case highlights the complex relationship between centralized federalism and democracy. Linguistic reorganization illustrates a process in which federalism and democracy have been mutually reinforcing. Despite the *lack* of regional veto powers, bottom-up-driven resistance (subnational democracy) has pushed forward linguistic reorganization (federal reform) and further processes of state reorganization. Generally, the same holds for state reorganization, which took place after 1966. Despite its centralizing tendencies, federalism has also opened the door to regional policy divergence – more so since liberalization – enabling regional variations in industrial policy, land management, schooling, health, food supply, and power. To the extent that these variations tie in with regional differences in social mobilization or party competition, they have bolstered democracy and federalism.

Yet our chapter has also described phases in India's post-independence trajectory when democracy (at least in its majoritarian manifestation) undermined federalism – or *federal* democracy – especially when central rulers interpreted their central majority as a mandate to rid themselves of politically hostile regional governments. Therefore, the pluralized party system in place between 1989 and 2014, which recurrently brought to power more inclusive national governments with the support of regionalist parties, provided the strongest safeguard of federal democracy. In that context, the Supreme Court was also more inclined to police substate political autonomy. Conversely, our chapter has also illustrated instances in which subnational governments acquired illiberal forms, sometimes with the implicit support of the centre, which condoned or even promoted efforts by local rulers to establish regional autocracies in exchange for stability and territorial integrity.

B.R. Ambedkar, the spiritual father of the Indian Constitution and chair of the drafting committee, once said that the Constitution could be read as unitary or federal, "depending on the requirements of time and circumstances" (quoted in Cheluva Raju 1991, 160). Therefore, and perhaps more so than for other federations, our chapter has shown that the operation of India as a federation and a democracy is contingent on its political leaders making a *political* commitment to both principles. Given the relative weakness of regional veto powers, the commitment to what the late Michael Burgess (2012) referred to as the "federal spirit" – and so, we might argue, also democracy – is strongest when the party system forces central (and regional) leaders into territorial (and non-territorial) modes of accommodation, built on a more multicultural understanding of the Indian nation.

NOTES

1 In addition, 12 per cent somewhat agreed, 5 per cent somewhat disagreed, and 15 per cent expressed no opinion.

2 Even the standing and ad hoc committees of the Lok Sabha (Lower House) have little influence and play a minimal role in executive oversight. Centrally Sponsored Schemes that are tied to ministerial departments could be scrutinized by departmentally related standing committees. Yet, as Kapur and Mehta point out (2006, 12–13), these committees have had little impact. Committee reports are often ignored by parliament, where they are rarely even tabled or discussed. Committee members are in post for only one year; therefore, they lack the inside knowledge of senior civil servants and policymakers. Furthermore, ministers rarely appear on parliamentary committees, and they cannot be summoned by committee members.

3 In *S.R. Bommai vs Union of India*, for example, it ruled that "the exercise of the power by the President under Article 356 to issue a proclamation is subject to judicial review at least to the extent of examining whether there existed material for the satisfaction of the President that a situation had arisen in which the Government of the State could not be carried out in accordance with the provisions of the constitution" (*S.R. Bommai vs Union of India*, 1994, All India Reporter (A.I.R), 1994 Supreme Court, p. 1918). For a discussion of the role of the Supreme Court and federalism and how the court managed to gain independence from the national executive, see Swenden and Saxena (2021).

13 Comparing Patterns of Federal Democracy

ARTHUR BENZ AND JARED SONNICKSEN

This volume has set out to explore institutional conditions and patterns of governance in federal democracies as well as the limits and possibilities put in place to make these complex governments work. Of central concern are linkages between institutions and processes in federalism and democracy that regularly cause tensions and are sources of conflict in politics and policymaking. Moreover, we are interested in finding out how these tensions materialize in different federations as well as how actors cope with them and manage the resulting conflicts. With respect to the quality of democracy, we have tried to discover whether the dynamics inherent in compounded institutions and the actors' responses to tensions lead to the unjustified dominance of executives or other actors lacking democratic legitimacy or whether they balance power and stabilize the democracy. In this final chapter, we re-examine the country studies collected in this volume from a comparative perspective, based on the analytical framework and normative premises outlined in chapters 2, 3, and 4.

Certainly, chapters on complex political systems that describe their history, change, and operation can provide only condensed empirical information. Moreover, this book is the result of a joint project of the authors, in which theory and empirical analyses evolved in parallel and which we still consider a first step in a work in progress. Therefore, our conclusion tries to summarize the main results, but it also indicates the need for further research. Yet we want to emphasize that this research has to avoid subjecting political practice to overly abstract normative ideals of either federalism or democracy, which ignore conflicting norms and the complexity of reality. When considering federal democracies at work, we need to understand the interference of politics in two institutionally different arenas. Moreover, we should not expect to find an ideal model of federal democracy, not only because of the variety of institutional configurations but also given the diverse patterns of interactions (governance) and different economic, societal, or political conditions.

For this reason, we refrain from rating either the quality of democracy or degrees of federalism according to an index. Instead, we conceive democratic federal governments as "multidimensional regimes" (see, e.g., Benz 2009, 2015), and the inherent tensions and dynamics preclude an aggregation of scores for individual dimensions. Our normative criteria constitute standards for evaluating federal democracies. We look at the ability of federal democracies to search for agreements on fundamental issues, to deal with distributive conflicts in a solidary way, and to balance power between levels of government (Hueglin, chap. 2). Moreover, power structures that emerge through the dynamics of federal democracies at work are justified if politics prevents arbitrary domination of executives, parties, or other actors (Fossum and Laycock, chap. 4).

From an empirical point of view, federalism and democracy need to be conceived as distinct dimensions of government. Each represents ordering principles for the division of powers with respectively different normative underpinnings as well as logics of operation. They can also comprise, each on their own and in combination, quite substantial varieties. The relationship between federalism and democracy is one that is neither inherently compatible nor necessarily contradictory (Benz and Sonnicksen 2017). They have a "tense relationship" with each other (Sonnicksen 2018, 31–6), which applies in multifarious ways. In the final analysis, the quality of democratic federalism depends on flexibility, adaptability, and, ultimately, the balancing of powers and interdependent mechanisms of governance in practice; it also depends on various arrangements and strategies for coping and, thus, effectively managing the tensions between the two regime dimensions.

To analyse structural and procedural interlinkages and their configuration, intensity, and flexibility in a comparative perspective, we introduced the concept of coupling between the institutions of federalism and democracy and the processes of politics shaped by these institutions. To make federal democracies work, governance on both dimensions needs to be linked. However, given the different actor constellations and patterns of interaction, when there is extensive tight coupling, or if powers are separated in all institutional dimensions, severe, negative consequences are not only to be theoretically expected but also observable. Therefore, we have to focus on patterns of loose coupling that provide the necessary conditions for coping with institutionalized tensions. Conceptualizing coupling arrangements not only explains to what extent tensions in various patterns of federal democracy affect politics and policymaking; it can also foster an enhanced approach to understanding what makes federal democracies work.

To summarize the findings outlined in the case studies, we start by systematizing the various structural configurations of the federal democracies examined, which we characterize by the intensity of coupling. This intensity depends on how political executives, which regularly act in a boundary-spanning role and are involved in processes in the arenas of both federalism and democracy, are constrained by structures, rules, or norms within these arenas. With regard to federalism, these structures, rules, or norms refer to the division of power and vertical and horizontal intergovernmental relations; as to democracy, it is the relation between the executive and the legislative or parliament that matters. Yet linkage structures are never fixed, and they can be shaped or circumvented by strategic actions. As outlined in the theoretical part of this chapter, systematizing these configurations requires examining the emergent structures and processes resulting from these dynamics – in particular, the relations constituted or enabled by the party system and intergovernmental relations. Finally, we discuss whether loosely coupled federal democracies can be stabilized or risk falling into the trap of executive dominance or disintegrative populist democracy.

The Structures of Federal Democracy

The particular types of federal democracy are surely affected by the constitutional parameters, institutional configurations, and structures of party politics. All these elements emerge and evolve over time, while the linkages between federalism and democracy result from the governance and strategic action of political actors. Of course, the developments in the interactions between federalism and democracy are influenced, but by no means determined, by the formal constitutional and institutional make-up. To grasp the coupling of federalism and democracy, let alone apply the concept to actual cases, we have to first describe the two governmental dimensions, their specific arrangements for the distribution of power with the corresponding functional logics of politics. Before going into greater detail, two remarks are necessary.

First, the intensity of coupling is a matter of degree. Hence, when we talk about uncoupled or tightly coupled patterns, we indicate extreme cases, which rarely exist in reality. In political systems, interactions and processes regularly cross the boundaries of institutions. However, the commitment of actors to their institutions, the binding power of rules, or the actual constraints are more or less strong. This situation also applies to the relations between executives and legislatures in a democratic system or between the executives of governments at the different levels of a federation. Moreover, the intensity of coupling can vary among policy fields, depending on the allocation of power, or over time. Therefore, our categorization describes the basic structures of a particular federal democracy that can be considered the predominating pattern, not the entirety of the actual variations within these structures.

Second, we are well aware that our theoretical approach reduces the complexity of governments by focusing on two institutional dimensions. Certainly, democratic systems do not include only executives and legislatures, particularly if we take into account the elements of direct democracy in Switzerland. Moreover, we do not ignore parties and intermediary associations or the role of courts. However, to understand the linkage between intergovernmental and democratic processes, the position of the political executive in a political system and its accountability to popularly elected parliaments must be examined. As for intergovernmental relations, they include the federal government and governments of the constituent states, but they may also include a "horizontal" dimension shaped by relations among the constituent units. The latter arrangement is especially important in multinational federations, where it may reveal some kind of asymmetry.

Keeping these remarks in mind, we can locate the eight cases of federal democracy covered by this volume in a two-dimensional scheme (see table 13.1).

Concerning the division of powers in democratic governments, the logic of politics correlates to executive-legislative checks and balances as well as stricter separation of powers – for instance, in the case of presidential – or non-parliamentary – governments. In this type of democracy, the executive cannot rely on a majority in the legislature, though it depends on budget appropriations by legislation. Yet, in its own domain, it is not responsible to the legislative assembly. More power-sharing applies in parliamentary systems, where the executive and the party or coalition supporting the government form a de facto alliance, usually pitted against the minority party or parties forming the opposition. The intensity of coupling between the executive and parliament is generally high in these systems, but de facto lower in one-party parliamentary governments, even if a party forms a minority government. This contrasts with multiparty governments, in which executives are committed to coalition agreements. In a one-party government, an executive can trust that its party in parliament will accept policies or proposals for legislation, whereas the leeway for policy change is more limited if the executive needs to broker an agreement between two or more parties.

Table 13.1. Structures of federal democracy

	Democratic government (executive-legislative) Weak ←——→ Tight Intensity of coupling			
	Non-parliamentary government		Parliamentary government	
Federalism (intergovernmental relations) Tight ←——→ Weak Intensity of coupling	Majoritarian	Consensus	Single-party government	Multi-party government
Separation of powers	United States		Spain	
Voluntary, intergovernmental cooperation		Switzerland	Canada India	Belgium
Joint-decision system			Australia	Germany

Concerning the federal dimension and its logic of politics, powers may be more prone to separation and, thus, strictly delineated or compartmentalized among the jurisdictions and levels of government. This model of dual federalism refers chiefly to the relations between levels of government, whereas horizontal relations among constituent states are usually more flexible, although tax competition can constrain a government's discretion in policymaking. Conversely, a more power-sharing predisposition to tight coupling is typical of a federal system with structural and functional interlocking, requirements of joint decision-making, or joint tasks between levels of government. Loosely coupled patterns include intergovernmental cooperation in voluntary negotiations, allowing bilateral agreements or allowing the governments of constituent states to opt out, coordination by standards, or governance by yardstick competition.

In the relations among the branches and levels of government, systems of complex government obviously demonstrate neither "watertight" insulation from one another nor mutual interlocking beyond distinguishability. This holds irrespective of how intensely interlinked or strictly disjointed by constitutional rule and institutional design they may be. Institutions of one democratic government, as well as the constituent units and their governments in a federal system, interact in numerous arenas and through various processes: through political parties, administrative networks, intergovernmental coordination, and interparliamentary relations. It is precisely these processes in governance and political practice, in combination with the structural configuration of democratic and federal government, that achieve the effective coupling arrangements in different federal democracies. They may be underlined, reinforced, or mitigated by different forms of fiscal federalism, which themselves can range from more separating or sharing of fiscal resources or their autonomous or joint administration.

Having established this framework, we address in the remaining sections of this chapter eight federal democracies, first with a view to their institutional patterns and then with regard to their established patterns of processes in democratic and intergovernmental politics. We first compare the two non-parliamentary democracies, the United States and Switzerland, before we turn to the federations with parliamentary governments. In this group, we start with Canada, Australia, and Germany before moving to the particularly diverse cases of Belgium, India, and Spain.

Federalism and Non-parliamentary Democracy

The first federal states were founded in the United States and Switzerland in the late eighteenth and mid-nineteenth centuries, respectively. Thus, they formed before the idea of parliamentary responsible government emerged in Great Britain and predominated the first wave of democratization. Accordingly, they combined the classical concept of the separation of powers between the executive and legislative branches of government with a "dual federalism" that divided powers between levels of government. In contrast with US democracy, in which a strong executive can govern independent of the confidence of Congress, the powers of Swiss executives are constrained by the need to negotiate policies with parties and civil society in the shadow of direct democracy.

While the non-parliamentary system remained in place in both countries, democracy in the United States was increasingly shaped by a party dualism, while in Switzerland, party pluralism and referendums formed a consensus democracy. Both federations unite an at least originally constituted predisposition to extensive autonomy, secured for the constituent units – the states and cantons, respectively – though their structure of federalism has likewise changed and even diverged significantly. Intergovernmental relations emerged in policy fields, but for a long time lacked an institutional basis, although this has changed in Switzerland during the last decades.

Turning to the US case first, federalism and democracy were founded foremost on the principles of the separation of powers. Each head of the executive and the legislative chambers at the national and state levels are endowed with direct and distinct electoral linkages to the people as their ultimate source of legitimacy, while formal, institutional interlocking among governmental levels is, by and large, absent since the appointment of senators by the state legislatures was abolished in 1913. In terms of structures, the United States represents a clear-cut composite of an uncoupled federal democracy, with a double dualism between parties and federal and state governments. As Timothy Conlan has argued in his case study (chap. 5), the "long arc" of both democratic and federal political development have followed majoritarian logics, but also revealed an incremental expansion of inclusiveness and political equality. The modernization of American federalism, on the whole, has appeared to coincide with the nationalization of democratic politics (Beer 1978). With this concurrence have come, in turn, recurring tensions – for instance, in balancing popular and state sovereignty, realizing national policy goals in the jurisdiction of state powers, and safeguarding the autonomy of states as laboratories of democracy.

In their basic structural predispositions, US federalism and democracy may still approximate the separation of powers. However, the dynamics established in the nineteenth, and especially throughout the twentieth, century moved towards cooperative federalism (see also Elazar 1964). This pattern intensified with the advent of the New Deal in the 1930s and the large-scale expansion of a welfare and regulatory state regime steered by the national government. Competitive, dual federalism is deemed to have "passed" (Corwin 1950) long ago, as federal regulations of state and local governments, grants in aid, or multi-level, administrative linkages and policy-coordination networks expanded among federal, state, and local governments, in both the vertical and the horizontal dimension ("picket-fence federalism").

However, by the late twentieth century, the competing dynamics of new federalism and strengthening states had not only re-emerged but also steadily increased in parallel. Inter-branch brinkmanship and deadlock have become more common in divided governments between president and Congress, while the effectiveness of cross-level administrative coordination and the "intergovernmental lobby" have declined. As Conlan's chapter on the United States has shown, the overall fragmentation of US federal democracy has intensified with political polarization, the "nationalization" of politics, and an erosion of federal government legitimacy. Virtually all offices of government have simple majoritarian electoral systems, and the resulting dualist, partisan competition has intensified during recent decades. It has encumbered cross-party, cross-branch, and cross-level negotiations as well as consensus-seeking, the hallmark of American federal democracy in the "heyday" of cooperative federalism and policymaking among legislative committees, executives, and interest associations. The strict separation of powers has rendered coordination across all levels of government not only complicated and unpredictable but also vulnerable to informal influence by special interest groups and lobbying (Robertson 2012, 134).

At the same time, while multi-level governance is dominated by executives and informal, more often than not bilateral, negotiations of "technocrats" (Beer 1978, 18), there is the possibility of legislatures counteracting, amending, or rejecting those agreements, leading to uncertainty in the negotiation and executive decision-making processes and an all-round tendency to internal fragmentation. Consequently, emerging patterns of loose coupling by, for example, policy networks, waivers in regulatory programs, and intergovernmental lobbying remain highly susceptible to deadlocks, especially in times of polarization. The multidimensional separation of powers in American federalism and democracy implies, in turn, that deadlocks are circumvented by decoupling, especially when, in response, states go their own way in various policy domains. Meanwhile, the resulting pattern appears to be not only one of institutional but also, increasingly, policy fragmentation, thereby favouring the dominance of private interests over the public good.

As mentioned, the original "default settings" of Swiss federal democracy overlap considerably with the US constitutional model. Although there is no popularly elected chief executive, the Federal Council (Bundesrat) constitutes a collective executive body, elected for a fixed term of office and representing all major parties in parliament. Hence, it does not depend on the confidence of a single party or a coalition in parliament. The bicameral legislature resembles the US Congress, with the National Council (Nationalrat) being configured to represent the Swiss people and the Council of States (Ständerat) representing the cantonal peoples through popularly elected councillors. On the other hand, Swiss democracy diverges considerably from the US case through its direct democracy, the strong influence of civil society, and a multiparty system.

Given the comparatively wide scope of cantonal authority, Swiss federalism exhibits a dual character. But it diverges from the dual model to a significant extent in that it establishes a division-of-labour-type distribution of powers as the cantons are charged by the Constitution with implementing most federal legislation. Yet, in contrast with German federalism, functional interdependence does not imply institutionalized, joint decision-making in Switzerland, although the federal government has recently gained a stronger role in intergovernmental coordination in some policy fields and the cantons have institutionalized their intergovernmental councils (Vatter 2018b, 63–83). Among the smaller cantons, coordination has become increasingly urgent, and it is achieved in multiple and still largely informal patterns of horizontal cooperation. Thus, Swiss federalism unites dual and cooperative institutional features, while its democratic model combines substantial elements of the separation of powers (e.g., mutual executive-legislative branch independence) with the extensive practice of power-sharing (e.g., proportional representation, multiple parties, strong bicameralism). In addition to the long-standing institutionalization of consociational governance (see, e.g., Lehmbruch 1993), the instruments of referendum democracy, as captured by Neidhart (1970), contribute to inducing not only cross-branch and multilateral but also cross-cantonal, multi-level consultations and coordination. This is why Swiss federal democracy at work constitutes a model case of a loosely coupled system (see, e.g., Armingeon 2000, 121–3).

As Sean Mueller has outlined in chapter 6, this loosely coupled federal democracy reveals tensions, arising from the strong power of minorities in consensus democracy and the limited power of parliaments against the cooperating executives. Yet flexible patterns of multidimensional cooperation and negotiation allow political actors in the federation to cope with the conflicts caused by these structural features (Vatter 2018b, 218–44). Because there are non-parliamentary, separation-of-powers forms of government at all levels, cross-branch and cross-level coordination appears highly complex: executives lack mechanisms like votes of confidence for instrumentalizing party discipline. But, in turn, they are not bound to one party or coalition majority, and the threat of a popular initiative and referendum motivates all actors to find an agreement. As recent decades have demonstrated, Swiss consensus democracy can be challenged by party polarization. So far, however, it has proved resistant to confrontation and the risk of deadlock.

To conclude, US and Swiss federalism, which are often idealized as models of a federal democracy, share a number of features but diverge in the linkages between democracy and federalism, and these linkages have significant consequences for the legitimacy of both governance and power structures. In both countries, policy coordination through negotiations between the executive and legislative branches and between levels of government has intensified. Yet, in the United States, the structural divides among the branches and levels of government have remained in place, and the dualist nature of politics has given rise to confrontation instead of consensus. In Switzerland, consensual negotiations link the executives and legislatures as well as the federal and cantonal governments. Though grounded in law, these negotiations have emerged outside the constitutional framework and in the shadow of referendum democracy, and they are supported by a political culture that has evolved in a society characterized by cross-cutting cleavages.

Federalism and Parliamentary Democracy

For a long time, scholars held that federalism was incompatible with parliamentary democracy. They argued that a federal constitution limited the sovereignty of governments and contradicted the principle of parliamentary sovereignty. For example, this issue was discussed during the making of the Australian Constitution (Aroney 2010) and is still a matter of constitutional debates in Canada (Webber 2015, 169). Similar concerns were raised in Germany, when, in 1919, the Weimar Constitution established a parliamentary system in the existing federation (Ritter 2005). Later, political scientists highlighted potentially disruptive frictions between the logics of competitive party politics in parliamentary democracy and intergovernmental negotiation and cooperation in federalism (Lehmbruch 2000; Sharman 1990). Against this backdrop, one could expect particular tensions to arise in this constellation of a federal democracy, and this is indeed the case. Upon closer inspection, however, the three federations with parliamentary democracy addressed in this volume reveal significant differences.

First, only the Canadian Constitution followed the Westminster model of parliamentary sovereignty and established a clear majoritarian democracy. Even the Upper House of the federal legislature, the Senate, essentially replicates the British House of Lords, while the provinces decided against bicameral legislatures altogether. In Australia, the Senate is popularly elected, since the reform of elections in 1948, by the rules of the proportional, single-transferable vote, which is a further departure from the Westminster system. In consequence, opposition parties can gain veto power and can also hold the executive accountable. Accordingly, legislative decisions have to be negotiated, and the executive requires the agreement of both Houses and multiple parties (see Sayers and Banfield 2013; Banfield and Sayers, chap. 9). The same applies – also in contrast with the Canadian provinces – to the parliamentary systems of the Australian states.

In Germany, we find a parliamentary government constrained by the powers of the Federal Council (Bundesrat), in which the Länder governments are represented by their members of Cabinet. This construction of the federal legislature tightly couples parliamentary democracy and intergovernmental relations in a unique way (Lehmbruch 2000, 30), whereas, in other federations, bicameral legislatures at the national level have only weak ties to the governments of the constituent units (Palermo 2018). Moreover, in contrast with Canada and Australia, the federal parliament (Bundestag) as well as the Länder parliaments are elected according to proportional representation. In consequence, to form a government, parties have to negotiate coalition agreements, and the executive is committed not only to a party but also to an agreement of parties. Hence, ties between the executive and the legislature are much stronger in Germany than in Canada, where the executive enjoys significant independence within the democratic system.

The patterns of intergovernmental relations reveal similar varieties. Canada, in its original adoption of federalism, largely emulated the dual federalism of the United States. Accordingly, intergovernmental relations are not institutionalized; instead, agreements are based on voluntary negotiations and concluded under the proviso of parliamentary assent. These rather flexible arrangements allowed governments to accommodate their conflicts with Quebec. This province has long demanded far-reaching autonomy, though other provinces have become more assertive, and the western provinces also demand self-rule and protect their powers against the federal government (see, e.g., Broschek 2009, 283–313).

In Australia, federalism is characterized by a functional division of powers, with legislation being made mainly at the federal level, whereas public services are delivered by the states, which increasingly depend on federal grants. In consequence, federal and state governments have engaged in intergovernmental negotiations and expanded "collaborative federalism" (Painter 1998), not least to guarantee a high level of equality in the Australian welfare state. Though federal and state governments have realized an objective need to cooperate, they are not legally compelled to make agreements. De facto, they coordinate their policies through joint decision-making in the executive and, as Banfield and Sayers show in chapter 9, manage to achieve an ongoing "recoupling" of institutions and interactions to pragmatically solve policy problems (see also Hollander and Patapan 2007).

In Germany, institutionalized forms of joint decision-making among the Länder governments, and later between the federal and Länder governments, have evolved over centuries and are entrenched in the Constitution of the Federal Republic. In federal legislation, Bundestag bills that concern Länder powers and shared taxes cannot pass without the assent of the Federal Council. While the constitutional theory of federalism assumes that federalism implies a ban on federal-Länder cooperation, in policies that require cooperation or in cases where governments prefer joint action or shared funding, the Constitution has to establish legal provisions. Accordingly, intergovernmental relations often turn into joint decision-making, a tightly coupled form of compulsory negotiations that prevents exit options.

Thus, federations with parliamentary democracies reveal various ways of linking both regime dimensions. The Australian and Canadian federal democracies are loosely coupled due to their particular features of either executive-Parliament or intergovernmental relations. As a result, competitive party politics need not contradict, but rather can facilitate, intergovernmental coordination. In Australia, the party system gives the regional party groups a significant voice. The need for intra-party consensus moderates federal-state conflicts, as do administrative networks. In Canada, the veto power of parliaments and the provinces' ability to opt out of intergovernmental agreements, or, on the other hand, the federal government's power to conclude bilateral, intergovernmental agreements with the provinces, foster shifts between the arenas of executive federalism and parliamentary democracy. Thus, we observe alternating patterns of federal-provincial cooperation and unilateral federal action in the first arena and between "court government" (Savoie 1999) dominated by prime ministers and assertive parliaments in the second, as Jörg Broschek has shown in chapter 8.

Germany represents an extreme case of tight coupling of executives, both to their parliament and party politics and to intergovernmental policymaking. This constellation can cause serious problems of governance under the conditions of polarized party competition or a disintegrated party system. Nonetheless, actors have found ways to circumvent the double constraints of joint decision-making and parliamentary democracy. One way is to modify intergovernmental policymaking by moving political negotiations into administrative networks or the other way around. As Sabine Kropp (chap. 7) asserts, this approach can help "soften" the otherwise rigid structures in German federal democracy, particularly under the current conditions of a pluralist party system. The other is to define policy issues as matters of constitutional law, to be decided by the Federal Constitutional Court. Both strategies risk undermining the power of parliaments; nonetheless, one should not underestimate the fact that parliamentary committees are able to scrutinize executive politics. Thus, serious frictions have been avoided through the adaptation of federal democracy.

Federalism and Parliamentary Democracy in Divided Societies

By now, we can conclude that parliamentary as well as non-parliamentary democracies operate in a way that can conflict with governance in federalism and prevent effective intergovernmental coordination. Moreover, it is clearly not only separation-of-power federalism but also power-sharing between levels that can constrain the demos and democratic politics. In the final analysis, how federal democracies work depends not only on institutions of federalism and democracy but also on how actors and their modes of interaction in both arenas adapt to constraining conditions. In addition, conflicts in society and societal dynamics influence the dynamics of federalism and democracy and how actors shape the pattern of coupling between these dimensions. This situation points to the particular federal-democratic challenges in multinational federations in divided societies, which find expression in subnational regionalism. Among the federations included in this volume, Belgium, Canada, India, and Spain fall into this category.

According to Stepan (1999), multinational federations enable democracy by giving distinct societies a voice, or veto power. The establishment of federalism, however configured, should allow spaces and places of democratic self-rule for minority groups, on the one hand, while democratic politicization of federalism should mobilize subnational parties, parliaments, and civil society and their intermediation into the "centre" on the other. Canadian federalism has long been considered a prototype of multinational federal democracy, given the large, territorially concentrated, French-speaking minority and many non-territorially organized Indigenous peoples. The growing assertiveness of Quebec regionalist parties and the demos of Quebec have successfully prevented the Canadian federation from becoming centralized during the rise of the welfare state. In addition, they have contributed to making intergovernmental relations compatible with provincial autonomy and pressed for constitutional reforms that included parliaments and civil society.

Belgium, Spain, and India are further multinational federations. They share with Canada the combination of federalism and parliamentary democracy. In India and Spain, the majoritarian logic and dualist party competition has prevailed despite the rise of regional parties and the increasing pressure to accommodate the diversity of regional societies. In Belgium, this diversity finds expression in a party system divided along linguistic lines, with the consequence that, in combination with veto powers for minority groups, a consensus democracy has evolved.

Since the transition to democracy established with the Constitution of 1978, Spain has conformed clearly to the majoritarian type of parliamentary government and has been prone to government versus opposition dualism, with rather strong executives and mostly single-party governments. The weak second chamber hardly moderates this majoritarianism. Yet, from the outset, democratization coincided with federalization, establishing a State of Autonomies and a right to self-government for the seventeen autonomous communities (ACs), including the three "historical nationalities" (Basque Country, Catalonia, Galicia) (Moreno 2001, 109–24). The Constitution separates powers, but it is "open ended" because it leaves the exact distribution to the statute reforms of the ACs, provided that the federal government agrees. Intergovernmental relations have subsequently developed but still lack coherent institutionalization. On the other hand, fiscal equalization is one of the rare features of de facto joint decision-making, whereas the reform of AC statutes is a matter of bilateral negotiations.

On the whole, these ambivalences are reflected in the highly dynamic relations between federalism and democracy in Spain. As in other cases, political contestation among political parties affects coordination and integration between the levels of government. As César Colino (chap. 11) points out, the loose coupling between governments at the central and regional levels can make governance in informal intergovernmental relations more cooperative and consensus-seeking since multi-level, intra-party coordination helps to moderate centrifugal tendencies. In line with competitive, partisan political dynamics, intergovernmental relations do become politicized, at times, by national opposition parties that are in government at the regional level, but national law-making processes or intergovernmental relations do not necessarily wind up in deadlock or joint-decision traps.

On occasion, minority governments moderate the competitive logics of parliamentary democracy. From this point of view, the escalation of the regionalist conflict with Catalonia in the last few years, which culminated dramatically in the vote to secede from Spain in 2017, ultimately appears exceptional rather than typical of relations between the central and AC governments because it was instigated by unresolved conflicts over fiscal equalization and the unilateral rejection by a conservative, unitarist federal government and the Constitutional Court of the Catalonians' 2006 reform of its statute of autonomy. This polarization between federal and regional parties, whose hands were tied by constitutional law and a referendum, respectively, caused a serious crisis of federal democracy in Spain.

India shares with Canada and Australia the combination of a federation with a parliamentary system and a majoritarian democracy. During the postcolonial process of state-building, a strong nationalism was deemed to integrate the divided society. Yet strong allegiances of people to their states and further diverse regional identities remained. Therefore, the Indian federation is much more variegated, both in its territorial structures and in the economic, religious, and ethnic diversity of its society. Moreover, Indian parliamentary democracy has some counter-majoritarian features, including bicameralism and judicial review. The interplay of these features led Lijphart (1996) to formulate the "puzzle of Indian democracy," which, in his view, could be "resolved" because of the recurring phases of consociational politics.

However, as Wilfried Swenden and Katharine Adeney assert, the adaptation of federal governance as well as readjusting the vertical division of powers and even constituent-unit boundaries has proved pivotal to balancing Indian federal democracy. The territorial reorganization along linguistic and ethnic lines, including the division and creation of new states, has turned societal conflicts into a matter of multi-level governance and made the federation considerably less centralized than in its original constitutional configuration (see also Singh and Saxena 2015).

However, Indian "cooperative federalism" (Majeed 2005) is based on loosely coupled structures. The second chamber has no veto power against the parliament. Intergovernmental coordination developed out of a largely hierarchical mode of governance – exemplified, for instance, by the use of President's Rule, or top-down economic planning – towards cooperative but informal and consultative modes, when the federal government was increasingly challenged by regional parties and looming conflicts. Moreover, while intergovernmental conferences have developed, albeit with a rather small degree of institutionalization, cross-level and interstate coordination has intensified, particularly as a result of administrative relations, which constitute an important pattern of loose coupling. Finally, intra-party and cross-level coordination also play a critical role in mediating regional interests. The dynamics in this more and more loosely coupled federal democracy have so far maintained a balanced system. However, one should not ignore the tendency towards authoritarian rule of the federal government over secessionist state governments and regional autocracies in certain states; these are instances where both federalism and democracy are threatened by domination.

Among not only multinational but also federal countries in general, Belgian federal democracy provides a unique case in several regards. Its historical development began with democratization in the nineteenth century, followed by a series of constitutional reforms, beginning in 1970, in which the unitary state turned into a federation. Since the formal transition to a federation in 1993, the process of federalization has continued to the present day. Geared towards linguistic-territorial accommodation, and spurred on particularly by Flemish regionalist demands, the six state reforms between 1970 and 2011 produced an undoubtedly particular pattern of federalism. It is organized not only by territorial but also by linguistic constituent units. As Petra Meier and Peter Bursens describe in chapter 10, the reforms have adhered to rather one-sided dynamics since they have been aimed at federalism, without making major efforts to adjust democratic institutions and processes accordingly.

Although Belgium is a parliamentary system, like Switzerland it had long represented a model case of consociational democracy, with oversized governmental coalitions and even broader cross-party and corporatist negotiation patterns in the unitary state (Anderweg 2000). When federalism rather than consociationalism became the prevailing mode of pacifying regional antagonisms, this led to increased decentralization (Deschouwer 2006), but also an incremental disconnection of federalism and democracy. This process is reflected in the separation of competences for the different policy areas, with governments actually avoiding interference and joint responsibilities, and the downgrading of the Senate as a second chamber.

As it stands, Belgian federal democracy is made up of a bifurcated party system as well as a civic society divided along regional-linguistic lines. Tight couplings such as joint decision-making have proved to be destabilizing arrangements, so that uncoupling offers a coping strategy for holding Belgium's federal democracy together. As Meier and Bursens conclude, the thrust of the developments favouring "the dominance of the demoï over the demos" has weakened parliamentary democracy at the central level, but also brought about few cross-governmental interlinkages. In consequence, political executives and party leaders have taken on a pivotal role in linking the federal and regional arenas through their coordination and coalition-building practices (see also, e.g., Deschouwer 2006; Swenden 2002). In the absence of statewide parties, and under the conditions of a structurally rather uncoupled intergovernmental dimension of government, these patterns of negotiation have proved appropriate for managing the tensions between self-rule in the territorial regions and linguistic communities, but they have seen agreements regularly benefiting the regions and communities at the cost of the federal government and democracy. Thus, these agreements put the stability of the federation at risk.

As the four cases of multinational federations demonstrate, the divides among regional societies increase the tensions in a federal democracy, both as regards majoritarian rule within governments and relations between governments. Tightly coupled intergovernmental structures hardly exist in these cases, for good reason, since they would only increase the probability of deadlock and ignite conflicts. Instead, we find different patterns of loosely coupled arrangements; only Belgium tends towards a distinctively informal, but routinized, joint-decision system among the regional coalition governments – a kind of executive-dominated federalism.

As already outlined above, Canadians cope with tensions in a multinational federation by pragmatically balancing parliamentary sovereignty with voluntary intergovernmental cooperation. In India and Spain, this balance is threatened by the unilateral politics of the regions aiming at secession and the reactions of the central government. Thus, maintaining a loosely coupled federal democracy is a continuous challenge, especially in divided societies, where tightly coupled structures would cause deadlocks but dissociated structures would increase the divides. This finding extends beyond this particular group of federations.

Loose Coupling: Democratic Politics and Intergovernmental Coordination

In constitutional terms, the structures of federal democracies vary between separation of powers and power-sharing. Power-sharing in parliamentary democracy is one cause of the tight coupling of intergovernmental relations to democracy. Joint decision-making between levels of governments constitutes a second constraint tying the hands of executives. As comparative research reveals, this combination of a tightly coupled federal democracy, which we find in Germany, is an exceptional case, as is, conversely, the separation of powers in both the democratic system and the federalism that characterizes the US federal democracy. Most cases exhibit a loosely coupled arrangement in at least one dimension.

When we take into account the operation of federal democracies, including the processes and patterns of interaction that emerge within their institutions, we discover even more loosely coupled patterns. Institutions define the rules of democratic governments and federalism, but effective linkages among them develop in practice and under varying conditions. Among these conditions, two are particularly relevant and affect how federal democracies work. In democracy, it is party politics in a particular party system that determines executive-legislative relations, but it also affects how executives coordinate policies between levels and constituent governments in a federation. The other condition relates to intergovernmental policymaking. Governments can aim to coordinate their policies in either institutionalized or informal processes (Bolleyer 2009; Poirier, Saunders, and Kincaid 2016), but whether and how they interact depends on the strategic action of political executives and administrations. Depending on the actor constellation in a democracy, governments provide more or fewer opportunities for executives to adjust intergovernmental policy to politics.

It has been discovered that party politics is a main determining factor in federations, and there is an extensive literature on different aspects of it, from the impact of federalism on party systems to party preferences for centralization and decentralization. To understand federal democracies at work, the structural features of party politics are relevant. They relate to the horizontal and vertical dimension of a party system. The first has been considered in numerous studies on party systems (summarized in Kitschelt 2011), the second in recent extensions of these approaches to federations (Chhibber and Kollman 2004; Detterbeck 2012; Thorlakson 2009). Without going into the details of the different categorizations of party politics, we assume that the degree of party-political polarization in the horizontal dimension, and the integration or disjointedness, or regionalization, of a party system in the vertical dimension, is most relevant for understanding how federal democracies actually work. This assumption is supported by the case studies collected in this volume.

Polarization in party competition is more likely in majoritarian democracies with two-party systems, but it can also arise in multiparty ones. In parliamentary systems, it increases the commitment of executives to parties in parliament and intensifies the contest between majority and opposition. In non-parliamentary systems with divided governments, polarization can obstruct legislation and constrain the executive, as exemplified in the United States, particularly since the mid-1990s. Tight coupling of political executives to parties also affects intergovernmental policymaking in federalism. In institutionalized negotiation systems, it can lead actors into the paradoxical situation of antagonistic cooperation or the joint-decision trap, a concept that Fritz

Table 13.2. Coupling by party politics

		Multi-level party organization	
		Integrated	Disjointed or regionalized
Party competition	Polarized	Tight coupling	Disconnection of levels
	Pluralist	Loose coupling	Loose coupling

Source: Benz (2019, 399).

W. Scharpf originally theorized in his research on Germany and the European Union (EU) (Scharpf 1988).

In federations with separation of powers and non-institutionalized intergovernmental relations, political executives tend to avoid cooperation when confronted with party polarization, with the consequence that informal patterns of coordination can temporarily dissolve, as occurred in Canada between 2009 and 2015. In multinational federal democracies, polarization typically manifests in confrontations between mainstream parties at the centre and regionalist parties that demand autonomy or threaten secession. Again, this political constellation encumbers intergovernmental relations, as can be observed in Canada during the 1980s and 1990s and in Spain since 2010.

Multiparty systems do not prevent polarization, but they generally favour pluralist competition. Under this condition, executives are always compelled to find compromises with partners from other parties, be it to form governments and implement their legislative program or to coordinate policies across levels of government. Due to the varying actor constellations in a pluralist party system, executives have to find procedures to circumvent the constraints of institutions and to establish flexible linkages. Accordingly, we observe loosely coupled patterns of interaction emerging under these conditions. For instance, governments can shift negotiations on agreements to informal processes among experts, bureaucrats, and stakeholders in a policy field. Switzerland is a case in point for this kind of governance, and similar tendencies can be observed in Germany. In Australia and India, bodies of experts have a significant impact on multi-level governance. In Belgium, where parties play a strong role in policies that shape the federal system, we observe a shift of decision-making from formal arenas of democratic government to negotiations among party leaders.

Parties generally, but evidently more so in integrated party systems, can also be an arena of coordination between levels of government.

They provide venues for exchanging information and opinions among members of parliament and the governments of the different levels. At the same time, parties represent overlapping cleavages between party politics and intergovernmental politics. Regardless of the institutional arrangements of the federal system and democracy, integrated party systems create loose ties between the two arenas.

From this point of view, the trend towards disjointed and regionalized parties, which is described in the relevant literature (Detterbeck, Renzsch, and Kincaid 2016; Swenden and Maddens 2009) and in most chapters of this book, seems to be problematic. In the United States, nationalization of the polarized parties has undermined their regional level and, thus, disrupted a formerly important channel of communication between the federal and state governments. This situation contrasts with the decentralized Australian party system, which still serves as a linkage structure between levels of government, and it moderates majority rule in that parliamentary democracy. In Canada, the regionalization of the party system has reinforced conflicts between the provinces and the central government. In Germany, integrated parties still exist, but integration has weakened in the last few decades. In Belgium, federal parties have been dissolved, and, in that pluralist party system, the remaining regional parties compete, usually with the aim of strengthening the regions. In Spain, the two mainstream parties are still integrated, but they are challenged by regional parties, not unlike what can be observed in India.

In principle, federalized or regionalized parties can become driving forces of decentralization and, in this way, also of democratizing regional politics. However, if they fail to link federalism and democracy to constitute a loosely coupled pattern of governance, they can also become a risk to the stability of a federal democracy.

Party politics, like the patterns of democracy, reveal a compound of conditions that policymakers cannot really influence. The disintegrative trends in party systems as well as political polarization reflect changes in society. However, in the complex and redundant structures of a federal system (Landau 1969, 1973), parties are not the only linkage structures. Most important are the patterns of intergovernmental policy coordination. In contrast with party systems, these patterns can be shaped in various ways as long as they are not strictly regulated in the constitution. As a rule, they can be adjusted to create a loosely coupled constellation, although change is constrained by the path dependency of the existing patterns of interaction or institutions. Waivers in the United States; opt-outs in Canada, which increase policy options in the case of highly politicized issues; cooperation among the cantons in the shadow of central regulation or referendums in Switzerland; and "soft governance" by guidelines, or by naming and shaming in German budget policy are examples of how multi-level governance can be made flexible. Adjustment is also possible if intergovernmental relations consist of layers of political and administrative relations or include actors from civil society and if party-political processes are complemented by bureaucratic or participatory processes.

The chapters collected in this volume have not focused on the role of administration, which is still not appropriately considered in research. There is, however, no doubt that what is summarized under the concept of intergovernmental relations includes administrative policymaking. In federations where powers are functionally separated, so that the federal government is responsible for legislation and the regional governments are responsible for implementation, central and regional administrations often communicate on drafts for legislation or on standards of implementation of the law. This is particularly the case in countries where equality of public services is considered a basic public value, as is the case in Australia (Painter 2001) and Germany (Behnke 2019), but also in the United States, where many intergovernmental programs are implemented by state or local administrations (Peterson, Rabe, and Wong 1995). In Switzerland, horizontal cooperation among the cantons is also prepared by administrations, whereas in India, vertical coordination rests to a considerable degree on expert bodies.

When administrations cooperate to implement programs or laws, they are, as a rule, separated from the democratic process and thus rarely influenced by politics. They participate in a kind of de facto joint-decision system and are motivated to find agreements to fulfil their tasks. This "bureaucratization" can make political control of administration rather difficult. However, if administrations are involved in intergovernmental policy, they prepare agreements to be concluded by the political members of their governments. Using their expertise, they can influence policymaking and moderate antagonistic negotiations among political executives. This enables the interplay of politics and administration to loosen the strong ties linking intergovernmental relations to party politics (Benz, Detemple, and Heinz 2016, 61–3, 190–1; Johns, O'Reilly, and Inwood 2006). However, administrative policymaking cannot prevent confrontation among governments in polarized party systems. There is also the risk that closed and opaque administrative networks undermine the autonomy of democratic politics in federal and regional governments. Executive dominance would be the consequence.

Dominance and Balance: Is Executive-Dominated Federalism Inevitable?

With growing interdependence between the levels of governments in a federal democracy, the respective executives have to coordinate their policies. In consequence, they can exploit informal processes and asymmetrical information to dominate the majority party or party coalition and, thus, the parliament. Although executive dominance has been discussed as a general problem in a functionally differentiated, complex, and dynamic society, it confronts federal democracies, as John Erik Fossum and David Laycock have outlined in chapter 4, in particular ways. Federalism increases institutional complexity, which adds to policy complexity. This problem cannot be solved merely by "bringing government closer to the people" through decentralization since decentralization would only increase interdependence between governments. Federalism is about balancing centralization and decentralization to reduce problems that transgress the borders of jurisdictions and to mitigate the external effects of policies, but it can never rule out interdependence. Therefore, tensions between federalism and democracy are inevitable, though they can be managed.

Executive federalism must not contradict democracy, as Thomas Hueglin has outlined (Hueglin 2013a), provided that parliaments can control the executive and that federal democracy is not "out of balance" (Fossum and Laycock, chap. 4). Balance is not only at risk in tightly coupled or uncoupled systems but also remains fragile in loosely coupled arrangements, which are always ambiguous (Fossum 2019, 319). Though such linkages prove highly flexible and thus allow actors to manage tensions, this is exactly what makes them susceptible to the volatility of power structures. Executive dominance is one effect of this instability, which, in this case, is caused by a shift towards tightly coupled intergovernmental relations. Another indication of imbalance is party polarization, which compels executives to adhere to the will of their party and extend the game of party competition to the arena of federalism. Other ways to cope with tensions in a federal democracy can also cause domination, be it by technocrats or by courts. In contrast, additional patterns of negotiation and deliberation within integrated parties, interparliamentary relations, or public forums, including experts and representatives of civil society, can contribute to stabilizing loosely coupled structures since they provide sufficient redundancy to countervail the domination of actors.

Balance and imbalance are the results of processes; thus, they cannot be secured. Domination of executives, technocrats, or parties is regularly contested, less so the dominance of courts. As a result, non-dominated federal democracies may result from shifts between executive governance in federalism and democratic politics, as can be observed in Canada (see Broschek, chap. 8). In the EU, scholars have also observed that national parliaments have reacted to multi-level governance by adjusting their capacities and rules of interaction with the executive (Hix and Raunio 2000). The rise of regionalist parties is a response to domination by majoritarian democracy or by executive federalism. These reactions against different instances of domination can cause instability on their own, particularly in divided societies, as exemplified in Spain. However, whereas loosely coupled federal democracies are particularly vulnerable to instability, they are also more prone to dynamics and thus to correcting destabilizing tendencies.

Conclusion: Prospects for Comparative Federalism

For a long time, the relationship between federalism and democracy remained underexposed in research. According to the mainstream of theorizing and the common assumptions that guided comparative research, the two constitutional principles should complement each other, and tensions and conflicts resulted from the misdirected implementation of both principles in institutions and practices. Scholars following this view did not recognize that the adopted normative concepts of federalism and democracy aimed to limit power as a means of securing liberty rather than enabling effective governance for the purpose of solving societal problems. They underestimated the fact that, in reality, federal democracies are confronted with incongruent structures and conflicting modes of operation. Whereas federalism constitutes a multi-level system of governance, irrespective of the particular division of powers, representative democracy is bound to a territory in which a congruent relationship between a community of citizens and governance by responsible representatives can be organized.

This institutional divide has been intensely discussed in the literature on the democratic deficits of international or European politics, but it was rarely reflected in research on federalism. At best, problematic tensions were recognized in federal states with parliamentary systems of government. Upon closer inspection, however, this inference holds neither across all cases nor even over time within particular ones, and it neglects similar tensions in federations with non-parliamentary governments.

As the chapters collected in this volume indicate, we need to revise the general assumption of an unproblematic complementarity of federalism and democracy. This assumption is still based on ideas of the

US model or of Swiss consensus democracy, which are either no longer confirmed by empirical research or not transferable to other cases. At the same time, the incompatibilities of parliamentary federalism should not be exaggerated. On the one hand, this model encompasses a range of configurations, as a closer look at Canada, Australia, India, Spain, Belgium, and Germany reveals. On the other hand, political actors in federal democracies react to the institutional tensions that exist, and they find procedures to reduce them or to avoid conflicts.

Future research must uncover these reactions in greater detail and analyse their conditions and effects. In addition, research must focus on societal changes that primarily affect federalism and democracy through changes in party systems. In this context, we need to learn more about how loosely coupled institutional arrangements can be stabilized in federations with deeply divided societies and to better understand the causes of the frictions resulting from the inevitable tensions in federal democracies that are confronted with ethnic, linguistic, and/or regional conflicts. Last but not least, the multiple patterns of intergovernmental relations need to be examined in terms of their compatibility with democratic governance. They can turn tightly coupled or disintegrated systems into loosely coupled constellations of a federal democracy, without resulting in a domination of executives or bureaucrats over parliaments. Rather, they can establish patterns of policy coordination that are open to agenda-setting and control by parliaments and may be adjusted to the dynamics of democratic politics.

The great relevance of this research becomes obvious if we acknowledge that democratic deficits in federations cannot be solved simply by strictly separating powers between levels of government, by minimizing external effects through territorial reforms, or by resolving fundamental conflicts through secession. In the complex societies in which we are living, many pressing political problems and public tasks cannot be territorially confined, and interdependences cannot be eliminated, regardless of the territorial organization of a political order. The idea that a return to the nation state would solve the complications and dilemmas of democracy in multi-level systems turns out to be the illusion of populist parties, as does the expectation of those arguing or fighting for regional autonomy. Federalism, like democracy, constitutes a sustainable principle of political order, one that cannot be realized only by the formal rules in a constitution, but has to be lived through governmental practice. Thus, the real challenge for a federal democracy is to reconcile the different purposes, structures, and mechanisms of policymaking in a pragmatic way and through the appropriate institutions, procedures, and patterns of interaction among those actors that make federal democracy work.

References

Abramovitz, Alan, and Steven Webster. 2016. "The Rise of Negative Partisanship and the Nationalization of U.S. Elections in the 21st Century." *Electoral Studies* 41 (March): 12–22. https://doi.org/10.1016/j.electstud.2015.11.001.

Abromeit, Heidrun. 1992. *Der verkappte Einheitsstaat*. Wiesbaden: VS Verlag für Sozialwissenschaften.

Adeney, Katharine. 2007. *Federalism and Ethnic Conflict Regulation in India and Pakistan*. Basingstoke, UK: Palgrave Macmillan.

– 2017. "Does Ethnofederalism Explain the Success of Indian Federalism?" *India Review* 16 (1): 125–48. https://doi.org/10.1080/14736489.2017.1279933.

– 2020. "How Can We Model Ethnic Democracy? An Application to Contemporary India." Nations and Nationalism. Published ahead of print, 24 July. https://doi.org/10.1111/nana.12654.

Adeney, Katharine, and Lawrence Sáez, eds. 2005. *Coalition Politics and Hindu Nationalism*. London: Routledge.

Adeney, Katharine, and Andrew Wyatt. 2004. "Democracy in South Asia: Getting beyond the Structure-Agency Dichotomy." *Political Studies* 52 (1): 1–18. https://doi.org/10.1111/j.1467-9248.2004.00461.x.

Aja, Eliseo, and César Colino. 2014. "Multilevel Structures, Coordination and Partisan Politics in Spanish Intergovernmental Relations." *Comparative European Politics* 12 (4–5): 444–67. https://doi.org/10.1057/cep.2014.9.

Ajenjo, Natalia, and Ignacio Molina. 2009. "Spain: Majoritarian Choices, Disciplined Party Government and Compliant Legislature." In *The Role of Governments in Legislative Agenda Setting*, edited by Bjørn Erik Rasch and George Tsebelis, 164–83. London: Routledge.

Albertazzi, Daniele, and Sean Mueller. 2013. "Populism and Liberal Democracy: Populists in Government in Austria, Italy, Poland and Switzerland." *Government and Opposition* 48 (3): 343–71. https://doi.org/10.1017/gov.2013.12.

Aldrich, John H. 1995. *Why Parties? The Origin and Transformation of Political Parties in America*. Chicago: University of Chicago Press.

Allan, Kate, and George Parker. 2017. "UK Lays Out Plans for Repealing and Replacing EU Laws." *Financial Times*, 30 March.

Alonso, Sonea. 2011. "Representative Democracy and the Multinational Demos." In *The Future of Representative Democracy*, edited by Sonia Alonso, John Keane, and Wolfgang Merkel, 169–90. Cambridge: Cambridge University Press.

Althusius, Johannes. 1995. *Politica: An Abridged Translation of Politics Methodically Set Forth and Illustrated with Sacred and Profane Examples*, edited by Frederick S. Carney. Foreword by Daniel J. Elazar. Indianapolis, IN: Liberty Fund. First published 1614.

Álvarez-Tardío, Manuel. 2005. *El camino a la democracia en España (1931 y 1978)*. Madrid: Gota a Gota.

Anderweg, Rudy. 2000. "Consociational Democracy." *Annual Review of Political Science* 3 (1): 509–36. https://doi.org/10.1146/annurev.polisci.3.1.509.

Arban, Erika. 2013. "La subsidiarité en droit européen et canadien: Une comparaison." *Canadian Public Administration* 56 (2): 219–34. https://doi.org/10.1111/capa.12015.

Arceneaux, Kevin. 2005. "Does Federalism Weaken Democratic Representation in the United States?" *Publius* 35 (2): 297–311. https://doi.org/10.1093/publius/pji015.

Arens, Alexander, Tobias Arnold, Sean Mueller, and Adrian Vatter. 2017. "Föderalismus und Dezentralisierung in der Schweiz: Die politischen Effekte der Föderalismusreform NFA." In *Jahrbuch des Föderalismus* 2017, edited by Europäisches Zentrum für Föderalismus-Forschung Tübingen, 184–97. Baden-Baden, Germany: Nomos.

Arias Maldonado, Manuel. 2019. "Divide y vencerás." *El Mundo*, 26 December.

Aristotle. 1962. *Politics*. London: Penguin. First date of publication unknown.

Armingeon, Klaus. 2000. "Swiss Federalism in Comparative Perspective." In *Federalism and Political Performance*, edited by Ute Wachendorfer-Schmidt, 112–29. London: Routledge. https://doi.org/10.1080/01402389708425223.

Aroney, Nicholas. 2010. "New Zealand, Australasia and Federation." *Canterbury Law Review* 31 (16): 31–46.

Aroney, Nicholas, and Campbell Sharman. 2018. "Statewide Parties in Western and Eastern Europe: Territorial Patterns of Party Organizations." In *Handbook of Territorial Politics*, edited by Klaus Detterbeck and Eve Hepburn, 388–400. Cheltenham, UK: Edward Elgar.

Arroyo Gil, Antonio. 2018. "Calidad democrática y distribución territorial del poder, con especial atención al reparto de competencias y a la cámara de representación territorial." In *Calidad democrática y Organización territorial*, edited by José Tudela, Mario Kölling, and Fernando Reviriego, 53–68. Madrid: Marcial Pons.

Aucoin, Peter, Mark Jarvis, and Lori Turnbull. 2011. *Democratizing the Constitution: Reforming Responsible Government*. Toronto: Emond Montgomery.

Auel, Katrin, and Christine Neuhold. 2017. "Multi-Arena Players in the Making? Conceptualizing the Role of National Parliaments since the Lisbon Treaty." *Journal of European Public Policy* 24 (10): 1547–61. https://doi.org/10.1080/13501763.2016.1228694.

Austin, Granville. 1966. *The Indian Constitution: Cornerstone of a Nation*. London: Clarendon Press.

Bach, Stanley. 2003. *Platypus and Parliament: The Australian Senate in Theory and Practice*. Canberra: Department of the Australian Senate.

Bächtiger, André, and Jürg Steiner. 2004. "Switzerland: Territorial Cleavage Management as Paragon and Paradox." In *Federalism and Territorial Cleavages*, edited by Ugo M. Amoretti and Nancy Bermeo, 27–54. Baltimore, MD: Johns Hopkins University Press.

Bajpai, Rochana. 2011. *Debating Difference: Group Rights and Liberal Democracy in India*. New Delhi: Oxford University Press.

Bakvis, Herman, and Grace Skogstad. 2012. "Canadian Federalism: Performance, Effectiveness, and Legitimacy." In *Canadian Federalism*. 3rd ed., edited by Herman Bakvis and Grace Skogstad, 2–19. Don Mills, ON: Oxford University Press.

Bakvis, Herman, and Steven B. Wolinetz. 2005. "Canada: Executive Dominance and Presidentialization." In *The Presidentialization of Politics: A Comparative Study of Modern Democracies*, edited by Thomas Poguntke and Paul Webb, 199–220. New York: Oxford University Press.

Balz, Dan. 2014. "National Governors Association Showing Deep Republican, Democratic Divisions." *Washington Post*, 25 February.

Banting, Keith. 2005. "Canada: Nation-Building in a Federal Welfare State." In *Federalism and the Welfare State: New World and European Experiences*, edited by Herbert Obinger, Stephan Leibfried, and Francis Castles, 89–137. Cambridge: Cambridge University Press.

Banting, Keith, and Robin Boadway. 2004. "Defining the Sharing Community: The Federal Role in Health Care." In *Money, Politics and Health Care: Reconstructing the Federal-Provincial Partnership*, edited by Harvey Lazar and France St-Hilaire, 1–78. Montreal: Institute for Research on Public Policy.

Baragona, Steve. 2017. "After US Climate Accord Exit, State, Local Governments Step Up." *Voice of America*, 2 June.

Barber, N.W. 2005. "The Limited Modesty of Subsidiarity." *European Law Journal* 11 (3): 308–25. https://doi.org/10.1111/j.1468-0386.2005.00261.x.

Baron, Nacima. 2017. "Le modèle institutionnel espagnol au point limite? L'échec de la loi Dépendance ou la solidarité à l'épreuve des crises." *Rives méditerranéennes* 53: 185–97. https://doi.org/10.4000/rives.5128.

Barrio, Astrid, Gabriel Colomé, and Jonatan Garcia. 2018. "El factor territorial y los nacionalismos." In *Las elecciones generales de 2015 y 2016*, edited by Francisco J. Llera, Baras Montserrat, and Juan Montabes, 273–97. Madrid: CIS.

Barrios-Suvelza, Franz Xavier. 2014. "The Case for Conceptual Dichotomies in Comparative Federalism: Can Political Science Learn from Comparative Constitutional Law?" *Territory, Politics, Governance* 2 (1): 3–29. https://doi.org/10.1080/21622671.2013.866595.

Bates, Crispin. 2007. *Subalterns and Raj: South Asia since 1600*. London: Routledge.

Baumer, Donald C., and Howard J. Gold. 2010. *Parties, Polarization, and Democracy in the United States*. Boulder, CO: Paradigm Publishers.

Beam, David, Timothy Conlan, and David B. Walker. 1983. "Federalism: The Challenge of Conflicting Theories and Contemporary Practice." In *Political Science: The State of the Discipline*, edited by Ada W. Finifter, 247–79. Washington, DC: American Political Science Association.

Bednar, Jenna. 2009. *The Robust Federation: Principles of Design*. Cambridge: Cambridge University Press.

Bednar, Jenna, and Scott Page. 2016. "Complex Adaptive Systems and Comparative Politics: Modeling the Interaction between Institutions and Culture." *Chinese Political Science Review* 1 (3): 448–71. https://doi.org/10.1007/s41111-016-0039-6.

Beer, Samuel. 1976. "The Adoption of General Revenue Sharing: A Case Study in Public Sector Politics." *Public Policy* 24 (2): 127–95.

– 1978. "Federalism, Nationalism, and Democracy in America." *American Political Science Review* 72 (1): 9–21. https://doi.org/10.2307/1953596.

– 1992. *To Make a Nation: The Rediscovery of American Federalism*. Cambridge, MA: Harvard University Press.

Behnke, Nathalie. 2019. "How Bureaucratic Networks Make Intergovernmental Relations Work: A Mechanism Perspective." In *Configurations, Dynamics and Mechanisms of Multilevel Governance*, edited by Nathalie Behnke, Jörg Broschek, and Jared Sonnicksen, 41–59. Cham, Switzerland: Palgrave Macmillan.

Behnke, Nathalie, and Arthur Benz. 2009. "The Politics of Constitutional Change between Reform and Evolution." *Publius* 39 (2): 213–40. https://doi.org/10.1093/publius/pjn039.

Behnke, Nathalie, and Sabine Kropp. 2016. "Arraying Institutional Layers in Federalism Reforms: Lessons from the German Case." *Regional and Federal Studies* 26 (5): 585–602. https://doi.org/10.1080/13597566.2016.1236026.

Behnke, Nathalie, and Sean Mueller. 2017. "The Purpose of Intergovernmental Councils: A Framework for Analysis and Comparison." *Regional and Federal Studies* 27 (5): 507–27. https://doi.org/10.1080/13597566.2017.1367668.

Behrend, Jacqueline, and Laurence Whitehead, eds. 2016. *Illiberal Practices: Territorial Variance within Large Federal Democracies*. Baltimore, MD: Johns Hopkins University Press.

Benz, Arthur. 2000. "Two Types of Multi-level Governance: Intergovernmental Relations in German and EU Regional Policy." *Regional and Federal Studies* 10 (3): 21–44. https://doi.org/10.1080/13597560008421130.

– 2009. "Ein gordischer Knoten der Politikwissenschaft? Zur Vereinbarkeit von Föderalismus und Demokratie." *Politische Vierteljahresschrift* 50 (1): 3–22. https://doi.org/10.1007/s11615-009-0123-8.

– 2012. "Yardstick Competition and Policy Learning in Multi-level Systems." *Regional and Federal Studies* 22 (3): 251–67. https://doi.org/10.1080/13597566.2012.688270.

– 2013. "Dimensions and Dynamics of Federal Regimes." In *Federal Dynamics: Continuity, Change, and the Varieties of Federalism*, edited by Arthur Benz and Jörg Broschek, 70–90. Oxford: Oxford University Press.

– 2015. "Making Democracy Work in a Federal System." *German Politics* 24 (1): 8–25. https://doi.org/10.1080/09644008.2014.921906.

– 2016. *Constitutional Policy in Multilevel Government: The Art of Keeping the Balance*. Oxford: Oxford University Press.

– 2017a. "Ein Verteilungskampf, in dem alle gewonnen haben? Oder ein Tauschgeschäft zum Nachteil von Föderalismus und Demokratie?" In *Jahrbuch des Föderalismus 2017: Föderalismus, Subsidiarität und Regionen in Europa*, edited by the Europäisches Zentrum für Föderalismus-Forschung Tübingen, 63–76. Baden-Baden: Nomos.

– 2017b. "Patterns of Multilevel Parliamentary Relations: Varieties and Dynamics in the EU and Other Federations." *Journal of European Public Policy* 24 (4): 499–519. https://doi.org/10.1080/13501763.2016.1273371.

– 2019. "Conclusion: Governing under the Condition of Complexity." In *Configurations, Dynamics and Mechanisms of Multilevel Governance*, edited by Nathalie Behnke, Jörg Broschek, and Jared Sonnicksen, 387–409. Cham, Switzerland: Palgrave Macmillan.

Benz, Arthur, and Jörg Broschek. 2013a. "Conclusion: Theorizing Federal Dynamics." In *Federal Dynamics: Continuity, Change, and the Varieties of Federalism*, edited by Arthur Benz and Jörg Broschek, 366–88. Oxford: Oxford University Press.

–, eds. 2013b. *Federal Dynamics: Continuity, Change, and the Varieties of Federalism*. Oxford: Oxford University Press.

– 2013c. "Federal Dynamics: Introduction." In *Federal Dynamics: Continuity, Change, and the Varieties of Federalism*, edited by Arthur Benz and Jörg Broschek, 1–23. Oxford: Oxford University Press.

Benz, Arthur, Jessica Detemple, and Dominic Heinz. 2016. *Varianten und Dynamiken der Politikverflechtung im deutschen Bundesstaat*. Baden-Baden: Nomos.

Benz, Arthur, and Sabine Kropp. 2014. "Föderalismus in Demokratien und Autokratien: Vereinbarkeiten, Spannungsfelder und Dynamiken." *Zeitschrift für Vergleichende Politikwissenschaft* 8 (1): 1–27. https://doi.org/10.1007/s12286-014-0179-8.

Benz, Arthur, and Jared Sonnicksen. 2015. "Federalism and Democracy: Compatible or at Odds with One Another? Re-examining a Tense Relationship." In *Citizen Participation in Multi-level Democracies*, edited by Christina Fraenkel-Haeberle, Sabine Kropp, Francesco Palermo, and Karl-Peter Sommermann, 15–30. Leiden, The Netherlands: Brill.

– 2017. "Patterns of Federal Democracy: Tensions, Friction, or Balance between Two Government Dimensions." *European Political Science Review* 9 (1): 3–25. https://doi.org/10.1017/s1755773915000259.

– 2018. "Advancing Backwards: Why Institutional Reform of German Federalism Reinforced Joint Decision-Making." *Publius* 48 (1): 134–59. https://doi.org/10.1093/publius/pjx055.

Berdahl, Loleen. 2013. "(Sub)National Economic Union: Institutions, Ideas, and Internal Trade Policy in Canada." *Publius* 43 (2): 251–74. https://doi.org/10.1093/publius/pjs036.

– 2014. "The West in Canada: Assessing the West's Role in the Post-2011 Federal System." In *Canada: The State of the Federation 2011; The Changing Federal Environment*, edited by Nadia Verelli, 45–63. Montreal and Kingston: McGill-Queen's University Press.

Bermann, George. 1994. "Taking Subsidiarity Seriously: Federalism in the European Community and the United States." *Columbia Law Review* 94 (2): 331–456. https://doi.org/10.2307/1123200.

Bernauer, Julian, and Adrian Vatter. 2019. *Power, Diffusion and Democracy: Institutions, Deliberation and Outcomes*. Cambridge: Cambridge University Press.

Beyers, Jan, and Peter Bursens. 2006. "The European Rescue of the Federal State: How Europeanisation Shapes the Belgian State." *West European Politics* 29 (5): 1057–78. https://doi.org/10.1080/01402380600968984.

– 2013. "How Europe Shapes the Nature of the Belgian Federation: Differentiated EU Impact Triggers Both Co-operation and Decentralization." *Regional and Federal Studies* 23 (3): 271–91. https://doi.org/10.1080/13597566.2013.773898.

Bhattacharyya, Harihar, and Jhumpa Mukherjee. 2018. "Bodo Ethnic Self-Rule and Persistent Violence in Assam: A Failed Case of Multinational Federalism in India." *Regional and Federal Studies* 28 (4): 469–87. https://doi.org/10.1080/13597566.2018.1478293.

Binder, Sarah. 2003. *Stalemate: Causes and Consequences of Legislative Gridlock*. Washington, DC: Brookings Institution Press.

Black, Edwin R., and Alan C. Cairns. 1966. "A Different Perspective on Canadian Federalism." *Canadian Public Administration* 9 (1): 27–44. https://doi.org/10.1111/j.1754-7121.1966.tb00919.x.

Blanco Valdés, Roberto. 2014. *El laberinto territorial*. Madrid: Alianza Editorial.

– 2017. "El año que vivimos peligrosamente: Del bipartidismo imperfecto a la perfecta ingobernabilidad." *Revista Española de Derecho Constitucional* (109): 63–96. https://doi.org/10.18042/cepc/redc.109.03.

– 2018. *Luz tras las tinieblas: Vindicación de la España constitucional*. Madrid: Alianza Editorial.

Blöchliger, Hansjörg, and Claire Charbit. 2008. "Fiscal Equalization." *OECD Journal: Economic Studies* 2008/1. https://doi.org/10.1787/eco_studies-v2008-art8-en.

Blyth, Mark. 2002. *Great Transformations: Economic Ideas and Institutional Change in the Twentieth Century*. Cambridge: Cambridge University Press.

Bochsler, Daniel. 2017. "Lo stemperamento dei contorni politici dei Cantoni svizzeri." In *Il federalismo svizzero: Attori, strutture e processi*, edited by Sean Mueller and Anja Giudici, 63–91. Locarno: Armanda Dadò.

Bogumil, Jörg, Falk Ebinger, and Linda Jochheim. 2012. "Spitzenbeamte und ihr Verhalten bei politisch relevanten Entscheidungen." In *Bürokratie im Irrgarten der Politik: Gedächtnisband für Hans-Ulrich Derlien*, edited by Dieter Schimanke, Sylvia Veit, and Hans-Peter Bull, 151–74. Baden-Baden: Nomos.

Bolleyer, Nicole. 2009. *Intergovernmental Cooperation: Rational Choices in Federal Systems and Beyond*. Oxford: Oxford University Press.

Bolleyer, Nicole, and Lori Thorlakson. 2012. "Beyond Decentralization: The Comparative Study of Interdependence in Federal Systems." *Publius* 42 (4): 566–91. https://doi.org/10.1093/publius/pjr053.

Bosco, Anna. 2018. *Le quattro crisi della Spagna*. Bologna, Spain: Il Mulino.

Bose, Sumantra. 1997. *The Challenge in Kashmir: Democracy, Self-Determination and a Just Peace*. New Delhi: Sage Publications.

Brass, Paul R. 1974. *Language, Religion and Politics in North India*. London: Cambridge University Press.

Braun, Dietmar, ed. 2000. *Public Policy and Federalism*. Aldershot, UK: Ashgate.

Breton, Albert. 1998. *Competitive Governments: An Economic Theory of Politics and Public Finance*. Cambridge: Cambridge University Press.

Brett, Judith. 2003. *Australian Liberals and the Moral Middle Class: From Alfred Deakin to John Howard*. Cambridge: Cambridge University Press.

Brock, Kathy. 2003. "Executive Federalism: Beggar Thy Neighbour?" In *New Trends in Canadian Federalism*, edited by François Rocher and Miriam C. Smith, 67–83. Petersborough, ON: Broadview Press.

Brody, David. 2012. "Only on Brody File: Paul Ryan Says His Catholic Faith Helped Shape Budget Plan." *thebrodyfile* (blog), CBN News. 4 October. https://www1.cbn.com/thebrodyfile/archive/2012/04/10/only-on-brody-file-paul-ryan-says-his-catholic-faith.

Broschek, Jörg. 2009. *Der kanadische Föderalismus: Eine historisch-institutionalistische Analyse*. Wiesbaden: VS Verlag.

– 2012. "Historical Institutionalism and the Varieties of Federalism in Germany and Canada." *Publius* 42 (4): 662–87. https://doi.org/10.1093/publius/pjr040.
– 2015a. "Exploring Authority Migration in Multilevel Architectures: A Historical-Institutionalist Framework." *Comparative European Politics* 13 (6): 656–81. https://doi.org/10.1057/cep.2014.17.
– 2015b. "Pathways of Federal Reform: Australia, Canada, Germany, and Switzerland." *Publius* 45 (1): 51–76. https://doi.org/10.1093/publius/pju030.
– 2016. "Federalism in Europe, America and Africa: A Comparative Analysis." In *Federalism and Decentralization: Perceptions for Political and Institutional Reforms*, edited by Wilhelm Hofmeister and Edmund Tayao, 23–50. Singapore: Konrad-Adenauer Stiftung; Makati City: Local Government Development Foundation.
– 2020. "Bicameralism and the Consequences of Political Structuring in Canada: Lost Alternatives, Future Options." In *Canadian Federalism and Its Future: Actors and Institutions*, edited by Alain-G. Gagnon and Johanne Poirier, 53–83. Montreal and Kingston: McGill-Queen's Univrsity Press.
Buchanan, James M. 1995. "Federalism as an Ideal Political Order and an Objective for Constitutional Reform." *Publius* 25 (2): 19–27. https://doi.org/10.2307/3330825.
Bunge, Mario. 1997. "Mechanism and Explanation." *Philosophy of the Social Sciences* 27 (4): 410–65. https://doi.org/10.1177/004839319702700402.
Burch, Traci, and Philip Edwards Jones. 2012. "Who Sings in the Heavenly Chorus? The Shape of the Organized Interest." In *The Unheavenly Chorus: Unequal Political Voice and the Broken Promise of American Democracy*, edited by Kay Lehman Schlozman, Sidney Verba, and Henry E. Brady, 312–46. Princeton, NJ: Princeton University Press.
Burgess, Michael. 2012. *In Search of the Federal Spirit: New Comparative, Empirical and Theoretical Perspectives*. Oxford: Oxford University Press.
Burgess, Michael, and Alain-G. Gagnon, eds. 2010. *Federal Democracies*. London: Routledge.
Burkhart, Simone. 2009. "Reforming Federalism in Germany: Incremental Changes Instead of the Big Deal." *Publius* 39 (2): 341–65. https://doi.org/10.1093/publius/pjn035.
Burkhart, Simone, and Philip Manow. 2006. "Kompromiss und Konflikt im parteipolitisierten Föderalismus der Bundesrepublik Deutschland." *Zeitschrift für Politikwissenschaft* 16 (3): 807–24. https://doi.org/10.5771/1430-6387-2006-3-807.
Burkhart, Simone, Philip Manow, and Daniel Ziblatt. 2008. "A More Efficient and Accountable Federalism? An Analysis of the Consequences of Germany's 2006 Constitutional Reform." *German Politics* 17 (4): 522–40. https://doi.org/10.1080/09644000802501349.

Burrell, Andrew. 2010. "The Raw Deal Is a Rich Resource in the West." *Weekend Australian*, 24 April. https://www.theaustralian.com.au/news/inquirer/the-raw-deal-is-a-rich-resource-in-the-west/news-story/3878298ecd5e33955ed1095699f9cdcd.

Bursens, Peter, Frederic Maes, and Matthias Vileyn. 2015. "Belgian Regional Assemblies in EU Policy-Making: The More Parliaments, the Less Participation in EU Affairs?" In *Subnational Parliaments in an EU Multi-level Parliamentary System: Taking Stock of the Post-Lisbon Era*, edited by Gabriel Abels and Annegret Eppler, 175–92. Innsbruck: Studienverlag.

Cairns, Alan C. 1968. "The Electoral System and the Party System in Canada, 1921–1965." *Canadian Journal of Political Science* 1 (1): 55–80. https://doi.org/10.1017/s0008423900035228.

– 1979a. *From Interstate to Intrastate Federalism in Canada*. Discussion Paper No. 5, Institute of Intergovernmental Relations. Kingston, ON: Queen's University.

– 1979b. "The Other Crisis of Canadian Federalism." *Canadian Public Administration* 22 (2): 175–95. https://doi.org/10.1111/j.1754-7121.1979.tb01811.x.

– 1992. *Charter versus Federalism: The Dilemmas of Constitutional Reform*. Montreal and Kingston: McGill-Queen's University Press.

Calhoun, John C. 2007. *A Disquisition on Government*. South Bend, IN: St. Augustine's Press. First published 1851.

Cameron, David. 2001. "Intergovernmental Relations in Canada." In *Intergovernmental Relations of Federal Countries*, edited by J. Peter Meekinson, 9–16. Ottawa: Forum of Federations.

Camissa, Anne. 1995. *Governments as Interest Groups: Intergovernmental Lobbying and the Federal System*. Westport, CT: Praeger.

Canadian Broadcasting Corporation. 2017. "The High Stakes of Philippe Couillard's Constitutional Project." https://www.cbc.ca/news/canada/montreal/the-high-stakes-of-philippe-couillard-s-constitutional-project-1.4141741.

Castellà, Josep M. 2006. "The Spanish Senate after 28 Years of Constitutional Experience: Proposals for Reform." In *A World of Second Chambers: Handbook for Constitutional Studies on Bicameralism*, edited by Jörg Luther, Paolo Passaglia, and Rolando Tarchi, 859–909. Milan: Guiffré.

– 2008. "El debate sobre la reforma del Senado y su incidencia en la forma de estado y la forma de gobierno." In *Estudios sobre la Constitucion Española: Homenaje al profesor Jordi Solé Tura*, edited by Congreso de los Diputados, 419–46. Madrid: Fundación Dialnet.

– 2018. *Estado autonómico: Pluralismo e integración constitucional*. Madrid: Macial Pons.

Castles, Francis G. 1985. *The Working Class and Welfare: Reflections on the Political Development of the Welfare State in Australia and New Zealand, 1890–1980*. Wellington: Allen & Unwin.

Celis, Karen, and Petra Meier. 2017. "Other Identities in Ethnofederations: Women's and Sexual Minorities' Advocacy in Belgium." *National Identities* 19 (4): 415–32. https://doi.org/10.1080/14608944.2016.1206068.

Chaqués Bonafont, Laura, Anna M. Palau, and Frank R. Baumgartner. 2015. *Agenda Dynamics in Spain*. Basingstoke, UK: Palgrave Macmillan.

Cheluva Raju, K.H. 1991. "Dr. B.R. Ambedkar and Making of the Constitution: A Case Study of Indian Federalism." *Indian Journal of Political Science* 52 (2): 153–60.

Cheneval, Francis, and Frank Schimmelfennig. 2013. "The Case for Demoicracy in the European Union." *JCMS: Journal of Common Market Studies* 51 (2): 334–50. https://doi.org/10.1111/j.1468-5965.2012.02262.x.

Chhibber, Pradeep K., and Ken Kollman. 2004. *The Formation of National Party Systems: Federalism and Party Competition in Canada, Great Britain, India, and the United States*. Princeton, NJ: Princeton University Press.

Churchill, Winston. 1947. United Kingdom. Parliament. House of Commons Debates. 11 November, vol. 444, column 207. https://hansard.parliament.uk/Commons/1947-11-11/debates/ac22a8ea-e202-4be6-b2b6-a5a448a12182/CommonsChamber.

Coleman, William, Selwyn Cornish, and Alf Hagger. 2006. *Giblin's Platoon: The Trials and Triumph of the Economist in Australian Public Life*. Canberra: ANU Press.

Colino, César. 2010. "¿Hacia la normalidad federal? La existencia y el surgimento reciente de nuevos mecanismos para la cooperación horizontal entre CC.AA." In *España y modelos de federalismo*, edited by José Tudela and Felix Knüpling, 341–60. Madrid: Centro de Estudios Juridicos y Constitucionales.

– 2013. "Intergovernmental Relations in the Spanish Federal System: In Search of a Model." In *The Ways of Federalism in Western Countries and the Horizons of Territorial Autonomy in Spain*, edited by Alberto López-Basaguren and Leire Escajedo San Epifanio, 111–24. Berlin: Springer.

– 2014. "Calidad democrática, crisis y reformas en el estado autonómico." In *Informe Comunidades Autónomas 2013*, edited by Eliseo Aja, Francisco Javier García Roca, and José Antonio Montilla Martos, 37–69. Barcelona: Instituto de Derecho Público.

– 2020. "Decentralisation in Spain: Federal Evolution and Performance of the Estado Autonómico." In *Oxford Handbook of Spanish Politics*, edited by Diego Muro and Ignacio Lago, 62–81. Oxford: Oxford University Press.

Colino, César, and Ramón Cotarelo. 2012. *España en crisis: Balance de la segunda legislatura de Zapatero*. Valencia: Tirant lo Blanch.

Colino, César, and Eloísa del Pino. 2010. *National and Subnational Democracy in Spain: History, Models and Challenges*. Working paper 7. Madrid: Instituto de Políticas y Bienes Públicos (IPP), CCHS-CSIC. http://hdl.handle.net/10261/24408.

– 2011. "Spain: Strong Regional Government and the Limits of Local Decentralization." In *The Oxford Handbook of Subnational Democracy in Europe*, edited by Frank Hendriks, Anders Lindström, and John Loughin, 356–83. Oxford: Oxford University Press.

Colino, César, and Angustias Hombrado. 2014. "Territorial Pluralism in Spain: Characteristics and Assessment." In *Territorial Pluralism: Managing Difference in Multinational States*, edited by Karlo Basta, John McGarry, and Richard Simeon, 171–95. Vancouver: UBC Press.

– 2017. "Spain: Complexity, Counteracting Forces and Implicit Change." In *Federal Power-Sharing in Europe*, edited by Ferdinand Karlhofer and Günther Pallaver, 181–205. Baden-Baden: Nomos.

Colino, César, and Mario Kölling. 2020. "Spanien." In *Handbuch der europäischen Verfassungsgeschichte im 20. Jahrhundert: Institutionen und Rechtspraxis im gesellschaftlichen Wandel.*Band 5, *Seit 1989*, edited by Arthur Benz, Stephan Bröchler, and Hans-Joachim Lauth, 451–81. Bonn: Dietz.

Collins, Hugh. 1985. "Political Ideology in Australia: The Distinctiveness of a Benthamite Society." *Daedalus* 114 (1): 147–69.

Colomer, Josep M. 2010. "Spain: A Partisan, Non-institutional Democratic Regime." In *Spain in America: The First Decade of the Prince of Asturias Chair in Spanish Studies at Georgetown University Library*, edited by Jesús M. De Miguel Gabriel Castro. Madrid: Georgetown University.

– 2017. "The Venturous Bid for the Independence of Catalonia." *Nationalities Papers: The Journal of Nationalism and Ethnicity* 45 (5): 950–67. https://doi.org/10.1080/00905992.2017.1293628.

– 2018a. *España: La Historia de una Frustracíon*. Barcelona: Anagrama.

– 2018b. "Ni coalición ni union." *El Páis*, 26 September.

Commonwealth of Australia. 2018. *Productivity Commission Inquiry into Horizontal Fiscal Equaliasation: Government Interim Response*. https://static.treasury.gov.au/uploads/sites/1/2018/07/HFE-Government-Response.pdf.

Conlan, Timothy J. 1998. *From New Federalism to Devolution: Twenty-Five Years of Intergovernmental Reform*. Washington, DC: Brookings Institution Press.

Conlan, Timothy J., Paul L. Posner, and Priscilla M. Regan. 2016. *Governing under Stress: The Implementation of Obama's Economic Stimulus Program*. Washington, DC: Georgetown University Press.

Coppedge, Michael, John Gerring, Carl Henrik Knutsen, Staffan Lindberg, Svend-Erik Skaaning, Jan Teorell, David Altman, et al. 2018. "V-Dem Dataset – Version 8: Varieties of Democracy Project." https://www.v-dem.net/en/data/data-version-8/.

Corwin, Edward. 1950. "The Passing of Dual Federalism." *Virginia Law Review* 36 (1): 1–24. https://doi.org/10.2307/1069035.

Costar, Brian. 1992. "Constitutional Change." In *Trials in Power: Cain, Kirner and Victoria, 1982–1992*, edited by Mark Considine and Brian Costar, 201–14. Melbourne: Melbourne University Press.

Costar, Brian, and Greg Gardiner. 2003. "From Breaking Governments to a Brake on Government: A New Bicameralism in Victoria?" *Australasian Parliamentary Review* 18 (1): 33–45.

Council of Australian Governments. 2020. "Announcements." Accessed 27 October 2020. https://www.coag.gov.au/.

Crisp, Leslie F. 1978. *Australian National Government*. Melbourne: Longman Cheshire.

Crum, Ben, and John Erik Fossum. 2009. "The Multilevel Parliamentary Field: A Framework for Theorizing Representative Democracy in the EU." *European Political Science Review* 1 (2): 249–71.

–, eds. 2013. *Practices of Inter-parliamentary Coordination in International Politics: The European Union and Beyond*. Colchester, UK: ECPR Press.

CSDS Data Unit. 2004. *National Election Study*. Delhi: Centre for the Study of Developing Societies/Lokniti.

Curtin, Deirdre. 2009. *Executive Power of the European Union: Law, Practices and the Living Constitution*. Oxford: Oxford University Press.

– 2014. "Challenging Executive Dominance in European Democracy." *Modern Law Review* 77 (1): 1–32.

Cutler, Fred. 2004. "Government Responsibility and Electoral Accountability in Federations." *Publius* 34 (2): 19–38. https://doi.org/10.1093/oxfordjournals.pubjof.a005028.

– 2008. "Whodunnit? Voters and Responsibility in Canadian Federalism." *Canadian Journal of Political Science* 41 (3): 627–54. https://doi.org/10.1017/s0008423908080761.

Cutler, Fred, and Matthew Mendelsohn. 2005. "Unnatural Loyalties of Native Collaborationists: The Governance and Citizens of Canadian Federalism." In *Insiders and Outsiders: Alan Cairns and the Reshaping of Canadian Citizenship*, edited by Gerald Kernermann and Philip Resnick. Vancouver: University of British Columbia Press.

Dahl, Robert. 1983. "Federalism and the Democratic Process." *Nomos* 25, 95–108.

– 1994. "A Democratic Dilemma: System Effectiveness versus Citizen Participation." *Political Science Quarterly* 109 (1): 23–34. https://doi.org/10.2307/2151659.

– 1998. *On Democracy*. New Haven, CT: Yale University Press.

Dahl, Robert, and Edward Tufte. 1973. *Size and Democracy*. Stanford: Stanford University Press.

Dandoy, Régis. 2013. "Belgium: Towards a Regionalization of National Elections?" In *Regional and National Elections in Western Europe: Territoriality of the Vote in Thirteen Countries*, edited by Régis Dandoy and Arjan Schakel, 47–67. Basingstoke, UK: Palgrave Macmillan.

Dardanelli, Paolo, John Kincaid, Alan Fenna, André Kaiser, André Lecours, Ajay Kumar Singh, Sean Mueller, et al. 2019. "Dynamic De/Centralization in Federations: Comparative Conclusions." *Publius* 49 (1): 194–219. https://doi.org/10.1093/publius/pjy037.

Dardanelli, Paolo, and Sean Mueller. 2019. "Dynamic De/Centralization in Switzerland, 1848–2010." *Publius* 49 (1): 138–65. https://doi.org/10.1093/publius/pjx056.

DeBardeleben, Joan, and Achim Hurrelmann. 2007. *Democratic Dilemmas of Multilevel Governance: Legitimacy, Representation and Accountability in the European Union*. New York: Palgrave Macmillan.

Decoster, André, and Willem Sas. 2012. "Feiten en cijfers over de nieuwe financieringswet." In *België, quo vadis? Waarheen na de zesde staatshervorming,?* edited by Patricia Popelier, Dave Sinardet, Jan Velaers, and Bea Cantillon, 311–42. Antwerp: Intersentia.

D-EDK (Deutschschweizer Erziehungsdirektoren-Konferenz). 2018. "Lehrplan 21: Entstehung."

Deem, C. Jacob. 2018. *Subsidiarity's Quest for Meaning: Understanding the Political Culture of Subsidiarity in Australia, Canada, Germany and the United Kingdom*. Brisbane: Griffith University.

Deeming, Christopher. 2013. "The Working Class and Welfare: Francis G. Castles on the Political Development of the Welfare State in Australia and New Zealand Thirty Years On." *Social Policy & Administration* 47 (6): 668–91. https://doi.org/10.1111/spol.12037. Medline:24436502.

De Grauwe, Paul, and Philippe Van Parijs, eds. 2009. *Electoral Engineering for a Stalled Federation:* A Country-Wide Electoral District for Belgium's Federal Parliament. Brussels: Re-Bel E-book.

–, eds. 2011. *Social Federalism: How Is a Multi-level Welfare State Best Organized?* Brussels: Re-Bel E-book.

–, eds. 2014. *The Malaise of Electoral Democracy and What to Do about It*. Brussels: Re-Bel E-book.

Delwit, Pascal, Emilie van Haute, and Jean-Benoit Pilet. 2011. *Les partis politiques en Belgique*. Brussels: Les éditions de l'Université de Bruxelles.

Democracy Barometer. 2016. "Quality of Democracy." Accessed 11 June 2017. http://www.democracybarometer.org/dataset_en.html.

Derthick, Martha. 1970. *The Influence of Federal Grants: Public Assistance in Massachusetts*. Cambridge, MA: Harvard University Press.

– 2001. *Keeping the Compound Republic: Essays on American Federalism*. Washington, DC: Brookings Institution Press.

Deschouwer, Kris. 2006. "And the Peace Goes On? Consociational Democracy and Belgian Politics in the Twenty-First Century." *West European Politics* 29 (5): 895–911. https://doi.org/10.1080/01402380600968760.

– 2012. *The Politics of Belgium: Governing a Divided Society*. Basingstoke, UK: Palgrave Macmillan.

Deschouwer, Kris, Pascal Delwit, Marc Hooghe, Pierre Baudewyns, and Stefaan Walgrave, eds. 2015. *De kiezer ontcijferd: Over stemgedrag en stemmotivaties*. Leuven, Belgium: LannooCampus.

Deschouwer, Kris, and Min Reuchamps. 2013. "The Belgian Federation at a Crossroad." *Regional and Federal Studies* 23 (3): 261–70. https://doi.org/10.1080/13597566.2013.773896.

Deschouwer, Kris, and Philippe Van Parijs. 2007. "Une circonscription fédérale pour tous les Belges." *Revue Nouvelle* 62 (4): 12–23.

De Schutter, Helder. 2011. "Federalism as Fairness." *Journal of Political Philosophy* 19 (2): 167–89. https://doi.org/10.1111/j.1467-9760.2010.00368.x.

Detterbeck, Klaus. 2012. *Multi-level Party Politics in Western Europe*. Houndmills, UK: Palgrave Macmillan.

– 2016. "The Role of Party and Coalition Politics in Federal Reform." *Regional and Federal Studies* 26 (5): 645–66. https://doi.org/10.1080/13597566.2016.1217845.

Detterbeck, Klaus, and Eve Hepburn, eds. 2018. *Handbook of Territorial Politics*. Cheltenham, UK: Edward Elgar.

Detterbeck, Klaus, Wolfgang Renzsch, and John Kincaid, eds. 2016. *Political Parties and Civil Society in Federal Countries*. Oxford: Oxford University Press.

De Winter, Lieven, and Patrick Dumont. 2006. "Do Belgian Parties Undermine the Democratic Chain of Delegation?" *West European Politics* 29 (5): 957–76. https://doi.org/10.1080/01402380600968844.

De Winter, Lieven, Marc Swyngedouw, and Patrick Dumont. 2006. "Party System(s) and Electoral Behaviour in Belgium: From Stability to Balkanisation." *West European Politics* 29 (5): 933–56. https://doi.org/10.1080/01402380600968836.

De Winter, Lieven, and Caroline Van Wynsberghe. 2015. "Kingdom of Belgium: Partitocracy, Corporatist Society, and Dissociative Federalism." In *Political Parties and Civil Society in Federal Countries*, edited by Wolfgang Renzsch, Klaus Detterbeck, and John Kincaid, 40–69. Oxford: Oxford University Press.

Diez, Thomas. 1995. *Neues Europa, altes Modell: Die Konstruktion von Staatlichkeit im politischen Diskurs zur Zukunft der europäischen Gemeinschaft*. Frankfurt: Haag + Herchen.

DiGiacomo, Gordon. 2005. *The Democratic Content of Intergovernmental Agreements in Canada*. Regina: Universitry of Regina, Saskatchewan Institute for Public Policy.

Dinan, Desmond. 2012. "Governance and Institutions: Impact of the Escalating Crisis." *Journal of Common Market Studies* 50 (S2): 65–92. https://doi.org/10.1111/j.1468-5965.2012.02268.x.

Docherty, David. 2010. "Legislatures." In *Auditing Canadian Democracy*, edited by William Cross, 65–92. Vancouver: University of British Columbia Press.

Dose, Nicolai, and Iris Reus. 2016. "The Effect of Reformed Legislative Competences on Länder Policy-Making: Determinants of Fragmentation and Uniformity." *Regional and Federal Studies* 26 (5): 625–44. https://doi.org/10.1080/13597566.2016.1244669.

Dunn, Christopher. 2002. "The Central Executive in Canadian Government: Searching for the Holy Grail." In *The Handbook of Canadian Public Administration*, edited by Christopher Dunn, 305–40. Don Mills, ON: Oxford University Press.

Dupré, Stefan. 1985. "Reflections on the Workability of Executive Federalism." In *Intergovernmental Relations*, edited by Richard Simeon, 1–32. Toronto: University of Toronto Press.

Easton, David. 1965. *A Systems Analysis of Political Life*. New York: Wiley.

EDK (Swiss Conference of Cantonal Ministers of Education). 2018. "HarmoS: Beitrittsverfahren und Inkrafttreten." Accessed 24 October 2018. http://www.edk.ch/dyn/14901.php.

Elazar, Daniel. 1964. "Federal-State Collaboration in the Nineteenth-Century United States." *Political Science Quarterly* 79 (2): 248–81. https://doi.org/10.2307/2146065.

– 1987. *Exploring Federalism*. Tuscaloosa: University of Alabama Press.

Elazar, Daniel J., and John Kincaid, eds. 2000. *The Covenant Connection: From Federal Theology to Modern Federalism*. Lanham MD: Lexington Books.

Elías Méndez, Christina. 2009. "Principales rasgos de las reformas estatutarias: ¿Hacia un Estado autonómico cooperativo?" *Revista valenciana d'estudis autonòmics* 52: 258–83.

Encarnación, Omar E. 2004. "Democracy and Federalism in Spain." *Mediterranean Quarterly* 15 (1): 58–74. https://doi.org/10.1215/10474552-15-1-58.

Endo, Ken. 1994. "The Principle of Subsidiarity: From Johannes Althusius to Jacques Delors." *Hokkaido Law Review* 44 (6): 553–652.

Eriksen, Erik O. 2018. "Political Differentiation and the Problem of Dominance: Segmentation and Hegemony." *European Journal of Political Research* 57 (4): 989–1009. https://doi.org/10.1111/1475-6765.12263.

Evans, Tim. 2006. *Compulsory Voting in Australia*. Kingston: Australian Electoral Commission.

Fabbrini, Sergio, ed. 2005. *Democracy and Federalism in the European Union and the United States: Exploring Post-National Governance*. London: Routledge.

Falleti, Tulia. 2005. "A Sequential Theory of Decentralization: Latin American Cases in Comparative Perspective." *American Political Science Review* 99 (3): 327–46. https://doi.org/10.1017/s0003055405051695.

Farrell, Henry, and Adrienne Héritier. 2003. *The Invisible Transformation of Codecision: Problems of Democratic Legitimacy*. Stockholm: Swedish Institute for European Policy Studies.

Fehrman, Craig. 2016. "All Politics Is National: How State Politicians Went from Solving the Problems in Their Own Backyards to Mimicking the Gridlock in Washington." *FiveThirtyEight* (website), 7 November 2016.

Fenna, Alan. 2019. "The Centralization of Australian Federalism 1901–2010: Measurement and Interpretation." *Publius* 49 (1): 30–56. https://doi.org/10.1093/publius/pjy042.

Ferreres, Victor. 2013. *The Constitution of Spain: A Contextual Analysis*. Oxford: Hart Publishing.

Field, Bonnie. 2014. "From Consensual to Complex Multi-level Democracy: The Contours of Contestation and Collaboration in Spain." *Comillas Journal of International Relations* 1: 41–52. https://doi.org/10.14422/cir.i01.y2014.004.

– 2015. "The Evolution of Sub-state Nationalist Parties as Statewide Parliamentary Actors: CiU and PNV in Spain." *Nationalism and Ethnic Politics* 21 (1): 121–41. https://doi.org/10.1080/13537113.2015.1003493.

– 2016. *Why Minority Governments Work:* Multilevel Territorial Politics in Spain. New York: Palgrave Macmillan.

Field, Bonnie, and Caroline Gray. 2019. "The Spanish Parliament in Context." In *The Iberian Legislatures in Comparative Perspective*, edited by Jorge Fernandes and Cristina Leston-Bandeira, 25–46. London: Routledge.

Field, Bonnie, and Kerstin Hamann. 2008a. "Conclusion: The Spanish Case and Comparative Lessons on Institutions, Representation, and Democracy." In *Democracy and Institutional Development: Spain in Comparative Theoretical Perspective*, edited by Bonnie Field and Kerstin Hamann, 203–16. Basingstoke, UK: Palgrave Macmillan.

– 2008b. "Introduction: The Institutionalization of Democracy in Spain." In *Democracy and Institutional Development: Spain in Comparative Theoretical Perspective*, edited by Bonnie Field and Kerstin Hamann, 1–22. Basingstoke, UK: Palgrave Macmillan.

Fiers, Stefaan. 2006. "Evoluties in het parlementair bestel." In *De geschiedenis van België na 1945*, edited by Els Witte, Alain Meynen, and Jaak Billiet, 263–88. Antwerp: Standaard Uitgeverij.

Filippov, Mikhail, Peter Ordeshook, and Olga Shvetsova. 2004. *Designing Federalism: A Theory of Self-Sustainable Federal Institutions*. Cambridge: Cambridge University Press.

Finke, Patrick, and Antonios Souris. 2017. "Die „Veralltäglichung" von Parteipolitik im Bundesrat? Ein neuer Datensatz zu den Voten in den Ausschüssen." *Zeitschrift für Parlamentsfragen* 48 (4): 773–84. https://doi.org/10.5771/0340-1758-2017-4-773.

Fishman, Robert. 2019. *Democratic Practice: Origins of the Iberian Divide in Political Inclusion*. New York: Oxford University Press.

Føllesdal, Andreas. 2018. "Federalism." In *The Stanford Encyclopedia of Philosophy*, Summer ed., edited by Edward N. Zalta. https://plato.stanford.edu/archives/sum2018/entries/federalism/.

Fossum, John Erik. 2017. "European Federalism: Pitfalls and Possibilities." *European Law Journal* 23 (5): 361–79. https://doi.org/10.1111/eulj.12250.
– 2019. "Extending the Coupling Concept: Slack, Agency and Fields." In *Configurations, Dynamics and Mechanisms of Multilevel Governance*, edited by Nathalie Behnke, Jörg Broschek, and Jared Sonnicksen, 311–27. Cham, Switzerland: Palgrave Macmillan.
Fossum, John Erik, and Markus Jachtenfuchs, eds. 2017. *Federal Challenges and Challenges to Federalism*. London: Routledge.
Fossum, John Erik, and David Laycock. 2013. "Democratic Governance and the Challenge of Executive Dominance in International and National Settings." In *Developing Democracies: Democracy, Democratization, and Development*, edited by Michael Böss, Jørgen Møller, and Svend-Erik Skaaning, 176–90. Aarhus, Denmark: Aarhus University Press.
Fossum, John Erik, and Agustín José Menéndez, eds. 2014. *The European Union in Crises or the European Union as Crises? ARENA Report No. 2/14*. Oslo: Centre for European Studies, University of Oslo.
Fowler, Anthony. 2013. "Electoral and Policy Consequences of Voter Turnout: Evidence from Compulsory Voting in Australia." *Quarterly Journal of Political Science* 8 (2): 159–82. https://doi.org/10.1561/100.00012055.
Free, Lloyd A., and Hadley Cantril. 1967. *The Political Beliefs of Americans: A Study of Public Opinion*. New Brunswick, NJ: Rutgers University Press.
Freedom House. 2017. "Freedom in the World 2017." https://freedomhouse.org/report/freedom-world/freedom-world-2017.
Friedrich, Carl Joachim. 1937. *Constitutional Government and Politics: Nature and Development*. New York: Harper & Brothers Publishers.
– 1959. *Demokratie als Herrschafts- und Lebensform*. Heidelberg: Quelle & Meyer.
– 1975. *Johannes Althusius und sein Werk im Rahmen der Entwicklung der Theorie von der Politik*. Berlin: Duncker und Humblot.
Frotscher, Werner, and Bodo Pieroth. 2018. *Verfassungsgeschichte*. 17th ed. Munich: C.H. Beck.
Gagnon, Alain-G., and Raffaele Iacovino. 2007. *Federalism, Citizenship, and Quebec: Debating Multinationalism*. Toronto: University of Toronto Press.
Gagnon, Alain-G., and James Tully, eds. 2001. *Multinational Democracies*. Cambridge: Cambridge University Press.
Gais, Thomas, and James Fossett. 2005. "Federalism and the Executive Branch." In *Institutions of American Democracy: The Executive Branch*, edited by Joel D. Aberbach and Mark A. Peterson, 486–524. New York: Oxford University Press.
Gale, William G., Aaron Krupkin, and Kim Rueben. 2015. "The Relationship between Taxes and Growth at the State Level: New Evidence." *National Tax Journal* 68 (4): 919–42. https://doi.org/10.17310/ntj.2015.4.02.
Ganghof, Steffen, Sebastian Eppner, and Alexander Pörschke. 2018. "Australian Bicameralism as Semi-parliamentarism: Patterns of Majority

Formation in 29 Democracies." *Australian Journal of Political Science* 53 (2): 211–33. https://doi.org/10.1080/10361146.2018.1451487.

García Morales, Maria J. 2013. "Intergovernmental Relations in Spain and the Constitutional Court Ruling on the Statute of Autonomy of Catalonia: What's Next?" In *The Ways of Federalism in Western Countries and the Horizons of Territorial Autonomy in Spain*, edited by Alberto López-Basaguren and Leire Escajedo San Epifanio, 83–109. Berlin: Springer.

Garmendia, Amuitz. 2019. "40 años de Gobiernos autonómicos en España: Competición política, feudos electorales y calidad de gobierno." In *Informe sobre la Democracia en España 2018*, edited by Jorge San Vicente Feduchi, 72–87. Madrid: Fundación Alternativas.

Gelman, Andrew. 2008. *Red State, Blue State, Rich State, Poor State: Why Americans Vote the Way They Do*. Princeton, NJ: Princeton University Press.

Gerber, Marlène, and Sean Mueller. 2018. "When the People Speak – and Decide: Deliberation and Direct Democracy in the Citizen Assembly of Glarus, Switzerland." *Policy & Politics* 46 (3): 371–90. https://doi.org/10.1332/030557317x14976099453327.

Gerring, John, and Strom C. Thacker. 2008. *A Centripetal Theory of Democratic Governance*. Cambridge: Cambridge University Press.

Gibson, Edward. 2013. *Boundary Control: Subnational Authoritarianism in Federal Democracies*. Cambridge: Cambridge University Press.

Giudici, Anja, and Nenad Stojanovi . 2016. "Die Zusammensetzung des Schweizerischen Bundesrates nach Partei, Region, Sprache und Religion, 1848–2015." *Swiss Political Science Review* 22 (2): 288–307. https://doi.org/10.1111/spsr.12214.

Godbout, Jean-François, and Monika Smaz. 2016. "Party Development in the Early Decades of the Australian Parliament: A New Perspective." *Australian Journal of Political Science* 51 (3): 478–95. https://doi.org/10.1080/10361146.2016.1182618.

Goeters, Johann Friedrich Gerhard, ed. 1971. *Die Akten der Synode der Niederländischen Kirchen zu Emden vom 4.–13. Oktober 1571*. Neukirchen-Vluyn, Germany: Neukirchener Verlag. First published 1571.

González, Juan L. 2017. "Crisis de la democracia de partidos y segunda transición." *UNED Revista de Derecho Politico* 100: 613–36. https://doi.org/10.5944/rdp.100.2017.20712.

Graefe, Peter, Julie M. Simmons, and Laura A. White, eds. 2013. *Overpromising and Underperforming? Understanding and Evaluating New Intergovernmental Accountability Regimes*. Toronto: University of Toronto Press.

Granovetter, Marc. 1985. "Economic Action and Social Structure: The Problem of Embeddedness." *American Journal of Sociology* 91 (3): 481–510. https://doi.org/10.1086/228311.

Grattan, Michelle. 1973. "The Australian Labor Party." In *Australian Politics: A Third Reader*, edited by Henry Mayer and Helen Nelson, 389–406. Melbourne: Cheshire.

Grau Creus, Mirea. 2000. "The Effects of Institutions and Political Parties upon Federalism: The Channeling and Integration of the Comunidades Autónomas within the Central-Level Policy Processes in Spain (1983–1996)." PhD diss., European University Institute, Florence.

– 2010. "The Spanish Lower Chamber of Parliament: An Intergovernmental Arena? The Representation and Integration of Territorial Interests within the Congreso de los diputados." In *Legislatures in Federal Systems and Multi-level Governance*, edited by Rudolf Hrbek, 11–33. Baden-Baden: Nomos.

Gray, Caroline. 2020. *Territorial Politics and the Party System in Spain: Continuity and Change since the Financial Crisis*. Abingdon, UK: Routledge.

Gray, Virginia. 2018. "The Socioeconomic and Political Context of States." In *Politics in the American States: A Comparative Analysis*, edited by Virginia Gray, Russell L. Hanson, and Thomas Kousser, 1–27. Thousand Oaks, CA: CQ Press.

Grodzins, Morton. 1966. *The American System: A New View of Government in the United States*. Chicago: Rand McNally.

– 1967. "American Political Parties and the American System." In *American Federalism in Perspective*, edited by Aaron Wildavsky, 109–43. Boston: Little, Brown.

– 1968. "Centralization and Decentralization in the American Federal System." In *A Nation of States*, edited by Robert Goldwin, 1–23. Chicago: Rand McNally.

Günther, Richard, José Ramón Montero, and Joan Botella. 2004. *Democracy in Modern Spain*. New Haven, CT: Yale University Press.

Habermas, Jürgen. 1992. *Faktizität und Geltung*. Frankfurt: Suhrkamp.

– 2012. *The Crisis of the European Union: A Response*. Cambridge: Polity Press.

Hahn, Heather, Aron Laudan, Cary Lou, Eleanor Pratt, and Adaeze Okoli. 2017. *Why Does Cash Welfare Depend on Where You Live? How and Why State TANF Programs Vary*. Washington, DC: Urban Institute.

Haider, Donald. 1974. *When Governments Come to Washington: Governors, Mayors, and Intergovernmental Lobbying*. New York: Free Press.

Hamilton, Alexander, James Madison, and John Jay. 1938. *The Federalist Papers*. New York: Modern Library. First published 1787.

– 1989. *The Federalist Papers*. New York: Bantam. First published 1787.

– 2003. *The Federalist Papers*. Cambridge: Cambridge University Press. First published 1787.

Hancock, William K. 1931. *Australia*. New York: C. Scribner's Sons.

Harguindéguy, Jean-Baptiste, Xavier Coller, and Alistair Cole. 2017. "Why Is the Spanish Upper Chamber So Difficult to Reform?" *Parliamentary Affairs* 70 (3): 530–47.

Harguindéguy, Jean-Baptiste, Gonzalo Sola, and José Cruz. 2018. "Between Justice and Politics: The Role of the Spanish Constitutional Court in the State of Autonomics." *Territory, Politics, Governance* 8 (2): 222–40.

Hasenöhr, Sàndor, Christa Pölzlbauer, and David F.J. Campbell. 2016. "Global Democracy Ranking." http://democracyranking.org/wordpress/rank/democracy-ranking-2016/.

Hausing, Kham Khan Suan. 2018. "Telangana and the Politics of State Formation in India: Recognition and Accommodation in a Multinational Federation." *Regional and Federal Studies* 28 (4): 447–68. https://doi.org/10.1080/13597566.2018.1473856.

Health Canada. 2004. "Asymmetrical Federalism That Respects Quebec's Jurisdiction." Report on the Progress Made Regarding the Bilateral Agreement Entered Into during the Federal-Provincial-Territorial Meeting of the First Ministers on Health, September 2004. https://publications.msss.gouv.qc.ca/msss/en/document-001266/.

Hedström, Peter, and Richard Swedberg, eds. 1998. *Social Mechanisms: An Analytical Approach to Social Theory*. New York: Cambridge University Press.

Hegele, Yvonne, and Nathalie Behnke. 2017. "Horizontal Coordination in Cooperative Federalism: The Purpose of Ministerial Conferences in Germany." *Regional and Federal Studies* 27 (5): 529–48. https://doi.org/10.1080/13597566.2017.1315716.

Heinemann, Friedrich, Eckhard Janeba, Marc-Daniel Moessinger, and Christoph Schröder. 2015. "Who Likes to Fend for Oneself? Revenue Autonomy Preferences of Subnational Politicians in Germany." *Publius* 45 (4): 653–85. https://doi.org/10.1093/publius/pjv022.

Held, David. 1996. *Models of Democracy*. Stanford, CA: Stanford University Press.

Herrnson, Paul. 2010. "The Evolution of National Party Organizations." In *The Oxford Handbook of American Political Parties and Interest Groups*, edited by Sandy L. Maisel and Jeffrey M. Berry, 245–64. Oxford: Oxford University Press.

Hershey, Marjorie R. 2011. *Party Politics in America*. New York: Longman.

Hesse, Konrad. 1962. *Der unitarische Bundesstaat*. Karlsruhe: C.F. Müller.

Heylen, Frederik, and Evelien Willems. 2019. "Writing Blank Checks? How Government Funding Affects Interest Organisations' Advocacy Behaviour in a Multi-layered Context." *Journal of European Public Policy* 26 (6): 863–82. https://doi.org/10.1080/13501763.2018.1495250.

Hildebrandt, Achim, and Frieder Wolf. 2016. "How Much of a Sea-Change? Land Policies after the Reforms of Federalism." *German Politics* 25 (2): 227–42. https://doi.org/10.1080/09644008.2016.1164842.

Hirst, John. 2002. *Australia's Democracy: A Short History*. Crows Nest, Australia: Allen & Unwin.

Hix, Simon, and Tapio Raunio. 2000. "Backbenchers Learn to Fight Back: European Integration and Parliamentary Government." *West European Politics* 23 (4): 142–68. https://doi.org/10.1080/01402380008425404.

Hobbes, Thomas. 1991. *Leviathan*. Cambridge: Cambridge University Press. First published 1651.

Hogg, Peter. 1998. *Constitutional Law of Canada*. Scarborough: Carswell.

Holbrook, Thomas, and Raymond LaRaja. 2018. "The Socioeconomic and Political Context of States." In *Politics in the American States: A Comparative Analysis*, edited by Virginia Gray, Russell Hanson, and Thomas Kousser, 57–98. Thousand Oaks, CA: CQ Press.

Hollander, Robyn, and Haig Patapan. 2007. "Pragmatic Federalism: Australian Federalism from Hawke to Howard." *Australian Journal of Public Administration* 66 (3): 280–97. https://doi.org/10.1111/j.1467-8500.2007.00542.x.

Hooghe, Liesbet, and Gary Marks, eds. 2016. *Community, Scale, and Regional Governance: A Postfunctionalist Theory of Governance*. Oxford: Oxford University Press.

Hooghe, Liesbet, Gary Marks, and Arjan Schakel. 2010. *The Rise of Regional Authority: A Comparative Study of 42 Democracies*. New York: Taylor & Francis.

Hooghe, Liesbet, Gary Marks, Arjan Schakel, Sandra Chapman Osterkatz, Sara Niedzwiecki, and Sarah Shair-Rosenfield. 2016. *A Postfunctionalist Theory of Governance*. Vol. 1 of *Measuring Regional Authority*. Oxford: Oxford University Press.

Hooghe, Marc. 2012. "Debate: How Do Countries Survive without a National Government? Theoretical Reflections on the Belgian Case." *European Political Science* 11 (1): 88–113. https://doi.org/10.1057/eps.2011.57.

Hopkins, Dan. 2014. "All Politics Is Presidential." *FiveThirtyEight* (website), 17 March.

Horsley, Thomas. 2012. "Subsidiarity and the European Court of Justice: Missing Pieces in the Subsidiarity Jigsaw?" *JCMS: Journal of Common Market Studies* 50 (2): 267–82. https://doi.org/10.1111/j.1468-5965.2011.02221.x.

Hough, Dan, and Charlie Jeffery, eds. 2006. *Devolution and Electoral Politics*. Manchester: Manchester University Press.

Hueglin, Thomas O. 1999. *Early Modern Concepts for a Late Modern World: Althusius on Community and Federalism*. Waterloo, ON: Wilfrid Laurier University Press.

– 2000. "From Constitutional to Treaty Federalism: A Comparative Perspective." *Publius* 30 (4): 137–53. https://doi.org/10.1093/oxfordjournals.pubjof.a030100.

– 2013a. "Federalism and Democracy: A Critical Reassessment." In *The Global Promise of Federalism*, edited by Grace Skogstad, David Cameron, Martin Papillon, and Keith Banting, 17–42. Toronto: University of Toronto Press.

– 2013b. "Treaty Fderalism as a Model of Policy Making: Comparing Canada and the European Union." *Canadian Public Administration* 56 (2): 185–202. https://doi.org/10.1111/capa.12013.

– 2015. "Social Justice and Solidarity as Criteria for Fiscal Equalization." In *Das Teilen beherrschen: Analysen zur Reform des Finanzausgleichs 2019*, edited by René Geißler, Felix Knüpling, Sabine Kropp, and Joachim Wieland, 35–48. Baden-Baden: Nomos.

– 2016. "Vertragsföderalismus in der EU: Sonderfall oder Normalfall." In *Föderalismen: Modelle jenseits des Staates*, edited by Eva-Marlene Hausteiner, 267–80. Baden-Baden: Nomos.

Hueglin, Thomas O., and Alan Fenna. 2015. *Comparative Federalism: A Systematic Inquiry*. 2nd ed. Toronto: University of Toronto Press.

Human Rights Watch. 2002. "'We Have No Orders to Save You': State Participation and Complicity in Communal Violence in Gujarat." *Human Rights Watch Short Report* 14 (3): 1–68. https://doi.org/10.1163/2210-7975_hrd-2156-0278.

IFF (Institute of Federalism Fribourg). 2018a. "Kantonale Volksabstimmungen vom 10. Juni 2018: Ergebnisse." https://www3.unifr.ch/federalism/fr/assets/public/files/Newsletter/Abstimmungen/Newsletter-10-06-2018-resultats.pdf.

– 2018b. "Kantonale Volksabstimmungen vom 23. September 2018: Ergebnisse." https://www3.unifr.ch/federalism/fr/assets/public/files/Newsletter/Abstimmungen/27-Newsletter-23-09-2018-Ergebnisse.pdf.

India. Commissioner for Linguistic Minorities. 2014. *51st Report of the Commissioner for Linguistic Minorities in India (July 2013–June 2014)*. New Delhi: Government of India. http://www.nclm.nic.in/.

Izadi, Elahe. 2014. "Congress Sets Record for Voting along Party Lines." *NationalJournal* (website), 3 February.

Jaffrelot, Christophe. 2017. "India's Democracy at 70: Toward a Hindu State." *Journal of Democracy* 28 (3): 52–63. https://doi.org/10.1353/jod.2017.0044.

Jeffery, Charlie, and Niccole Pamphilis. 2016. "The Myth and the Paradox of 'Uniform Living Conditions' in the German Federal System." *German Politics* 25 (2): 176–92. https://doi.org/10.1080/09644008.2016.1164843.

Jeffery, Charlie, Niccole M. Pamphilis, Carolyn Rowe, and Ed Turner. 2014. "Regional Policy Variation in Germany: The Diversity of Living Conditions in a 'Unitary Federal State.'" *Journal of European Public Policy* 21 (9): 1350–66. https://doi.org/10.1080/13501763.2014.923022.

Jensenius, Francesca Refsum, and Pavithra Suryanarayan. 2015. "Fragmentation and Decline in India's State Assemblies: A Review, 1967–2007." *Asian Survey* 55 (5): 862–81. https://doi.org/10.1525/as.2015.55.5.862.

Jiménez Asensio, Rafael. 2016. *Los frenos del poder*. Madrid: Marcial Pons.

Jochheim, Linda, and Falk Ebinger. 2009. "Wessen loyale Diener? Wie die große Koalition die deutsche Ministerialbürokratie veränderte." *der moderne staat: Zeitschrift für Public Policy, Recht und Management* 2 (2): 335–53.

John, Stefanie, and Thomas Poguntke. 2012. "Party Patronage in Germany." In *Party Patronage and Party Government in European Democracies*, edited by Petr Kopecky, Peter Mair, and Maria Spirova, 121–43. Oxford: Oxford University Press.

Johns, Carolyn M., Patricia L. O'Reilly, and Gregg Inwood. 2006. "Intergovernmental Innovation and the Administrative State in Canada." *Governance* 19 (4): 627–49. https://doi.org/10.1111/j.1468-0491.2006.00331.x.

Jörke, Dirk. 2019. "The Democratic Federalism of the Anti-Federalists." In *The Theories of Modern Federalism*, edited by Skadi Siiri Krause, 109–36. Baden-Baden: Nomos.

Juliá, Santos. 2019. *Demasiados retrocesos: España 1898–2018*. Barcelona: Galaxia Gutenberg.

Kant, Immanuel. 1996. "Groundwork of the Metaphysics of Morals." In *Practical Philosophy*, edited by Mary Gregor, 37–108. Cambridge: Cambridge University Press. First published 1785.

Kapur, Devesh, and Pratap Bhanu Mehta. 2006. *The Indian Parliament as an Institution of Accountability*. Geneva: United Nations Research Institute for Social Development.

Kapur, Devesh, and Milan Vaishnav, eds. 2018. *Costs of Democracy: Political Finance in India*. New Delhi: Oxford University Press.

Karmis, Dimitrios, and Wayne Norman, eds. 2005. *Theories of Federalism: A Reader*. New York: Palgrave Macmillan.

Katz, Richard, and Peter Mair. 2009. "The Cartel Party Thesis: A Re-statement." *Perspectives on Politics* 7 (4): 752–66. https://doi.org/10.1017/s1537592709991782.

Kellow, Aynsley. 2003. "Tasmania." In *Australian Politics and Government: The Commonwealth, the States and the Territories*, edited by Jeremy Moon and Campbell Sharman, 131–53. Cambridge: Cambridge University Press.

Kelly, Paul, and Troy Bramston. 2015. *The Dismissal: In the Queen's Name*. Hawthorn, Australia: Penguin Books.

Kettl, Donald F. 1988. *Government by Proxy: (Mis?)Managing Federal Programs*. Washington, DC: Congressional Quarterly Incorporated.

KFF (Kaiser Family Foundation). 2017. "Status of State Action on the Medicaid Expansion Decision," 17 August. https://www.kff.org/health-reform/state-indicator/state-activity-around-expanding-medicaid-under-the-affordable-care-act/?currentTimeframe=0&sortModel=%7B%22colId%22:%22Location%22,%22sort%22:%22asc%22%7D.

Kiiver, Philipp. 2011. "The Early-Warning System for the Principle of Subsidiarity: The National Parliament as a Conseil d'Etat for Europe."

European Law Review 36 (1): 98–108. https://doi.org/10.4324/97802031 27001.

Kim, Junghun, and Hansjörg Blöchliger. 2015. *Institutions of Intergovernmental Fiscal Relations: Challenges Ahead*. OECD Fiscal Federalism Studies. Paris: OECD Publishing.

Kincaid, John, ed. 2011. *Federalism*. 4 vols. Los Angeles: Sage.

Kincaid, John, and Richard Cole. 2011. "Citizen Attitudes toward Issues of Federalism in Canada, Mexico, and the United States." *Publius* 41 (1): 53–75. https://doi.org/10.1093/publius/pjq035.

King, Desmond, and Robert C. Lieberman. 2009. "American Political Development as a Process of Democratization." In *Democratization in America: A Comparative-Historical Analysis*, edited by Desmond King, Robert C. Lieberman, Gretchen Ritter, and Laurence Whitehead, 3–27. Baltimore, MD: Johns Hopkins University Press.

King, Preston. 1982. *Federalism and Federation*. Baltimore, MD: Johns Hopkins University Press.

Kingdon, Robert. 1994. "Calvinism and Resistance Theory 1550–1580." In *The Cambridge History of Political Thought 1450–1700*, edited by J.H. Burns, 193–218. Cambridge: Cambridge University Press.

Kitschelt, Herbert. 2011. "Party Systems." In *Oxford Handbook of Political Science*, edited by Robert E. Gooding, 616–47. Oxford: Oxford University Press.

Kochanek, Stanley. 1976. "Mrs. Gandhi's Pyramid: The New Congress." In *Indira Gandhi's India: A Political System Reappraised*, edited by Henry Hart, 93–124. Boulder, CO: Westview Press.

Kommers, Donald P., and Russell A. Miller. 2012. *The Constitutional Jurisprudence of the Federal Republic of Germany*. Durham, NC: Duke University Press.

Koop, Royce, and Campbell Sharman. 2015. "National Party Structure in Parliamentary Federations: Subcontracting Electoral Mobilisation in Canada and Australia." *Commonwealth and Comparative Politics* 53 (2): 177–96. https://doi.org/10.1080/14662043.2015.1013294.

Korioth, Stefan. 2016. "A Path to Balanced Budgets of Bund and Länder? The New Shape of the 'Debt Brake' and the 'Stability Council.'" *Regional and Federal Studies* 26 (5): 687–705. https://doi.org/10.1080/13597566.2016 .1214130.

Kothari, Rajni. 1964. "The Congress 'System' in India." *Asian Survey* 4 (12): 1161–73. https://doi.org/10.1525/as.1964.4.12.01p00302.

Kropp, Sabine. 2010. *Kooperativer Föderalismus und Politikverflechtung*. Wiesbaden: VS Springer.

Kropp, Sabine, and Nathalie Behnke. 2016. "Marble Cake Dreaming of Layer Cake: The Merits and Pitfalls of Disentanglement in German Federalism

Reform." *Regional and Federal Studies* 26 (5): 667–86. https://doi.org/10.1080/13597566.2016.1236335.

Kropp, Sabine, and Roland Sturm. 1998. *Koalitionen und Koalitionsvereinbarungen: Theorie, Analyse und Dokumentation*. Opladen, Germany: Leske + Budrich.

Kymlicka, Will. 1995. *Multicultural Citizenship: A Liberal Theory of Minority Rights*. Oxford: Oxford University Press.

– 2001. *Politics in the Vernacular: Nationalism, Multiculturalism, and Citizenship*. New York: Oxford University Press.

– 2005. *"Federalism, Nationalism and Multiculturalism."* In *Theories of Federalism: A Reader*, edited by Dimitrios Karmis and Wayne Norman, 269–92. New York: Palgrave Macmillan.

Lacey, Joseph. 2017. *Centripetal Democracy: Democratic Legitimacy and Political Identity in Belgium, Switzerland and the European Union*. Oxford: Oxford University Press.

Lacina, Bethany. 2009. "The Problem of Political Stability in Northeast India: Local Ethnic Autocracy and the Rule of Law." *Asian Survey* 49 (6): 998–1020. https://doi.org/10.1525/as.2009.49.6.998.

– 2017. *Rival Claims: Ethnic Violence and Territorial Autonomy under Indian Federalism*. Ann Arbor: University of Michigan Press.

Ladner, Andreas. 2016. *Gemeindeversammlung und Gemeindeparlament: Überlegungen und empirische Befunde zur Ausgestaltung der Legislativfunktion in den Schweizer Gemeinden*. Lausanne: IDHEAP.

Ladner, Andreas, Nicolas Keuffer, and Harald Baldersheim. 2016. "Measuring Local Autonomy in 39 Countries (1990–2014)." *Regional and Federal Studies* 26 (3): 321–57. https://doi.org/10.1080/13597566.2016.1214911.

Landau, Martin. 1969. "Redundancy, Rationality, and the Problem of Duplication and Overlap." *Public Administration Review* 29 (4): 346–58. https://doi.org/10.2307/973247.

– 1973. "Federalism: Redundancy and System Reliability." *Publius* 3 (2): 173–96. https://doi.org/10.1093/oxfordjournals.pubjof.a038278.

Lane, Jan-Erik, and Svante Ersson. 2005. "The Riddle of Federalism: Does Federalism Impact on Democracy?" *Democratization* 12 (2): 163–82. https://doi.org/10.1080/13510340500069220.

Laski, Harold. 2005. "The Obsolescence of Federalism." In *Theories of Federalism: A Reader*, edited by Dimitrios Karmis and Wayne Norman, 193–8. New York: Palgrave Macmillan. First published 1939.

Laycock, David. 2014. "Understanding the Impact of Executive Dominance on Political Parties: Lessons from the Canadian Case." Paper presented at the 23rd IPSA World Congress, 20–4 July, Montreal.

LeDuc, Lawrence, and Jon Pammett. 2016. *Dynasties and Interludes: Past and Present in Canadian Electoral Politics*. Toronto: Dundurn Press.

Lehmbruch, Gerhard. 1976. *Parteienwettbewerb im Bundesstaat*. Stuttgart: Kohlhammer.

– 1993. "Consociational Democracy and Corporatism in Switzerland." *Publius* 23 (2): 43–60. https://doi.org/10.2307/3330858.

– 2000. *Parteienwettbewerb im Bundesstaat: Regelsysteme und Spannungslagen im Institutionengefüge der Bundesrepublik Deutschland*. Wiesbaden: Westdeutscher Verlag.

Leigh, Andrew. 2000. "Factions and Fractions: A Case Study of Power Politics in the Australian Labor Party." *Australian Journal of Political Science* 35 (3): 427–48. https://doi.org/10.1080/713649348.

Léon, Sandra. 2017. "Intergovernmental Councils in Spain: Challenges and Opportunities in a Changing Political Context." *Regional and Federal Studies* 27 (5): 645–65. https://doi.org/10.1080/13597566.2017.1354850.

León, Sandra, and Mónica Ferrín Pereira. 2011. "Intergovernmental Cooperation in a Decentralised System: The Sectoral Conferences in Spain." *South European Society and Politics* 16 (4): 513–32. https://doi.org/10.1080/13608746.2011.602849.

Lerner, Hannah. 2011. *Making Constitutions in Deeply Divided Societies*. Cambridge: Cambridge University Press.

Leslie, Peter. 1987. *Federal State, National Economy*. Toronto: University of Toronto Press.

Levy, Jacob T. 2007. "Federalism, Liberalism, and the Separation of Loyalties." *American Political Science Review* 101 (3): 459–77. https://doi.org/10.1017/s0003055407070268.

– 2008. "Self-Determination, Non-domination, and Federalism." *Hypatia: A Journal of Feminist Philosophy* 23 (3): 60–78. https://doi.org/10.2979/hyp.2008.23.3.60.

Lewis, Jeffrey. 2013. "The Council of the European Union and the European Council." In *European Union Politics*, edited by Michelle Cini and Nieves Pérez-Solórzano Borragán, 142–58. Oxford: Oxford University Press.

Lieberman, Robert C. 2002. "Ideas, Institutions, and Political Order: Explaining Political Change." *American Political Science Review* 96 (4): 697–712. https://doi.org/10.1017/s0003055402000394.

– 2009. "Civil Rights and the Democratization Trap: The Public-Private Nexus and the Building of American Democracy." In *Democratization in America: A Comparative-Historical Analysis*, edited by Desmond King, Robert C. Lieberman, Gretchen Ritter, and Laurence Whitehead, 211–29. Baltimore, MD: Johns Hopkins University Press.

Lienhard, Andreas, Daniel Kettiger, Lacques Bühler, Loranne Mérillat, and Daniela Winkler. 2017. "The Federal Supreme Court of Switzerland: Judicial Balancing of Federalism without Judicial Review." In *Courts in*

Federal Countries: Federalists or Unitarists,? edited by Nicholas Aroney and John Kincaid, 404–39. Toronto: University of Toronto Press.

Light, Paul. 1999. *The True Size of Government.* Washington, DC: Brookings Institution Press.

Lijphart, Arend. 1977. *Democracy in Plural Societies: A Comparative Exploration.* New Haven, CT: Yale University Press.

– 1979. "Consociation and Federalism: Conceptual and Empirical Links." *Canadian Journal of Political Science* 12 (3): 499–515. https://doi.org/10.1017/s0008423900051714.

– 1996. "The Puzzle of Indian Democracy: A Consociational Interpretation." *American Political Science Review* 90 (2): 258–68. https://doi.org/10.2307/2082883.

– 1999a. "Australian Democracy: Modifying Majoritarianism?" *Australian Journal of Political Science* 34 (3): 313–26. https://doi.org/10.1080/10361149950254.

– 1999b. *Patterns of Democracy: Government Forms and Performance in Thirty-Six Countries.* New Haven, CT: Yale University Press.

– 2012. *Patterns of Democracy: Government Forms and Performance in Thirty-Six Countries.* 2nd ed. New Haven, CT: Yale University Press.

Linder, Wolf, and Sean Mueller. 2017. *Schweizerische Demokratie: Institutionen – Prozesse – Perspektiven.* Bern: Haupt.

Livingston, William. 1956. *Federalism and Constitutional Change.* Oxford: Clarendon.

Lokniti Programme for Comparative Democracy. 2008. *State of Democracy in South Asia: A Report.* New Delhi: Oxford University Press.

López-Basaguren, Alberto. 2018. "The Secession Issue and Territorial Autonomy in Spain: Bicameralism Revisited." *Perspectives on Federalism* 10 (2): 238–67. https://doi.org/10.2478/pof-2018-0025.

Loveday, Peter, Allan Martin, and Robert Parker, eds. 1977. *The Emergence of the Australian Party System.* Sydney: Hale & Ironmonger.

Luyckx, Marc. 1992. *Histoire philosophique du concept de subsidiarité: Note de Dossier 64/92.* Brussels: Commission of the European Union.

Machiavelli, Niccoló. 1970. *Discourses.* London: Penguin. First published 1531.

Maciag, Mike. 2014. "Voter Turnout Plummeting in Local Elections." *Governing* (website), October.

Mackerras, Malcom, and Ian McAllister. 1999. "Compulsory Voting, Party Stability and Electoral Advantage in Australia." *Electoral Studies* 18 (2): 217–33. https://doi.org/10.1016/s0261-3794(98)00047-x.

Macpherson, Crawford. 1977. *The Life and Times of Liberal Democracy.* Oxford: Oxford University Press.

Mahmood, Zaad, and Rahul Ganguli. 2017. "The Performance of Indian States in Electoral Integrity." *Electoral Integrity Project* (blog), 1 January.

Mahoney, James, Erin Kimball, and Kendra Koivu. 2009. "The Logic of Historical Explanation in the Social Sciences." *Comparative Political Studies* 42 (1): 114–46. https://doi.org/10.1177/0010414008325433.

Mahoney, James, and Kathleen Thelen, eds. 2010. *Explaining Institutional Change: Ambiguity, Agency, and Power*. New York: Cambridge University Press.

Mair, Peter. 1997. "E.E. Schattschneider's 'The Semisovereign People.'" *Political Studies* 45 (5): 947–54. https://doi.org/10.1111/1467-9248.00122.

Majeed, Akhtar. 2005. "Republic of India." In *Constitutional Origins, Structure, and Change in Federal Countries*. Vol. 1, *A Global Dialogue on Federalism*, edited by John Kincaid and G. Alan Tarr, 180–208. Montreal and Kingston: McGill-Queen's University Press.

Mann, Thomas E., and Norman J. Ornstein. 2016. *It's Even Worse Than It Looks: How the American Constitutional System Collided with the New Politics of Extremism*. New York: Basic Books.

Manow, Philip, and Simone Burkhart. 2007. "Legislative Self-Restraint under Divided Government in Germany, 1976–2002." *Legislative Studies Quarterly* 32 (2): 167–91. https://doi.org/10.3162/036298007780907941.

Marriott, Peter Anthony John. 2011. *Dome Diseases: Party Competition, Legislative Oversight and Government Accountability in Three Canadian Provinces*. Burnaby, BC: Simon Fraser University.

Marshall, Thomas. 1950. *Citizenship and Social Class*. Cambridge: Cambridge University Press.

Martínez-Tapia, Óscar. 2016. *Los problemas no resueltos de la democracia:* Centro y periferia en España. Madrid: Arrebato.

Matia Portilla, Francisco Javier. 2011. "La cooperación horizontal: Un impulso tan necesario como esperado." *Revista Jurídica de Castilla y León* (23): 105–44.

Maxwell, Phillip. 2018. "The End of the Mining Boom? A Western Australian Perspective." *Mineral Economics* 31 (1): 153–70. https://doi.org/10.1007/s13563-017-0116-9.

Mayhew, David. 1974. *Congress: The Electoral Connection*. New Haven, CT: Yale University Press.

Mayntz, Renate. 2004. "Mechanisms in the Analysis of Social Macro-phenomena." *Philosophy of the Social Sciences* 34 (2): 237–59. https://doi.org/10.1177/0048393103262552.

McAllister, Ian. 1991. "Party Adaptation and Factionalism within the Australian Party System." *American Journal of Political Science* 35 (1): 206–27. https://doi.org/10.2307/2111444.

– 2014. "ANU-SRC Poll: Changing Views of Governance: Results from the ANUpoll, 2008 and 2014." http://csrm.cass.anu.edu.au/sites/default/files/docs/ANU_SRC_Poll_Governance_1_0.pdf.

McAtee, Andrea, and Jennifer Wolak. 2011. "Why People Decide to Participate in State Politics." *Political Research Quarterly* 64 (1): 45–58. https://doi.org/10.1177/1065912909343581.

McCarthy, Justin. 2016. "Americans Still More Trusting in Local over State Government." *Gallup* (website), 19 September.

McGarry, John, and Brendan O'Leary. 2007. "Federation and Managing Nations." In *Multinational Federations*, edited by Michael Burgess and John Pinder, 180–212. Oxford: Routledge.

Menéndez, Agustín José. 2013. "The Existential Crisis of the European Union." *German Law Journal* 14 (5): 453–525. https://doi.org/10.1017/s2071832200001917.

Mettler, Suzanne. 2011. *The Submerged State: How Invisible Government Policies Undermine American Democracy*. Chicago: University of Chicago Press.

Miller, Peter, and Ruth Dassonneville. 2016. "High Turnout in the Low Countries: Partisan Effects of the Abolition of Compulsory Voting in the Netherlands." *Electoral Studies* 44: 132–43. https://doi.org/10.1016/j.electstud.2016.07.009.

Miragliotta, Narelle, and Campbell Sharman. 2017. "Managing Midterm Vacancies: Institutional Design and Partisan Strategy in the Australian Parliament, 1901–2013." *Australian Journal of Political Science* 52 (3): 351–66. https://doi.org/10.1080/10361146.2017.1325441.

Moeckli, Silvano. 2009. "Parlamente und die Interkantonalisierung der Politik." *Parlament, Parlement, Parlamento: Mitteilungsblatt der Schweizerischen Gesellschaft für Parlamentsfragen* 3 (9): 5–11.

Molina, Ignacio. 2020. "Encomio de la mesura." *Agenda pública*, 7 January. http://agendapublica.elpais.com/encomio-de-la-mesura/.

Montani, Guido. 2012. "No to a Phoney Fiscal Union, Yes to a Federal Government." *EURACTIV*, 9 January. https://www.euractiv.com/section/euro-finance/opinion/no-to-a-phoney-fiscal-union-yes-to-a-federal-government/.

Montesquieu. 1961. "Spirit of the Laws: Extracts." In *The Great Political Theories*, edited by Michael R. Curtis, 389–401. New York: Avon Books.

Moon, Jeremy, and Anthony Sayers. 1999. "The Dynamics of Governmental Activity: A Long-Run Analysis of the Changing Scope and Profile of Australian Ministerial Portfolios." *Australian Journal of Political Science* 34 (2): 149–67. https://doi.org/10.1080/10361149950344.

Morden, Michael, Jane Hilderman, and Kendall Anderson. 2018. *Flip the Script: Reclaiming the Legislature to Reinvigorate Representative Democracy*. Toronto: Samara Centre for Democracy.

Moreno, Luis. 2001. *The Federalization of Spain*. Abingdon, UK: Routledge.

Moreno, Luis, César Colino, and Angustias Hombrado. 2019. "Spain: Constitutional Transition through Gradual Accommodation of Territories." In *Territory and Power in Constitutional Transitions*, edited by Sujit Choudhry and George Anderson, 237–54. Oxford: Oxford University Press.

Morrissey, Christopher. 2016. "The Truth about Plato's 'Noble Lie.'" *The Imaginative Conservative*, 15 November.

Mueller, Sean. 2014. "Shared Rule in Federal Political Systems: Conceptual Lessons from Subnational Switzerland." *Publius* 44 (1): 82–108. https://doi.org/10.1093/publius/pjt009.

– 2015. "Switzerland: Federalism as an Ideology of Balance." In *Understanding Federalism and Federation*, edited by Alain-G. Gagnon, Soeren Keil, and Sean Mueller, 105–24. New York: Routledge.

– 2018. "Catalonia: The Perils of Majoritarianism." *Journal of Democracy* 30 (2): 142–56. https://doi.org/10.1353/jod.2019.0031.

Mueller, Sean, and Julian Bernauer. 2016. "Einheit in der Vielfalt? Ausmass und Gründe der Nationalisierung von Schweizer Parteien." In *Wahlen und Wählerschaft in der Schweiz*, edited by Adrian Vatter and Markus Freitag, 325–54. Zürich: NZZ Libro.

Mueller, Sean, and Marlène Gerber. 2016. "The Parliamentary and Executive Elections in Switzerland, 2015." *Electoral Studies* 43: 194–97. https://doi.org/10.1016/j.electstud.2016.06.002.

Musgrave, Thomas. 2003. "The Western Australian Secessionist Movement." *Macquarie Law Journal* 3: 95–129.

Neidhart, Leonhard. 1970. *Plebiszit und pluralitäre Demokratie:* Eine Analyse der Funktionen des schweizerischen Gesetzesreferendums. Bern: Francke.

Neyer, Jürgen. 2003. "Discourse and Order in the EU: A Deliberative Approach to Multi-level Governance." *Journal of Common Market Studies* 41 (4): 687–706. https://doi.org/10.1111/1468-5965.00441.

Nicholson-Crotty, Sean. 2012. "Leaving Money on the Table: Learning from Recent Refusals of Federal Grants in the American States." *Publius* 42 (3): 449–66. https://doi.org/10.1093/publius/pjs022.

Niclauß, Karlheinz. 1998. *Der Weg zum Grundgesetz: Demokratiegründung in Westdeutschland 1945–1949*. Paderborn, Germany: Schöningh.

Nicolaïdis, Kalypso, and Robert Howse, eds. 2001. *The Federal Vision: Legitimacy and Levels of Governance in the United States and the European Union*. Oxford: Oxford University Press.

Noël, Alain. 2006. "Social Justice in Overlapping Sharing Communities." In *Dilemmas of Solidarity: Rethinking Redistribution in the Canadian Federation*, edited by Lorne Sossin, Jean-François Gaudreault-DesBiens, and Sujit Choudhry, 57–72. Toronto: University of Toronto Press.

– 2009. "Balance and Imbalance in the Division of Financial Resources." In *Contemporary Canadian Federalism: Foundations, Traditions, Institutions*, edited by Alain-G. Gagnon, 273–302. Toronto: University of Toronto Press.

Nolte, Paul. 2012. *Was ist Demokratie? Geschichte und Gegenwart*. Munich: C.H. Beck.

Norris, Pippa. 2008. *Driving Democracy: Do Power-Sharing Institutions Work?* Cambridge: Cambridge University Press.

Novo Arbona, Ainhoa, and Sergio Pérez Castaños. 2018. "Building a Federal State: Phases and Moments of Spanish Regional (De)centralization." *Italian Political Science Review* 49 (3): 263–77. https://doi.org/10.1017/ipo.2018.23.

Nugent, John D. 2009. *Safeguarding Federalism: How States Protect Their Interests in National Policymaking*. Norman: University of Oklahoma Press.

NZZ (*Neue Zürcher Zeitung*). 2007. "Degressive Steuern sind illegal: Bundesgericht kippt die umstrittene Obwaldner Regelung," 7 June.

– 2015. "Tessin: Burka-Verbot ohne Pardon," 24 November.

– 2016. "Wichtiges Signal für Harmos," 25 September.

– 2018. "St. Galler 'Burka-Verbot' gilt ab Anfang Jahr," 28 October.

Oates, Wallace E. 1972. *Fiscal Federalism*. New York: Harcourt Brace Jovanovich.

– 2005. "Toward a Second-Generation Theory of Fiscal Federalism." *International Tax and Public Finance* 12 (4): 349–73. https://doi.org/10.1007/s10797-005-1619-9.

Obinger, Herbert, Stephan Leibfried, and Francis Castles, eds. 2005. *Federalism and the Welfare State: New World and European Experiences*. Cambridge: Cambridge University Press.

Obydenkova, Anastassia, and Wilfried Swenden. 2013. "Autocracy-Sustaining versus Democratic Federalism: Explaining the Divergent Trajectories of Territorial Politics in Russia and Western Europe." *Territory, Politics, Governance* 1 (1): 86–112. https://doi.org/10.1080/21622671.2013.763733.

O'Leary, Brendan, Ian Lustick, and Thomas Callaghy, eds. 2001. *Right-Sizing the State: The Politics of Moving Borders*. Oxford: Oxford University Press.

Olmeda, José A. 2019. "¿Hacia una desconsolidación de la democracia en España?" *Cuadernos de Pensamiento Político* 61: 5–16.

Olsen, Johan P. 2009. "Change and Continuity: An Institutional Approach to Institutions of Democratic Government." *European Political Science Review* 1 (1): 3–32. https://doi.org/10.1017/s1755773909000022.

O'Malley, Eoin. 2007. "The Power of Prime Ministers: Results of an Expert Survey." *International Political Science Review* 28 (1): 7–27. https://doi.org/10.1177/0192512107070398.

Orren, Karen, and Stephen Skowronek. 1994. "Beyond the Iconography of Order: Notes for a 'New Institutionalism.'" In *The Dynamics of American Politics: Approaches and Interpretations*, edited by Lawrence Dodd and Calvin Jillson, 311–30. Boulder, CO: Westview Press.

– 2004. *The Search for American Political Development*. Cambridge: Cambridge University Press.

Orton, J. Douglas, and Karl E. Weick. 1990. "Loosely Coupled Systems: A Reconceptualization." *Academy of Management Review* 15 (2): 203–23. https://doi.org/10.5465/amr.1990.4308154.

Painter, Martin. 1991. "Intergovernmental Relations in Canada: An Institutional Analysis." *Canadian Journal of Political Science* 24 (2): 269–88. https://doi.org/10.1017/s0008423900005084.

– 1997. "Federalism." In *Politics in Australia*, edited by Rodney Smith, 194–211. St. Leonards, Australia: Allen & Unwin.

– 1998. *Collaborative Federalism: Economic Reform in Australia in the 1990s*. Cambridge: Cambridge University Press.

– 2001. "Multi-level Governance and the Emergence of Collaborative Federal Institutions in Australia." *Policy & Politics* 29 (2): 137–50. https://doi.org/10.1332/0305573012501260.

Palau, Anna, and Luz Moñoz. 2018. "Spain: Government and Opposition Cooperation in a Multi-level Context." In *Opposition Parties in European Legislatures*, edited by Elisabetta De Giorgo and Gabriella Ilonszki, 113–32. London: Routledge.

Palermo, Francesco. 2018. "Beyond Second Chambers: Alternative Representation of Territorial Interests and Their Reasons." *Perspectives on Federalism* 10 (2): 49–70. https://doi.org/10.2478/pof-2018-0016.

Pallarés, Francesc, Javier Astudillo, and Tània Verge. 2015. "Spain: Unresolved Integration Challenges in a Party-Led Decentralization." In *Political Parties and Civil Society in Federal Countries*, edited by Wolfgang Renzsch, Klaus Detterbeck, and John Kincaid, 227–53. Toronto: Oxford University Press.

Papadopoulos, Yannis. 2010. "Accountability and Multi-level Governance: More Accountability, Less Democracy?" *West European Politics* 33 (5): 1030–49. https://doi.org/10.1080/01402382.2010.486126.

Parkin, Andrew. 1983. "Party Organisation and Machine Politics: The ALP in Perspective." In *Machine Politics in the Australian Labor Party*, edited by Andrew Parkin and John Warhurst, 15–29. Sydney: Allen & Unwin.

Parkin, Andrew, and Vern Marshall. 1994. "Frustrated, Reconciled or Divided? The Australian Labor Party and Federalism." *Australian Journal of Political Science* 29 (1): 18–39. https://doi.org/10.1080/00323269408402278.

Parkin, Andrew, and John Warhurst, eds. 1983. *Machine Politics in the Australian Labor Party*. Sydney: Allen & Unwin.

Peterson, Paul E. 1996. *The Price of Federalism*. Washington, DC: Brookings Institution Press.

Peterson, Paul E., Barry Rabe, and Kenneth Wong. 1995. *When Federalism Works*. Washington, DC: Brookings Institution Press.

Pettit, Philip. 1997. *Republicanism*. Oxford: Oxford University Press.

– 2012. *On the People's Terms: A Republican Theory and Model of Democracy*. Cambridge: Cambridge University Press.

Pew Research Center. 2014. "Political Polarization in the American Public," 12 June. https://www.people-press.org/2014/06/12/political-polarization-in-the-american-public/.

– 2015. "Beyond Distrust: How Americans View Their Government." 23 November. https://www.people-press.org/2015/11/23/beyond-distrust-how-americans-view-their-government/.

Phillimore, John, and Jeffrey Harwood. 2015. "Intergovernmental Relations in Australia: Increasing Engagement within a Centralizing Dynamic." In *Intergovernmental Relations in Federal Systems: Comparative Structures and Dynamics*, edited by Johanne Poirier, Cheryl Saunders, and John Kincaid, 42–79. Oxford: Oxford University Press.

Piattoni, Simona, ed. 2015. *The European Union: Democratic Principles and Institutional Architectures in Times of Crisis*. Oxford: Oxford University Press.

Pierson, Paul. 2004. *Politics in Time: History, Institutions and Social Analysis*. Princeton, NJ: Princeton University Press.

Pilet, Jean-Benoit, and Petra Meier. 2018. "Ze halen hun slag wel thuis: Over particratie en het aanpassingsvermogen van Belgische partijen." *Res publica* 60 (4): 321–45. https://doi.org/10.5553/rp/048647002018060004002.

Pilet, Jean-Benoit, and Teun Pauwels. 2010. "De vertegenwoordiging van taalgroepen in België: De weg naar een hyperinstitutionalisering." In *Gezien, gehoord, vertegenwoordigd? Diversiteit in de Belgische politiek*, edited by Karen Celis, Petra Meier, and Bram Wauters, 47–68. Ghent: Academia Press.

Pitkin, Hannah. 1972. *The Concept of Representation*. Berkeley: University of California Press.

Plato. 1955. *The Republic*. London: Penguin. First date of publication unknown.

– 1997. "Statesman." In John M. Cooper, ed. *Plato: Complete Works*. Indianapolis, IN: Hacket Publishing. First date of publication unknown.

Poirier, Johanne, Cheryl Saunders, and John Kincaid, eds. 2016. *Intergovernmental Relations in Federal Systems: Comparative Structures and Dynamics*. Oxford: Oxford University Press.

Polity IV. 2014. *Individual Country Regime Trends, 1946–2013*. http://www.systemicpeace.org/polity/polity4.htm.

Popelier, Patricia, and Bea Cantillon. 2013. "Bipolar Federalism and the Social Welfare State: A Case for Shared Competences." *Publius* 43 (4): 626–47. https://doi.org/10.1093/publius/pjt005.

Popelier, Patricia, Dave Sinardet, Jan Velaers, and Bea Cantillon, eds. 2012. *België, quo vadis? Waarheen na de zesde staatshervorming?* Antwerp: Intersentia.

Posner, Paul L. 1998. *The Politics of Unfunded Mandates: Whither Federalism?* Washington, DC: Georgetown University Press.

Potoski, Matthew. 2001. "Clean Air Federalism: Do States Race to the Bottom?" *Public Administration Review* 61 (3): 335–43. https://doi.org/10.1111/0033-3352.00034.

Potter, David. 1996. *India's Political Administrators: From ICS to IAS*. New Delhi: Oxford University Press.

Powell, Charles. 2001. *España en democracia, 1975–2000: Las claves de la produnda transformación de España*. Barcelona: Plaza y Janés.

PRS Legislative Research. 2014. "Legislative Performance of State Assemblies." *The PRS Blog*, 27 May. http://prsindia.org/theprsblog/legislative-performance-state-assemblies.

– 2017. "Committees in State Legislatures." *The PRS Blog*, 31 October. https://www.prsindia.org/blog-category/states-and-state-legislatures.

Putnam, Robert. 1988. "Diplomacy and Domestic Politics: The Logic of Two-Level Games." *International Organization* 42 (3): 427–60. https://doi.org/10.1017/s0020818300027697.

Radcliff, Pamela. 2017. *Modern Spain: 1808 to the Present*. Hoboken, NJ: Wiley-Blackwell.

Radin, Beryl A. 2007. "The Indian Administrative Service (IAS) in the 21st Century: Living in an Intergovernmental Environment." *International Journal of Public Administration* 30 (12–14): 1525–48. https://doi.org/10.1080/01900690701229848.

Rama, José. 2016. "Ciclos electorales y sistema de partido en España, 1977–2016." *Revista Jurídica de la Universidad Autónoma de Madrid* 34: 241–66.

Rao, Govinda. 2007. "Republic of India." In *The Practice of Fiscal Federalism: Comparative Perspectives*, edited by Anwar Shah, 151–77. Montreal and Kingston: McGill-Queen's University Press.

Reid, Gordon S., and Martyn Forrest. 1989. *Australia's Commonwealth Parliament, 1901–1988: Ten Perspectives*. Melbourne: Melbourne University Press.

Renan, Ernest. 1882. "Qu'est-ce qu'une nation?" Lecture delivered at the Sorbonne, Paris, 11 March 1882.

Renzsch, Wolfgang. 2000. "Bundesstaat oder Parteienstaat: Überlegungen zu Entscheidungsprozessen im Spannungsfeld von föderaler Konsensbildung und parlamentarischem Wettbewerb in Deutschland." In *Zwischen Wettbewerbs- und Verhandlungsdemokratie*, edited by Everhard Holtmann and Helmut Voelzkow, 53–78. Wiesbaden: Westdeutscher Verlag.

Requejo, Ferran. 2005. *Multinational Federalism and Value Pluralism: The Spanish Case*. London: Routledge.

– 2010. "Revealing the Dark Side of Traditional Democracies in Plurinational Societies: The Case of Catalonia and the Spanish 'Estado de las Atonomia.'" *Nations and Nationalism* 16 (1): 148–68. https://doi.org/10.1111/j.1469-8129.2010.00414.x.

Requejo, Ferran, and Miquel Caminal, eds. 2012. *Federalism, Plurinationality and Democratic Constitutionalism: Theory and Cases*. London: Routledge.

Riker, William H. 1964. *Federalism: Origin, Operation, Significance*. Boston: Little, Brown.

Riklin, Alois. 2006. *Machtteilung: Geschichte der Mischverfassung*. Darmstadt: Wissenschaftliche Buchgesellschaft.

Riley, Patrick. 1973. "The Origins of Federal Theory in International Relations Ideas." *Polity* 6 (1): 87–121. https://doi.org/10.2307/3234183.

Ritter, Gerhard. 2005. *Föderalismus und Parlamentarismus in Deutschland in Geschichte und Gegenwart*. Munich: C.H. Beck.

Robertson, David B. 2012. *Federalism and the Making of America*. New York: Routledge.

Rocher, François. 2009. "The Quebec-Canada Dynamic or the Negation of the Ideal of Federalism." In *Contemporary Canadian Federalism: Foundations, Traditions, Institutions*, edited by Alain-G. Gagnon, 81–131. Toronto: University of Toronto Press.

Rodgers, Steven. 2013. *Accountability in State Legislatures: How Parties Perform in Office and State Legislative Elections*. Nashville, TN: *Center for the Study of Democratic Institutions*, Vanderbilt University.

Rodríguez, Emilio, Jean-Baptiste Harguindéguy, and Almudena Sánchez. 2019. "The Perfect Storm? How to Explain the Rise of Intergovernmental Conflicts in Spain? (1984–2014)." *Innovation: The European Journal of Social Science Research* 32 (2): 211–30. https://doi.org/10.1080/13511610.2018.1520628.

Romero, Joan, and Joaquín Farinós. 2006. *Gobernanza territorial en España*. Valencia: Universidad de València.

Rose, Shanna, and Greg Goelzhauser. 2018. "The State of American Federalism 2017–2018: Unilateral Executive Action, Regulatory Rollback, and State Resistance." *Publius* 48 (3): 319–44. https://doi.org/10.1093/publius/pjy016.

Rousseau, Jean-Jacques. 1966. *Du contrat social*, edited by Pierre Burgelin. Paris: Flammarion. First published 1762.

– 1968. *The Social Contract*. London: Penguin. First published 1762.

Rüb, Friedbert, ed. 2014. *Rapide Politikwechsel in der Bundesrepublik: Theoretischer Rahmen und empirische Befunde*. Baden-Baden: Nomos.

Rummens, Stefan, and Stefan Sottiaux. 2014. "Democratic Legitimacy in the Bund or 'Federation of States': The Cases of Belgium and the EU." *European Law Journal* 20 (4): 568–87. https://doi.org/10.1111/eulj.12053.

Ruperalia, Sanjay. 2015. *Divided We Govern: Coalition Politics in Modern India*. London: Hurst.

Russell, Peter. 2004. *Constitutional Odyssey: Can Canadians Become a Sovereign People?* Toronto: University of Toronto Press.

– 2017. *Canada's Odyssey: A Country Based on Incomplete Conquests*. Toronto: University of Toronto Press.

Sáenz, Eva. 2012. "Parlamento, partidos y Estado autonómico: Sobre la Conveniencia de suprimir el senado." *Revista de Derecho Politico* (85): 171–94. https://doi.org/10.5944/rdp.85.2012.10248.

– 2013. "Relaciones interguvernamentales de carácter vertical en el Estado Autonómico: El Ser, El Deber ser y posibles retos de future." *Reviste española de Derecho Constitucional* (97): 45–71.

Saldanha, Alison. 2017. "2017 Deadliest Year for Cow-Related Hate Crime since 2010: 86% of Those Killed Muslim." *India Spend*, 8 December. Accessed 26 September 2018. http://www.indiaspend.com/2017-deadliest-year-for-cow-related-hate-crime-since-10-86-of-those-killed-muslim-12662/.

Salmon, Pierre. 2019. *Yardstick Competition among Governments: Accountability and Policymaking When Citizens Look across Borders*. Oxford: Oxford University Press.

Sánchez Barrilao, Juan Francisco. 2009. "La participación de las CCAA en la elección por el Senada de los Magistrados constitucionales." *Teoría y Realidad Constitucional* (23): 387–424. https://doi.org/10.5944/trc.23.2009.6852.

Sartori, Giovanni. 1976. *Parties and Party Systems*. Cambridge: Cambridge University Press.

Savoie, Donald. 1999. *Governing from the Centre: The Concentration of Power in Canadian Politics*. Toronto: University of Toronto Press.

– 2008. *Court Government and the Collapse of Accountability in Canada and the United Kingdom*. Toronto: University of Toronto Press.

Sawer, Marian. 2003. *The Ethical State? Social Liberalism in Australia*. Melbourne: Melbourne University Press.

Saxena, Rekha. 2013. "Intergovernmental Relations in India." In *Public Administration in South Asia: India, Bangladesh, and Pakistan*, edited by Meghna Sabharwal and Evan Berman, 73–89. New York: CRC Press.

Sayers, Anthony. 1986. *The Debate over Representation in Western Australia 1983–1985: The Proposals for Reform of Labor's First Term*. Perth: University of Western Australia.

Sayers, Anthony, and Andrew Banfield. 2013. "The Evolution of Federalism and Executive Power in Canada and Australia." In *Federal Dynamics: Continuity, Change, and the Varieties of Federalism*, edited by Arthur Benz and Jörg Broschek, 185–208. Oxford: Oxford University Press.

Sayers, Anthony, and Jeremy Moon. 2002. "State Government Convergence and Partisanship: A Long-Run Analysis of Australian Ministerial Portfolios." *Canadian Journal of Political* Science 35 (3): 589–612. https://doi.org/10.1017/s0008423902778360.

Saywell, John. 2002. *The Lawmakers: Judicial Power and the Making of Canadian Federalism*. Toronto: University of Toronto Press.

Scharpf, Fritz W. 1970. *Demokratietheorie zwischen Utopie und Anpassung*. Konstanz, Germany: Universitätsverlag.

– 1988. "The Joint-Decision Trap: Lessons from German Federalism and European Integration." *Public Administration* 66 (3): 239–78. https://doi.org/10.1111/j.1467-9299.1988.tb00694.x.

– 1993. "Versuch über Demokratie im verhandelnden Staat." In *Verhandlungsdemokratie, Interessenvermittlung, Regierbarkeit: Festschrift für Gerhard Lehmbruch*, edited by Roland Czada and Manfred G. Schmidt, 25–50. Opladen, Germany: Westdeutscher Verlag.

– 1997. *Games Real Actors Play: Actor-Centered Institutionalism in Policy Research.* Boulder, CO: Westview Press.
– 1999. *Governing in Europe: Effective and Democratic?* Oxford: Oxford University Press.
– 2009. *Föderalismusreform: Kein Ausweg aus der Politikverflechtungsfalle?* Frankfurt: Campus.
Scharpf, Fritz W., Bernd Reissert, and Fritz Schnabel. 1976. *Politikverflechtung: Theorie und Empirie des kooperativen Föderalismus in der Bundesrepublik.* Kronberg, Germany: Scriptor Verlag.
Schattschneider, Elmer E. 1960. *The Semisovereign people: A Realist's View of Democracy in America.* New York: Holt, Rinehart and Winston.
Schaub, Hans-Peter. 2016. *Landsgemeinde oder Urne: Was ist demokratischer? Urnen- und Versammlungsdemokratie in der Schweiz.* Baden-Baden: Nomos.
Schiller, Friedrich. 1998. *Wilhelm Tell.* Munich: DTV. First published 1804.
Schmidt, Vivien A. 2008. "Discursive Institutionalism: The Explanatory Power of Ideas and Discourse." *Annual Review of Political Science* 11 (1): 303–26. https://doi.org/10.1146/annurev.polisci.11.060606.135342.
– 2013. "Democracy and Legitimacy in the European Union Revisited: Input, Output and 'Throughput.'" *Political Studies* 61 (1): 2–22. https://doi.org/10.1111/j.1467-9248.2012.00962.x.
Schnabel, Johanna, and Sean Mueller. 2017. "Vertical Influence or Horizontal Coordination? The Purpose of Intergovernmental Councils in Switzerland." *Regional and Federal Studies* 27 (5): 549–72. https://doi.org/10.1080/13597566.2017.1368017.
Schram, Sanford, and Joe Soss. 1998. "Making Something out of Nothing: Welfare Reform and a New Race to the Bottom." *Publius* 28 (3): 67–88. https://doi.org/10.1093/oxfordjournals.pubjof.a029985.
Schultze, Rainer-Olaf. 1982. "Politikverflechtung und konföderaler Föderalismus: Entwicklungslinien und Strukturprobleme im bundesrepublikanischen und kanadischen Föderalismus." *Zeitschrift für Kanada-Studien* 2: 111–44.
– 1999. "Föderalismusreform in Deutschland: Widersprüche – Ansätze – Hoffnungen." *Zeitschrift für Politik* 46 (2): 173–94.
Schwaller, Urs. 2003. "Incidences de la RPT sur les parlements: Prise de position du point de vue de la Conférence des gouvernements cantonaux." *Parlament, Parlement, Parlamento: Mitteilungsblatt der Schweizerischen Gesellschaft für Parlamentsfragen* 3 (3): 12–14.
Schwanke, Karina, and Falk Ebinger. 2006. "Politisierung und Rollenverständnis der deutschen administrativen Elite 1970 bis 2005: Wandel trotz Kontinuität." In *Politik und Verwaltung: Politische Vierteljahresschrift*, Sonderheft Nr. 37, edited by Jörg Bogumil, Werner Jann, and Frank Nullmeier, 228–46. Wiesbaden: VS Verlag für Sozialwissenschaften.

Scott, Kyle. 2011. *Federalism: A Normative Theory and Its Practical Relevance*. London: Continuum International Publishing Group.

Scott, William Richard. 2014. *Institutions and Organizations: Ideas, Interests, and Identities*. New York: Sage Publications.

SGI (Sustainable Governance Indicators). 2018. "Quality of Democracy." https://www.sgi-network.org/2019/Democracy/Quality_of_Democracy.

Shah, Anwar, ed. 2007. *The Practice of Fiscal Federalism: Comparative Perspectives*. Montreal and Kingston: McGill-Queen's University Press.

Shani, Ornit. 2010. "Conceptions of Citizenship in India and the 'Muslim Question.'" *Modern Asian Studies* 44 (1): 145–73. https://doi.org/10.1017/s0026749x09990102.

Shannon, John. 1987. "The Return to Fend-for-Yourself Federalism: The Reagan Mark." *Intergovernmental Perspective* (Summer/Fall): 34–7.

Shapiro, Ian. 1999. *Democratic Justice*. New Haven, CT: Yale University Press.

– 2012. "On Non-domination." *University of Toronto Law Journal* 62 (3): 293–335. https://doi.org/10.3138/utlj.62.3.293.

– 2016. *Politics against Domination*. Cambridge, MA: Belknap Press.

Sharma, Chanchal Kumar. 2017. "A Situational Theory of Pork-Barrel Politics: The Shifting Logic of Discretionary Allocations in India." *India Review* 16 (1): 14–41. https://doi.org/10.1080/14736489.2017.1279922.

– 2020. "The Political Economy of Fiscal Federalism and Indirect Tax Reform in India." Unpublished manuscript.

Sharma, Chanchal Kumar, and Wilfried Swenden. 2018. "Modi-fying Indian Federalism? Centre-State Relations under Modi's Tenure as Prime Minister." *Indian Politics & Policy* 1 (1): 51–82. https://doi.org/10.18278/inpp.1.1.4.

Sharman, Campbell. 1990. "Parliamentary Federations and Limited Government: Constitutional Design and Redesign in Australia and Canada." *Journal of Theoretical Politics* 2 (2): 205–30. https://doi.org/10.1177/0951692890002002004.

– 1999. "The Representation of Small Parties and Independents in the Senate." *Australian Journal of Political Science* 34 (3): 353–61. https://doi.org/10.1080/10361149950272.

Sharman, Campbell, and Anthony Sayers. 1998. "Swings and Roundabouts? Patterns of Voting for the Australian Labor Party at State and Commonwealth Lower House Elections, 1901–96." *Australian Journal of Political Science* 33 (3): 329–44. https://doi.org/10.1080/10361149850507.

Shastri, Sandeep. 2006. "Representing the States at the Federal Level: The Role of the Rajya Sabha." In *A World of Second Chambers: Handbook for Constitutional Studies on Bicameralism*, edited by Jörg Luther, Paolo Passaglia, and Rolando Tarchi, 587–612. Milan: Giuffrè.

Sheingate, Adam. 2014. "Institutional Dynamics and American Political Development." *Annual Review of Political Science* 17: 461–77. https://doi.org/10.1146/annurev-polisci-040113-161139.

Shugart, Matthew Soberg, and John Carey. 1992. *Presidents and Assemblies: Constitutional Design and Electoral Dynamics*. Cambridge: Cambridge University Press.

Simeon, Richard. 1972. *Federal-Provincial Diplomacy: The Making of Recent Policy in Canada*. Toronto: University of Toronto Press.

– 1978. "Opening Statement to the Special Committee on the Constitution." Institute of Intergovernmental Relations Working Paper. Kingston, ON: Queen's University.

Simeon, Richard, and David Cameron. 2008. "Intergovernmental Relations and Democracy: An Oxymoron If There Ever Was One." In *Canadian Federalism: Performance, Effectiveness, and Legitimacy*, edited by Herman Bakvis and Grace Skogstad, 278–95. Oxford: Oxford University Press.

Simeon, Richard, and Amy Nugent. 2008. "Parliamentary Canada and Intergovernmental Canada: Exploring the Tensions." In *Canadian Federalism: Performance, Effectiveness, and Legitimacy*, edited by Herman Bakvis and Grace Skogstad, 89–111. Don Mills, ON: Oxford University Press.

Simmons, Julie. 2008. "Democratizing Executive Federalism: The Role of Non-governmental Actors in Intergovernmental Agreements." In *Canadian Federalism: Performance, Effectiveness, and Legitimacy*, edited by Herman Bakvis and Grace Skogstad, 355–79. Oxford: Oxford University Press.

Simmons, Julie, and Peter Graefe. 2013. "Assessing the Collaboration That Was 'Collaborative Federalism' 1996–2006." *Canadian Political Science Review* 7 (1): 25–36.

Sinardet, Dave, and Peter Bursens. 2014. "Democratic Legitimacy in Multilevel Political Systems: The Role of Politicization at the Polity-Wide Level in the EU and Belgium." *Acta Politica* 49 (3): 246–65. https://doi.org/10.1057/ap.2013.17.

Singh, Ajay Kumar. 2019. "Dynamic De/Centralization in India, 1950–2010." *Publius* 49 (1): 112–37.

Singh, Mahendra P., and Rekha Saxena. 2013. *Federalizing India in the Age of Globalization*. New Delhi: Primus Books.

– 2015. "Intergovernmental Relations in India." In *Intergovernmental Relations in Federal Systems*, edited by Johanne Poirier, Cheryl Saunders, and John Kincaid, 239–71. Don Mills, ON: Oxford University Press.

Smiley, Donald V. 1971. "The Structural Problem of Canadian Federalism." *Canadian Public Administration/Administration publique du Canada* 14 (3): 326–43. https://doi.org/10.1111/j.1754-7121.1971.tb00284.x.

– 1972. *Canada in Question: Federalism in the Seventies*. Toronto: McGraw-Hill Ryerson.

– 1979. "An Outsider's Observation of Intergovernmental Relations among Consenting Adults." In *Confrontation and Collaboration: Intergovernmental Relations in Canada Today*, edited by Richard Simeon, 105–13. Toronto: Institute of Public Administration of Canada.

Smiley, Donald V., and Ronald L. Watts. 1985. *Intrastate Federalism in Canada*. Toronto: University of Toronto Press.

Smith, Jennifer. 1988. "Canadian Confederation and the Influence of American Federalism." *Canadian Journal of Political Science* 21 (3): 443–63. https://doi.org/10.1017/s0008423900056778.

– 2007. "Federalism and Democratic Accountability." In *Democratic Dilemmas of Multilevel Governance: Legitimacy, Representation and Accountability in the European Union*, edited by Joan DeBardeleben and Achim Hurrelmann, 38–58. New York: Palgrave Macmillan.

Smith, Rodney. 2018. "New South Wales: An Accidental Case of Semi-parliamentarism?" *Australian Journal of Political Sciences* 53 (2): 256–63. https://doi.org/10.1080/10361146.2018.1451486.

Smith, Troy E. 2008. "Intergovernmental Lobbying: How Opportunistic Actors Create a Less Structured and Balanced Federal System." In *Intergovernmental Management for the 21st Century*, edited by Timothy J. Conlan and Paul L. Posner, 310–37. Washington: Brookings Institution Press.

Sonnicksen, Jared. 2018. "Federalism and Democracy: A Tense Relationship." In *Calidad democrática y organización territorial*, edited by José Tudela, Mario Kölling, and Fernando Reviriego Picón, 31–52. Madrid: Marcial Pons.

Sørensen, Eva, and Jacob Torfing, eds. 2007. *Theories of Democratic Network Governance*. Basingstoke, UK: Palgrave Macmillan.

Sottiaux, Stefan. 2011. *De Verenigde Staten van België: Reflecties over de toekomst van het grondwettelijk recht in de gelaagde rechtsorde*. Mechelen, Belgium: Kluwer.

– 2014. "De federale staatshervorming: Van federale staat naar verenigde staten van België." In *Het federale België na de Zesde Staatshervorming*, edited by André Alen, Benjamin Dalle, Koen Muylle, Wouter Pas, Jeroen Van Nieuwenhove, and Willem Verrijdt, 635–51. Bruges: Die Keure.

SRF (Schweizer Radio und Fernsehen). 2018. Umsetzung Lehrplan 21: "Der Einführung steht nun nichts mehr im Weg." https://www.srf.ch/news/schweiz/umsetzung-lehrplan-21-der-einfuehrung-steht-nun-nichts-mehr-im-weg.

Stecker, Christian. 2016. "The Effects of Federalism Reform on the Legislative Process in Germany." *Regional and Federal Studies* 26 (5): 603–24. https://doi.org/10.1080/13597566.2016.1236334.

Stepan, Alfred. 1999. "Federalism and Democracy: Beyond the U.S. Model." *Journal of Democracy* 10 (4): 19–34. https://doi.org/10.1353/jod.1999.0072.

Stepan, Alfred, Juan Linz, and Yogendra Yadav, eds. 2011. *Crafting State-Nations: India and Other Multinational Democracies*. Baltimore, MD: Johns Hopkins University Press.

Stie, Anne Elizabeth. 2012. *Democratic Decision-Making in the EU: Technocracy in Disguise*. London: Routledge.

Stoker, Robert P. 1991. *Reluctant Partners: Implementing Federal Policy*. Pittsburgh, PA: University of Pittsburgh Press.

Stone, Bruce. 2002. "Bicameralism and Democracy: The Transformation of Australian State Upper Houses." *Australian Journal of Political Science* 37 (2): 267–81. https://doi.org/10.1080/10361140220148142.

– 2005. "Changing Roles, Changing Rules: Procedural Development and Difference in Australian State Upper Houses." *Australian Journal of Political Science* 40 (1): 33–50. https://doi.org/10.1080/10361140500049222.

Strangio, Paul. 2009. "Introduction: From Confusion to Stability." In *Confusion: The Making of the Australian Two-Party System*, edited by Paul Strangio and Nick Dyrenfurth, 1–22. Melbourne: Melbourne University Press.

Stuligross, David, and Ashutosh Varshney. 2002. "Ethnic Diversities: Constitutional Designs and Public Policies in India." In *The Architecture of Democracy: Constitutional Design, Conflict Management, and Democracy*, edited by Andrew Reynolds, 429–58. Oxford: Oxford University Press.

Sturm, Roland. 1999. "Party Competition and the Federal System: The Lehmbruch Hypothesis Revisited." In *Recasting German Federalism: The Legacies of Unification*, edited by Charlie Jeffery, 197–216. London: Pinter.

Supreme Court of Canada. 2001. *114957 Canada Ltée (Spraytech, Societé d'arrosage) v. Hudson (Town)*, SCC 40 (CanLII), [2001] 2 SCR 241.

Swenden, Wilfried. 2002. "Asymmetric Federalism and Coalition-Making in Belgium." *Publius* 32 (3): 67–87. https://doi.org/10.1093/oxfordjournals.pubjof.a004960.

– 2016. "Centre-State Bargaining and Territorial Accommodation: Evidence from India." *Swiss Political Science Review* 22 (4): 491–515. https://doi.org/10.1111/spsr.12233.

– 2018. "Governing Diversity in South Asia: Explaining Divergent Pathways in India and Pakistan." *Publius* 48 (1): 102–33. https://doi.org/10.1093/publius/pjx058.

– 2019. "'Team India' and the NITI Aayog." In *Seminar*, no. 717 (May), *The Union and the States: A Symposium on the Changing Federal Dynamic in India*, edited by Yamini Aiyar and Louise Tillin, 28–33. https://www.india-seminar.com/2019/717.htm.

Swenden, Wilfried, and Maarten Theo Jans. 2006. "'Will It Stay or Will It Go?' Federalism and the Sustainability of Belgium." *West European Politics* 29 (5): 877–94. https://doi.org/10.1080/01402380600968745.

Swenden, Wilfried, and Bert Maddens, eds. 2009. *Territorial Party Politics in Western Europe*. Basingstoke, UK: Palgrave Macmillan.

Swenden, Wilfried, and Rekha Saxena. 2017. "Rethinking Central Planning: A Federal Critique of the Planning Commission." *India Review* 16 (1): 42–65. https://doi.org/10.1080/14736489.2017.1279925.

– 2021. "Policing the Federation: The Supreme Court and Judicial Federalism in India." *Territory, Politics, Governance* (forthcoming).

Swenden, Wilfried, and Simon Toubeau. 2013. "Mainstream Parties and Territorial Dynamics in the UK, Spain and India." In *Federal Dynamics: Continuity, Change, and the Varieties of Federalism*, edited by Arthur Benz and Jörg Broschek, 249–74. Oxford: Oxford University Press.

Switzerland. BFS (Bundesamt für Statistik). 2017. "Volksabstimmungen (Ergebnisse Ebene Gemeinde seit 1981)." https://www.bfs.admin.ch/bfs/de/home/statistiken/politik.assetdetail.7646485.html.

Switzerland. Bundeskanzlei. 2018a. "Ungültig erklärte Volksinitiativen." https://www.bk.admin.ch/ch/d/pore/vi/vis_2_2_5_6.html.

– 2018b. "Volksabstimmungen." https://www.bk.admin.ch/bk/de/home/politische-rechte/volksabstimmungen.html.

– 2018c. "Von Volk und Ständen angenommene Volksinitiativen." https://www.bk.admin.ch/ch/d/pore/vi/vis_2_2_5_8.html.

Switzerland. SPK (Staatspolitische Kommission des Ständerats). 2017. "Standesinitiativen – Kt.Iv.ZG: Wiederherstellung der Souveränität der Kantone bei Wahlfragen; Änderung der Bundesverfassung; Kt.Iv.UR: Souveränität bei Wahlfragen." https://www.parlament.ch/centers/documents/de/bericht-spk-s-14-307-14-316-2017-06-21-d.pdf.

Taflaga, Marija. 2018. "What's in a Name? Semi-parliamentarism and Australian Commonwealth Executive-Legislative Relations." *Australian Journal of Political Science* 53 (2): 248–55. https://doi.org/10.1080/10361146.2018.1451484.

Tajadura Tejada, Javier. 2013. "Horizontal Cooperation: Unfinished Business for the Spanish Autonomic State Framework." In *The Ways of Federalism in Western Countries and the Horizons of Territorial Autonomy in Spain*, edited by Alberto López-Basaguren and Leire Escajedo San Epifanio, 211–26. Wiesbaden: Springer.

Talbot, Ian, and Gurharpal Singh. 2009. *The Partition of India*. Cambridge: Cambridge University Press.

Telford, Hamish. 2003. "The Federal Spending Power in Canada: Nation-Building or Nation-Destroying?" *Publius* 33 (1): 23–44. https://doi.org/10.1093/oxfordjournals.pubjof.a004976.

Thomas, Paul E.J., and J.P. Lewis. 2018. "Executive Creep in Canadian Provincial Legislatures." *Canadian Journal of Political Science* 51 (1): 1–21.

Thompson, Frank. 2013. "The Rise of Executive Federalism: Implications for the Picket Fence and IGM." *American Review of Public Administration* 43 (1): 3–25. https://doi.org/10.1177/0275074012461561.

Thompson, Frank J., Kenneth K. Wong, and Barry G. Rabe. 2020. *Trump, the Administrative Presidency, and Federalism*. Washington, DC: Brookings Institution Press.

Thorlakson, Lori. 2007. "An Institutional Explanation of Party System Congruence: Evidence from Six Federations." *European Journal of Political Research* 46 (1): 69–95. https://doi.org/10.1111/j.1475-6765.2006.00647.x.

– 2009. "Patterns of Party Integration, Influence and Autonomy in Seven Federations." *Party Politics* 15 (2): 157–77. https://doi.org/10.1177%2F1354068808099979.

Thucydides. 1934. *The Peloponnesian War*. New York: Modern Library. First date of publication unknown.

Tiebout, Charles M. 1956. "A Pure Theory of Local Expenditures." *Journal of Political Economy* 64 (5): 416–24. https://doi.org/10.1086/257839.

Tillin, Louise. 2013. *Remapping India: New States and Their Political Origins*. London: Hurst.

– 2019. *Indian Federalism*. New Delhi: Oxford University Press.

Tillin, Louise, Rajeshwari Deshpande, and K.K. Kailash, eds. 2015. *Politics of Welfare: Comparisons across Indian States*. New Delhi: Oxford University Press.

Tillin, Louise, and Anthony W. Pereira. 2017. "Federalism, Multi-level Elections and Social Policy in Brazil and India." *Commonwealth & Comparative Politics* 55 (3): 328–52. https://doi.org/10.1080/14662043.2017.1327928.

Tocqueville, Alexis de. 1969. *Democracy in America*. Garden City, NY: Anchor Books. First published 1835–40.

– 2000. *Democracy in America*. Chicago: University of Chicago Press. First published 1835–40.

– 2010. *Democracy in America*. Indianapolis, IN: Liberty Fund. First published 1835–40.

Toubeau, Simon, and Emanuele Massetti. 2013. "The Party Politics of Territorial Reforms in Europe." *West European Politics* 36 (2): 297–316. https://doi.org/10.1080/01402382.2013.749657.

Townson, Nigel. 2001. *The Crisis of Democracy in Spain: Radical Centrist Politics under the Second Republic 1931–1936*. Brighton: Sussex Academic Press.

Trein, Philipp. 2017. "A New Way to Compare Horizontal Connections of Policy Sectors: 'Coupling' of Actors, Institutions and Policies." *Journal of Comparative Policy Analysis: Research and Practice* 19 (5): 419–34. https://doi.org/10.1080/13876988.2016.1225342.

Tsebelis, George. 1991. *Nested Games: Rational Choice in Comparative Politics*. Berkeley: University of California Press.

– 2002. *Veto Players: How Political Institutions Work*. Princeton, NJ: Princeton University Press.

Tucker, Eric. 2017. "2 States Lobby against Travel Ban." *U.S. News & World Report*, 6 February. https://www.usnews.com/news/politics/articles/2017-02-06/white-house-expresses-confidence-travel-ban-will-be-restored.

Tudela, José. 2016. *El fracasado éxito del Estado autonómico: Una historia española*. Madrid: Marcial Pons.

Tudor, Maya. 2013. *The Promise of Power: The Origins of Democracy in India and Autocracy in Pakistan*. Cambridge: Cambridge University Press.

Tully, James. 1995. *Strange Multiplicity: Constitutionalism in an Age of Diversity*. Cambridge: Cambridge University Press.

Tuschhoff, Christian. 1999. "The Compounding Effect: The Impact of Federalism on the Concept of Representation." *West European Politics* 22 (2): 16–33. https://doi.org/10.1080/01402389908425300.

Tusell, Javier. 2007. *Spain: From Dictatorship to Democracy; 1939 to the Present*. Oxford: Wiley Blackwell.

United States. Congressional Budget Office. 2011. "Estimated Impact of the American Recovery and Reinvestment Act on Employment and Economic Output from July 2011 through September 2011." Washington, DC: Congressional Budget Office.

Urbinati, Nadia. 2006. *Representative Democracy: Principles and Genealogy*. Chicago: University of Chicago Press.

Vallès, Josep. 2016. "El Estado de las autonomías: Una apuesta fallida." In *Ciencia y politica: Una aventura vital*, edited by César Colino, Jaime Ferri Durá, José A. Olmeda, Paloma Román Marugán, and Josefa Rubio Lara, 391–418. Valencia: Tirant lo Blanch.

Van Aelst, Peter, and Tom Louwerse. 2014. "Parliament without Government: The Belgian Parliament and the Government Formation Processes of 2007–2011." *West European Politics* 37 (3): 475–96. https://doi.org/10.1080/01402382.2013.832953.

van Biezen, Ingrid, and Jonathan Hopkin. 2005. "The Presidentialization of Spanish Democracy: Sources of Prime Ministerial Power in Post-Franco Spain." In *The Presidentialization of Politics: A Comparative Study of Modern Democracies*, edited by Thomas Poguntke and Paul Webb, 107–28. Oxford: Oxford University Press.

Van Dyck, Ruth. 1996. "Divided We Stand: Regionalism, Federalism and Minority Rights in Belgium." *Res Publica* 38 (2): 429–46.

van Haute, Emilie, and Kris Deschouwer. 2018. "Federal Reform and the Quality of Representation in Belgium." *West European Politics* 41 (3): 683–702. https://doi.org/10.1080/01402382.2017.1399320.

Varoufakis, Yanis. 2016. *And the Weak Suffer What They Must?* London: Bodley Head.

Vatter, Adrian. 2018a. *Das politische System der Schweiz*. Baden-Baden: Nomos.

– 2018b. *Swiss Federalism: The Transformation of a Federal Model*. New York: Routledge.

V-Dem (Varieties of Democracy). 2018. *Democracy for All? V-Dem Annual Democracy Report 2018*. Gothenburg, Sweden: V-Dem Institute. https://www.v-dem.net/media/filer_public/3f/19/3f19efc9-e25f-4356-b159-b5c0ec894115/v-dem_democracy_report_2018.pdf.

Verrijdt, Willem. 2014. "Algemene beschouwingen bij de zesde staatshervorming." In *Het federale België na de Zesde Staatshervorming*, edited by André Alen, Benjamin Dalle, Koen Muylle, Wouter Pas, Jeroen Van Nieuwenhove, and Willem Verrijdt, 1–16. Bruges: Die Keure.

Victorian Labor. 2020. *Australian Labor Party: Victorian Branch Rules*. Updated 14 September. Accessed 17 November 2020. https://www.viclabor.com.au/resources/.

Vipond, Robert C. 1985. "Constitutional Politics and the Legacy of the Provincial Rights Movement in Canada." *Canadian Journal of Political Science* 18 (2): 267–94. https://doi.org/10.1017/s0008423900030250.

– 1989. "1787 and 1867: The Federal Principle and Canadian Confederation Reconsidered." *Canadian Journal of Political Science* 22 (1): 3–26. https://doi.org/10.1017/s0008423900000810.

Vírgala, Eduardo. 2013. "The Participation of Autonomous Communities in the Central Bodies of State." In *The Ways of Federalism in Western Countries and the Horizons of Territorial Autonomy in Spain*, vol. 2, ed. Alberto López-Basaguren and Leire Escajedo San-Epifanio, 63–82. Berlin: Springer.

Völkl, Kerstin. 2016. "Länder Elections in German Federalism: Does Federal or Land-Level Influence Predominate?" *German Politics* 25 (2): 243–64. https://doi.org/10.1080/09644008.2016.1157863.

voteviewblog. 2016. "The End of the 114th Congress," 18 December. https://voteviewblog.com/2016/12/18/the-end-of-the-114th-congress/.

Wagener, Frido. 1979. "Der Öffentliche Dienst im Staat der Gegenwart." *Verfassungstreue und Schutz der Verfassung: Der Öffentliche Dienst im Staat der Gegenwart*. Veröffentlichungen der Vereinigung der Deutschen Staatsrechtslehrer, no. 37, 215–66. Berlin: De Gruyter.

Walker, David B. 1995. *The Rebirth of Federalism: Slouching toward Washington*. Chatham, NJ: Chatham House Publishers.

Ward, Lee. 2007. "Montesquieu on Federalism and Anglo-Gothic Constitutionalism." *Publius* 37 (4): 551–77. https://doi.org/10.1093/publius/pjm018.

Watts, Ronald L. 1998. *Comparaison des régimes fédéraux des années 1990*. Kingston: Institute of Intergovernmental Relations, Queen's University.

– 1999. *The Spending Power in Federal Systems: A Comparative Study*. Kingston: Institute of Intergovernmental Relations, Queen's University.

– 2008. *Comparing Federal Systems*. Kingston: School of Policy Studies, Queen's University.

Weale, Albert. 2018. "What's So Good about Parliamentary Hybrids? Comment on 'Australian Bicameralism as Semi-parliamentarianism: Patterns of Majority Formation in 29 Democracies.'" *Australian Journal of Political Science* 53 (2): 234–40. https://doi.org/10.1080/10361146.2018.1451489.

Webber, Jeremy. 2015. *The Constitution of Canada: A Contextual Analysis*. Oxford: Hart.

Weichlein, Siegfried. 2012. "Föderalismus und Bundesstaat zwischen dem Alten Reich und der Bundesrepublik Deutschland." In *Handbuch Föderalismus: Föderalismus als demokratische Rechtsordnung und Rechtskultur in Deutschland, Europa und der Welt*, edited by Ines Härtel, 101–27. Vol. 1 of *Grundlagen des Föderalismus und der deutsche Bundesstaat*. Berlin: Springer.

– 2019. *Föderalismus und Demokratie in der Bundesrepublik*. Stuttgart: Kohlhammer.

Weick, Karl. 1976. "Educational Organizations as Loosely Coupled Systems." *Administrative Science Quarterly* 21 (1): 1–19. https://doi.org/10.2307/2391875.

Weinstock, Daniel. 2001. "Towards a Normative Theory of Federalism." *International Social Science Journal* 53 (167): 75–83. https://doi.org/10.1111/1468-2451.00295.

– 2006. "Liberty and Overlapping Federalism." In *Dilemmas of Solidarity: Rethinking Redistribution in the Canadian Federation*, edited by Lorne Sossin, Jean-François Gaudreault-DesBiens, and Sujit Choudhry, 167–74. Toronto: University of Toronto Press.

Welsh, Helga. 2014. "Education, Federalism and the 2013 Bundestag Elections." *German Politics* 23 (4): 400–14. https://doi.org/10.1080/09644008.2014.953065.

Whitaker, Reginald. 1992. "Federalism and Democratic Theory." In *A Sovereign Idea: Essays on Canada as a Democratic Community*, edited by Reginald Whitaker, 165–204. Montreal and Kingston: McGill-Queen's University Press.

White, Graham. 2010. "Cabinets and First Ministers." In *Auditing Canadian Democracy*, edited by William Cross, 40–64. Vancouver: UBC Press.

White, Jonathan. 2015. "Emergency Europe." *Political Studies* 63 (2): 300–18. https://doi.org/10.1111/1467-9248.12072.

Wieland, Joachim. 2013. *Neuordnung der Finanzverfassung nach Auslaufen des Solidarpakts II und Wirksamwerden der Schuldenbremse: Rechtsgutachten im Auftrag der Bertelsmann Stiftung*. Speyerer Arbeitsheft Nr. 211. Speyer: Deutsche Universität für Verwaltungswissenschaften.

Wilkinson, Steven. 2002. "Ethnic Mobilization and Ethnic Violence in Post-Independence India." Paper presented at the annual conference of the American Political Science Association, Boston.

– 2015. "Where's the Party? The Decline of Party Institutionalization and What (If Anything) That Means for Democracy." *Government and Opposition* 50 (3): 420–45. https://doi.org/10.1017/gov.2015.5.

Wills, Garry. 2006. *Lincoln at Gettysburg: The Words That Remade America*. London: Simon & Schuster.

Witte, Els, Jan Craeybeckx, and Alain Meynen. 2010. *Politieke Geschiedenis Van Belgie: Van 1830 tot heden*. Antwerpen: Standaard Uitgeverij.

Wolfers, Justin. 2014. "What Debate? Economists Agree the Stimulus Lifted the Economy." *New York Times*, 29 July.

Wright, Gerald, Robert Erikson, and John McIver. 1987. "Public Opinion and Policy Liberalism in the American States." *American Journal of Political Science* 31 (4): 980–1001. https://doi.org/10.2307/2111232.

Wyatt, Andrew. 2009. *Party System Change in South India: Political Entrepreneurs, Patterns and Processes*. Abingdon, UK: Routledge.

Yee, Vivian. 2017. "Judge Blocks Trump Effort to Withhold Money from Sanctuary Cities." *New York Times*, 25 April.

Young, Iris Marion. 2005. "Self-Determination as Non-domination: Ideals Applied to Palestine/Israel." *Ethnicities* 5 (2): 139–59. https://doi.org/10.1177/1468796805052112.

Ziegfeld, Adam. 2016. *Why Regional Parties? Clientelism, Elites, and the Indian Party System*. Cambridge: Cambridge University Press.

Contributors

Katharine Adeney is a professor and director of the Institute for Asia-Pacific Studies at the University of Nottingham, United Kingdom. Her main research interests include the countries of, and democratization in, South Asia, especially India and Pakistan; ethnic-conflict regulation and institutional design; the creation and maintenance of national identities; and the politics of federal states.

Andrew Banfield is a senior lecturer in the School of Politics and International Relations at the Australian National University, Canberra, and was the director of the Australian Centre for Federalism between 2012 and 2015. His research interests are judicial politics, comparative federalism, and political elites.

Arthur Benz is a professor emeritus of comparative politics and German government at the Institute for Political Science, Technical University of Darmstadt, Germany. His research focuses on German politics, comparative federalism, multi-level governance, policy learning, and institutional change.

Jörg Broschek is an associate professor and Canada Research Chair in Comparative Federalism and Multilevel Governance at Wilfrid Laurier University, Waterloo, Canada. His research has primarily centred on the dynamics of Canadian and German federalism, comparative federalism, and theories of institutionalism.

Peter Bursens is a professor of political science at the Department of Political Science, University of Antwerp, Belgium. He is a senior member of the Politics and Public Management Research Group and of the GOVTRUST Centre of Excellence. His research focuses on Europeanization and democratic legitimacy in the multi-level political systems and regions of the European Union.

César Colino is a professor in the Department of Political Science and Public Administration at the Spanish National Distance-Learning University in Madrid, Spain. His recent research and publications have revolved around comparative federalism – in particular, constitutional reform, diversity management and secessionism, intergovernmental relations, fiscal federalism and regional finance, and the effects of the 2008–9 financial crisis on federal systems.

Timothy Conlan is a university professor emeritus of government and public policy at George Mason University, Virginia, United States, and a fellow of the US National Academy of Public Administration. His research focuses on American politics and public policymaking, federalism, and intergovernmental relations.

John Erik Fossum is a professor of political science at ARENA Centre for European Studies at the University of Oslo, Norway. His research focuses on democracy, constitutionalism, and federalism in the European Union and Canada.

Thomas O. Hueglin is a professor of political science at Wilfrid Laurier University in Waterloo, Canada. His research interests are the history of political thought and comparative federalism. His most recent book provides a new view on Canadian federalism.

Sabine Kropp is a professor of political science at the Freie Universität Berlin, Germany. Her research interests include comparative federalism, the political system of Germany, parliaments, and autocracy and democracy in comparative perspective.

David Laycock is a professor emeritus of political science at Simon Fraser University, Burnaby, British Columbia, Canada. His research focuses on political ideologies; democratic theory; the comparative study of populism, conservatism, and socialism; Canadian party politics; and public policy.

Petra Meier is a professor of politics at the Department of Political Science and dean of the Faculty of Social Sciences, University of Antwerp, Belgium. She is a senior member of the Politics and Public Management Research Group and of the GOVTRUST Centre of Excellence. Her research focuses on the representation of gender in politics and policies, with a particular interest in how institutions (re)produce inequality and how to promote equality.

Sean Mueller is an assistant professor at the Institute of Political Science, University of Lausanne, Switzerland, funded by the Swiss National Science Foundation ("Eccellenza" program). His main areas of research are Swiss and comparative federalism, regionalism, local government, and direct democracy.

Anthony Sayers is an associate professor in the Department of Political Science at the University of Calgary, Canada. His research encompasses electoral systems, political parties, federalism, comparative politics, and Canadian and provincial politics.

Jared Sonnicksen is a senior researcher at the Institute for Political Science at the Technical University of Darmstadt, Germany, in the area of comparative politics. His research interests include comparative federalism, European integration, US politics, and democratic theory.

Wilfried Swenden is a professor of South Asian and comparative politics in the School of Social and Political Science at the University of Edinburgh, Scotland, UK. His areas of research interest are comparative federalism and territorial politics, intergovernmental relations as well as political parties in multi-level states, institutional engineering for divided societies, and centre-state relations and party politics in India.

Index

accountability, 12–14, 23–6, 29, 34, 44–6, 54, 67–74, 101, 242; Belgium, 190–4; Canada, 161, 248; Germany, 123, 133–4, 136–7; India, 226–7; Spain, 217; Switzerland, 115; United States, 84, 97
adaptation, 165, 213, 253
administration, 7, 54–5, 256; German Länder, 134–7; India, 222, 226; intergovernmental, 95, 210, 245, 250, 253, 259; Spain, 215; United States, 93
Althusius, Johannes, 30–1, 33, 35, 43
Anti-Federalists, 5, 80
Australian Loan Council (ALC), 173, 176
autocracy, regional, 3, 147, 234–7
autonomous communities (ACs) (Spain), 204, 209–11, 252
autonomy, 144; Belgium, 184, 190–1, 194; cantonal (Switzerland), 108, 111, 115, 118–19; democratic (political), 15–16, 89, 259; fiscal, 50; German Länder, 133, 137–9; Indian states, 219–22, 237; individual, 40–62; parliamentary, 46, 56; provincial (Canada), 154, 249, 251; regional (Spain), 201–3, 209–10; United States, 87–8, 90–1, 245

balance, 12–13, 56, 120, 157–9, 181–2, 260–1; of federalism and democracy, 16–17, 56–7, 67, 75, 120, 142, 255, 260–1; of power, 38, 46, 88, 177, 200
Basic Law (German Constitution), 107, 110–12
Basque Country, 202, 206, 213, 252
Bavaria, 131, 133
Bharatiya Janata Party (BJP) (India), 221–3, 225, 230–1, 234–6
bicameralism. *See* legislature: bicameral
British North America Act, 24, 149–50, 156. *See also* Constitution: of Canada
Brussels Capital Region, 182–6, 188, 190–2
Bundesrat (Upper House, Germany), 124–7, 135, 140–1, 248
Bundestag (Lower House, Germany), 124–5, 128–9, 249
Burgess, Michael, 8, 76

Cairns, Alain, 150–1, 154–5
Calhoun, John C., 82
Canadian Charter of Rights and Freedoms, 77, 149, 160
cantons (Switzerland), 103, 106–8, 112, 115–18, 246–8, 258–9

Catalonia, 22, 198, 202–6, 209, 211–13, 215, 252
centralization, 32, 38, 42, 76, 99, 111, 152, 256; Australia, 177; Germany, 134; India, 222, 226, 233, 237; Spain, 217
checks and balances, 3, 7, 28, 38, 78, 242
citizen, 5, 11–14, 17, 21, 31–4, 37–8, 40–5, 56, 59, 61, 67, 72–4, 99, 102–4, 145, 261; Belgium, 184, 192; India, 224, 233–6; Spain, 202, 204, 211; Switzerland, 106–8, 112, 115–20; United States, 84–5
citizen assembly, 99, 198, 112
citizen participation. *See* participation
citizenship, 9, 58, 100–2, 146, 220, 235–6
civil society, 5, 7–8, 18, 31, 41, 54, 185, 200–1, 220, 244, 251, 259
coalition government, 14, 242; Australia, 173; Belgium, 182–3, 188, 255; Germany, 124–30, 249; India, 223, 230; Spain, 208, 216
Commonwealth Grants Commission (CGC) (Australia), 173, 176
communities (Belgium), 184–5, 193, 196
community, 40, 48–50, 67, 110–11, 153, 219, 236, 261; ethnolinguistic, 20, 180, 183, 185, 188, 193–5, 220; religious, 30, 117, 220, 234
competences, 44, 46; concurrent, 66, 212, 220, 223, 254; exclusive, 107, 134, 149, 154–7, 162, 184–6, 203, 220, 222–3; shared, 14, 48, 51, 53, 66, 73, 123, 224
compulsory voting, 166, 167–9, 179
concentration of power, 3–4, 71, 148–9, 160–1, 204
Concertation Committee (Belgium), 186–7, 189, 195
confederation, 79, 108, 149–50, 156, 196
Congress (United States), 84, 88–9, 93–4, 97, 244–6
Congress of Deputies (Spain), 203, 205–7, 210
Congress Party (India), 219–23, 228–32
congruence principle, 13, 41–2, 48–50, 214
consensus, 6, 34–6, 82, 124, 169, 217, 246, 250
consensus democracy, 6, 47–8, 50, 52, 70, 105; Australia, 178; Belgium, 181–3, 186–7, 252; Germany, 124–30, 137–9; Spain, 209; Switzerland, 104–5, 244, 247–8
constitution, 14, 18, 24, 45, 65–7, 74–5, 144, 241
Constitution: of Belgium, 183–4; of Canada, 24, 32, 157–60; of Germany (*see* Basic Law); of India, 218–21, 223–4, 231–4; of Spain, 198, 202–3, 209; of Switzerland (*see* Federal Constitution); of United States, 37, 79–83
constitutional amendment, 35–6, 74; Belgium, 195; Canada, 36, 163; India, 228, 230–1; Spain, 210, 213; Switzerland, 102–3, 106–7, 110, 114; United States, 83
constitutional change, 79, 110, 112, 119, 131–2, 161, 178, 195
Constitutional Court: of Belgium, 187, 189, 195; of Spain, 206–7, 209, 211–13, 252
constitutionalism, 8, 61, 63, 76
constitutional principle, 5, 33, 59, 139, 203
constitutional rules, 14, 18, 34, 132, 203, 262
constitution-making, 74–5, 79, 205

Cortes Generales (parliament, Spain), 205
Council of Australian Governments (COAG), 166, 172–4, 176, 179
Council of States (Upper House, Switzerland), 105–6, 112–13, 118–19, 246
coupling, 15–16, 49–51, 60, 88, 96, 153, 165–6, 178, 200, 213–14, 240–4. *See also* loose coupling; tight coupling
covenant, 6, 35, 65

decentralization, 5–7, 38, 45, 92, 111, 113, 256, 258, 260; Belgium, 195, 254; Germany, 127, 133; Spain, 203–8, 212; United States, 89
decoupling, 49–50, 53, 66, 87, 132, 175, 190, 200, 245, 254
defederalization, 65, 124, 130–1, 134, 137–8
delegitimation, 96–7
deliberation, 40–1, 57, 71, 99, 145, 260
democracy: concept of, 26, 37, 40–1, 59, 101–14, 144–5, 181, 240; consensus (*see* consensus democracy); direct (*see* referendum); federal, 8, 11–14, 22, 39, 47, 172, 201, 237, 240–2, 262; liberal, 3, 5, 110–11; majoritarian, 48, 62, 70, 83, 145, 203, 205, 252; multinational, 9, 38, 162; non-parliamentary, 15, 242, 244–51, 257–61; parliamentary, 27–8, 68, 123, 202–9, 223, 242, 248–55; quality of, 10, 104; representative, 13, 25, 41; republican, 5, 17–18
democratization, 146, 201–4
demoï, 37, 44, 160, 181–2, 190–4, 233, 236, 254
demoïcracy, 10
demos, 37, 40–1, 44, 79, 81, 102–3, 219
devolution. *See* decentralization
discrimination, 5, 85, 145
disparities. *See* inequality
diversity, 4, 7, 9, 13, 32, 36–7, 43, 46, 111, 118, 151, 169, 172, 198, 218–20, 253; accommodation of, 233, 252
division of power, 7, 101–2, 120, 242. *See also* separation of power; sharing of power
domination, 56, 61–9, 187–93, 260–1

elections, 41; Australia, 168–70, 175; Belgium, 189–90, 194; Germany, 125, 128–30; India, 218–19, 223, 229, 231; Spain, 206, 209; Switzerland, 102, 105–6, 119; United States, 83–4, 92–4
electoral system, 25, 70, 105–6, 112, 150–3, 170–1, 182, 203, 233
equality, 4–5, 83, 98, 217; of citizens, 12–13, 36, 40, 45, 111–12; of peoples, 12–13, 45, 111; social, 4, 145, 249, 259
Eriksen, Erik, 62–3
ethno-federation, 193, 220
European Parliament (EP), 69, 71, 77
European Union (EU), 10, 32, 35–6, 59, 67–72, 75–6, 99, 130, 147, 186, 257
executive dominance, 15, 58–76, 259–60; Australia, 178; Belgium, 187–90; Canada, 148; Germany, 123; India, 221, 225; Spain, 205; Switzerland, 104; United States, 87, 94
executive-legislative relations, 15, 51, 53, 66–72, 242
externality, 42, 45, 189, 194

federal comity, 16, 33, 35, 123
Federal Constitution (Switzerland), 107, 110–12

Federal Constitutional Court (Germany), 33, 250
Federal Council (government, Switzerland), 105, 112–13
federal democracy. *See* democracy: federal
federal dynamics, 52–5, 160, 168, 177
federalism: administrative, 134–7; competitive, 6, 87, 90–1; concept of, 38, 42–4, 59, 64, 101–4, 144, 240; cooperative, 95, 107, 122–3, 135, 138, 159, 245–6, 253; demos-constraining, 113–15; dual, 87, 165, 243; executive, 29, 56, 73, 190, 225–6, 260; fiscal, 132–5, 173, 223–4, 228; laboratory, 6, 43; multinational, 9, 20–1, 251, 254
Federalist, The, 80–2, 101
Federalists, 5
federalization, 99, 144, 182–3, 185–6, 188, 193, 201–4, 211, 217, 252, 254
federal spirit, 8, 65, 100, 150, 238
Federal Supreme Court (Switzerland), 105, 111–12, 114–15
federation: centralized, 222–4; centrifugal, 157, 184–7, 217, 252; defect, 3; multinational, 9, 45, 62, 242, 251–4
Finance Commission (India), 222, 228, 231
fiscal equalization, 33–4, 84, 90–1, 131, 133–4, 173–5, 252
Flanders, 184–5, 250
freedom, 60–2, 65, 103
friction, 11, 15, 20–1, 51, 53, 148, 248; Australia, 166; Canada, 148, 151, 156, 160–2; Germany, 123–5; Spain, 213, 217; Switzerland, 104, 119–20

Gandhi, Indira, 229
Gandhi, Mahatma, 219
Gibson, Edward, 147
governance, 4, 6–7, 9, 11, 13; indirect, 97. *See also* multi-level governance
grants-in-aid (United States), 88, 91, 93, 97, 173, 245

Harper, Stephen, 70–1, 76, 154, 159
House of Commons (Canada), 151–3
House of Representatives: of Australia, 170; of Belgium, 191, 196; of United States, 31, 80

identity, 9, 32, 118, 185, 192, 220–30, 233
Indian National Congress. *See* Congress Party (India)
Indigenous peoples, 64, 160, 162, 251
inequality, 4, 25, 44–5, 50, 86, 91
input legitimacy, 27, 123, 135, 142, 145–6, 148, 161–2, 181
inter-cantonal cooperation, 108, 115–16
intercurrence, 143, 146–8, 150, 153–4, 162
interest groups, 12, 16, 48–9, 54, 89–90, 193, 204, 246
intergovernmental agreement, 36, 56, 72, 174
intergovernmental coordination, 7, 15, 42, 46, 48, 250–1, 255–9
intergovernmental council, 135, 159, 172–4, 210, 225, 228
intergovernmental lobby, 87, 89–90, 94, 117, 245
intergovernmental relations, 9, 28–9, 50–6, 72–3, 249–50; Australia, 172–7; Belgium, 186–9, 194; Canada, 155–9; Germany, 135; India, 225–8; Spain, 203–4, 209–13; Switzerland, 115–16, 119–20; United States, 93–4, 245–6
interparliamentary relations, 74, 77
Inter-State Council (ISC) (India), 225, 227

Jammu, 222, 230–2, 234–6
joint decision-making, 50, 56, 66, 123, 134, 138–9, 212, 243, 250
joint-decision trap, 34, 53, 252, 257

Kashmir, 222, 230–2, 234–6
King, Preston, 65–6

Labor Party (Australia), 167–71, 177
Länder (German states), 36, 124–37
legislature: Australia, 165, 169–72, 178; Belgium, 183, 191; bicameral, 248–9; Spain, 205; Switzerland, 105, 246–7
legitimacy, 11, 27, 31, 34–6, 85, 100–1, 119, 170–2, 177, 194, 200–2; democratic, 7–10, 12, 17, 22, 27–8, 38, 40–1, 46, 68, 73, 79–81, 87, 115, 120, 170, 181, 239, 245. *See also* input legitimacy; output legitimacy; throughput legitimacy
Levy, Jacob, 64–5
liberty, 4, 5, 23, 37, 40, 43–4, 79–82, 101, 261
Lincoln, Abraham, 37
Lok Sabha (Lower House, India), 227, 238
loose coupling, 16, 50–5, 65–6, 103, 120, 143, 159–61, 247, 255–9

Madison, James, 80–1, 85
majority, 25, 81; concurrent, 82; countervailing, 125; double, 107, 110, 114, 187, 191, 195; tyranny by, 5, 85
majority rule, 4, 13, 24, 31, 35–6, 44, 62–3, 76, 82, 123–4, 137–8, 151–2, 221, 258
minority, 25, 81–3, 85, 205, 234–6
minority government, 14, 21, 55, 76, 129, 154, 199–200, 203, 214–16, 242, 252
minority rights, 9, 20, 66, 82, 145, 190–1, 235
Montesquieu, 5, 80
multi-level governance, 4, 7–10, 16, 21, 47–56, 72, 99–100, 257–9. *See also* intergovernmental coordination
multinationalism, 37–8, 198

nation, 79, 81, 94, 118–19, 146, 219, 221–2, 233, 238
nation state, 37, 99, 262
National Council (Lower House, Switzerland), 105, 111
nationalism, 118, 201–2, 206–7, 253, 258
nationalization, 19, 78, 92–3, 245–6
Nehru, Jawaharlal, 219, 229
non-domination, 12, 18, 59–66, 75, 83, 104, 261

Obama administration, 94–5, 97
"open federalism," 154
opposition parties, 125, 205–6, 212, 229, 242, 248
output legitimacy, 6, 16, 27, 38, 45, 123, 135–7, 142, 145–6, 148, 151, 161–2, 181, 217

parliament, 27–8, 54–7, 69–73, 135, 156, 188–90; supremacy of, 27–8, 56, 156, 248, 255
parliamentary government, 56, 68, 172, 243–4, 249, 252
participation: of citizens, 5, 38, 61, 100, 117; in elections, 84, 99, 119
parties, 24, 51–4, 242, 257–8; Australia, 164, 166–71, 177–8; Belgium, 182–94; Canada, 150–3; fragmented, 150, 183, 201, 203; Germany, 124–5, 127–31; India,

221, 225–30; integrated, 51–2, 127, 142, 167–9, 175–7, 200, 213, 250, 257–8; nationalist, 207–10, 213–16; opposition (*see* opposition parties); regional, 182–3, 194, 200, 208–10, 213, 215, 230, 233, 261; Spain, 202–17; statewide, 206, 208, 215; Switzerland, 117; United States, 89, 92, 94
party competition, 48, 125, 256–7
party congruence, 214
party democracy, 164
party system, 7–8, 50–2, 147, 256–8; Australia, 164–9, 175, 250; Belgium, 20, 182–3, 193–5, 254; Canada, 150–2; Germany, 127–30, 139, 250; India, 221, 228–33, 237–8; Spain, 201–5, 214; Switzerland, 117; United States, 89, 92–5
people. *See* demos
peoples. *See* demoï
Pettit, Philip, 60–4
picket-fence federalism, 88, 95, 245
Plato, 24–6
polarization, 93–6, 136–7, 139, 208, 246, 257
populism, 99–100, 130, 153, 233, 241, 262
power. *See* division of power; separation of power; sharing of power
presidential government, 28, 87, 101, 242
presidentialization, 73, 87, 208
President's Rule (India), 220, 229–31, 235, 253
provinces (Canada), 36, 149, 151, 153, 156–7, 162, 248–9, 258
Punjab, 219, 222, 229, 233–4

Quebec, 36, 148, 151–2, 162, 249, 251

Rajya Sabha (Upper House, India), 227
recoupling, 165, 249
redundancy, 16, 55, 165–6, 258, 260
referendum, 15, 41, 74, 103–7, 112, 114, 116–17, 247–8
reform, 55–7, 177–8, 251–4, 262
reform, constitutional, 57, 165, 195, 210
reform, institutional: Australia, 166–7, 169–71; Spain, 213
reform of federalism: Canada, 152–4; Germany, 130–9; Spain, 211–13, 252
reform policy: Australia, 174–6; Germany, 124–5, 128–30; Spain, 198–9; United States, 83, 90
reform state: Belgium, 180–3, 189, 195
regionalism, 9, 51, 150, 205, 251–2, 254, 257, 261
regional nationalities, 9, 191, 198, 202–4, 206, 213–15, 252
regions (Belgium), 184–5
religion, 9, 30, 113, 117–18, 220–1, 233, 235–6
re-parliamentarization, 131–3
representation, 44–6, 67, 81; citizens, 192–4, 217; minority, 185, 190–1; territorial, 85, 113, 119, 144, 148–53, 169, 204, 217, 227
republic, 80–2, 85. *See also* democracy: republican
responsibility, 45–6, 64, 72, 74, 133–4
responsiveness, 26, 32, 58, 94, 150–1, 217
Rousseau, Jean-Jacques, 24, 40
rule of law, 29, 82, 110–1, 118, 202

Scharpf, Fritz W., 55, 257
secession, secessionism, 5, 22, 173, 198, 209, 212–15, 220, 234–5
self-determination, 18, 64, 66, 145, 162
self-government, 59, 64, 80, 144, 202, 211, 219, 225, 232

self-rule, 15, 20, 30, 59, 103, 251, 255; Canada, 143–5, 148–50, 159–61; Germany, 122–3; Spain, 204, 211, 218; Switzerland, 120
separation of power, 15, 34, 44–5, 55, 242–7, 255, 257; Belgium, 193; Switzerland, 103, 247; United States, 78, 80, 87–8, 254–6
Shapiro, Ian, 61–4
shared rule, 30, 59, 103, 144–5, 243; Canada, 149, 151, 159–61; Germany, 122–3; Spain, 208, 211, 218; Switzerland, 120
sharing of power, 10, 13, 15, 19, 44, 51, 120, 129, 242, 247, 255
small-republic theory, 80–1, 84–6
solidarity, 4, 13, 17–18, 32–4, 43, 83, 120, 131, 203, 240
sovereignty: parliamentary (*see* parliament); popular, 24, 28, 30, 79, 82, 110, 245; state, 30, 60, 64, 79, 81, 112, 245
spending power, 34, 157, 162
states: Australia, 164–5, 172–5; India, 223–4, 228, 231–6; United States, 85–7, 90–1, 94–6, 245
statutes of autonomy (Spain), 203, 207, 209–11, 213, 252
subsidiarity, 6, 31–2, 34, 42–3, 110–11
Supreme Court: of Canada, 32, 160; of India, 224, 231–2, 237; of United States, 88

tensions, 14–15, 23, 38, 44–7, 52–3, 145–6, 200
throughput legitimacy, 27–8, 163, 177
tight coupling, 50–2, 123, 129, 139, 249–50
Tocqueville, Alexis de, 5, 24–5, 78, 82
Trudeau, Justin, 70, 159
Trudeau, Pierre, 157
Trump administration, 93–4, 96

unilateralism, 20, 35, 143, 150, 154–7, 161–2, 217

veto player, 48, 130

welfare policies, 83–6, 90–1, 120, 130, 223, 230
welfare state, 27, 83–4, 181, 198, 202, 249, 251
Western Australia, 173–4
Westminster democracy, 20, 27–8, 68, 143, 145, 248; Canada, 148–56, 159–61

Young, Iris Marion, 64–6

www.ingramcontent.com/pod-product-compliance
Lightning Source LLC
LaVergne TN
LVHW090151080826
844660LV00013B/755/J